Praise for *The Irish Assassins*

"Lively and suspenseful . . . Ms. Kavanagh's narrative of high politics and low intrigue, ranging from Dublin to Downing Street and the high seas, brings to vivid life a bloody chapter in the troubled history of Britain and Ireland."
—*Wall Street Journal*

"Julie Kavanagh has done an adroit unpicking of the intricacies of the history, and her book is at once admirable for its scholarship and immensely enjoyable in its raciness."
—*New York Times*

"Kavanagh's is a sweeping and compelling narrative of a story that more than bears retelling. What she has sought to do, which has not been done before, is to try to connect in time the political and social lives of what is an extended and diverse cast of characters in Britain and Ireland, spanning from the Gladstone household (of which Lucy Cavendish, wife of the murdered Frederick, was a close member), to Parnell's relationship with Katharine O'Shea, and encompassing the poverty-stricken background in Gweedore of Patrick O'Donnell and his people."
—*Irish Times*

"With a novelist's eye for detail, Kavanagh reminds us in her new book, *The Irish Assassins*, how English rule in Ireland not only diminished the lives of the oppressed Irish natives but how it also unmoored the moral compass of centuries of English colonists too . . . pacy and deeply learned . . . brilliantly entertaining."
—*Irish Central*

"Julie Kavanagh, in her terrific new book, *The Irish Assassins*, does a masterful job of sorting through the complexities and making the history accessible and comprehensible . . . a gripping story, well and clearly told."
—*Minneapolis Star Tribune*

"You could think of this as the prequel to Patrick Radden Keefe's best seller *Say Nothing* . . . Although the events in these two books are set nearly a hundred years apart, they are linked by the push and pull in that country between Protestant and Catholic, between peace and violence, between independence and accord."   —Amazon

"[M]arvelously engaging . . . Kavanagh vividly presents the innumerable players in this saga. And she never neglects the thorny human dimension of her story: the acts of impulse, folly, and desperation, of betrayal and heroism. In a nutshell, she has built a narrative that's faithful to the flow of events, both overt and behind-the-scenes, while never losing sight of the frailties and passionate commitments behind them."   —*Washington Independent Review of Books*

"The tale of the Phoenix Park murders is not unfamiliar, but Kavanagh recounts it with a great sense of drama . . . Kavanagh's account reminds me of the very best of true crime, the sort that Dominick Dunne used to write for Vanity Fair. Like Dunne, Kavanagh never hurries; she takes the time to describe characters and places with exquisite detail. An engaging story is rendered beautiful because of the tiny ephemera that a less sensitive author might have carelessly discarded."   —*Times* (UK)

"The dramatic story of the Phoenix Park murders — including the background to the killings and their cataclysmic aftermath — is told with novelistic panache by Julie Kavanagh . . . This is not just the fascinating tale of the shadowy group of determined killers and their victims, but it also paints a picture of some of the key political figures of the time."   —*Irish Independent*

"Journalist Julie Kavanagh's account of the murders of two members of the British authority in Ireland in 1882 has the plot and intrigue of a sweeping 19th-century novel . . . *The Irish Assassins* is a colourful, ambitious book."   —*Sunday Business Post* (UK)

"What Julie Kavanagh has done here is to bring this most extraordinary of assassinations to life. The research is meticulous . . . The writing is clear and yet warm, leaving the reader in no doubt as to how much personalities, foibles and mere coincidence affect law, politics and history. This is one of the best researched and most enjoyable historical reads I have come across in quite some time." —*Sunday Independent* (UK)

"[Kavanagh] draws in the strands of the story with extraordinary dexterity. She portrays the poverty and the brutality inflicted upon the starving, disease-ridden communities of rural Ireland. She describes in the most touching terms the devastation among the families of both the murdered and those men caught up in the conspiracy who paid for it with their lives." —*Air Mail*

"Kavanagh delivers a page-turning history of the murders of the chief secretary and the undersecretary for Ireland in May 1882 . . . This entertaining and richly detailed chronicle offers fresh insights into a conflict whose repercussions are still felt today." —*Publishers Weekly*

"This entertaining and informative narrative is populated by colorful characters on both sides of the conflict, all of whom are brought to vivid life by Kavanagh's stellar writing." —*Booklist*, starred review

"[A] riveting tale that is both deeply researched and unforgettable . . . [Kavanagh] skillfully tells a complex story of ambition, conspiracy, betrayal, and coercion that was centuries in the making, with implications that reach to the 21st century . . . Expertly blending history and true crime, this is an essential read for anyone wanting to understand modern Irish history. Kavanagh's writing is engaging from start to finish."

—*Library Journal*, starred review

fragility of that solution of partition is evident in this time, in the Irish border. It is part of the history of our islands made of course all the more interesting by the extraordinary characters with the leading roles in the drama."

—Tony Blair

"This is one of those rare books that is superbly written, tells me something I need to know, and which grips the imagination from first word to last. Julie Kavanagh has produced an engrossing account of revolutionary violence, political folly and human weakness. It is a powerful work."

—Fergal Keane, BBC correspondent and author of *Wounds: A Memoir of War and Love*

"Julie Kavanagh has taken a violent and sensational event, the assassination of two senior government official in Dublin in 1882, and placed it in a richly contextualized and many-layered historical setting. Using a wide range of sources and opening up new avenues of enquiry, she vividly demonstrates the convulsive reverberations of one violent act, tracing the shock-waves it sent into political salons at Westminster, cabins in County Donegal, court circles at Windsor, revolutionary cabals in Paris, the Irish leader Parnell's secret life in a London suburb, and the complex world of the transatlantic Irish diaspora. Consummately well-written and full of novel insights, this is the best kind of historical detective story."

—R.F. Foster, Emeritus Professor of Irish History, University of Oxford

"In *The Irish Assassins*, Julie Kavanagh has brilliantly succeeded in making a complex sequence of events irresistibly accessible, providing an engrossing narrative that is violent, tragic, sometimes funny, extremely astute and remarkably well written."

—Selina Hastings, author of *Sybille Bedford: A Life*

THE
IRISH
ASSASSINS

Also by Julie Kavanagh

Secret Muses:
The Life of Frederick Ashton

Rudolf Nureyev:
The Life

The Girl Who Loved Camellias:
The Life and Legend of Marie Duplessis

THE
IRISH
ASSASSINS

Conspiracy, Revenge, and
the Phoenix Park Murders
That Stunned
Victorian England

JULIE KAVANAGH

Grove Press
New York

FIRST EDITION

Published simultaneously in Canada
Printed in Canada

First Grove Atlantic hardcover edition: August 2021
First Grove Atlantic paperback edition: August 2022

The book is set in 13-point Centaur MT by Alpha Design & Composition of Pittsfield, NH.

Library of Congress Cataloging-in-Publication data is available for this title.

ISBN 978-0-8021-4937-4
eISBN 978-0-8021-4938-1

Grove Press
an imprint of Grove Atlantic
154 West 14th Street
New York, NY 10011
Distributed by Publishers Group West
groveatlantic.com

22 23 24 25 26   10 9 8 7 6 5 4 3 2 1

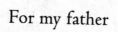

For my father

CONTENTS

CONTENTS

A BRIEF HISTORY

E VERY READER of this book will know about the age-old hostility between the Irish and the English, but not everyone will know how, when, and where it started. It was in 1170, to be precise, that Anglo-Normans first invaded Ireland, going on to grab the best land and introduce their own feudal system—a hierarchy of master and serf, landlord and tenant that was still in place more than seven hundred years later. Since then, the theme of violence between the two places—erupting, receding, erupting again—has never entirely disappeared. The muraled "peace walls" separating Catholic and Protestant neighborhoods in Northern Irish cities like Belfast and Derry had been prefigured in the fourteenth century by the thorny hedges and ten-foot ditches bounding "The Pale," an area covering Dublin and its surroundings, under protection of the Crown and governed by its rules. It was considered to be a pocket of safety and civilization in marked contrast to the barbarous conditions of Irish life outside (and is the origin of the expression "beyond the pale").

This "Us and Them" divide, "their religion" or "our religion," intensified during the Reformation, when Protestantism replaced Roman Catholicism as the national church in England and Ireland, and Irish Catholics were seen as dangerous worshippers of the anti-faith. Henry VIII had broken ties with Rome when the pope refused to annul his first marriage and made himself supreme head of the English Church. He was also named king of Ireland, but his daughter, Queen Elizabeth, took much firmer control of their neighboring island. Fearing that her enemy—the Spanish Catholic King Philip—would use Ireland as a foothold to launch an attack on England, she decided to populate the country with loyal subjects. This involved confiscating vast quantities of land from powerful Gaelic families in the province of Munster and planting Irish estates with English and Scottish settlers.

One of the first arrivals was the great Elizabethan poet Edmund Spenser. Appointed a colonial official, he was a party to what was literally a war of extermination by the English—the 1580 suppression of a rebellion against the queen in Munster. More than six hundred Spanish and Irish soldiers were massacred; ordinary people systematically butchered; Catholic priests, hanged until "half dead," were then decapitated, their heads fixed on poles in public places to instill fear in the native inhabitants. "So the name of an Inglysh man was made more terrible now to them than the sight of an hundryth was before," remarked Sir Humphrey Gilbert, the queen's ruthless military governor. The appalling famine that resulted from the merciless destruction of crops and cattle by Elizabeth's troops left an estimated thirty thousand inhabitants dying of starvation—"anatomies of death," who crawled along the ground because their legs were too weak to support them and feasted on carrion and carcasses they had dug out of graves. Spenser was one of the queen's most ardent devotees, and his masterpiece, the allegorical epic *The Faerie Queene*, an extravagant homage to her sovereignty. And yet, his horror of what he saw in Munster is embedded in his writing: the hollow-eyed character of Despair wearing rags held together with thorns, his "raw-bone cheeks . . . shrunk into his jaws," is the very image of the Irish famine victim.

It was as if the English felt themselves absolved from all ethical restraints when dealing with the Irish. The divine right of kings legitimized the use of force in maintaining the dominion of the sovereign, and as the insurrections of the Irish amounted to treason, Englishmen had God's sanction to keep the rebellious natives in their thrall. Right of conquest had also validated England's confiscation of Irish land.

*

Ultimately, in 1641, the long-suppressed Irish retaliated with a wave of horrific attacks. Queen Elizabeth's successor, James I, had followed her policy of planting Irish estates with English and Scottish settlers and was concentrating on Ulster, the center of residual Gaelic resistance. Native resentment erupted: a County Armagh widow was captured by insurgents, who drowned five of her six children; in Portadown, one hundred English Protestants were herded from the sanctuary of a church, marched to a bridge over the River Bann, and forced into the wintry waters, where they died of exposure, drowned, or were shot by musket fire. As always, though, Britain, with its far superior military resources, had the upper hand. Retaliation for the 1641 uprising, and the reconquest of Ireland (which, following the English Civil Wars, had become the monarchy's last chance of retaining the throne), resulted in one of the most shocking war crimes ever recorded.

In August 1649, six months after the execution of King Charles I, the parliamentarian General Oliver Cromwell decided to crush any remaining Royalist loyalty among Irish Catholics by conducting a massive campaign of ethnic cleansing. During his nine-month rampage, six hundred thousand perished, including fifteen hundred deliberately targeted civilians. Landowners, given the choice of going "to hell or to Connaught," were forcibly driven west to the bleakest and poorest of the provinces, where they were allowed 10 percent of their original acreage. And yet, the vast majority of Cromwell's contemporaries applauded his ruthless mission. To Irish Protestants, he was a brave deliverer who put down popery and set them free, while the celebrated English poet and parliamentarian Andrew Marvell endorsed Cromwell's view of himself as a divine agent, regarding him as an elemental firebrand who could not have been held back. "'Tis madness to resist or blame / The force of angry Heaven's flame," he wrote, in "An Horatian Ode upon Cromwell's Return from Ireland."

No other figure in nine centuries of Anglo-Irish history has so starkly embodied the divide between the two nations: Ireland's view of Cromwell as a monstrous tyrant is countered by England's admiration of the soldier and statesman—today considered "one of the ten greatest Britons of all time"—who steered his country toward a constitutional government. A 1946 spy film, *I See a Dark Stranger*, gently satirizes this polarity, pairing the naïvely romantic Irish heroine (a dewy Deborah Kerr) with a British army type (Trevor Howard). He is writing a thesis in his spare time on Cromwell, explaining that the "underrated general" is a highly neglected character. "Huh! Not in Ireland!" snorts Kerr's Bridie Quilty. "Do you know what he did to us?" Her private war against Britain has been provoked by hearing Guinness-fueled tales of Cromwell's terrible deeds, and although she ends up marrying the Englishman, she still retains her fierce nationalist principles. On the first night of their honeymoon she storms off with her suitcase after spotting the inn sign beneath their window: "The Cromwell Arms." Fifty years later, in much the same spirit, Irish prime minister Bertie Ahern is said to have marched out of the British foreign secretary's office, refusing to return until a painting of "that murdering bastard" had been removed. (It was a political gaffe likened to "hanging a portrait of Eichmann before the visit of the Israeli Prime Minister.")

*

Accounts of appalling suffering have been handed down from generation to generation, mythologized in folklore, poems, and patriotic songs. It was this historical grievance against the English—the "taunting, long-memory, back-dated, we-shall-not-forget . . . not letting bygones be bygones"—that Tony Blair decided to address when he was elected prime minister in 1997. The year marked the 150th anniversary of the Great Famine, when Ireland lost two million of its population through death or emigration—the most cataclysmic chapter of its history. The Irish had always blamed the disaster on Britain, which in the interest of protecting its economy, continued to import food from Ireland when its population were starving. Blair conceded that his country had indeed been accountable. In a message of reconciliation, read at a memorial concert by the actor Gabriel Byrne, he said, "That one million people should have died in what was then part of the richest and most powerful nation in the world is something that still causes pain. Those who governed in London at the time failed their people through standing by while a crop failure turned into a massive human tragedy." Hailed as a landmark in Anglo-Irish relations, Blair's admission coincided with a breakthrough in the Irish peace process—a few weeks later, the Irish Republican Army (IRA) restored its cease-fire.

*

The Great Famine had begun in 1845, when a virulent fungus, *Phytophthora infestans*, migrated from America to the potato fields of Ireland, Britain, and Europe, reducing entire crops to a black stinking mush. Nineteenth-century science had no remedies for such epidemic infestations, and as potatoes were the staple diet for at least half the people, the impact of the crop's massive failure was more catastrophic in Ireland than anywhere else. "The Almighty, indeed, sent the potato blight, but the English created the famine," was a typical nationalist response at the time, the accusation being that the apathy of English politicians, combined with their laissez-faire economic doctrine, had decimated the Irish peasantry. Even more incriminating was the belief that their campaign had been deliberate. The minister in charge of charitable relief, Charles Trevelyan, was demonized by the twentieth century, his much-quoted remark that "God had sent the calamity to teach the Irish a lesson" used as evidence by conspiracy theorists. In 1996, New York governor George Pataki ordered the Irish Famine to be included in the state's school curriculum, saying that children were to be taught that hunger had been used by Britain as a tool of subjection, "as a means of keeping people down." The Irish Famine/ Genocide Committee, founded in the United States a year earlier, looked into the possibility of forming an international tribunal to rule on legal accountability for the human loss.

Ordinary people's resentment was directed not so much at the British government as at local agents, land-grabbers, and moneylenders— the avaricious "gombeen men," who exploited the situation to their own advantage. What can be in no doubt, however, is the culpability of many Irish landlords. Regarding the removal of the poor from their estates as a prerequisite to making agricultural improvements, they used the Famine as an opportunity for mass clearances, evicting an estimated quarter of a million people. With nowhere to go, desperate tenant families built temporary shelters near their former homes, only to have them burned down or destroyed by bailiffs and hired crowbar brigades emboldened by the support of police and soldiers. In March 1846, responding in Parliament to complaints of inhumanity, the home secretary sided with the landlords, rejecting the notion that they were liable for criminal proceedings: as property owners, each had the right to do as he pleased.

*

In post-Famine Ireland, most smallholders were in arrears with their rent, and while numerous employers went out of their way to treat their workers with compassion—"Feed your family first, then give me what you can afford when times get better," said one Bantry-based man—landlords continued to be much despised. The most prominent were often absent from their properties, the MPs in London while Parliament sat, the wealthiest moving between their various estates and delegating the management to land agents, who notoriously exploited their power over the tenants. Less prosperous owners did not have the cash to invest in improvements, and consequently, the country's farming methods had stagnated. The umbrella term for

the situation was "landlordism," an entirely pejorative word implying abuse of authority, from rack-renting to mercilessly arbitrary
evictions.

And then, in the late 1870s, when rural Ireland—especially the
west—was again threatened with starvation and eviction, a radical
change took place. Determined never again to make "a holocaust"
of themselves, smallholders began collectively rising up and fighting for ancestral territory that was theirs by right. The Land War
of 1879–82 became the greatest mass movement Ireland had ever
known, a social revolution led by a messianic land activist and an
inspirational new political leader whose mission to bring down feudalism was funded by what today would be millions of American
dollars. For the first time in seven hundred years, Irish tenant farmers
stood together to destroy the landlord system, mounting an anarchic
campaign of intimidation, which the British tried to suppress with
hateful new coercive measures.

By the beginning of the 1880s, the Irish land issue had reached a
crisis point, occupying an astonishing nine-tenths of Britain's political agenda. What is less known is that the first rumblings of resistance took place more than two decades earlier—not in Dublin, the
hub of revolutionary fervor, but in a wild, wind-battered corner of
County Donegal, in Ireland's northwest.

BEFORE

ALL ALONG Donegal's Bloody Foreland, the Atlantic surf was seething and hurling itself against the rocks. It was the winter of 1857, and most of the inhabitants were down on the shore—men, women, and children, braving the gale to scythe seaweed from the shingles or wade into the foaming brine to gather it in armfuls. Draping the granite boulders with slimy, reddish-brown matting, these tangles of kelp were a commodity valuable enough for the locals to risk their lives in every storm. As the breakers boomed around them, sucking up seaweed from the deep, the families went out in force to collect it—soaked to the bone and aching with windchill and exhaustion.

Less than ten miles away, in the warm glow of a gaslit, mahogany-paneled room, a Belfast journalist was enjoying a glass of punch served by a fetching young barmaid. The door opened, and Lord George Hill, the owner of the Gweedore Hotel, looked inside to ask whether there was anything he could do to make the guest more comfortable. A convivial host, Hill had opened the hotel sixteen years earlier, modeling it on a Scottish Highlands lodge to provide salmon fishing and grouse shooting for the gentry. He had been enchanted by the vast open spaces, lakes, rivers, dramatic mountains, and savage seas of Gweedore, a small Roman Catholic community in northwest Donegal, and had bought land comprising twenty-four thousand acres, intending to create a kind of oasis there. The hotel he opened offered English tourists a pampering but adventurous alternative to Cheltenham's Promenade or the Pump Room in Bath, and with the arrival of guests as eminent as the Scottish historian and writer Thomas Carlyle, Hill could claim to be bringing metropolitan manners and culture to a place that had long been cut off from the world outside.

Situated in the northern province of Ulster—the most Protestant part of Ireland—and geographically distant from the rest of the Republic, Donegal has a unique spirit of independence. The parish of Gweedore, located in the heart of the Gaeltacht, where Irish is still the first language, is even more distinctive. It has none of the soft pastoral lushness of the south but is a remote area of blanket bog and primeval rocks, with a harsh, architectural beauty of its own. For centuries, its people had clung to the coast, struggling to make a living from land not meant to be worked, many of them living in mud hovels shared with a farm animal. Potatoes were their regular diet, and their main source of income was kelp, which they burned in kilns until the ashes could be compressed into hard blocks to be shipped to Scotland, where they were used to make iodine. Some traded in woolen goods, eggs, and corn (much of which was distilled into the illegal whiskey poteen), and it was this small local industry that Lord Hill decided to expand on a massive scale.

On the twenty-five hundred families who lived on his land, Hill launched what he called "a curious social experiment." He found overseas buyers for Gweedore's seafood, poultry, dairy products, and knitwear, commissioning a London firm to purchase homespun goods. He created a model farm, employing an agriculturist to introduce new methods, and miraculously reclaimed acres of spongy bog and impermeable granite to cultivate a number of different crops. He improved the roads, constructed a harbor, built bridges and mills for flax, wood, and corn, set up an icehouse to store the fish, opened a bakery, a tavern, a schoolhouse, and a general store. Not only involved with the running of the estate on a daily basis, Hill had learned enough Irish to speak to his tenants in their own language—an extraordinary departure in the context of the times. Unlike the malign stereotype, Lord Hill was a landlord of outstanding benevolence and vision. Or so it first appeared.

The Great Famine had been felt most desperately in the west (where there were even reports of cannibalism), and with ruin affecting countless estate owners, the more entrepreneurial among them had begun seeking ways to increase their revenue. One of Hill's first innovations was to reorganize his Gweedore acreage. Until then, under an ancient form of property division known as "rundale," arable land was held in joint tenancy by all its occupiers, who lived in clusters of houses with no fences separating their plots. It was a communistic arrangement that inevitably led to disputes, but it also forged a strong sense of solidarity. To Hill, these old ways were a barrier to any progress. He gave each smallholder his own strip of land and ordered him to demolish his house and construct a new one. This caused tremendous discontent. Not only were people asked to pay four times more rent for these rectangular "cuts," but they were expected to build the new houses at their own expense. Worse was to come.

Seeing the commercial potential, Hill imported large numbers of Scottish sheep, accompanied by their foreign owners, to graze on his mountain pastures. Tenants whose animals previously had access to land used by their ancestors for centuries now found themselves either charged a fee for entry or fined for straying stock. This provoked the Gweedore Sheep Wars—a campaign of furious retaliation in which hundreds of imported livestock were stolen, killed, or brutally maimed.

Hill's neighbor, a wealthy land speculator named John "Black Jack" Adair, followed his lead. Owner of the stunningly beautiful land around Lough Veagh, Adair rearranged its boundaries for the grazing of imported sheep, and in November 1860, his Scottish land steward was found beaten to death on the mountain. Holding his tenants collectively responsible, Adair decided to exact revenge. Over three days in April 1861, around two hundred rifle-carrying constables, soldiers with bayonets, and a hired crowbar brigade descended on the district. Declaring that they had legal hold, the men forced their way into every cottage and drove whole families onto the road. An entire community of 244 people was left at the mercy of relatives, friends, or the poorhouse, their possessions buried under the demolished walls and thatch of their homes. Although news of the scandal was raised in Parliament, no action was taken because Adair had broken no law. "The Crown could pardon a murderer, but could not prevent an eviction."

In the winter of 1857, the Adair evictions were still to come, but already the landlord-tenant conflict was alarming enough to have brought the editor of the *Ulsterman*, Denis Holland, to Gweedore to see things for himself. His guide would be Father John Doherty, an ardent defender of tenants' rights who had played a critical role in the sheep war by encouraging his parishioners in their anti-grazier revolt. Lately, however, the priest had decided that a more effective form of activism would be a newspaper propaganda campaign led by journalists like Holland, who were sympathetic to the cause, and could help to discredit Donegal's despotic landlords.

*

The gale had lost none of its force when the two men, priest and journalist, set off in the morning, the sleet lashing their faces with the viciousness of a knotted cord. As they drove away from the hotel, Holland noted the picturesque cottages nearby, learning they were not inhabited by smallholders but were show homes, rented to local bureaucrats—the first sign that Hill's philanthropy might be something of a facade. Farther afield, on the wild mountain road to Derrybeg, they passed the straight furrows of the new cuts, which Father Doherty declared to be evidence of Hill's self-promoting destruction of the community—"a means of generating pauperism." Here and there, scarcely distinguishable from the boulder-strewn bogland, was a stray cabin of peat sod or unmortared stone. Stopping to inspect one, they entered a single, sunken chamber and found a ragged man sitting by the fire with a sickly toddler in his arms, another child lying on a mound of turf. Simmering in a hanging pot was a brew of seaweed and foul-smelling liquid, and behind a screen, there was a mountain cow. The only furniture was a pine table and a bundle of rags in a corner serving as a couch in the day and a bed at night. Every dwelling they visited during the tour was just as abominably wretched.

Father Doherty was eager for Holland to talk to an angry tenant farmer who had been radicalized after spending seven or eight years in the United States. They headed north to the hamlet of Meenacladdy, where the rocky mountain road comes to an end. With its bleak stony beach overlooking Tory Island, and with the haunting, ashen cone of Errigal Mountain to the east, Meenacladdy was then—and still is—a place out of time. Michael Art O'Donnell and his wife, Margaret, had settled in the parish in the mid-1830s to build a house and start a family. Their first son, Patrick, was born around 1838. Daniel followed three years later, and they also had two daughters, Mary and Nancy. All went well, with O'Donnell cultivating his arable patch, until 1844, when a Dublin solicitor and property speculator, Lord John Obin Woodhouse, bought up Meenacladdy's thousand acres, taking away the tenants' grazing rights and sectioning off the land. "We got it out of rundale with great difficulty," Woodhouse would later remark. "The people were so much opposed to it."

For Michael Art O'Donnell, not being able to subdivide his property meant not providing a legacy for his sons, and he decided to emigrate. Selling his leasehold to Woodhouse's manager for twenty pounds, he paid his way to America, settling with his family in Janesville, Pennsylvania. They were away for the Famine years and doing fairly well in the States, but a yearning for home brought them back to Meenacladdy in the mid-1850s. O'Donnell repurchased his "tenant right" to the land, only to discover that Woodhouse had quadrupled the rent, justifying this by the amount of money he had spent on improvements in the interim. "Sure if it wasn't for burning the

kelp we couldn't pay the rent at all," exclaimed O'Donnell. "An' even
on that the landlords want to put a tax if they can." He uttered some
angry words in Irish, which to Holland sounded like oaths, surprising
him, as he'd encountered only crushed acquiescence until now. Father
Doherty smiled. "I fear Mihil learned to curse a little in America,"
he said.

It was hard for an outsider to understand what could have driven
Michael Art O'Donnell back to the hardships of Donegal and its
implacable landlord rule. His explanation was simple. He and his wife
had been disturbed by the "immorality" they had seen in the States
and became increasingly frightened that their children would "lose
their religion." Anti-Catholic forces in 1850s America were stronger
than at any other time in its history, with roving street preachers zeal-
ously working to convert new immigrants to Protestantism. It was a
decade in which enemies of Catholicism far outnumbered the Catholics themselves; churches were violated by fanatics who whipped up
hatred and hysteria about "a bigoted, a persecuting and a superstitious religion." And with most impoverished Irish immigrants gravi-
tating toward the tenement districts of American cities, alcoholism
and crime were rife. "Better for many of our people they were never
born than to have emigrated from the 'sainted isle of old' to become
murderers, robbers, swindlers and prostitutes here," one Boston Irishman exclaimed.

So, the O'Donnells were far from alone in believing that the option
of one meal a day of potatoes and seaweed in Ireland was better than
the sinful temptations of American urban life. And yet, they must
have known that Meenacladdy could offer their sons no future. None
of the four siblings was able to read or write; the two girls could
marry, but with hundreds of families in the region facing destitution,
what prospects were there for the boys?

Between 1858 and 1860 hundreds of single young people began
leaving Gweedore and the adjoining parish of Cloughaneely, carrying
tufts of grass or lumps of turf as mementos of their homeland. The

departure ritual was always the same. The night before, there would be drinking, singing, and dancing, but when daylight broke the *caoine* (keening) would start in earnest, its eerie sound fading as the young emigrant left the village, watched by family and friends until he or she could no longer be seen.

Sponsored by a relief fund, the teenage Dan O'Donnell emigrated to Australia; Paddy went to America—"the New Ireland across the sea"—just one of millions of anonymous immigrants driven to seek a better future. Or, at least, so he was until the name Patrick O'Donnell became infamous throughout the world—a name that still resonates in Donegal to this day.

ONE

The Leader

Twenty years later

FROM WELL before dawn on a rainy Sunday in June 1879, tenant farmers from miles around began converging on the coastal town of Westport in County Mayo. By mid-morning a procession had formed of men wearing green scarfs patterned with the Irish harp and shamrock and brandishing banners with the words IRELAND FOR THE IRISH! SERFS NO LONGER! THE LAND FOR THE PEOPLE! A brass band accompanied them as they made their way in a heavy downpour to a field near the town, where a crowd of about eight thousand had gathered. Taking the platform, the chairman introduced the first speaker as "the great Grattan of this age," shrewdly predicting that, like Henry Grattan, the pioneering statesman who won new legislative freedom for Ireland in 1782, this was another Irish Protestant who would leave his mark on history.

> We have here amongst us today Charles Stewart Parnell [*cheers*] whose high character is well known to all of you [*cheers*]. He left the county of Wicklow yesterday to be here today [*He is welcome!*] and he will leave Westport tonight to be in the British Parliament tomorrow night [*cheers and a shout, "And a good man he is in it!"*].

A slim, proud, inscrutable figure with fire in his eyes, Parnell had all the authority of a natural ruler, and yet, unlike the electrifying

Grattan, he was no orator. His speech was plain, his voice quite soft, but his clenched fists conveyed the anger he felt about Ireland's feudalism as forcefully as eloquent words.

> You must show the landlords that you intend to hold a firm grip of your homesteads and lands [*applause*]. You must not allow yourselves to be dispossessed, as you were dispossessed in 1847. . . . Above all things remember that God helps him who helps himself, and that by showing such a public spirit as you have shown here today, by coming in your thousands in the face of every difficulty, you will do more to show the landlords the necessity of dealing justly with you than if you had 150 Irish members in the House of Commons [*applause*].

Five years earlier, Parnell could not have held this audience. He was a landlord himself, the owner of Avondale, a family estate in softly rolling County Wicklow, and never happier than when riding, hunting, shooting, or playing cricket. Three of his ancestors had been distinguished politicians, his American mother voiced blazing anti-British views, and two of his sisters were militant nationalists, but Charles did not know or care about Anglo-Irish affairs—in fact, with his aloof manner and Oxbridge accent he could easily be mistaken for an Englishman. His priority throughout his twenties had been to turn his five-thousand-acre property into a paying proposition and become a progressive landowner while maintaining good relations with his tenants. If he ever set foot in Avondale's well-stocked library, it was not to consult the texts on vital Irish issues written by his grandfather and great-uncle but to expand his own interests—geology, mining, mechanics, and country sports. The only book his favorite brother ever saw him read was William Youatt's *History, Treatment and Diseases of the Horse*.

*

Sir John Parnell, Charles's great-grandfather, a passionate supporter of Irish independence, had been a member of Grattan's Parliament but forfeited his post as chancellor of the exchequer when he opposed the merging of Ireland with England—the 1801 Act of Union that brought Irish administration under the control of Westminster. Sir John had not engaged with the cause of Catholic political emancipation—the right to sit in Parliament—but his two sons, Henry and William, both parliamentarians, had thrown themselves into the fight (finally won in 1829 by the legendary Irish leader Daniel O'Connell).

Henry's book on the penal laws chronicling England's legal persecution of Irish Catholics during the eighteenth century is regarded as a classic, while William's pamphlet *An Historical Apology for the Irish Catholics* was reprinted at least three times. In it, Queen Elizabeth is reviled as an oppressive and vindictive tyrant whose bigotry toward Catholics and confiscation of Irish land was the main cause of the country's lasting discord. William's only fictional work, *Maurice and Berghetta; or, The Priest of Rahery: A Tale*, is dedicated to the Catholic priesthood, and what the novel lacks in human interest is made up for in the "aching pity" of the introduction. A cry from the heart, it inveighs against the deplorable state of the Irish peasantry—a people degraded, oppressed, and forbidden any connection with the civil business of their country—and pleads for compassion from the Anglo-Irish class: "The unfeeling society in whose narrow circle they pass their time; they eat pineapples, drink champagne, shoot woodcocks, are assiduously flattered and feeling themselves very well off, forget how other people suffer."

It was William Parnell, Charles's grandfather, who inherited Avondale from a cousin and combined his role of country gentleman with that of politician and proselytizer—"Constantly thinking, studying, writing, talking in hope that by exertion or good fortune he might be the means of bettering [Ireland's] condition." His son, John Henry, Charles's father, while also free of the usual supremacist attitudes, did not involve himself in anything other than parochial administrative affairs. He aimed simply to be a liberal and innovative landlord of Avondale and his two other Irish properties, relishing local society, proud of his position as master of the hounds, and indulging his great passion for cricket. But on a tour of the United States and Mexico, his eyes were opened to the world beyond Wicklow—an adventure that led to "the one impetuous act on the part of a generally sober and predictable young man." This was his heady marriage in 1835 to a vivacious Washington belle, whom John Henry brought back to live with him at Avondale.

Nineteen-year-old Delia Stewart, the daughter of Admiral Charles Stewart, famous for his naval victories against Britain in 1812, can only have been impressed by the beauty of Avondale's surroundings —the magnificent park and woodlands sloping down to a deep gorge in the winding River Avon. The house itself was comfortable, if not particularly grand, with the bleak facade common to Irish Georgian architecture—a bleakness that worsened in the incessant rain. Before long, John Henry's new bride was feeling melancholy and isolated; she was "a flaring exotic," accustomed to far greater freedom than young women of the Irish gentry were. Not sharing her husband's interest in country sports, and bored by his circle, she began spending more and more time in Paris with her brother, whose Champs-Élysées apartment was a social hub of the American colony. Inevitably, the Parnells grew apart, although their marital relations must have continued, as Delia gave birth to twelve babies before the age of thirty-six (two did not survive).

Born in 1846, one of four brothers and six sisters, Charles was regarded as the household pet, his every whim indulged. He was delicate in health yet headstrong in manner, bullying his sisters and domineering even his brother John, who was four years older, mercilessly imitating his stammer so often that he started stammering himself. John and their younger sister Fanny were his constant companions, much closer to him than anyone outside the family, apart from his nurse, a firm but affectionate Englishwoman known as Mrs. Twopenny (pronounced "Tup'ny"). In line with upper-class custom of the time, Charles was sent to boarding school at the age of six or seven. With

Delia mostly absent from Avondale, John Henry—wanting to find a kindly surrogate, someone "who would mother [Charles] and cure his stammering"—enlisted the help of the principal of a girls' school in Somerset. When Charles contracted typhoid fever during his second term, she devotedly nursed her small charge back to health, but then felt it her duty to send him home. Over the next few years, he was tutored mostly at Avondale, and when his father died unexpectedly in 1859, Delia stepped in to supervise the education of the two older boys in preparation for university.

John, who was being schooled in Paris, accompanied thirteen-year-old Charles to a private cramming academy in the Cotswolds, whose regimentation contrasted harshly with their comfortable, if haphazard home life. To the masters, Charles was a reserved, edgy boy, while his fellow pupils disliked him for his arrogance and aggressiveness. Only while riding, hunting, or playing cricket did he distinguish himself, although John enviously noted that "Charley's" adroitness on the dance floor had made him quite a catch among the local girls. Seemingly untroubled by remaining in his younger brother's shadow, John was a kind, self-effacing youth who was nevertheless prone to occasional eruptions of the Parnell temper. Of the two, only Charles appears to have inherited elements of a much darker ancestral strain: he suffered all his life from melancholia, anxiety, sleep-walking, and night terrors that would cause him to "spring up panic-stricken out of deep sleep and try to beat off an imaginary foe." But he would be spared the mental disintegration of two forebears—Thomas Parnell, an eighteenth-century clergyman and minor poet afflicted with manic depression, and their great-uncle Henry Parnell, whose depression spiraled into psychosis and suicide.

*

The 1860s saw the rise of the Irish Republican Brotherhood, a secret movement formed in Dublin on St. Patrick's Day, 1858, with the aim of overthrowing British rule by armed insurrection.

In homage to the Fianna warriors of Irish mythology, the IRB's oath-bound members became known as "Fenians," and their crusade expanded so fast that they decided to launch a newspaper as a mouthpiece—the *Irish People*. Fanny Parnell, the family bluestocking, a petite, dark-haired sixteen-year-old, was swept up by this new wave of nationalism and began contributing passionately patriotic poems. Charles disapproved, refusing to accompany his sister to the paper's offices—"the Fenian stronghold"—and making fun of her verses, just as he chided their mother for her gullible support of members of the movement, whom he suspected were vagrants, turning up at the door for handouts. "He distinctly resented the idea of being stamped as a Fenian," John remarked, "[and] finally declared that he would leave the house if anything more was said about the Fenians."

As it happened, Charles was not in Dublin during a frenzy of Fenianism in the fall of 1865. The British government had suppressed the *Irish People* and arrested its editors for high treason; Fanny and John attended every day of their trial, and the Parnell house in Temple Street was searched by police, whose suspicions had been alerted by Delia's flamboyant complicity with the rebel cause. Charles had just started his first term at Cambridge, having been accepted by Magdalene College, a small, sporty establishment whose undergraduates were mostly rowing hearties, "sons of monied parvenus from the North of England." He made himself unpopular from the start, disdaining student antics and furiously throwing out a group who burst into his room to carry out some prank. The teaching at Magdalene was as lax as its admissions standards, but that suited Charles, who had no academic ambitions and was described by one contemporary as "keen about nothing."

His real education took place during university vacations. He had inherited Avondale on coming of age (John was left an estate in County Armagh), which brought him close to tenant farmers and deepened his attachment to the Irish land. He loved to spend time at a rough mountain shooting lodge, a former military barracks used to house troops involved in the suppression of the 1798 uprising. Drawing inspiration from the revolutions in France and America, this bloody fight for independence, lasting a few concentrated weeks, had disastrously rebounded, leading to the abolition of the Dublin-based Irish Parliament and opening the way for the union of the two nations. Britain's savage crushing of the insurrection was entrenched in Irish memory, and Charles would have heard tales from his old retainers of rebel soldiers ruthlessly tortured and executed (there were at least ten thousand Irish fatalities to England's six hundred). He is said to have taken pride in the tattered Irish Volunteer banner hanging in Avondale's baronial hall—relic of the Grattanite movement of the 1770s and '80s pushing for increased Irish autonomy. But it was a contemporary incident, not the discovery of history close to home, that triggered Parnell's political awakening.

In February 1867, as preparation for a nationwide revolution, there was an abortive Fenian raid on the armory wing of England's Chester Castle, and once again, the rising was suppressed by the British. The perpetrators were deported or imprisoned without trial, and during a Fenian ambush in Manchester to free two comrades from a police van, an officer was killed. What had been just an accident unleashed a wave of anti-Irish hysteria in England, leading to a notoriously prejudiced trial, and in November, three Irishmen—not one had fired the fatal shot—were hanged in front of at least a thousand spectators. The British government's execution of the "Manchester Martyrs" touched off a global outpouring of protest, the ferocity of which shook Parnell into engaging with Irish history for the first time. "Driven wild" by the injustice of inflicting the death penalty on men who had not committed willful murder, he began to learn of seven centuries of Irish victimization, and what had previously been no more than a faint Anglophobia—an aversion to that almost tangible sense of superiority and entitlement in the English character—intensified into an obsession.

"These English despise us because we are Irish," he told John. "But we must stand up to them. That's the way to treat the Englishman—stand up to him." Charles's temper was easily ignited, and during his last two years at Cambridge, he was involved in many physical fights. One night, after too much sherry and champagne, he assaulted a stranger in the street, who pressed charges. In May 1869, Parnell was summoned to court, fined twenty guineas, and suspended by the university for misconduct.

He was more than happy to spend a long summer at Avondale. In addition to building sawmills to capitalize on its timber assets, he intended to quarry the hills, situated in Ireland's ancient gold-bearing region, for mineral deposits (finding gold became a lifelong dream). Still not ready to renounce English society, Parnell continued to go to parties in Dublin, to British embassy balls in Paris, and even attended an event at Dublin Castle—the bastion of British rule—where he was seen chatting about cricket to the lord lieutenant, the Crown's representative in Ireland. He did, however, take a stand about not returning to England. He had been rusticated, not expelled, and so was entitled to take his degree, but Cambridge had come to symbolize what he most disliked about the English, and he had no further use for their elitist institutions. Besides, the twenty-four-year-old Parnell's horizons were still confined to his estate: his prime concerns were to focus on his landowning interests and find a bride to bring back home.

*

The Anglo-American colony in Paris was renowned as a marriage market, and Parnell's uncle, Charles Stewart, had a particular young heiress in mind for his nephew. A lucrative match would not only help with improvements to Avondale; it would ease the financial burden of the profligate Delia, who had been left nothing in her husband's will and whose support was a responsibility now felt acutely by her son. But if Parnell's designs on Abigail Woods had initially been mercenary, he was also seriously smitten at first sight. The daughter of a

Rhode Island art collector, she had rather a schoolmistressy face but created an aura of beauty by dressing exquisitely and imaginatively styling her blond hair. Her father had brought her along on his Grand Tour of Europe and the Middle East with the idea of introducing her to art, culture, and—more crucially—a future husband. Already feeling that she was on the shelf at twenty-one—"I am sure that if I do not marry soon, I shall never marry at all!"—Abby did not hesitate to respond to the advances of the tall, refined Charles Parnell, delightedly accompanying him on evening walks alongside other courting couples in the Bois de Boulogne. For several weeks they were inseparable, and in February 1870, when the Woodses traveled to Venice, Parnell followed them and presented Abby with a gold ring. "I am glad I came for more reasons than one," she wrote to her mother. "I think how anxious I know you will be but I am very prudent."

Back in Paris after a visit to Egypt, she found herself being urged to marry a titled foreigner, mostly by her father, who was determined to separate her from this nondescript young Irishman. Mrs. Woods seems to have been more open-minded about the match, and Abby frequently confided in her. "The more I think of it, the more worried I become. Just think of the letter that I should have to send!" she wrote in June, adding a few days later: "You cannot tell how perplexed I am about him." In August, when Charles's gold ring broke in two, it seemed like a startling presage, but he hastened to reassure her that he was "not at all superstitious" and hoped that she was not either.

Always fearful of omens ("How could you expect a country to have luck that has green for its colour?" he later demanded), Parnell was in fact appalled, and the letter from Abby that arrived soon afterward, questioning their future together, seemed all too inevitable. His insecurity showed in his angry antipathy toward potential rivals; one, an American male friend, felt impelled to caution Abby about her choice of such an offensive fiancé. "He cannot bear him. I do not wonder for [Charles] treats people so coldly and contemptuously," she told Mrs. Woods, asking, "What can I do to get out of this?" By September, she was relying on divine guidance—clearly not in Parnell's favor—as she then wrote calling off the engagement and sending copies of the letter to her mother and grandfather (whom she was sure would be "very much pleased that it is all over").

By now, Abby had returned to America, and Parnell, convinced that he could permanently win her over if he confronted her face-to-face, did not think twice about following her. Arriving at the Woods family mansion in Newport, he was so affectionately welcomed by Abby that he got the impression that "things were as they had been." One night, however, when a rakishly handsome young man came into the room, he could tell by her reaction that there was some kind of bond between them. Sure enough, Samuel Abbott, a wealthy, Harvard-educated lawyer, much approved of by her parents, would be Abby's husband within eighteen months. What shattered Parnell was not so much the idea of losing his fiancée to another man as the reason she gave for rejecting him. She had decided not to marry him, she said, because "he was only an Irish gentleman without any particular name in public."

*

John Parnell, then living in Alabama, was surprised to receive a telegram from Charles announcing that he was coming to see him. A year earlier, John had bought a cotton plantation in West Point and, wanting to expand the business into a fruit farm, had just planted new orchards of peach trees, which he proudly showed his brother when he arrived. Almost the first thing Charles said was, "I want you to come home with me; you have been over here long enough." But John, excited by his new enterprise, had no intention of leaving. He felt sure he knew the reason behind his brother's sullen, dejected manner, and finally, after being pressed, Charles "poured forth the pitiful tale." To distract him, John took him out shooting and on tours of the great Alabama cotton factories, gristmills, coalfields, and iron mines. Commerce—and in particular mining—fascinated Charles, and he wanted to know minute details of production methods in each place they visited. Instructed in American finance by his uncle, he had already taken a stake in Virginian coalfields and intended to invest a further £3,000 to become part owner of a mine in Warrior, Alabama. He might well have pursued a career as a mining magnate, had the brothers not been involved in a serious rail accident, which left Charles unhurt but injured John so badly that he should have been killed on the spot. Charles nursed John tenderly for over a month, and sleeping together in a small hotel bed, the brothers grew closer than ever before.

On New Year's Day, 1872, they sailed back to Ireland, John to take over the running of his County Armagh estate, Charles determined to make a name for himself. Eventually, he would admit "it was a jilting" that had driven him into politics, and if the humiliation of Abby Woods's dismissal still stung, the timing of it could not have been better.

*

Since the spring of 1870, there had been a major advance in Irish politics with the formation of a pressure group, the Home Government Association, fiercely campaigning for freedom from British control. Behind it was a brilliant barrister and MP named Isaac Butt, who was not only fighting for legislative independence but also taking the side of tenant farmers. At last it seemed as if the Irish might make themselves felt in England's Parliament; a new form of nationalism was emerging—a distinct change of direction that combined a respect for the Fenian tradition of physical force with a commitment to English constitutional methods.

In front of the fire at Avondale one night, the Parnell brothers had discussed the consequences of Butt's crusade. John, having gained insight into landlord-tenant relations by managing his own estate, stressed the importance of extending the tenants' rights system throughout Ireland. In July, the perfect opportunity presented itself. Until this moment, smallholders, the mass of the population, had faced reprisal if they did not vote according to the will of their landlords, but the passing of a momentous new bill—the Ballot Act of 1872—allowed these employees to vote in secret for the first time. "Now," Charles said, "something can be done."

A direct result was the spectacular success in the 1874 general election of Butt's movement, which had been reconstituted a year earlier as an official political organization, the Home Rule Party. Although Butt was still at the helm, he was proving to be conservative and overcautious, and both Parnells questioned whether he had the mettle to break though constitutional boundaries. "Charley and myself agreed that Butt was, if not too weak a man, at any rate too unenterprising to be leader of what then appeared to be a forlorn hope." Although neither had any experience, they decided the time had come to try to enter the political field themselves: Charles's position as high sheriff of Wicklow ruled out his candidacy for the county, and so John stood in his place. Unsurprisingly, he finished at the bottom of the polls, as Charles did when he took part in a Dublin County by-election later that year. In a result that surprised no one, the Parnell debut had been a disaster.

"He broke down utterly," recalled the Irish MP and lawyer A. M. Sullivan.

> He faltered, he paused, went on, got confused, and pale with intense but subdued nervous anxiety, caused everyone to feel deep sympathy for him. The audience saw it all, and cheered him kindly and heartily; but many on the platform shook their heads, sagely prophesying that if ever he got to Westminster . . . he would either be a "silent member" or be known as "single-speech Parnell."

Parnell did succeed in getting into Parliament the following year, his arrival on the Westminster benches on April 22, 1875, coinciding with a groundbreaking Irish victory. At the time, Ireland's politicians, hugely outnumbered and treated with mild contempt by their English counterparts, had no say over their own legislation—let alone any influence on constitutional decisions. Home Rulers—with one exception, a boorish, fearless man who had no respect for Britain's revered institutions—had resigned themselves to obeying Westminster rules. In a speech lasting a full four hours, barely comprehensible in his thick Belfast accent, Joseph Biggar deliberately blocked the day's business, making a mockery of parliamentary procedures. Watching with admiration and amusement, Parnell realized that Biggar, a former pork butcher with a round, jovial face, had inaugurated a formidable new Irish weapon: the tactic of obstruction, which, in more sophisticated hands, could be turned into a powerful system of political warfare.

Four days later, Parnell made his maiden speech. It was short and modest, spoken with evident nervousness, but he got across what he wanted to say—that Ireland was a nation in itself, not a geographical fragment of England. For the rest of the year, Parnell remained an undistinguished spectator. He was using the time to watch and learn the rules and customs of Parliament, studying its strengths and weaknesses in order to launch an effective attack. Slowly, by voicing advanced ideas, he attracted attention of the Fenians (his sympathy for the Manchester Martyrs was hailed as "a revelation"), and by 1877, the diffident neophyte had thrust himself to the fore. He had conquered his fear of public speaking and had begun adopting Biggar's new strategy, his calm, tactical delivery raising bumbling verbiage into a fine art. "Even a critical colleague admitted he was a beautiful fighter. He knew exactly how much the House would stand."

It had become obvious that Parnell should be leading the Irish party; Isaac Butt was an honorable politician, a gentle, kindly soul, who "could not bear to see even his enemies wince," but having reached his sixties, he was battle-weary and unwilling to condone the obstruction tactic of the radicals. Parnell, by comparison, had all the dynamism and effrontery of youth, and although he endorsed Butt's formula for a successful nationalist movement—the physical-force spirit working in tandem with constitutional methods—he knew that the government would never concede to Irish aspirations unless intense pressure was applied.

All that was missing now was Parnell's alliance with an Irish trail-blazer who had made it his life's mission to bring down feudalism. "Everything was ready, or would shortly be, for the conjunction of a great agrarian leader with the great political chief."

*

Michael Davitt, his face furrowed, hair thinned, and eyes sunken by seven horrific years in English prisons, was exactly the same age as Parnell, but the two men's backgrounds could not have differed more. The son of tenant farmers in Famine-stricken County Mayo, Davitt had been four years old when his family was evicted for failure to pay its rent. Michael, his father, mother, sister, and a new baby just a few days old were all thrown out onto the roadside as their cottage was set on fire. When they were turned away from Galway's poorhouse because Sabina Davitt refused to be separated from her children, the parish priest let them take shelter in his barn, and her husband went to England to find employment. He fell ill, and during the nine months he was hospitalized, Sabina labored in the fields by day and spun flax at night to pay for his return fare. Eighteen months later, the Davitts emigrated to Lancashire, in northwest England, and nine-year-old Michael went to work in a cotton mill, ordered to operate machinery that should never have been in the hands of a child. His right arm was crushed between cogwheels, and after a home amputation, to save his life, Michael was bedridden for several months. To pass the time, his mother used to tell him stories about "the wrongs committed by England on Ireland"—the brutal evictions she had witnessed, and an account of the 1798 rebellion, vengefully crushed by British troops. These tales "so fired his youthful imagination," his sister recalled, "that he didn't want to listen to anything else."

A decade later, at the age of nineteen, Davitt joined the Irish Republican Brotherhood, and in February 1867 led a platoon of fifty Fenians who planned to raid Chester Castle for arms. Learning in time about a tip-off to the British, Davitt managed to extricate his men without being caught, but he continued to deal in IRB weapons, and a London transaction led to his arrest for treason felony in 1870. As a result of an informer's false testimony, he was sentenced to fifteen years penal servitude—more than twice as long as his fellow gunrunner, who was an Englishman. In atrocious conditions of the notoriously desolate Dartmoor Prison, Davitt was singled out as an Irish political inmate and given such needlessly cruel and degrading treatment that it was impossible not to develop a loathing for the system that had allowed it.

In December 1877, he was released for good conduct on a ticket-of-leave for the remaining years of his imprisonment (his weight had dropped to 122 pounds, and his six-foot height had shrunk by an inch and a half). Davitt rejoined the Irish Republican Brotherhood and six months later, on a visit to New York, came under the influence of the exiled activist John Devoy, leader of the IRB's American sister organization, the Clan na Gael. Convinced that constitutional and revolutionary nationalism could unite in the battle for self-government and a peasant proprietary—the "New Departure of 1878"—Devoy promised Irish American support for a more aggressive parliamentary party. Under Isaac Butt, the land question had taken second place to Home Rule, but Davitt believed that only when feudalism was abolished could Ireland achieve independence.

Back home, on a visit to his native County Mayo, he was so horrified by the plight of the smallholders that he organized what turned out to be a historic public meeting. Held in Irishtown in April 1879, it was this rebellious gathering that struck the match to an incendiary new movement soon to set Ireland ablaze.

Davitt knew that if he were to build on the momentum, it was essential to involve Parnell. The Dublin press had not reported the Irishtown demonstration, but an appearance at an upcoming tenants' rights meeting by the most influential Irishman in the House of Commons would guarantee national coverage. Parnell's prestige would not only give the nascent land campaign an enormous boost, but it would almost certainly guarantee the backing of Irish America.

Persuading Parnell to participate in the demonstration in Westport had not been easy. As a Protestant landlord himself, Parnell feared that he would be ridiculed for siding with the tenants, and it was only after several conversations that he gave his consent. To Davitt's grateful surprise, Parnell kept to his word, even after a virulent attack on the proposed meeting by a prominent archbishop. "This was superb. Here was a leader at last who feared no man who stood against the people, no matter what his reputation or record might be. . . . I have always considered it the most courageously wise act of his whole political career."

The Westport crowd that day was just as indifferent to clerical opposition. Raised on memories of the Great Hunger, this was a new, tough-minded, nationalistic generation of Irishmen who refused to be swayed. Their pent-up mass power excited Parnell, who agreed to take on the role of president of Davitt's organization. And so it was that the Land League came about, its aim to achieve security of tenure, fair rents, and freedom for tenants to become property owners themselves. In just over a year, this mighty force of radical politics and angry populace would begin ruthlessly challenging the British domination of Ireland by decimating its landlord system.

✻

Bertie Hubbard was a twenty-three-year-old cub reporter reluctantly covering an Irish political convention in Buffalo, New York, when he found himself transfixed by Parnell's magnetism onstage: "The speech was so full of sympathy and rich in reason, so convincing, so pathetic, so un-Irishlike, so charged with heart . . . that everybody was captured by his quiet, convincing eloquence. The audience was melted into a whole."

This was to be the case in all sixty cities Parnell visited over the first three months of 1880 on a triumphant fundraising tour of the United States and Canada. With Michael Davitt temporarily out of action because of an arrest for sedition, Parnell had taken with him a passionate, scholarly young campaigner named John Dillon. Never the picture of health, with his scrawny limbs, dark-shadowed eyes, and concave cheeks, Dillon had become more emaciated than ever during the storm-battered Atlantic crossing, spent prostrate in his cabin. But as news reached North America of imminent famine in the West of Ireland, money for food became a priority, and Dillon's pitiful appearance proved excellent propaganda. In the words of one US governor: "When I saw this sleek young dude [Parnell] as well fed as you or I and a damn sight better groomed, I said to myself: 'The idea of sending out a man like that to tell us they are all starving!' But when the other man, poor Dillon, came along, with hunger written on every line of his face, I said, 'Ah! That's a different thing. There's the Irish famine right enough.'"

Intent on convincing audiences that land agitation was vital to the struggle for national independence, Parnell took every opportunity to drive home the point that the main cause of Irish poverty was its feudal tenure. In Cincinnati, on February 23, he said, "I feel confident that we shall kill the Irish landlord system, and when we have given Ireland to the people of Ireland we shall have laid the foundation upon which to build up our Irish nation." Henry George's book *Progress and Poverty* had recently been published, and quoting from it, Parnell made the link between Irish tenants and America's slaves. "Man is a land-animal. . . . Therefore, he who holds the land on which and from which another man must live is that man's master; and the man is his slave." He gained strong support from the influential journalist Patrick Ford, who took the view that Irish peasants and the American working class were facing the same struggle. "The cause of the poor in Donegal is the cause of the factory slave in Fall River [Massachusetts]."

Parnell's commitment at Westport had impressed Ford, who heralded his arrival in the United States in his newspaper, the *Irish World and American Industrial Liberator*. COLUMBIA'S WELCOME TO PARNELL was the front-page headline above a large sketch showing the symbolic figure enticing the Irishman up the steps of Liberty Hall. Distributed throughout Ireland as well as the United States, with a vast, mostly subsidized circulation, *Irish World* gave up much of its American news coverage in the interest of promoting the Land League. Its "Million Fund," set up expressly "to help the Irish people to obtain their Land from the Land-Thieves, and their liberty from the political thieves," became the greatest single channel of funds for the Irish cause.

✽

Early in March, during the Canadian stage of the tour, Parnell returned to his Montreal hotel to find a cablegram waiting him. "Parliament dissolved," Joseph Biggar had written. "Return at once." This changed everything. Isaac Butt had died the previous spring, to be succeeded by a chairman who had no qualities as a leader but was elected largely to keep out Parnell and his obstructionist clique. Split between militant Home Rulers and moderate, pro-British MPs, the Irish party badly needed to be recast and refashioned, and Parnell saw that it was crucial to summon candidates who would favor a more confrontational strategy. Leaving John Dillon in charge in North America, he caught a train to New York the following morning; a snowstorm delayed the departure of the steamship on which he had booked his passage home, but finally it set sail, and as Parnell stood on the bridge, bareheaded in the swirling snow, he was formally saluted by veteran Irish soldiers of the Sixty-Ninth Infantry Regiment. It was a magnificent sight, and Parnell's regal wave in response was visible proof of his belief in his destiny: the uncrowned king of Ireland was coming home to fight for his people's land.

TWO

That Half-Mad Firebrand

QUEEN VICTORIA had scarcely arrived for a holiday in the German spa of Baden-Baden when she learned the alarming news of Britain's dramatic election results; there was no longer any doubt—her Conservative government was about to fall.

The previous few days had been taxing enough. She had traveled to Darmstadt, where her daughter Alice, grand duchess of Hesse, and one of her grandchildren had died of diphtheria a little over a year ago. She made a pilgrimage to the mausoleum holding the coffins, attended the confirmation of her two motherless granddaughters, and revisited Schloss Darmstadt to see Alice's sitting room, where all her belongings were just as she had left them. With her mind filled with poignant images, the queen had just returned to the sanctuary of her Baden-Baden villa when, on April 2, she received Prime Minister Benjamin Disraeli's "terrible telegram."

Convinced that the Liberal opposition in power would be a calamity for the country, Victoria was plunged into despair, but as the days went by, she could not help being lulled by her surroundings. She felt cozy in "dear little" Villa Hohenlohe, a spacious alpine chalet, and the rising hills reminded her of the view she loved in Scotland; it was delightful to go for walks and pass people who recognized her but never stopped and stared or followed her, as they did at home. She was enjoying the spa town's recreations and the daily sightseeing expeditions, particularly a visit to a small chapel, where she had been intrigued by the instruments of self-torture used by an eighteenth-century duchess during Lent: "A whip with sharp nails, with which she scourged herself—a girdle with sharp nails, which she wore next to her skin, & knee plates, also with nails, on which she knelt!!" But there was no escaping the political drama. "I grieve at the thought of parting with friends," she wrote in her journal that night. "Especially Lord Beaconsfield."

Queen Victoria had recently rewarded Disraeli with the title "Earl of Beaconsfield," as a formal acknowledgment of her esteem. When he came to power, in 1874, she had been a virtual recluse, still in deep mourning for Prince Albert. Disraeli, although now seventy-six, was young at heart and relished playing troubadour to susceptible dowagers; from the beginning, he set out to please and amuse Queen Victoria. They exchanged sentimental Valentine's Day cards, and the queen eagerly looked forward to Disraeli's long, informative, gossipy letters. On visits to Windsor, he thrilled her with his "poetry, romance and chivalry," deferentially dropping on one knee, his head lowered, his dyed black ringlets falling over his temples as he kissed her hand and earnestly declared his loving loyalty and faith. Disraeli knew that he overdid the flattery, mostly tongue-in-cheek, but it charmed the queen, who saw that beneath the flirtatious courtesy was genuine devotion.

More importantly, Disraeli shared and indulged Queen Victoria's pride in her empire. He hastened an act through Parliament that gave her the right to style herself empress of India, a title she had long coveted; and when Her Majesty's Treasury bought the bankrupt khedivate of Egypt's shares in the Suez Canal, Disraeli presented her with Britain's new acquisition as if it were a personal gift: "It is just settled. You have it, Madam." In the summer of 1879, encouraging Disraeli in his imperialistic foreign policy, she wrote, "If *we* are to *maintain* our position as a *first-rate* Power, we must, with our Indian Empire and large Colonies, be *Prepared for attacks* and *wars, somewhere* or *other* CONTINUALLY."

Disraeli needed little goading. By the end of the decade he was threatening the Russians with military action, occupying Cyprus, and waging war in Afghanistan and against the Zulu in South Africa.

It was this brash jingoism that had brought the former Liberal prime minister William Gladstone out of retirement to take down the government. In 1876, when reports reached Disraeli that thousands of Bulgarians had been murdered by Turkish troops, he cynically dismissed the atrocities as nothing but coffeehouse babble. Gladstone, on the other hand, was outraged. He believed that Disraeli was capable of entangling Britain in a war on Turkey's behalf and decided that he would make it his duty to put a stop to this imprudence while siding with the world's oppressed nations and racial minorities. Choosing the Scottish constituency of Midlothian to win his parliamentary seat, Gladstone embarked on what was more moral crusade than political campaign. From November 24 to December 7, 1879, his impassioned speeches vented his anger at "Beaconsfieldism," attacking its inhumane foreign policy and economic profligacy. "Everybody knew the great invisible antagonist with whom the orator before them was with all his might contending," wrote the MP John Morley, Gladstone's first biographer.

Queen Victoria, needless to say, had been distressed and angered by Gladstone's "unpatriotic ravings," which she considered to be little short of treason. Now, with the Conservatives fast losing to the Liberals, there loomed the unthinkable prospect of the People's William replacing Disraeli as prime minister. Writing in a fury to her private secretary, the queen brandished her stock threat of abdication and insisted that she would have nothing to do with Gladstone: "*That half-mad firebrand* who would soon ruin everything & be a *Dictator*. Others but herself *may submit* to his democratic rule but *not the Queen*."

*

Gladstone's premature retirement in 1874 had come as a shock—even to his wife, Catherine, who was certain he was making the wrong decision. He pleaded ill health, although he was strong and fit enough to think nothing of embarking on a twenty-five-mile mountain hike. But Gladstone was a fervent Christian and a classical scholar as well as a great statesman, and he yearned for time to devote to the study of theology and to indulge his private passions: the exposition of Homer interspersed with regular tree-felling. After five years, however, it was his religious faith that led him to "forget all rest and selfish thoughts," in Catherine's words. Believing himself to be a missionary of God, he felt he was being personally summoned to topple Disraeli and to restore right and justice. Gladstone's Midlothian campaign, launched a month before his seventieth birthday, was the first major step, and throughout the two-week tour, he had convinced himself that he was being sustained for the work by a power from above.

Gladstone's daughter Mary was astonished by the public's spontaneous outburst of feeling.

We are told the Queen has never had anything approaching to it—the surging crowds at the stations (even when the train doesn't stop) the illuminations and decorations and gifts. . . . The triumphant entry into Edinburgh on a dark, bitter winter's night with thousands and thousands of people behind barricades, street after street with its crowds of shouting multitudes, our four horses galloping on with 5 or 6 policemen outriders, hundreds having escaped from the barricades and running breathlessly alongside of the carriage. . . . You can hardly imagine the wild beauty and excitement of one of these galloping drives, the lurid light of the torches and bonfires, the brilliant glare of the electric lights and fireworks, the eager faces and waving hands and shouting voices. He has certainly stood it all wonderfully. . . . All Scotland is panting for a look at him. . . . Mama and I have been thumped, patted, stroked, had our hands and arms nearly shaken off by hundreds.

The display of support on Gladstone's second Midlothian tour in mid-March 1880 had been just as extraordinary. Even before his train left London's King's Cross Station, hundreds of enthusiasts had swelled to thousands; the intensive press coverage, drama, and spectacle of Gladstone's campaign were a foretaste of today's election extravaganzas. The raw spring weather, the hills covered in snow, had made no difference to the mass turnout in market squares, town halls, streets, and station platforms—great crowds enthralled by the blast of the Grand Old Man's oratory. Disraeli, bored by the electioneering process, had made few public speeches and had virtually no firsthand knowledge of popular feeling. Not so Gladstone. Standing with flying white locks and wild eyes, he rallied the multitudes of working-class men, never speaking down to them but holding forth with the same breadth of knowledge and sincerity with which he would address members of Parliament. It was this that had won him the country's confidence.

On April 6, Gladstone was on a night train heading south, so euphoric that he was unable to sleep. He was en route to his country home, and in the long hours before arrival he found himself ruminating once again "on the great hand of God so evidently displayed." From Chester station it was a brief journey to Hawarden Castle, an imposing estate on the borders of Cheshire, England, and North Wales that was his wife's childhood home and Gladstone's own center of gravity. The weather was unseasonably frosty, the lake iced over, and Catherine went straight to bed with a bad chill. Gladstone, still fired up with youthful energy, retired to his study, his "temple of peace," and set to work at once on a mass of papers, letters and congratulatory telegrams.

*

Waiting at Hawarden for the Gladstones' return was Catherine's niece, Lucy Cavendish, who was immediately struck by a difference in her uncle, noting in her diary:

> For the first time in my recollection he seems a little *personally* elated! It has always hitherto been the cause, or the moment, or the circumstances,

or *something*, that he thinks he is the mere mouthpiece of; but this unheard-of enthusiasm for his name, in his own country . . . and after the long time of abuse and loss of influence, has deeply moved him. Of course it was impossible to foresee—no one did—the *immense* victory brought about so mainly by his means. Even the autumn Midlothian campaign only made one hope that the tide was beginning to turn.

Thirty-nine-year-old Lucy was virtually a member of the Gladstone family. When her mother, Mary Lyttelton, died giving birth to her twelfth child, Catherine had taken charge of her sister's brood. "I must keep my promise and do what I can for her darlings," Catherine told Gladstone. "It is a sacred duty. . . . And you, poor dear, must share some of it." Catherine grew closest to Lucy, of all the Lyttelton children, closer even than she was to any of her own four daughters and four sons; they had the same unconventional, compassionate nature and worked side by side during hospital visits and the setting up of soup kitchens. "How marvelously, miraculously, you jumped with her, crept with her, flew with her," Mary Gladstone told Lucy, acknowledging the rapport. "Whatever her pace, you kept up; whatever she needed, there you were."

To Gladstone, too, Lucy was a surrogate daughter and more. He valued her political intelligence, frequently using her as a sounding board for his crusades; but their strongest bond was their religion. As a girl attending a service in Hawarden's chapel, Lucy had experienced a transcendent moment, "an unchangeable certainty" that had never left her. Governing every thought and action, her faith was so tangible that friends described an atmosphere of spiritual beauty about her that could fill a room with light.

*

A few days later, Lucy was joined at Hawarden by her husband, the Liberal MP Lord Frederick Cavendish, younger son of the Duke of Devonshire and practically a fifth son to Gladstone. Appointing

Cavendish his private secretary in 1872 and lord of the Treasury a year later, Gladstone had appeared to be grooming him for high office, telling Lucy, "He's such a compound of gallantry and good sense." A nervous public speaker (and hindered by a speech impediment), Cavendish would never be an impressive performer in the House, but he had made himself indispensable to Gladstone. Prone to what Lucy described as "having his blinkers on," Gladstone often became so completely absorbed by a situation, person, or even a book that he excluded thought of anything else. With a shrewd eye for the important factor in a tangled situation, Cavendish was one of few people who could get Gladstone to see things in proportion.

Since Gladstone's retirement, Frederick Cavendish's elder brother, Lord Hartington, had been leading the opposition in tandem with the former foreign secretary Lord Granville, and the two were now rivals for the position of prime minister. Although the people of Britain regarded the election as Gladstone's victory, he had made it clear that he would not resume the leadership without "a very general, a nearly unanimous, call from the Liberals with the appearance of a sort of national will." There was no sign of this. One of the most powerful ministers, Sir William Harcourt, was pressuring Hartington to push himself forward, insisting, "If you were staunch there could be no question of Mr. Gladstone resuming his old position." Hartington was not unambitious, but he could not bring himself to seize this opportunity of power. He was waiting for Gladstone to hint that he was willing to return as leader, but Gladstone was being obstinately passive. The situation had reached a deadlock, and it was Lucy Cavendish who was prevailed on to act as catalyst.

On April 10, Catherine Gladstone wrote Lucy a letter, knowing that she would show it to Frederick, who in turn would be likely to pass it on to his brother.

Can Father, having brought up his soldiers, run away? Now, however excellent Hartington and Granville are, would it not be cowardly to think of self when the giant's hand is needed? . . . If the country calls for Father and Lord Hartington wishes it! Surely it would be no disparagement of Lord Hartington to compare him with an experienced giant of power.

Mary Gladstone followed her mother's lead, writing Lucy a hastily penciled note clearly intended for Hartington.

Every person I meet, every letter I open says the same thing, "He must be Prime Minister." But no one seems to see it is no good saying it to *him*; they must say it to the Queen, Lord Granville and Lord Hartington. There is one thing I am certain of and that is that Papa will never take the smallest step *towards it*. The steps must be taken *towards him*. I have never doubted that in the event of a huge crisis of this sort he would never let personal longing for rest and retirement affect his coming forward again if he saw that the general feeling was in favour of it. . . . You will think it so silly, my writing to you and saying all the things everybody knows by heart, but I have always rather understood Lord Granville was the difficulty, that he longed to be Prime Minister. And now I hear he would dread it excessively. And so I don't see what the obstacle is.

Lucy knew exactly what it was: the small, stout, stumbling block of Queen Victoria, who "would far prefer either of the existing leaders to Uncle William, whom Dizzy has bamboozled her into dreading above all things." So certain was Lucy that the queen would not officially invite Gladstone to form a government that she had placed a two-pound bet on it (around $250 today).

*

It had been a wrench for Queen Victoria to leave Villa Hohenlohe, and three days later, on April 18, her melancholy was matched by a gloomy Disraeli, whom she received that afternoon at Windsor

Castle. Informing her that he and his cabinet proposed to resign immediately, Disraeli advised the queen to ask Lord Hartington to succeed him as prime minister. This was a slight to Lord Granville, who was older and more experienced than Hartington and generally regarded as the actual leader of the party (Hartington was leader of the House of Commons). Granville, however, was a close friend and ally of Gladstone's, whereas Hartington was thought more likely to be flattered into forming an administration independent of Gladstone.

The queen's eldest son, the Prince of Wales, was also championing Hartington as the next prime minister. "He is, as you know, the most moderate man of the Liberal Party." Her private secretary, Henry Ponsonby, however, was hedging his bets. Writing to her in Baden-Baden, he had said, "Almost all the newspapers assume that the Queen will send for Lord Granville, who will be acceptable to all sections of the Liberal Party (as will also Lord Hartington). But it must not be concealed that every day the cry becomes stronger for Mr. Gladstone." This may have been the case, but the queen knew that the final decision was hers; the selection of a new prime minister is the Crown's constitutional prerogative, and Queen Victoria was not one to yield to outside pressure.

On the afternoon of April 22, she met Lord Hartington, with whom she spoke frankly, declaring her lack of confidence in Gladstone. Hartington was equally frank, and told her that the Liberals had no chance of success if Gladstone were not in the government, and outside it he would only be a destabilizing force. Her son Arthur had already warned her of this. "I can't understand what is to be done with Mr. Gladstone if he is not to be in the new Ministry," he wrote. "Won't he be a terrible thorn in their side out of office?" But Arthur had also reminded her that people were "mad about him," intimating that Gladstone's appointment was inevitable. "It is indeed very hard for you to bear, dearest Mama, but I know how nobly you can sacrifice your own feelings at the call of duty."

The queen, still not giving in, sent Hartington off to find out whether Gladstone would agree to play a secondary role.

*

Queen Victoria had not always been hostile toward Gladstone—in fact, when Prince Albert was alive, she, like her husband, had held him in high esteem: "Such a *good* man," she had said. The disintegration set in during Disraeli's leadership, when, Iago-like, he began turning Queen Victoria's mind against his adversary, crowing with satisfaction, "She seems now really to hate Gladstone." The queen dated her dislike to 1876, the start of Gladstone's "violent, passionate invective against and abuse of Lord Beaconsfield." She blamed his conduct on venom and personal hatred, but her own self-interest was a factor too, as any attack on Disraeli's foreign policy was by implication an attack on the queen. In recent months, the remarkable public clamor for Gladstone had angered Victoria even further. "She can't bear to see the large type which heads the columns of newspapers by 'Mr. Gladstone's movements' while down below in small type is the Court Circular," noted Edward Hamilton, soon to be appointed Gladstone's private secretary.

In the early evening of April 22, Gladstone was visited by Lord Hartington, who gave a brief summary of his meeting with the queen and, as instructed, went through the motions of asking Gladstone to serve under him. This must have taken courage. Everyone knew that Gladstone had won the general election for the Liberals, and that none but he could head a new government. Gladstone shared this view: if God had called him out from retirement, it was not to be "the subordinate of one 20 years my junior and comparatively little tested in public life." The men's exchange was icy, and Gladstone made his displeasure known by implying that the party would have his support only if he agreed with its policies. He would, in other words, be a terrible thorn in the party's side.

The following afternoon, Hartington came to see him again, this time accompanied by Lord Granville. Together they had gone to Windsor in the morning to try to persuade the queen that Gladstone was the only possible prime minister, consoling her by saying that his age and failing health would prevent him from holding office for long.

*

Queen Victoria received Gladstone with studied courtesy while going through the motions of asking him to form a government. She waspishly described him to Disraeli as looking ill and haggard, but in fact, Gladstone had been animated by their encounter, noting in his journal, "She seemed to me, if I may say so, 'natural under effort.'" They briefly discussed the cabinet, in which Hartington was to be minister for India, Granville head of the Foreign Office, and Gladstone his own chancellor of the exchequer. Hartington had urged the queen not to reveal her lack of confidence in Gladstone, but she could not resist a moment of candor. She said that she hoped Gladstone would be "conciliatory," and he, admitting that he had indeed used strong language at times, assured her that any acrimony belonged to the past. "I ended by kissing Her Majesty's hand." (Describing a contemporary sketch of this exchange, the queen's biographer Elizabeth Longford wrote, "A look of detached disgust is depicted upon the royal features, as if the hand which suffered such indignity could no longer be her own.")

Gladstone had assembled his second administration within a few days. He gave the key appointment of home secretary to Sir William Harcourt, magnanimously overlooking their differences, and for the most part cocooned himself with family, friends, and trusted colleagues. Making financial reform a priority, he immediately set up a dinner with Frederick Cavendish, inviting him to become financial secretary, and admitting to Catherine that he could not undertake the chancellorship of the exchequer without Cavendish's help. As

Gladstone's unconventional wife did not fit the mold of first lady, their daughter Mary took on the role instead, given the title of honorary private secretary but in essence serving as political hostess. Looking like an earnest schoolgirl with a touch of Pre-Raphaelite beauty, Mary oversaw the Gladstones' move from their rented house in Harley Street to Number 10 Downing Street, furnishing the rooms, supervising the garden, and hosting "spicy and high bred" dinners. While Number 10 was still filled with workmen and a mass of flowers, "arranged in hideous untidiness, some in jugs, some in basins, some in pots," the new Parliament met for the first time on May 20, 1880.

Writing more than a half century later, Winston Churchill envisaged the members of Gladstone's government triumphantly taking their seats on the Treasury bench and looking around them. On the western horizon, Churchill wrote, they saw "the dark thunderclouds of Irish storm; an agrarian campaign backed by outrage; a national movement enforced by dynamite; an Irish parliamentary party using the weapon of Obstruction." In fact, they noticed no such thing. As Gladstone admitted later, neither he nor anyone else in the House of Commons realized the severity of the Irish crisis "that was already swelling upon the horizon and that shortly after rushed upon us like a flood."

THREE

The "Irish Soup" Thickens

I N THE spring of 1880, the West of Ireland verged on catastrophe. Disease had again struck the potato crop, and the winter's torrential rain had made the cutting and drying of turf for fuel almost impossible; cottagers threatened with starvation now faced the double calamity of hypothermia as well.

In Gweedore the crisis was exceptionally severe. A total collapse in the demand for seasonal laborers—the "tattie-hokers" who went en masse to harvest potatoes on Scottish estates—had left most families without a supplementary income, forcing them to buy goods on credit from local shopkeepers. Some of these acted as the district's bankers—the hated "gombeen men," who were regarded by the community as money-grabbing usurers. They, too, were refusing further loans. From Dublin a certain amount of aid was being organized by two influential private charities; in London a group of Quakers who had provided relief during the Great Famine stepped in again. One was led by a gentle, white-whiskered philanthropist named James Hack Tuke, who set off for Donegal at the beginning of March.

With his journey blasted by gales, rain, hail, and snow, Tuke was extremely relieved when he spotted the lights of the Gweedore Hotel. He had stayed there during the Great Famine years, appreciating the "admirable zeal and enlightened benevolence" of its owner, but Lord George Hill had died a year earlier, and his son, Captain Arthur Hill, had taken over. The new proprietor was rarely there, leaving his bailiff in charge as manager, and by the following spring, the Gweedore Hotel had become the epicenter of popular agitation. On this particular evening, however, it again provided Tuke with a welcoming refuge. He had arranged a meeting with the local priest—not Father Doherty, whose radicalism had led to his transfer to another parish—but Father James MacFadden, who was just as indefatigable a force. A stocky, handsome man of immense charisma, MacFadden spoke of the urgent need for seed supplies and grants for the construction of bog roads. He told Tuke that out of a thousand families, six hundred had no resources whatsoever and would starve.

The following morning, encountering the full force of the storm, Tuke collected Father MacFadden and headed toward Meenacladdy. In the distance, Mount Errigal was covered with snow, while along the coast, Atlantic waves were thrashing the cliffs as locals braved the elements to gather seaweed. Previous harvests spread out along low stone walls were turning from russet to blue like a bruise, but there was little hope that the kelp would ever be dry enough to burn this year.

Access to most of the dwellings to which MacFadden took Tuke was over sodden bogland, and as he followed the priest in his long, black flapping coat, Tuke was forced to jump over ditches and from clod to clod to avoid deep holes. It was hard for him to believe that one hovel they visited was a human habitation, and although there was more light in another, it only made the wretchedness more unsettling—the haunting image of five children wearing MacFadden's gifts of calico shirts that barely covered their malnourished bodies. Scrambling again across the bog, they came upon the worst sight of all—"if worse could be"—an old man and woman living in a hole scooped three feet below ground level. Not even the destitution and misery he had witnessed during the Great Famine years had prepared Tuke for this: "I feel, after a lapse of 24 hours, that I can hardly bring myself to write. It is not merely the unusual distress of today . . . but the everyday life, the normal condition of hundreds, nay thousands, of families on the west coast of Donegal, and of many other parts of the west of Ireland which oppresses me."

One smallholder he spoke to saw no alternative but to take his wife and children back to America: "We are beaten—everything is against us. Nature binds a man to his own counthrey [*sic*]—but I can't stand it any longer." Tuke himself was coming around to the idea of emigration as the only survival strategy for the destitute. Although it robbed Ireland of its most active and enterprising young people, many then found themselves in a position to help relatives they had left behind. "I would be a long time in the old country before I could give you the enclosed (£2)," one daughter remarked in a letter to her mother. Tuke, however, wanted to look into the feasibility of sending whole families abroad. Over the next three years he would raise enough funds for hundreds of families to emigrate, and his negotiations with the Canadian government resulted in free grants to new settlers, in addition to 160 acres of land. Thanks to Tuke, victimized Irish tenants would be offered the option to trade "the most minute subdivision and strife for the possession of a strip of bog" for a new life "on broad acres of fertile prairie-land to be had for the asking." It hardly seemed to be a choice.

*

Emigration had certainly paid off for Michael Art O'Donnell's younger son, Dan. His years in Australia and then America had earned him enough money to return to Gweedore as a wealthy man. He learned to read and write by sharing a classroom with ten-year-olds and married a local widow. In Briney's Town, near Derrybeg, he opened a shop, a bakery, and an alehouse; he also bought several acres of land from Father MacFadden. "He had a lot of people working for him, and his name was well known within the community," remarks the historian Dónall Ó Baoill.

But if Dan had elevated himself into becoming a respectable member of the parish's new middle class, his brother had fared less well.

Patrick O'Donnell's experience was likely to have been that of many other young arrivals in America, who crossed vast territories to find work in Irish enclaves. They would beg rides on goods trucks or travel for days on trains where it was not safe to sleep, as fellow passengers "thought no more of killing a human than they thought of killing a midge . . . particularly those that looked as if they had something in their pockets." In the Rocky Mountains of Montana, covered for most of the year with ice and snow, conditions were as dangerous as they were harsh, and on one occasion mine workers had to rescue the wife of a Donegal O'Donnell who had been abducted from their camp. Starting off as a laborer, Patrick went on to herding cattle on horseback outside Allentown, Pennsylvania, becoming the image of a homegrown American in his cowboy outfit.

Around 1867, Patrick O'Donnell returned home to Meenacladdy for a few years, living in an adjoining cottage to his parents', where he kept a huckster's shop. He had met and married a woman from neighboring Cloughaneely, Margaret O'Brien, who had dark brown hair and a fair, freckled Irish complexion. When O'Donnell's father died in 1871, and his mother went to join Dan in America, the couple followed, settling in Pennsylvania, where they both had family. A relative of Margaret's who worked in the steel-rolling mills at Ironton helped O'Donnell find a job there. Jack Curran, who with his family had also emigrated from Gweedore, later remembered, "Everything was good enough, Paddy worked away like that and he was married, but even so he wasn't very fond of the work and he went off herding cattle again."

Having married "such a restless rover," Margaret O'Donnell was often left to take care of herself. The couple was childless, and she found work as a maid in Philadelphia, passing herself off as single because employers distrusted married women whose husbands' whereabouts were unknown. Patrick O'Donnell would boast of having made a fortune investing in mines in Pennsylvania and California—earning enough with one venture to open an alehouse on the Canadian frontier—but by the end of 1879 he had lost almost every cent. Leaving Margaret alone again in Philadelphia, he went to Scotland and was employed for a short while by the Edinburgh tramways. In the spring, after developing Milroy's disease, a lymphatic disorder, he was hospitalized at the Royal Infirmary and had to convalesce for several months. Dan lent him the money to pay his fare back home to Donegal.

In the 1850s, the O'Donnells' father, Michael Art, had been one of the few smallholders to vent his fury about the injustice of landlordism, but now virtually all Gweedore's inhabitants were resisting the hardships imposed on them. The parish was soon to be in open rebellion, its people no longer resigned to being impoverished victims but collectively rising up to stage what even the nationalist press would describe as "an absolute reign of terror."

*

When Gladstone first became prime minister, in 1868, his mission, he famously declared, was to pacify Ireland. The Fenian Rising of '67 had thrust Irish discontent into the foreground, and Gladstone began systematically addressing issues of land, education, and religion. At the start of his second term, however, with his mind focused on foreign policy, he was confident that the appointment of one of his most senior colleagues as chief secretary, the representative of English rule, would allow him to turn his back on Ireland for a while.

William Forster, a paragon of Victorian liberalism, had been one of the main contenders for leadership on Gladstone's retirement from the party in 1874, but he stood down in favor of Hartington. Formerly a Yorkshire mill owner, Forster was MP for the northern city of Bradford and embodied the gruff, plainspoken characteristics of a stereotypical Yorkshireman. Known as "Long Forster" because of his exceptional height, he was as physically ungainly as he was socially gauche, but few people knew that his crabby manner and stern moral integrity were softened by humor and a tender heart. (His father had described him as a boy as "almost too full of feeling.") Both Forster's parents had been Quaker preachers, and, as he was their only son, his upbringing had been strangely solitary. As one of "those queer-dressed strange-talking little Friends, with their stumpy hats and strait collars and demure gait," he was different from other children, his sense of alienation compounded by the fact that he was homeschooled for many years.

Forster grew into a man of high ideals, and as a politician was responsible for the Education Act of 1870, the foundation of today's British system of state schooling, and, two years later, the ground-breaking Irish Ballot Act. Unlike his parliamentary colleagues, he went out of his way to learn about foreign political crises by observing situations at first hand (visiting Serbia and Turkey, better to understand the Great Eastern Crisis after the 1876 massacre of Bulgarian rebels by Ottoman Empire troops).

With the Liberals' return to power in April 1880, Forster had accepted the low-ranking but critical office of chief secretary on condition that it came with a cabinet seat. He had a sound knowledge of Ireland's problems, a genuine sympathy for the poor and oppressed, and showed no sign of the usual British superciliousness and patronizing goodwill. In his youth he had gone on holiday to Galway to see for himself the ravages of the Great Hunger, and had never forgotten the half-naked semi-skeletons he saw clamoring for soup tickets outside the poorhouse, the lifeless children whose faces were so haggard they looked geriatric; or the supplicating mob that surrounded him, "more like famished dogs than fellow creatures." So graphic and compassionate were the reports he sent home that his philanthropic father, William Forster Sr., was prompted to take immediate action. William Sr. spent five months in Ireland distributing aid, joined by young volunteers including his son and twenty-seven-year-old James Tuke.

Now, over three decades later, it was Tuke who told Forster of the appalling conditions he had just witnessed in Gweedore, and other reports were equally disturbing. General Charles Gordon claimed that nothing he had been exposed to while governing Britain's most impoverished colonies in Africa and the East even approached the horrors of what he had seen in the West of Ireland. "The state of our fellow country-men is worse than that of any people in the world, . . . lying on the verge of starvation in places where we would not keep cattle." An emergency measure was crucial, and Forster took it on himself to provide it. On June 8, 1880, he introduced a new act intended to force landlords to recompense tenants unjustly evicted for nonpayment of rent. It was a moderate, peacemaking gesture intended to tide over a year of particular hardship and seemed to the Irish to be a promise of better things to come. In Parliament, however, it caused an outcry.

"That wretched Bill of Forster's has done incalculable harm to the party," Edward Hamilton noted in his journal. "It has frightened the landlords; brought discredit on the Government and satisfied no-one." As many peers in the House of Lords were themselves Anglo-Irish landlords, they viewed the Compensation for Disturbance Bill as unacceptable discrimination; their condescension toward the Irish was summed up by one disagreeable individual's complaint that the bill would "retain in the country those who ought to be shipped off to America . . . and it will be impossible to get Paddy to resume the habit of paying of rent at the end of the time." On August 4, the bill was rejected by a massive majority of 231 to 51, prompting Queen Victoria to write in glee to Lord Beaconsfield: "Do *you* EVER remember *so many* voting against the government to whose party they belong? *I* do *not*."

This "wild excess of landlordism," as Gladstone called the rejection of the bill, was not only a grave personal blow to Forster, it disastrously sabotaged the placatory new attitude. Radical Irish MPs, who of late had been treating the government with restraint, now started using this as an excuse to advocate for violent resistance to English rule.

✳

When Parliament adjourned, Parnell, who in April 1880 had been elected leader of the Irish party by a small majority, went home to Avondale, appearing "more interested in partridges than in agitation." Typically, he was biding his time, and on the night of Sunday, September 19, standing in the streamer-festooned town square of Ennis, County Clare, Parnell broke his silence, making the speech that provoked a malevolent new form of warfare. Evangelically urging the people in the crowd to band themselves together in local branches of the Land League and ruthlessly adhere to its principles, he quietly and deliberately asked the keynote question: What would they do to a land-grabber—a man who took over the farm of an evicted tenant? Waiting with hands behind his back until the tumult subsided, Parnell calmly resumed:

> Now I think I heard somebody say, "Shoot him!" [*Cheers*] but I wish to point out to you a very much better way, a more Christian and a more charitable way. . . . You must shun him on the roadside when you meet him, you must shun him in the streets of the town, you must shun him at the shop counter, you must shun him in the fair and in the market-place, and even in the house of worship, by leaving him severely alone, by putting him into a moral Coventry, by isolating him from his kind as if he was a leper of old.

There was already a precedent for social ostracism, a technique used against carpetbaggers in America's southern states, one both John Dillon and Michael Davitt had advocated. But it was only after Parnell's Ennis speech that it was practiced on a nationwide scale.

The first known target was not a land-grabber but an unpopular English land agent, Captain Charles Boycott, whose victimization gave the new strategy its name. In an expansive letter to the London *Times* of October 14, 1880, Boycott outlined the kind of activities that would soon wreak havoc on England's rule over Ireland.

Sir,—The following details may be interesting to your readers as exemplifying the power of the Land League. On the 22nd of September a process-server, escorted by a police force of 17 men, retreated on my house for protection, followed by a howling mob of people, who yelled and hooted at the members of my family. On the ensuing day, September 23, the people collected in crowds upon my farm, and some hundred or so came up to my house and ordered off, under threats of ulterior consequences, all my farm labourers, workmen, and stablemen, commanding them never to work for me again. . . . My blacksmith has received a letter threatening him with murder if he does any more work for me, and my laundress has also been ordered to give up my washing. A little boy, 12 years of age, who carried my post-bag to and from the neighbouring town of Ballinrobe, was struck and threatened on September 27, and ordered to desist from his work, since which time I have sent my little nephew for my letters, and even he, on the 2nd of October, was stopped on the road and threatened. . . . The shopkeepers have been warned to stop all supplies to my house. . . . My farm is public property; the people wander over it with impunity. My crops are trampled upon, carried away in quantities and destroyed wholesale. The locks on my gates are smashed, the gates thrown open, the walls thrown down, and the stock driven out on the roads. I can get no workmen to do anything, and my ruin is openly avowed as the object of the Land League, unless I throw up everything and leave the country. I say nothing about the danger to my own life, which is apparent to anybody that knows the country.

Charles C. Boycott
Lough Mask-house, Ballinrobe, county Mayo, Oct. 14.

Three weeks later, it was rumored that a workforce of about three hundred armed Ulstermen was heading for Boycott's farm—members of the Protestant Orange Order, intent on defending civil liberty. Alarmed by the likelihood of violence, Forster wrote to

Gladstone, telling him that he had ordered detachments of five hundred infantrymen and three squadrons of cavalry to be sent to the district as a precaution. This vast show of military force guarding the workers harvesting Boycott's turnips made world headlines and caused considerable mirth—the ludicrous aspect was scorned by the Land League, whose power the "relief" effort had only served to underline.

But what began as passive resistance against tyranny and injustice worked effectively, in the view of extremists, only when militarized by intimidation. At night a grave might be dug in the garden of a boycotted shopkeeper, and in daylight masked men would show themselves behind hedges along the road by which he or his family traveled. A tenant who had paid a portion of his rent to a boycotted landlord woke to hear shots fired into the bedroom where he and his wife were sleeping. Another farmer was dragged into the street by a party of thirty men who had kicked down his door and beaten him with sticks. A boycotted publican's business was ruined because nobody would enter his premises, and in church the antipathy of the congregation was so threatening that the man left before the service ended (the pew on which he had sat was later smashed to pieces). After threats were made to his life, armed constables were called in to give twenty-four-hour protection.

In Anthony Trollope's unfinished novel *Land Leaguers*, the menacing weapon of boycotting results in the murder of a ten-year-old child. The boy, Florian, had witnessed the flooding of his father's land and crops by local members of the Land League but refused to testify, having fallen under the influence of a zealous young priest and been threatened by the agitators themselves. When he finally gives way and names the culprits, the family is boycotted, its servants and estate workers all leaving, with exception of an old retainer. The shooting of Florian from behind a hedge recalled the September 1880 murder by masked assassins of Captain Boycott's neighbor Lord Mountmorres, and in both cases no culprit was brought to justice. So it was with most agrarian crimes of the time: no witness dared provide the police with information, and anyone appointed on a jury would be too frightened to convict.

*

"The Irish 'soup' (as Mr. Gladstone terms it) is thickening, and becoming what the brewers would call Treble X," Edward Hamilton wrote in early December 1880, adding ten days later: "Lord Granville said that no other human being could have kept the Cabinet together over this Irish business save The Great Man, whose tact and influence with others is something certainly extraordinary. It is indeed plain that if he had his own free will he would retire from politics." Hamilton was right, of course, and Gladstone was now admitting this himself. "I was talking to Homer . . ." he remarked to one of his colleagues, adding after realizing his slip, "Ah if I could talk to the old chap how soon would I give up all this business."

The Irish problem was the responsibility of one man alone, William Forster, who was also feeling the strain. To Michael Davitt, he had largely himself to blame. While praising his good intentions, Davitt believed that Forster was blind to the difference that now existed between two generations of Irishmen—the spiritless victims of the Great Famine versus the semi-revolutionary followers of the Land League. "Had there been no Land League . . . he would probably have taken sides against the landlords, and helped the people in his own way to some ameliorative measures. . . . But he found himself in a situation which, in a sense, compelled him to defend an impossible system of rule and of land tenure against the leanings of his personal sympathies, because law and order were menaced."

Forster had convinced himself that Land League leaders, now the most powerful figures in Ireland, had tacitly incited the agrarian violence, and he was determined to bring them to trial. An Irish jury was highly unlikely to convict the men, but Forster felt that the government needed to demonstrate its determination to enforce the law. On

October 23, it was announced that Parnell and thirteen other associates were to be prosecuted.

From this point on, Irish MPs began insulting and ridiculing Forster. He had defended the conduct of the Royal Irish Constabulary, whose officers were compelled to protect eviction servers against angry mobs, but because they were dealing with violence at close quarters, he recommended that ball cartridges be replaced by the less deadly buckshot—a term with which he was instantly branded. "Buckshot" Forster was now regarded as Ireland's greatest foe, even though his weekly voyages to consult Dublin's administrators had put him in much closer contact with the Irish than their own MPs.

The strain was taking its toll on him. To one observer, Forster seemed "broken in mind and body," and he had been spotted in London's Athenaeum club, talking wildly and confusedly, as if in a world of his own. Forster had never been particularly popular with his peers, who found him vain and volatile, but now they watched as he conducted himself "more like an inebriated or demented man than one merely who has lost his nerves." Gladstone had also noticed that his chief secretary was "getting [in] a twist," and yet the prime minister remained loyal, admiring the stouteheartedness Forster had shown in his isolation and the way he endured constant vilification with calm stoicism, even a degree of wit.

The inability of the government to provide the people with protection so distressed Forster that on November 3 he wrote a letter to Gladstone, urging him to summon Parliament without delay to call for emergency legislation. What he had in mind was harsh and extreme—a motion to suspend the writ of habeas corpus, which would allow suspects to be imprisoned without trial. "It is impossible for anyone to dislike it more than I do," he told Gladstone. "But I doubt if in any way we can keep peace and protect life and prevent anarchy." The cabinet met on Monday, December 14, listened to Forster's reasons, and voted unanimously to resort to coercion.

*

On the night of December 15, Lucy Cavendish was lingering in a corridor of Windsor Castle talking to Queen Victoria. Having briefly served as maid of honor, she was not intimidated by the queen and had always experienced "very much more pleasure than terror" in her presence; once, having been moved at dinner by Victoria's sorrowful expression, she had spontaneously pressed her hand when taking her leave. The affection was reciprocal. On Lucy's first day at court, Victoria had kissed her before getting into the carriage, and a week later, singled her out to dine with her.

Lucy owed the court appointment to her paternal grandmother, Sarah Spencer (Lady Lyttelton), who had supervised the education of Victoria and Albert's children and become almost a member of the family (the royal siblings called her "Laddle"). Receiving the offer, Lucy had "shrieked and kicked and jumped about between delight and fright," and her family hoped that the required discipline and decorum would help tame her high spirits. After holding the position for only six months, however, Lucy left to marry Frederick Cavendish.

They had met at a Chatsworth dinner in early December 1863, and Frederick had followed her a few days later to stay with the Gladstones at Hawarden, where they discussed church issues at a "capital little dance." By New Year's Eve, they were in love. On January 17, 1864, Lucy began her tenure at Osborne House, the queen's retreat on the Isle of Wight, where she received her first letter from Frederick, "grave and simple, like himself." Their courtship continued at Windsor Castle, and they became engaged. On a rainy day in May 1864, Frederick arrived at Osborne with Lord Granville, to whom he was private secretary, and the young couple was given the afternoon to themselves. They made plans for a June wedding at Westminster Abbey. When Lucy gave in her notice, Victoria sent for her to say goodbye.

She came towards me with a beautiful Indian shawl and a jewel-case in her hands: kissed me and gave them to me with many kind words about her regret that I was going. . . . She kissed me again and again, saying she thought and felt the more for me because I had no mother. The ornament she gave me was a beautiful amethyst locket bordered with pearls; on it a little diamond cross. . . . She said, "It is an emblem of what I have to bear day after day." . . . I thanked her as well as I was able; kissed her dear hand many times and began to cry. . . . [Then I] went up to my room and had it out.

In the spring of 1869, Lucy was invited to Windsor for three days as a guest in her own right. "The dear Queen hasn't seen me since I married," she wrote. "She won't have Fred. I feel sure she has never forgiven him for standing on one leg and forgetting his manners that courting time at Osborne." Over a decade later, however, in December 1880, Victoria had wanted Lucy's husband to accompany her and made a point of asking about Lord Frederick and his work. This visit to Windsor was a restful break for Lucy—"Sweet peace in snug little rooms with tea and books till dinner-time"—but during their long conversation in the corridor, she had been made aware of the gravity of Queen Victoria's mood. "And no wonder. Ireland is a great distress to her."

*

Gladstone and Catherine had also been invited to Windsor that weekend, and before dinner, he spoke at length with the queen. Until now, Ireland had never interested her—"People only go who have their estates to attend to," she once declared—but with battalions of Coldstream and Scots Guards being dispatched in preparation for war, she realized that it was a country she could no longer dismiss. The prime minister looked unwell, she thought, but she was impressed by the seriousness with which he viewed the situation and by his loyalty to colleagues. Gladstone had launched into an explanation of a carrot-and-stick policy the government was considering: a new act promising tenants concessions over their land, to be introduced alongside stronger coercive measures. It had taken some effort to follow Gladstone's long, labyrinthian account, but Queen Victoria had been relieved by its main thread: the assurance that Parliament was making provisions for her to empower Ireland's viceroy to suppress further agitation.

The following day, William Forster came to see the queen. Listening to him describe a massive increase in lawlessness and terrorism in Ireland, she told him it was imperative that he take a firm stance, following this up in a forceful letter written on Christmas Day.

> There is to be a Cabinet very shortly, and it will be Mr. Forster's duty to *insist* on the *immediate* suspension of the Habeas Corpus Act and probably other coercive measures, and these being brought in and *pushed* strenuously through Parliament before *any attempt* at *any* Land Measure being brought in can *even* be thought of. Mr. Forster should *insist* on this and threaten to resign *unless* it *is complied with.* Nothing *else* will do now. . . . If the radicals want a democratic monarchy; they must look for another monarch. And she doubts they will find one.

*

Christmas Day, 1880, in Dublin was frosty and brilliantly sunny. After a musical service at Christ Church, Forster walked home to his lodge in Phoenix Park accompanied by his daughter Florence. Orphaned as children, she and one of her brothers had been adopted by Forster and his wife, their uncle and aunt, and brought up in a caring, stimulating environment. As the daughter of the renowned educational reformer Dr. Thomas Arnold and sister of the poet Matthew Arnold, Jane Forster had always been surrounded by scholars and writers, and her marriage to William, whose quick mind and depth of reading matched her own, was a bedrock of intellectual companionship. Florence had blossomed under the couple's influence;

politically astute and gifted as a writer, she began keeping a journal of her father's Irish experience, often acting as his unofficial private secretary.

"By this time next week," Forster told her, "I shall very likely have ceased to be Irish Secretary"—a remark that took Florence by surprise, as she had not realized that his proposed coercion bill was quite so contentious. After dinner, at Forster's dictation, she wrote the memorandum he would be submitting to the cabinet in the New Year, and its gravity stayed with her. Two days later, driving through the city, she found herself studying the surly faces of men in the streets, her sense of their antipathy toward her as an Englishwoman bringing to mind lines from a Wordsworth poem she knew:

> I, with many a fear—for my dear country, many heart-felt sighs—
> Amongst men who do not love her, linger here.

✻

December 29 was Gladstone's seventy-first birthday, and confined to bed with a bad cold and a touch of lumbago, he was feeling his age. When Lucy Cavendish saw her "poor Uncle W" on New Year's Eve, she was alarmed by his fatigue and poor spirits. Another guest at 10 Downing Street that night, Gladstone's friend and future biographer, the Liberal statesman Viscount Morley, discovered the main reason for his dejection:

> After dinner he took me into a corner and revealed his Coercion [scheme] much as a man might say (in confidence) that he found himself under the painful necessity of slaying his mother—it was downright piteous—his wrung features, his strained gesture, all the other signs of mental perturbation in an intense nature. I walked away in a horribly gloomy state.

The prospect of an act of Parliament suppressing the Irish people's liberty was abhorrent to Gladstone, who had always believed in the natural goodness and dignity of humankind. He felt that the interests of the many should not be sacrificed to the violence of the few, but his ministers were convinced that the suspension of habeas corpus was the only way to suppress sedition: Hartington was threatening to resign unless coercion was enforced; Lord Spencer, a calm, serious-minded man with valuable Irish experience, was strongly in favor of repressive measures; and the two most radical MPs, John Bright and Joseph Chamberlain, were themselves now failing to support Glad-stone. "I finally acquiesced. . . . My resistance would have broken up the government or involved my own retirement." But the great man's instincts had been sound, and his surrender to the cabinet would pre-cipitate a crisis from which he would not emerge with credit.

*

When Parliament reconvened on January 24, 1881, Forster set out to explain the urgent necessity for the legislation, named the Protection of Person and Property (Ireland) Bill. It was, without question, the Coercion Act it came to be called, but Forster adroitly reapplied the word to the Land League, whose supreme power "rests on coercion, and coercion alone." In every Irish town and village, he said, league-appointed constables were spying on inhabitants and reporting any infringement of its rules; their own courts blacklisted anyone who refused to join the society or who paid his rent. "The fact is," said Forster, "that those who defy the existing law and break it are safe, whilst those who keep it—the honest men in short—are in danger." He acknowledged that there had as yet been few resulting deaths but that intimidation had made murder unnecessary; people lived in fear of the ruffians who maimed their livestock, burned down their hay-stacks, or broke into their houses at night.

Some MPs had discounted Forster's alarm about the Land League's escalating campaign of violence, but he provided the House with proof in the form of sobering statistics. Even more persuasive were the graphic accounts of individual cases that he read aloud from constabulary reports; the House heard about animals maliciously killed by a blade piercing through the eye into the brain; a man who worked for a land-grabber and was stabbed in the face, struck with a spade, and burned on the back with a white-hot iron; and a farmer who was dragged out of bed by an armed party of masked men, who then beat and "carded" him.

> I do not know whether Honorable Members know what "carding" means, and perhaps I had better explain it. An iron comb, used for agricultural purposes, is applied to a man's naked body, and the torture must be very great. Then the man is threatened and warned against disobeying the orders of the organization any longer. Shots are fired over his head, and sometimes at him. Let Honorable Members think of the terror thus produced. . . . There is no help near; no police station is at hand; and the man himself is powerless to resist. Naturally, he submits to this cruel tyranny and intimidation.

The Land League's unwritten law was now the law of the land, Forster said; those who committed the crimes did so with impunity, as they knew no victim would dare give evidence against them. What he believed would result in an immense diminution of crime was "an immediate temporary remedy"—the eighteen-month imprisonment of men suspected of acts of violence or high treason. "We want the power we ask for and we want it now. . . . Every day of delay is a great increase of danger. . . . The Irish people cannot wait for protection."

Lasting an hour and forty minutes, Forster's speech was acknowledged even by his adversaries to be one of the most compelling they had ever heard. "His earnestness was so deep and burning that it caught the House," Lord Randolph Churchill remarked. When it was Gladstone's turn to speak, his words were measured and moderate by comparison and yet, to his daughter Mary, had "a ring of intense fervor which was soul-piercing."

Meanwhile, the Irish members were about to make their own indelible impact. The Land Leaguers' state trials in Dublin had concluded on January 25 in dismal failure, as the jury failed to reach a verdict, and Parnell and his colleagues had victoriously taken their seats in Parliament determined to disrupt the introduction of the offensive new bill. Their obstruction—an event that made history—lasted no fewer than forty-one hours. It was described with bombastic pride by a rabid nationalist, Patrick Tynan, soon to take center stage.

The dinner hour came and the thinned House listened to the monotonous sound of one of the Parnellite speakers talking against time determined to stand upon his feet as long as human endurance could sustain him. The morning came—still on went the monotonous, unceasing flow of words. Words! Words! Words! Gatling guns of talk, rolls of musketry, sweeping volleys of verbiage . . . shrapnel shells of denunciation, huge bombs of argument. . . . Midnight arrived, but still the Parnellites kept up the fight. . . . This is a Parliamentary coup d'etat—as violent an assault on Parliamentary liberties, as when Louis Napoleon assaulted French opinion by sweeping the Parisian boulevards with his artillery, to establish the Second Empire.

Having started at four p.m. on Monday, January 31, the obstruction campaign ended at nine thirty a.m. Wednesday, February 2, and proved to be the last stand the Irish politicians took before resorting to tactics that were more effective—and far more sinister.

*

Sitting in the Ladies' Gallery, her girlishly plump face veiled by its latticed grating, was Katharine O'Shea, the wife of an Irish MP, intently watching the speaker on the floor. She was looking out for a special gesture—not by her husband, William O'Shea—but by her lover. Way down below in the House, Charles Parnell could not see her but, as if by some strange telepathy, seemed to know she was there. A lift of his head, twiddle of his handkerchief, or lingering touch of the white rose in his buttonhole would be their private signal for her to leave and wait for him at one of the places at which they had been meeting in secret over the past three months. "The lonely man fighting the might of Britain . . . drew his life from her smile and presence," Winston Churchill wrote in his essay on Parnell. This was no exaggeration. Katharine O'Shea was Parnell's Cleopatra, his passion for her as obsessive and self-destructive as Mark Antony's. Theirs was not just another adulterous affair but a great political, middle-aged love story, which a decade later would cause Parnell's downfall and alter the course of Irish history.

FOUR

Fire Beneath the Ice

I T HAD been one of the century's most potent seduction scenes. After Parnell had persistently failed to respond to invitations to attend the O'Sheas' political dinner parties, Katharine set out to persuade him. On a sunny day in early July 1880, taking her sister, Anna Steele, as chaperone, she drove to the House of Commons and sent a message asking Parnell to come into the yard to speak to them. What followed was nothing less than a *coup de foudre*. "He looked straight at me smiling and his curiously burning eyes looked into mine with a wonderful intentness that there came into my brain the sudden thought: 'This man is wonderful—and different.'" Parnell, too, was captivated within seconds—not by Anna, the beauty, but by the petite, rather plump, thirty-five-year-old Katharine, whose merry eyes revealed the vivacity and charm of her nature. He apologized for not opening his correspondence and promised he would come to their next dinner if the invitation still stood.

As Katharine leaned forward in the carriage to say goodbye, a rose fastened in her bodice dropped onto her skirt. Whether this was by design or just a lucky accident can never be known, but the impact was intoxicating. Picking it up, Parnell touched it with his lips and slipped it into his buttonhole, initiating what became a private ritual. (Throughout the seasons, Katharine would keep a white rose bush blooming in her conservatory so that he might always have their

emblem on display. After Parnell's death, she found the original shriv-
eled rose in a dated envelope with her name on it. It was buried with
him in his coffin.)

*

For at least half the year while Parliament sat, Parnell's London existence was as lonely as it was for all the other Irish parliamentarians.
Cut off from his beloved Avondale and living in "miserable" Blooms-
bury lodgings, he craved domestic comfort and female company. John
Parnell maintained that ever since Abby Woods's rejection, his brother's attitude toward women had been "cold and suspicious," but if so,
Katharine O'Shea had instantly reversed this. Parnell's first letter to
her, written on July 17, was playfully flirtatious, as he explained that
he had been unable to leave the House of Commons to attend one of
the O'Sheas' soirées, "notwithstanding the powerful attractions which
have been tending to seduce me from my duty towards my country in
the direction of Thomas's Hotel." This small, semi-club in Berkeley
Square was the O'Sheas' favorite place to entertain and the location
of their first dinner with Parnell—a quiet gathering of about a half
dozen guests. Parnell had arrived late, looking pale and exhausted,
and had focused on Anna, seeming to be revived and amused by her
spirited conversation. Later, however, when the group moved on to
the Gaiety Theatre, he had gravitated toward Katharine, and they sat
together in a dark back corner of the box, where, ignoring the performance and the presence of her husband, they began a long, intimate
conversation.

This was exactly what Captain William O'Shea had planned.
Pompous and politically self-serving, he had no qualms about using
his lively wife to help forward his career: "He would urge me, again
and again, to make full use of my 'fascinations' to induce specially
wanted persons to embark on his schemes."

As a girl, Katharine had been infatuated by the handsome young
cavalry officer of the Eighteenth Hussars, with his soft eyes,

gold-braided uniform, and jingling spurs, but even on their honey-moon, O'Shea had bored her. This was hardly surprising, as their tastes and temperaments were completely at odds: Katharine, the daughter of an Anglican vicar, had been raised in cultured, intellec-tual surroundings; O'Shea, born into the Irish Catholic landowning class and expelled from university, had little time for learning and a lot for steeplechasing and profligate spending. His wife had been glad when he decided to enter politics—at least it would give them something to talk about.

After thrusting himself forward as a candidate for one of two seats in County Clare and promising to finance—"with someone else's money"—a swashbuckling old politician known as the O'Gorman Mahon, O'Shea had entered Parliament during the recent general election. His manifesto promised that he would act loyally for the Home Rulers, but he never became a fully pledged member of the party; he was more of a Liberal at heart than a committed nationalist —the epitome of an anglicized Irishman, with a clipped colonial accent, barbed wit, and superior sense of his own worth. A dilettante and adventurer, O'Shea may not have been particularly intelligent, but a European education had given him an impressively urbane manner. In his late thirties, with a dashing mustache and dark, wavy hair, he was still an attractive man, and he knew it. Within a few years of the marriage, Katharine became aware of Willie's philandering; she suspected him of frequenting prostitutes and claimed to know the names of at least two French mistresses. In 1875 she had been humiliated to discover that O'Shea had seduced their parlor maid under the family roof.

Katharine's wealthy widowed aunt had come to the rescue. Mrs. Benjamin Wood was a reclusive octogenarian who lived in a fine Geor-gian manor in Eltham, a small town in Kent, where she had bought a neighboring property for her niece—Wonersh Lodge, a large, ivy-clad suburban villa with a gate in its garden wall that led into the Wood estate. The arrangement was that Katharine would become a regular companion to "Aunt Ben," who in return offered to provide her with an income generous enough to cover the O'Shea children's education (their father contributed nothing). Early in the year, Katharine, her son and two daughters, a governess, an Irish cook, and a new parlor maid began life in Eltham, which was secure but tediously predictable and very lonely.

For quite some time the O'Shea marriage had been little more than a facade—as she put it, "Sex love between us was long dead." The couple lived separate lives, the captain visiting their three children only on weekends to take them to Mass. Nevertheless, they had managed to maintain an affectionate rapport, writing chatty letters to each other that used their pet names (she was "My Dick," and he "Your Boysie"). Katharine was glad that her husband valued her support of his political ambitions, but while she willingly traveled to London to host his parties, she resented being pressed into service like a courtesan: "I did what I could but I did not like it. And we had angry words sometimes because I drew the line as strictly as I did." With Parnell, of course, it would be different.

*

On that first evening, Parnell was unlikely to have been given a full picture of the O'Sheas' marital situation, but he must have sensed Katharine's dissatisfaction with her limited life. He had been brought up in a family of liberated women: his unconventional mother, influenced by the American woman suffrage movement, had allowed her daughters an unusual degree of freedom. Of the six sisters, only the eldest (also named Delia) and the youngest (Theodosia) had made conventional marriages. Emily was "the prototype of 'the wild Irish girl,'" disinherited by her father, who suspected she planned to elope; and Sophia had run away with the family solicitor; while Fanny, the family's "arch-rebel," and Anna, who epitomized the "new woman" of that era, both remained single. Parnell himself scorned the prim morality of the English bourgeoisie and completely accepted Katharine's yearning for risk and revolt.

Wanting to let her know that he was not romantically involved, he began to speak about his broken engagement to a young American woman, describing her as "very pretty with golden hair, small features and blue eyes." He said that he had sought her out during his recent tour of the United States and felt only cold disillusionment on seeing her again. But this encounter almost certainly did not take place (Mrs. Samuel Abbott, married for seven years, was heavily pregnant with her fourth daughter in the spring). Late that summer, however, John Parnell and their sister Theodosia did pay Abby a visit in Newport, where they found her to be extremely welcoming but very nervous. They could not have known that her marriage was in trouble, her lawyer husband having begun to roam, but they learned how much she regretted having cast aside their "great brother Charles" when, suddenly, she stopped mid-sentence, and cried out, "How famous he has become! . . . Oh why did I not marry him? How happy we should have been together!"

Parnell's account to Katharine of the courtship mixed truth with wishful fiction. Her father had opposed the match, refusing to provide a dowry for her to go to Ireland, he told her, but it had been *his* vacillation that had ended the relationship. His commitment to the Irish cause would not allow him to settle in America or succumb to his fiancée's all-consuming demands on his emotion: "I could not do all that, so I went home." Convinced by Parnell's sincerity and unperturbed by "his desertion," Katharine was completely won over. They felt as if there were no barriers to what they could say, and she sensed a complete understanding between them, "as though I had always known this strange, unusual man."

They began to meet frequently. O'Shea was busy in his constituency, and in his absence, Katharine would attend the Irish debates, and Parnell would come up to see her in the Ladies' Gallery. They went for afternoon drives, and one day when they sat side by side in the meadows by the river, Katharine, clearly acting on O'Shea's orders, asked for Parnell's help if there were to be another election. "He promised he would do his best to keep Willie in Parliament, and to secure County Clare for him should the occasion arise." Very soon, however, the courtship took on a life of its own, progressing more rapidly and more intensely than either had anticipated. Letters from Avondale throughout September expressed Parnell's urgent need to meet with Katharine, and his failure to turn up for engagements in Ireland was forcing colleagues to cover for him. "There must be a lady in the case," mused Tim Healy.

It is likely that the Parnellite MP Justin McCarthy was in on the secret. He had been present at the Gaiety Theatre evening; he had been the only other guest at a lunch given by Anna; and he gave a dinner at his house for the couple when O'Shea was away. This went on so late that Katharine missed her train, but Parnell hailed a cab and insisted on accompanying her on the hour-long drive back to Eltham. When they reached Wonersh Lodge, he expected to come inside, but afraid of compromising herself with her children and the servants in the house, Katharine declined to invite him in. His impatience to consummate their relationship was becoming all too clear. They had planned to dine at Thomas's Hotel the following week, but when Parnell met her train, he surprised her by directing the cab to the Cannon Street Station Hotel, where he had booked a suite—"I was under the impression that he lived at Keppel Street"—using the excuse of the presence of Irish MPs in the public rooms to take her straight upstairs. This was predatory behavior, and yet Katharine was struggling with her own desires, admitting that the long, charged silences between them were "dangerous." In her memoirs, she intimates that her mind was made up by Parnell's tenderness toward her during a train journey from London to Eltham, when sensing that she was cold, he took off his coat and tucked it closely around her, whispering, as he leaned over, how much he loved her. "I slipped my hand into his, and knew I was not afraid."

Parnell had been asked to stay at Wonersh Lodge by William O'Shea, who believed that a very public friendship with the Irish leader would guarantee his reelection for County Clare. Ostensibly, the visit was to help Parnell recuperate from a taxing Land League campaign, whose open-air mass meetings had taken their toll on his already fragile health. Arriving in a state of exhaustion and with a sore throat, he was nursed by Katharine, who provided nourishing meals and took care not to disturb him when he nodded off in an armchair. O'Shea was present for some of the time but, wanting his wife to establish an influence over Parnell, then encouraged what she called "unchaperoned companionship." (Their guest had been given a bedroom conveniently connecting through a small dressing room to Katharine's own.) Once Parnell left Eltham, his letters to Katharine were no longer addressed to "Dear Mrs. O'Shea" but to "My own love."

Their clandestine meetings in London became more regular. During all-night sessions, before Parnell was due to take a break of a few hours, he would signal to Katharine in the Ladies' Gallery, and she would leave to wait for him at a hotel or railway station. Waterloo Junction was open until the early hours, and porters thoughtfully stoked the waiting room fire for her, but at other stations she might be forced to keep warm by tramping up and down the platform until Parnell arrived. Knowing how taxing this was for her, and with Eltham only eight miles from the city center, he began making Wonersh Lodge his English base. Katharine, who found London society as tiresome as he did, welcomed their cocooned existence, and even at three a.m. would be waiting to serve Parnell supper in front of the fire, helping him out of his boots and frock coat and into slippers and an old cardigan.

More for her three children's sake than out of a need to conform, Parnell obligingly complied with Katharine's precautions to keep up appearances, but the fact that he was cuckolding a member of his own party was of absolutely no consequence to him. This is illustrated by an episode that occurred on an evening the three were together in Eltham; Katharine, the first to retire, was joined in her bedroom by O'Shea, who wanted to continue the discussion they had been having downstairs. Suddenly, the door banged violently open, and Parnell, without saying a word, marched up to Katharine, flung her over his shoulder, and carried her into his own room, where he threw her on the bed and shut the door. It may read more like a bodice-ripping fantasy than fact, but it was this account, published forty years later, that captured the imagination of the poet W. B. Yeats, who was intrigued by the story of "A husband that had sold his wife."

"It was a mixture of secrecy and recklessness," wrote Winston Churchill. "From a very early stage the complaisance of the husband was indispensable. . . . O'Shea accepted the position. He even profited by it. . . . He too was under the spell of the great man." Of this Katharine herself was completely convinced. "Of course he knew. . . . There was no bargain; there were no discussions; people do not talk of such things. But he knew. I remember especially one particular occasion, very early in the affair, when he wanted to get Mr. Parnell's assent to something. . . . He said, 'Take him back with you to Eltham and make him all happy and comfortable for the night and just get him to agree.'"

Parnell's worshipping of Katharine was almost palpable. A guest at a dinner they attended soon after they met watched her chatting and laughing, while "the dour, silent, handsome man opposite devoured her with his flaming eyes." Katharine came across as a clever woman with wide-ranging interests, although few of these were shared by the uncultured, poorly read Parnell. When Katharine gave him lines from Shakespeare to use in a speech, he sheepishly admitted to having forgotten "the fellow's name," and on rare occasions when he did quote from poetry, he made it sound awkward, "as though he were making a joke," a colleague said. Politics was their topic, and as they sat talking into the early hours, Parnell telling Katharine of the night's debate or describing the terrible reality of mass evictions, the intensity of his repressed anger allowed her to understand for the first time Ireland's deep-rooted resentment of England's colonization.

Only with Katharine—his soul mate, mistress, nurse, and surrogate mother—could Parnell unreservedly confide his thoughts and fears. She alone was able penetrate the unwavering reserve and to elicit passions equal to her own. John Parnell believed that his brother's sphinxlike exterior was his most valuable asset: "He was always a man apart, and in his isolation lay his strength." This remoteness served as a barrier against the English and added to his mystique, attracting "the loyalty, and even the wild enthusiasm, of his own countrymen, while at the same time repelling their intimacy." Katharine, who understood Charles Parnell even better, believed that his noble character—"the exquisite beauty, tenderness and strength"—could not be fully appreciated by people who saw only the public man. "He was so absolutely self-controlled that few knew of the volcanic force and fire that burned beneath his icy exterior."

*

At the beginning of 1881, aware that his authority as Ireland's leader was under threat, Parnell was becoming increasingly ill at ease. Two warring factions of militant Irish organizations in America were planning dynamite campaigns in English cities, and rumors had reached Parnell that his life was in danger. Compounding his agitation was information he had received that the government was considering his arrest for sedition.

All the Land League leaders were expecting to be arrested at any moment. As an emergency measure, Michael Davitt had come up with the plan of forming a committee of women to take over the running of the organization. The Ladies' Land League would be led by Parnell's youngest sister, Anna, whose knowledge of Ireland's economic and social conditions—"of the lights and shades of Irish peasant

life"—was profound. She and her lieutenants would keep in touch
with local branches, continue to encourage boycotting, and support
families that had been evicted or whose men had been imprisoned.
Parnell at first vehemently opposed the idea, but he and other skeptics were finally persuaded of the propaganda value of having a large
number of respectable women eager to promote agrarian revolt and
risk imprisonment without trial.

The other major decision was to move the league's financial center
from Dublin to Paris, and its treasurer, Patrick Egan, left immediately, with funds and essential records. On February 2, the executives met at London's Westminster Palace Hotel to discuss Ireland's
response to the impending Coercion Act. A general strike against rent
was thought by Michael Davitt to be the most effective counterblow,
and more radical still was the suggestion that the time had come
to consider secession. In an uncharacteristic display of extremism,
Parnell proposed that when the last stage of the act was reached, the
Irish members should withdraw for good from Parliament, return to
their constituencies, and establish a forceful new movement in Ireland. Davitt was deputed to return to Dublin at once to start making
arrangements.

*

After working throughout the morning of February 3, 1881, in the
Land League's new Dublin offices in Upper Sackville Street, Davitt
was crossing Carlisle Bridge to have lunch with his friend, the MP
Thomas Brennan, when a detective approached him, saying that he
was wanted at Dublin Castle by Superintendent Mallon. A high-
ranking member of the Dublin Metropolitan Police, John Mallon
had arrested Davitt for sedition in November 1880, and yet the two
men had immediately established a mutual liking and respect. (During
that arrest, when Davitt had asked to be allowed to finish his breakfast, Mallon had not only agreed but, mindful of Davitt's amputated
arm, even offered to cut up his chop for him.) The Dublin police had

been good to Davitt recently, alerting him to their suspicion of a plot against his life and lending him a handgun for his self-protection. On this occasion, however, Davitt arrived at Mallon's office in Lower Castle Yard to find that he had walked into a trap: waiting for him were two English officers, who told him he was under arrest for breach of the conditions of his ticket-of-leave. Davitt made no protest but spoke quietly to Mallon, saying that he wanted Brennan to have the handgun and asking if the detective would go to his lodgings to collect his overcoat—which Mallon later did.

The prospect of serving his remaining term in an English jail must have been terrifying for Davitt. Even before his first sentence was passed in 1870, he had been treated in ways "almost too disgusting to describe," frequently strip-searched, probably anally, and kept for days in a dark cell with no bed or bedding. After ten months in Millbank Prison, in a ten-by-eight-foot cell with the only furniture a bed made of three raised planks and a covered bucket serving as a seat/lavatory, he was transferred to Dartmoor Prison, where he received no visitors for seven years. His disability ignored, Davitt was forced into the severest physical labor—breaking stones, pulling a coal cart to which he was harnessed like a mule, and pounding decomposing bones for fertilizer. For over a year, he was kept in solitary confinement in a foul, unventilated "chokey," reduced to crouching on all fours near a gap at the bottom of the door to breathe fresh air. These conditions, together with the inhalation of noxious bone dust and the damp chill of Dartmoor, enveloped in almost perpetual fog, had left Davitt with chronic bronchial problems. Lately, his cough had been so severe that it kept him awake most nights.

Davitt's doctor, Joe Kenny, was allowed to visit his patient before the mail steamer had left Dublin's ferry port of Kingstown and found him physically worn out, although in surprisingly good spirits. Imprisonment, Davitt believed, was saving him from assassination, and his relief was intensified by the discovery that he was not being sent back to Dartmoor but would be lodged in Portland Prison on the

Dorset coast. The note he wrote to Brennan, asking him to pack up his belongings, was even jokey. "The sudden and involuntary nature of my departure from Dublin has left my affairs in such delightful confusion that I must trouble you with the task of restoring order," said Davitt. "If Dr. J. P. Kenny comes to London this week and cares to run down [to Portland] he is pretty certain to find No W822 at home."

※

On February 3, while Davitt was en route to Portland Prison, Parnell was on his feet in the House of Commons challenging the home secretary, Sir William Harcourt, to name the conditions his colleague had violated. Harcourt refused to give him an answer. It was in the queen's power to revoke a ticket-of-leave without providing a reason —and this is what had happened. Davitt, the most revolutionary member of the Land League, was considered too dangerous to be at large. Two days earlier, Harcourt was heard to remark, "Do you see that scoundrel next to Beaconsfield [Disraeli] in the gallery? Well, I will have that fellow back in penal servitude tomorrow."

To the Home Rule members, Davitt's arrest was an act of open war, and their anger led to an unprecedented scene in the House of Commons. After their forty-one-hour obstruction fiasco, Gladstone had felt compelled to introduce a drastic change of procedure, enabling the Speaker to stop a debate if he felt it had gone on too long—"a gagging," the Irish called it. As Gladstone started to explain the new resolution, he was interrupted by John Dillon, who shouted him down and had to be forcibly removed from the House. Parnell then took over in ensuring that "the Right Honourable gentleman be no longer heard" and was marched out by the sergeant at arms and three doorkeepers, amid raucous cheers of the Irish MPs, who had risen to their feet and were waving their hats above their heads. Queen Victoria was shocked when she heard of Parnell's "monstrous" breach of parliamentary etiquette, and as if acknowledging this himself, Parnell paused on his way out and bowed respectfully to the Speaker. By the end of the session, thirty-six members of the Home Rule Party had been suspended.

At a meeting the following day, Parnell arrived late, took the chair, and read a statement in which he appeared to be retracting his support of secession. He was now urging a policy of restraint, proposing that the party should continue to fight the proposed Coercion Act fiercely in Parliament but not to the point of getting expelled. His final decision as to an effective course of action was deferred until the next meeting of the Land League's executives, which, for safety's sake, was to be held in Paris.

*

The Irishmen's chosen place of rendezvous was the Hotel Brighton, overlooking the site of the Tuileries Palace, once the primary residence of the rulers of France, to which the Paris Commune had set fire a decade earlier. This magnificent extension of the Louvre complex was now a ruined shell, the symbol of populist revolution at a moment in history when France was poised between monarchy and republic. But while the Land League members may have been drawing inspiration from the hotel's view, their leader was not among them. Parnell, who had last been seen in London on February 5, had been missing for almost a week. "Some attribute it to a fear (an ungrounded one) of being arrested," wrote Edward Hamilton. "Others to something in connection with a misappropriation of the Land League funds; others to the charms of women to which he is supposed to be much addicted; and another story is that he has gone out of his mind & has been quietly detained somewhere by his friends."

Needless to say, Parnell was with Katharine. He told her that he had to disappear, and in her memoirs, she makes much of concealing him at Wonersh Lodge, bringing food to him in the little boudoir adjoining her bedroom so that not even the servants knew he was in the house. And while his Land League colleagues were settling into the Hotel Brighton in Paris, Parnell appears to have spent a day or two in the seaside resort of Brighton itself. Katharine had gone ahead to find rooms for a holiday she planned there with her children, and Parnell caught a train to join her, disguising himself on the journey by cutting off his beard. "Don't you know me?" he said quietly, when she looked alarmed to be approached at the station by a tall stranger. At their hotel, Parnell self-consciously wrapped a muffler around his jaw, telling the manageress that he was suffering from toothache, and signed himself in the register as "Mr. Stewart," his middle name.

Katharine claimed to have hidden Parnell for a fortnight, but in fact his mysterious absence lasted no more than a week. On Saturday, February 12, he joined the Irish MP Andrew Kettle on the crossing from Dover to Calais, then traveled in a crowded train to Paris, reaching the Hotel Brighton late that night. Kettle was woken in the morning by Tim Healy, Parnell's secretary, who came rushing into his room to ask "where the blazes" he had found Parnell. "We were going to get detectives to look for him. We thought he was done away with!" Parnell's colleagues had been so concerned, in fact, that Healy was asked if he could produce a letter that might provide a clue to his whereabouts. With great reluctance, and "in the national interest," Healy handed over to Patrick Egan and John Dillon an envelope in a woman's hand among a batch of unopened correspondence that he had brought to Paris. Hearing of this later, Katharine was certain the letter was hers, but in Healy's account, it was from a barmaid who had given birth to Parnell's child and was imploring him to send her the means to exist.

The identity of the correspondent was less important than the fact that the letter had been opened at all. Healy was mortified enough to resign his post of secretary when back in London. Only he, Dillon, and Egan were aware of its contents, but the atmosphere at the executive meeting after Parnell's arrival was so tense, it seemed as if everyone in the room knew of this violation of the party leader's privacy. The London-based Press Association had published an unconvincingly convoluted itinerary of Parnell's movements, which included a visit to Frankfurt, but Parnell himself offered no explanation for his disappearance nor any apology for the alarm he had caused. Smoking a cigar, he looked at no one, and they all sat in terrible silence until in desperation someone blurted out to Kettle, "Well, what have you got to say, now?" There followed a heated debate about whether or not the Irish had anything to gain from their presence in Parliament, causing Parnell to protest, "Gentlemen, if we get into personal wrangles we cannot get on with the business." Dillon wanted Parnell to go to America, ostensibly to appeal for aid but with the real purpose of removing their circumspect leader from the fray. Parnell refused, saying that his first duty was to return to the House of Commons to oppose the coercion bill—a decision that bitterly disappointed Home Rule members who believed he had been on the brink of advocating a policy of open revolution. It was the first clear sign of Katharine's moderating influence, but it was not only that: Parnell was now intent on looking beyond the confines of the Land League. Over the coming weeks, he and James O'Kelly, his most cosmopolitan, visionary colleague, would concentrate on winning the support of the radical Parisian press for *l'Agitation Irlandaise*.

*

Paris was a city Parnell had come to know well. His uncle Charles was no longer alive, but Parnell's sister Delia lived in a grand house on St-Germain, having married a wealthy American. As Parnell had mixed only in the expatriate community, his command of French was poor, but nevertheless, he managed to impress a *Figaro* journalist, mostly by the distinction of his appearance. Although a little startled by Parnell's beardless new look—the cleanly razored chin, with sidewhiskers attached to his pale brown mustache—the reporter noted his pale, manicured hands and the way his black frock coat cut across the immaculate whiteness of a collared shirt and, like many people meeting

Parnell for the first time, was particularly struck by the hard glint in his eyes. "It's the slow rolling gaze of a great crouching predator who follows the movements of people passing in front of its iron cage."

Accompanied by the bilingual O'Kelly, Parnell visited republican newspaper offices and made appointments with several *grands français*. Formerly drama critic and war correspondent of the *New York Herald*, O'Kelly had excellent contacts and was a close friend of Henri Rochefort, the playwright and politician, whom Parnell was particularly anxious to meet. In a café near rue Drouot, the former *communard*, a portly figure with a shock of graying hair, shook Parnell's hand with evident emotion, comparing this encounter with "the idol of the Irish people" to embracing the legendary Giuseppe Garibaldi some months earlier. Rochefort too was unnerved by the steely eyes and even more by Parnell's slim physique, which made him think of the dangerously lean and hungry Cassius. For more than three hours, he listened as the two Irishmen explained their country's feudal land system and told him of the implication of the coercion bill. "It will be pure despotism just as with the Shah of Persia," Rochefort said, and before taking his leave, he promised he would try to involve his friend the great Victor Hugo in their cause. All three attended one of Hugo's regular Tuesday at-homes on the avenue d'Eylau (now the avenue Victor Hugo) and dined there the following night. Regarding Ireland's problems as "strictly a social question—rich against poor," Hugo suggested that Parnell should write him an open letter about conditions in Ireland and said he would respond with a manifesto calling on all the countries of Europe for their support.

Parnell left the next morning for London but made a second trip to Paris toward the end of the month in time to witness the city's apotheosis of Hugo—the greatest public tribute ever paid to a living writer. At midday on Sunday, February 27, the day after the poet's seventy-ninth birthday, over half a million Parisians, braving arctic temperatures and snow flurries, marched in a procession from the arc de Triomphe to Hugo's flower-bedecked house. That same day, on its front page, Rochefort's paper *L'Intransigeant* published Parnell's letter of appeal to the "Honoured Monsieur, who is so well known for inspiring the sympathy of the human race for 'les Miserables.'" Couched throughout in sycophantically formal French, it ended by saying that Parnell felt sure that the writer would use his voice to help "a brave but unfortunate nation." He was mistaken. Apparently influenced by an English acquaintance, Hugo had been persuaded that Home Rule "entailed the betrayal of the principles of the French revolution" and decided not to involve himself in Irish affairs. The promised manifesto was never written.

Parnell, meanwhile, was starting to regret his public courtship of famous French radicals, which, while adding continental dash to his image, was causing resentment at home. Tim Healy complained to O'Kelly that Westminster, not the *boulevards*, was Parnell's first duty, while others were actually scandalized by what seemed an attempt to affiliate Ireland with European "anarchists and communists." With money pouring into the Land League in Paris—the latest remittances to Egan from Patrick Ford in New York totaled 50,000 francs— Parnell now turned his attention to Irish America. Aware of the need to appease his allies by adopting a more militant stance, he arranged to meet the fanatical William Mackey Lomasney, then in Paris preparing the groundwork for the bombing campaign in England (three years later he blew himself up while attempting to destroy London Bridge). Parnell could be as deft as a master poker player adopting a strategy of bluff—the act of deception known as "floating" (Conor Cruise O'Brien called it "the cape-work of the pseudo-revolutionary gesture"). Lomasney was so impressed he wrote an enthusiastic report of their encounter to the Clan na Gael activist John Devoy in America. "I feel he is eminently deserving of our support . . . ," said Lomasney. "As soon as he secured the means he would start in business with us, and smash up the opposition firm"—that is, the rival dynamite venture.

The process of quite literally playing with fire was putting Parnell even more on edge. He had told Katharine that his second trip to

Paris had been prompted by the threat of imminent arrest and also said that he had been warned of "some plot on foot against us." He knew that the director of Scotland Yard's criminal investigation department, Howard Vincent, had tailed him to Paris, and the plain-clothesmen on the pavement outside the hotel were making themselves comically obvious. When the detectives followed Parnell and O'Kelly's cab, the Irishmen decided to make a game of it by going up to their vehicle and "laughing in the face of the spies." When parting from Rochefort, Parnell bade him "*adieu*," adding, "I dare not say *au revoir*, for O'Kelly and I will perhaps be in prison before a month is over."

Parnell was bringing back to Katharine a wide, hollow gold brace-let that had been specially made in Paris, intending to insert inside papers that she believed would incriminate him if he were arrested. She was already hiding some sensitive political correspondence in a box kept in the locked room adjoining her bedroom, but these were documents that he wished to keep even safer. When Parnell arrived at Wonersh Lodge, he concealed the two papers inside the bracelet and fastened it on her arm. "There it remained for three years, and was then unscrewed by him and the contents destroyed."

FIVE

Captain Moonlight

O N MARCH 2, 1881, the Coercion Act received the royal assent, causing a surge of fury on both sides of the Atlantic. AMERICA'S ANSWER TO COERCION, bellowed the *Irish World*: EVERY TOWN AND HAMLET IN THE LAND BOUND TO BE ORGANISED!

In Gweedore the people needed no goading. A huge demonstration had taken place in January, when the parish turned out en masse to march in procession to Derrybeg. Standing on a platform erected in the churchyard was Father MacFadden, head of its Land League branch. "I never saw in my life any man have,such power over his fellow-men as he has over them," remarked Somerset Ward, manager of the Gweedore Hotel and estate. "I heard him say to the tenants in my presence that the League had brought the English ministers down to their knees and that it would bring the landlords down into the dust."

The smallholders' methods of preventing eviction had been primitive at best: they tried blocking up doors and windows, or balancing pans of scalding water on them, and preventing access to their property by trenching or booby-trapping lanes; MacFadden, however, would show up in person, confronting and belittling the bailiffs and police. "This was the great heroic man who took the people of Gweedore out of slavery," wrote one resident. "Who ended hunger and hardship in the parish, who put backbone into them, who marshaled them and who did not draw breath until he had finished rackrents, unjust laws and eviction." Discouraging violence, MacFadden advocated passive resistance in the people and obedience to his orders. "You consider me the enemy of the landlords," he told the bailiff of Captain Hill's Gweedore estate. "I consider myself their greatest friend. . . . If it was not for me both landlords and agents would have been shot."

In the summer of 1880, MacFadden became a hero, inspiring "a reverence and awe scarcely credible." He had been celebrating Mass in Derrybeg when a violent storm broke out, causing a culvert under the church floor, into which mountain streams were diverted, to overflow within minutes. Under pressure of the downpour, the masonry gave way, and the pent-up floodwater cascaded through the door, rising to a height of six feet. Some women in the gallery hung down their shawls to help people clamber up, other people broke glass panes, but five parishioners were drowned, and all the horses tethered to the church wall were swept away. Ignoring the chaos, MacFadden calmly continued saying Mass until he had administered general absolution, and then he smashed the nearest window and climbed out. From this moment he was looked upon as a messiah, arousing an idolatrous, almost supernatural faith in his flock. "Optimistic and impatient, arrogant and autocratic, MacFadden was profoundly reassuring in uncertain times," wrote the historian Breandán Mac Suibhne. "A symbol of achievement in ordinary years, in the [Land War] crisis of 1881 he became a saviour. Formerly admired, he was now adored."

It was MacFadden who directed Gweedore's insurrection in May of that year. He had instructed the smallholders not to pay rent until the landlords had given back their "confiscated" acres—a threat that resulted in legal proceedings. Starting on Captain Hill's estate, a process server and a bailiff, accompanied by at least fifty policemen, nailed writs on the tenants' doors or forced them through windows. Moving on to the next property, they were met by a furious horde of about six hundred people who threw stones and "clodded" them with handfuls of mud. The police were forced to retreat to their barracks, which the jeering crowd surrounded, smashing the windows.

Early on the Sunday morning of May 22, 1881, nine cars with reinforcements of over thirty police arrived in Derrybeg and took up quarters in an empty house belonging to Captain Hill, where bales of straw had been delivered for them to sleep on but no provisions left of any kind. The van of a merchant from nearby Gortahork bringing supplies of bread and groceries had been overturned on the road, its driver warned on peril of his life never to return. No publican would serve the police; the village bakers had stopped making bread until they left the district; and it was rumored that the wells used by the police had been poisoned. Daniel Keown, lessee of the large store in Bunbeg, had shut it down, and for two days the garrison's men were forced to survive on dry sea biscuits and stream water. "Mr. Keown gave the hungry policemen their breakfast on Sunday morning," reported the *Londonderry Sentinel*, "but informed them that he could not, or dare not, attempt to give them anything more. For this act he has been Boycotted, his servants and workmen leaving his employment."

At the Gweedore Hotel too, every employee had left with the exception of one loyal carriage driver who had worked there for twenty years. One hundred more constables were drafted into the area, together with the same number of cavalrymen from the Scots Greys and another hundred from the Rifles infantry. In Bunbeg, the people waited for instructions from Father MacFadden, who spoke to them in the churchyard, telling them to ignore the police provocations and stay calm.

Go on with your ordinary work, whether it be gathering seaweed or working in the fields at your crops. Regard all this force as harmless cabbage heads. [*Laughter*] Let them disperse like men having the plague, that you would not associate with; you have only to keep away from them, and let them go about their business. . . . Now, I tell you again, not to give the enemy any excuse for the importation of more force.

On the following Tuesday morning, May 24, four jaunting cars from Letterkenny, accompanied by a heavy escort, arrived in Derrybeg bringing rations to the garrison, while a gunboat with further provisions was sent by the government to Bunbeg harbor. No attempt was made to prevent the consignment from reaching the police, as the locals were following MacFadden's counsel to the letter, resuming their usual occupations and not even opposing the serving of writs. "They are absolutely under his authority, ready to do anything he tells them," said Somerset Ward, the hotel manager. "If I ask them to do a thing, they say at once, as simply as children, 'I must go and ask Father MacFadden and see what he says.'"

Resistance to the landlords involved risk and loss; Ward claimed that several tenants had told him that it was causing their ruin: "They said they wished that things were again as they used to be in the old times." The knitting industry that had been started by Lord George Hill, who had arranged with a London firm to send over yarn to be knitted into socks and stockings by Gweedore's women, had been forcibly shut down; one of the women had come into Bunbeg's store and handed over a couple of pairs, saying, "This is the last I can do, for the order has gone out through the country that we are to knit no more." Messrs. Allan & Solly had paid out to local knitters nearly £500 a year, and now the sum had shrunk to £60. "The only difficulty experienced by us was when 'Ireland's Curse,' the Land League, visited the district," said a representative. Somerset Ward had challenged MacFadden about the boycotting of local industries, saying, "How is it that the League has prevented them from working at 2s a day for the hotel, and 2s 6d at the fisheries? If they are so poor, is it not a strange thing to prevent them from earning wages?'" MacFadden had no answer.

Among the prosperous shopkeepers who had closed their businesses rather than serve the police was Dan O'Donnell. He had joined the mass Land League rally in Derrybeg but four months later had found himself a victim of its implacable regime. Boycotted for serving drinks to the constabulary, he then had his publican license revoked in revenge by the police (at a court appeal, it was reinstated, but only after "the appellant had expressed his regret and promised not to repeat the offence"). It must have seemed that he could not win.

For reasons of his own, Pat O'Donnell, who was living at Dan's house in Derrybeg, along with their mother, had kept away from the January rally. "I didn't go to it but took my brother's gun and went out fowling on the mountain." Today, Gweedore folklore has him menacing a bailiff by pacing up and down outside the man's house with a gun. "It's said that Patrick Michael Art was asked to bump off the bailiff Sean O'Donnell," according to one resident. "If the stories are to be believed, Patrick had the opportunity to kill him more than once, but he didn't have it in his heart to fire the shot."

*

In Dublin, in late May, Florence Forster was on a walk with her father when she noticed his grim expression. Confessing that he was struggling with a particularly troubling decision, Forster told her that he was considering whether or not to order police and soldiers to use their weapons in cases of violent resistance at evictions. There had been riots in which eighty constables had been outnumbered by a furious horde of five or six hundred, and the demonstrators fought with pitchforks and hurled not only stones and handfuls of mud but a hive of swarming bees. "If [the people] drive us to it, we must fire on them," Forster told a colleague. "I think by striking blow after blow every day I may make the law prevail." But in doing so, he was only honing his image as a tyrant. "The Irish have always said Force is no remedy," wrote one observer. "And now they add: 'nor is Fors-ter.'" The chief secretary had begun receiving threatening letters, and the police knew of plots against his life, and yet he refused any additional protection. If anything, the personal intimidation and the realization that his Coercion Act was failing had made Forster more combative

than ever. "I have had to put the Act into much more active operation, and indeed, to arrest right and left," he remarked in mid-July.
"For this I am, of course, much hated."

*

By now, the Land Law (Ireland) 1881 had been introduced by Gladstone, its main aims known as "the three Fs": fixity of tenure, free
sale, and fair rents. An improvement on his Landlord and Tenant (Ireland) Act 1870, it was intended to be a gesture of appeasement, but
it left tenant farmers uncertain whether to use the new legislation to
secure rent reductions in court, or to continue their allegiance to the
Land League. Extremist opinion was hostile. Father Eugene Sheehy,
a fiery curate adored by the Irish people for his support of their land
issues, admonished: "Oh, my friends, beware of the Land Act, for it
is a lawyers' Act. . . . Mr. Parnell, and he ought to know, distrusts this
Act. Well, we share that distrust." On May 21, 1881, the clergyman
was arrested for his seditious rhetoric and sentenced to four months
in prison.

In fact, Parnell was being as circumspect as ever. A landlord himself,
he counted on the Avondale rents, disliked the fact that all tenants
would have to litigate, and yet wished to give Gladstone's new Land
Act a fair trial. He suggested that selective cases should be submitted
so that this latest land law's efficacy could be tested—an equivocal
response that infuriated Irish American extremists. Sounding off in
the *Irish World*, Patrick Ford saw this as a watershed moment, one that
would determine the failure or victory of the Land Wars.

We tell the people of Ireland that anything like a general acceptance of
Gladstone's quack remedy for Irish grievances will alienate them from
the goodwill of those who on this side of the Atlantic have stood by
them in their fight against Landlordism. . . . If they now make a truce
with Landlordism on the basis of the Land Bill they will disappoint as

well as disgust the great majority of those who have swelled the Land
League Fund to its present magnificent proportions.

The message could not be clearer: the flow of funds from America
would almost certainly cease if Parnell endorsed Gladstone's Land
Act. At a Dublin Land League convention in September, Parnell
insisted that the tenantry would be in the league's control, and in a
follow-up telegram to the president of the American Land League
intimated that their choice of test cases would be sure to reveal "the
hollowness of the Act." To the Irish MP William O'Brien, Parnell was
acting like a trade union leader, striving to get better terms for his
workers, but Forster considered Parnell's intervention to be intolerable. He urged Gladstone that the time had come to make a drastic
decision: if Parnell continued to disparage the Land Act, he must be
arrested—and as swiftly as possible.

✳

The northern English city of Leeds, Gladstone's former constituency, had named a newly constructed hall after the prime minister,
who had decided to make its inaugural banquet the occasion for a
forceful speech expressing his condemnation of Parnell. A vast crowd
gave Gladstone a rousing welcome, but sitting close to him, Lucy
Cavendish sensed his deep unease. "For what he had to do was warn
Parnell and Co, that the 'long patience' of the Government had all
but reached its term. He had to say that now the Land Act was law it
was to have fair play. Parnell has been inciting the people to take no
advantage of it until he is pleased to give them leave."

Tremendous applause followed Gladstone's long, grave address,
and he and his entourage were escorted through the packed streets
by a procession of torchbearers. The following afternoon, Saturday,
October 8, Gladstone Hall was crammed mostly with working men
standing shoulder to shoulder. "I was frightened to death for the

1st half hour," wrote Lucy. "The atmosphere was horrible; and the people, tired of waiting . . . took to that dreadful *swaying* which is the most awful thing to see in a great crowd. Air, however, was let in and all went well when once Uncle W. got up. The 25 thousand cheers were something never-to-be-forgotten!"

Gladstone's appearance in Leeds had been stressful, and he was hoarse and exhausted by Saturday night, although greatly relieved that "the anxious effort about Ireland had been made." Writing to Forster, he said, "You will see that I dealt with the Irish case at length & made much more of it in order to lay the ground hard & broad for any measures however strong that may become necessary. I hope you will be fortified with this: perhaps you may even think I went too far."

✳

At his shooting lodge in County Wicklow, Parnell knew nothing of Gladstone's attack until the following day, when he met colleagues on a train, and Tim Healy read the transcript aloud from the *Cork Herald*. They were on their way to a Land League convention in the town of Wexford, where it was Parnell's turn to receive a hero's welcome. In an open carriage drawn through the narrow streets by four horses, he passed under triumphal arches of evergreens and under windows from which women waved handkerchiefs and showered him with flowers. At a meeting ground outside town, where a scarecrow effigy lampooned "the last landlord," Parnell prepared himself to upstage his mighty English antagonist. In words clearly aimed across the Atlantic, he poured scorn on Gladstone's philanthropy and hatred of oppression, calling him "the greatest coercionist . . . a pretended champion of the liberties of every other nation except those of the Irish"; the Grand Old Man was "perfidious and cruel," Parnell declaimed, his Leeds speech "unscrupulous and dishonest." Privately, though, Parnell resented the position of extremism he felt forced into, telling Healy, "We have pushed this movement as far as it can constitutionally go!" But afterward, dining with two Irish MPs, who asked him for instructions in the likelihood of his imprisonment, Parnell maintained his air of calculated audacity. "Ah," he said, gazing contemplatively through his glass of champagne, "If I am arrested, Captain Moonlight will take my place."

*

Threatening notes signed "Captain Moonlight" and embellished with crude sketches of skulls, dripping daggers, coffins, or graves were becoming more and more prevalent—the signature communication of outrage-mongers who sought revenge on those who had breached Land League rules. (Punishments now extended to women, whose heads were shaved—"clipped"—for infractions such as contact with a boycotted man or the police.)

On Monday, October 10, the day after Parnell's Wexford performance, James Tuke arrived in Dublin to stay overnight with the Forsters, still shaken by the intimidation he had witnessed during a tour of the West of Ireland. During dinner, Tuke told them that men known to have planned or committed murder were going free, as no one dared denounce them for fear of being boycotted or killed themselves; priests were tolerating if not actively encouraging the general lawlessness; land agents went about the countryside fully armed, their drivers instinctively ducking and lashing their horses when passing a wood or hedge to avoid bullets, which might at any moment be fired. Some landlords, having received no rent, were now almost as destitute as their evicted tenants, one woman hardly able to afford to buy food, she and her family targets of the whole district's concentrated hatred. Recording this in her diary, Florence Forster remarked, "Even such a benevolent, liberal-minded Quaker as Mr. Tuke, fresh from his recent experience would be almost prepared to tolerate the introduction of Martial law, and the complete suppression of the Land League."

Forster spent much of the following day at Dublin Castle in secret consultation with the commander of the British forces in Ireland,

Sir Thomas Steele, and that evening he made the crossing to London. The cabinet had been summoned for an emergency meeting to sanction the arrest of Parnell and key Land League leaders, and having obtained this, Forster walked to Westminster's telegraph office. The message he dispatched to Steele contained just a single word: "Proceed."

✻

On the morning of Thursday, October 13, Superintendent Mallon rose at four o'clock and went to the castle to await Forster's arrival from the overnight ferry. Dapperly dressed, with foxy features and a trim, salt-and-pepper-flecked beard, Mallon was a familiar figure in Dublin's smoky bars, where he mingled easily with the city's underworld, his republican, south Armagh accent and courteous manner winning the trust of even the hardest of men. Eventually known as "the Irish Sherlock Holmes" on account of his idiosyncratic, highly effective working methods, Mallon often countered the usual police procedures, and it was one such departure that he now brought into play.

The military had proposed ambushing Parnell with a massive presence of infantry and cavalry in Naas, County Kildare, where he was due to address a meeting later that day. Mallon, however, suggested a low-key alternative: he would take Parnell into custody himself, with no backup other than one constable. On Wednesday evening he had posted plainclothesmen at the railway station, so that when Parnell arrived from Wicklow, they could follow him to wherever he was staying. It was the Irish leader's usual Dublin residence, Morrison's Hotel, on the corner of Dawson and Nassau Streets, and sometime between six and seven o'clock on Thursday morning, Mallon, accompanied by a sturdy, red-haired detective, arrived at the hotel with a signed arrest warrant.

✻

Parnell had spent a late night with the MP William O'Brien, a brilliant young man whom he had chosen to edit *United Ireland*, the newspaper he had recently founded as a Land League mouthpiece. The post office clock was striking two when they broke off their "final excited colloquy," and Parnell returned to Morrison's, where he asked the porter to wake him at eight thirty. After only a few hours' sleep, he heard a knock on his door and was told that two gentlemen wanted to see him. Instructed to ask their names and business, the porter came back in a few minutes, saying they were policemen, and urged Parnell to escape over the rooftops, as he could easily reach the attic window of a safe house. Parnell declined, telling the man that the police would be watching every possible exit. In fact, he had no intention of resisting arrest. This was what he was expecting, what he had intentionally provoked by publicly defying Gladstone, and what he knew would redeem him in the eyes of Irish Americans.

And yet, he dreaded the confinement of prison, because foremost in his mind was the long separation it would mean from Katharine. "When I heard that the detectives were asking for me, a terror—one which has often been present with me in anticipation—fell upon me," he later confided to her. "For I remembered that my darling had told me that she feared it would kill her." There was a reason for their extreme agitation: Katharine was now five months pregnant with Parnell's child.

*

Superintendent Mallon had brushed aside the porter's initial insistence that the hotel guest had gone out for a Turkish bath, demanding to be shown up to room 20. Although still half-dressed when he opened the door, Parnell was perfectly composed when told that he was under arrest, asking merely for a little time to write a few urgent letters. Telling Parnell that his instructions were to escort him to the station, not to prevent him from writing letters, Mallon then politely withdrew into the corridor.

Morrison's Hotel Dublin,
October 13, 1881

My own Queenie,

I have just been arrested by two fine-looking detectives, and write these words to wifie to tell her that she must be a brave little woman and not fret after her husband.

The only thing that makes me worried and unhappy is that it may hurt you and our child.

You know, darling, that on this account it will be wicked of you to grieve, as I can never have any other wife but you, and if anything happens to you I must die childless. Be good and brave, dear little wife, then.

YOUR OWN HUSBAND

Politically it is a fortunate thing for me that I have been arrested, as the movement is breaking fast, and all will be quiet in a few months, when I shall be released.

Time was getting on, and the porter must have spread the word of the chief's arrest, as people were gathering in the street outside. Anticipating trouble, Mallon mentioned his concern to Parnell, who suggested slipping out some other way. "However, I had a cab at the front door and we walked straight down and out of the building, Mr. Parnell making no sign to the people." Mallon had promised Parnell that he could post the letters himself, but seeing the throng heading toward them, he rushed him straight into the waiting vehicle.

"Mr. Mallon, you have deceived me!"

"Nothing of the sort, sir. You asked that you might post your letters personally. There is a pillar box close to the court and, if there is not, I will bring you back to the post-office myself, at all risks."

For Mallon and his colleague, the journey to Kilmainham Gaol seemed endless; had Parnell sought help he would have been rescued by the onlookers, or their driver could have turned the horse's head and set off in whatever direction he wanted to go. But Parnell said nothing, sitting well back on the seat as if anxious not to be recognized. When the carriage reached the quay at the end of Parliament Street, a number of horse guards closed in behind the cab, forming a barrier between the people and their leader; at the Bank of Ireland, two police carriages drove in front of theirs; and on the steps of the courthouse adjoining the bleak gray limestone jail stood a detachment of the Queen's Foot Guards. True to his word, Mallon waited as Parnell posted his letters and then accompanied him through the iron gate over which writhed five stone serpents—The Five Devils of Kilmainham.

*

Gladstone had decided to make a *coup de théâtre* of Parnell's capture. With the full panoply of British pageantry, the prime minister was being honored that day in the City of London, a ceremony marking his fiftieth year of public service. Arriving at the Guildhall in the lord mayor's state carriage, Gladstone was led by the city marshal in a procession of sword and mace bearers to a raised dais. He listened to a lengthy tribute, made a speech of thanks, and then launched into the Irish troubles. He had just got to the point of stressing the government's determination to act more aggressively, when, right on cue, a telegraph boy appeared on stage. Gladstone continued:

Even within these few moments, I have been informed that towards the vindication of law, of order, and the rights of property, of the freedom of the land, of the first elements of political life and civilization the first step has been taken in the arrest of the man [*Long and prolonged cheering, accompanied by the waving of hats and handkerchiefs*] of the arrest of the man who, unhappily, from motives which I do not challenge . . . has made himself beyond all others, prominent in the attempt to destroy the authority of the law [*Cheers*] and to substitute what would end in being nothing more or less than anarchical oppression exercised upon the people of Ireland. [*Loud cheers*]

One journalist wrote of the incident's appearance of "well-contrived effect," which is exactly what it was: Gladstone would have received information from Dublin several hours before the Guildhall event, and yet even to Queen Victoria he made the claim, "As the news of Mr. Parnell's arrest arrived when he was speaking, he announced it in his speech."

*

On October 13, the queen was at Glassalt, her Scottish retreat on the shores of Balmoral's Loch Muick, surrounded by moors and snow-dusted hills. It was a beautiful day, and after a walk she sat sketching the view, returning just as a messenger arrived with a telegram from Forster and a letter from Gladstone. The news of Parnell's arrest delighted her, but the following morning it must have seemed as if the elements were raging against the government's action, for she wrote: "The most dreadful [day] I ever remember, a perfect gale of wind, with constant blinding snow showers, which drifted on to the windows, quite blocking them up. . . . The Loch looked very dark, & was covered with foam, the water, being all blown up, like smoke." In England, and Ireland too, the storm was the most violent for decades, with wind speeds of nearly one hundred miles per hour, telegraph poles ripped from the earth, and several ships run aground.

*

The apocalyptic weather had kept Katharine awake most of the night. Venturing out early the next morning, as gales swirled autumn leaves high in the air and a huge branch fell dangerously close, she hung onto railings as she struggled to walk to her aunt's house, looking up to see an entire avenue of ancient elms uprooted. It came as a relief to spend a peaceful day indoors with Aunt Ben, but Katharine hardly listened to the old lady's reminiscences, hearing only Parnell's voice in her head, trying to prepare her for his inevitable arrest. She returned home for dinner with O'Shea, who had written telling her to expect him that evening, and as soon as she saw his expression, she knew what had happened.

> Willie was so fiercely and openly joyful that my maids, who were ardent Parnellites, were much shocked, and I, being terribly overwrought, laughed at their disgusted faces as I went to dress for dinner. It was really the laugh of tears but that laugh of jangled nerves and misery did me good service with Willie, and we got through dinner amicably enough.

The O'Shea marriage had taken a new turn. In July, arriving unannounced at Wonersh Lodge, the captain had made an ugly scene, striking Katharine and threatening to challenge Parnell to a duel. The reason she gives is that he had discovered Parnell's portmanteau in the room connected to hers, but this makes no sense; her husband had long been aware of the sleeping arrangements and had actively encouraged the affair. It is far more likely that Katharine told O'Shea that she was expecting Parnell's child (thought to have been conceived in Brighton in mid-May 1881). The realization that the liaison, which should have been fleeting, had developed into something far deeper was not only a blow to O'Shea's pride; it put in jeopardy his political ambition and his income from Aunt Ben—both of which would disappear if there were a scandal. From now on, he reclaimed his conjugal rights—a situation that appeased his ego and also allowed him the self-deception that the child might be his.

*

When Parnell arrived at Kilmainham, he looked at no one as he passed through the courtyard, and standing imperiously in the hall, he barely acknowledged the acquaintances who came up to greet him. But when the officers attempted the customary body search of new prisoners, his pent-up anger erupted. A colleague asked afterward what he would have done if the head warder had persisted: "I should have killed him," he muttered.

Later, in what was more of a room than a cell—double-windowed, with a good fire in the grate, a table with a few books, and bowl of fruit—a reporter from the *Freeman's Journal* interviewed Parnell, noting the respect shown by prison staff, who knocked before entering, but struck mostly by the leader's cheerfulness. Imprisonment had bestowed a new power on Parnell, as martyrdom elevated him into a symbol of the Irish nation. "Let them manacle the body of our beloved chief," *United Ireland*'s editor William O'Brien declared. "His spirit is abroad in a million Irish-hearts. His work is done; his lesson taught. It has sunk into our souls."

＊

In Dublin, Forster wasted no time in acting on his new powers, and by October 15, O'Brien, and his fellow radical MPs, John Dillon and James O'Kelly, had joined Parnell in Kilmainham. Heavy military reserves were being held in case of a violent uprising, with troops numbering around twenty-five thousand stationed around the city. Two field guns were positioned inside the castle gates, and all the staff was armed. Forster himself carried a handgun in his pocket; two mounted police followed him when he walked through Phoenix Park, as well as a policeman on foot behind and a plainclothesman across the road. Herbert Gladstone, who had been sent by his father to assist Forster and was staying at the Chief Secretary's Lodge, had also bought a handgun. "A remark I made that Dublin seemed like a city in revolutionary Russia was not received with favor."

＊

Queen Victoria had rejoiced that "Mr. Parnell was safe in Kilmainham Jail," but she could not have been more mistaken: by locking up the Land League's leader and his deputies, the government was playing into the hands of the most dangerous extremists. Four days after Parnell's arrest came an order from Patrick Ford in New York to issue a retaliatory manifesto calling for a general strike against rent. If the entire population of tenant farmers refused to pay their landlords, banding together in fearless spirit of passive resistance, England's coercive regime would be powerless. "Your suggestion is approved," wrote Patrick Egan in reply. "Prompt measures are now in preparation. . . . The manifesto will be issued throughout the land. It is the only weapon in our hands."

At Parnell's request, a group secretly assembled in the hospital wing of Kilmainham Gaol to compose the manifesto, written by O'Brien with a blunt pencil on the back of a pink telegram form. The paper, smuggled out and circulated on October 18, elicited an ecstatic response from Patrick Ford: "A thousand cheers for that glorious Manifesto!" he cabled Egan. "It is the bravest act of the Land War. The document recalls Lincoln's Emancipation Proclamation. God bless you all. Count on America."

Forster, however, was so outraged that, without the knowledge or approval of Gladstone, he issued a proclamation the following day declaring the Land League to be illegal and warning that any meetings would be suppressed by force. This was a move its leaders had already anticipated. Asked in Wexford what would happen if the government suppressed the league, Parnell said that it would force the people to form secret organizations—a remark echoed by William O'Brien: "Captain Moonlight and his murder clubs began again to walk the night."

But it was a conversation Patrick Egan had with Superintendent John Mallon during the state trials in January 1881 that proved most prescient of all.

"Well John, what is to be the outcome of all this?"

"I don't know."

"I'll tell you. You will get no verdict here. Then you will suppress the League, and try to manufacture some way of effecting the imprisonment of the leaders of the people. And then you may look out."

SIX

The Invincibles

I N OCTOBER 1881, the chief commissioner of the Dublin Metropolitan Police, George Talbot, received an intelligence report that Patrick Egan was in town.

> His business most important. . . . Received a very large sum of money from America according to some new arrangement. . . . I am assured that the money alleged to have been brought by Egan is altogether independent of the weekly receipts and it is supposed to be over £5.000 [about $600,000 today].

Talbot's source was almost certainly Superintendent Mallon, who had learned from a reliable informer in November 1880 of the emergence of a secret society calling itself the Mooney Volunteers, after Thomas Mooney, the *Irish World*'s transatlantic columnist, who offered cash rewards for killing landlords, published bomb-making instructions, and was described by Patrick Ford as perhaps the most intense Irishman who ever lived. Mallon had reported that the society's members were "a set of assassins and desperadoes" and would be armed—some with handguns, daggers, and bayonets, and some with dynamite.

Now, in the fall of 1881, Mallon was warning of a plan to murder "persons in high places"—the prime minister, home secretary, and chief secretary at the top of the list. He told Talbot that the Land

League was not implicated, although "they could not control the fanatics who contemplate such things [and] would accept them as inevitable and for the good of their cause."

Talbot passed Mallon's report on to Forster, and in a postscript he added:

I have received further confirmation of the truth of this statement. There is no longer any [Land League] Executive; all is chaos; no control. . . . As to the atrocious crimes in contemplation, it will be observed they are no longer under any control of the League. They are in the hands of unscrupulous miscreants, whose movements it is not only necessary to watch, but to endeavor to become acquainted with their intentions. To effect this, I have spared no effort, and taken all the precautions at my disposal.

What neither Mallon nor Talbot knew at this point was that key Land Leaguers were very much involved. An initial gathering in London in October was attended by Patrick Egan and two advanced nationalist MPs, John Barry and Joseph Biggar (the inventor of the obstruction strategy), who met emissaries from America to discuss the formation of a murder society. "This was the first occasion that such a proposition was made," reported Mallon. "And the first occasion, moreover, that the Supreme Council party proposed an assassination of any kind."

The Supreme Council was the governing body of the Irish Republican Brotherhood, the secret revolutionary society, which, with its Masonic-style rituals, clan lodges, passwords, and alphabet ciphers, was virtually impossible for an outsider to infiltrate. The whereabouts of conventions were communicated only at the last moment; the insiders never attached signatures to any document, instead using a common seal. Mallon, nevertheless, had managed to ascertain Supreme Council names from top to bottom, including that of Patrick Egan, whom he said was by far the most effective organizer.

Highly intelligent, with shrewd administrative and executive abilities combined with great personal charm, Egan had been nominated three times to enter Parliament but had chosen not to run because he refused to swear allegiance to what he considered a foreign power. Although active in the ranks of the IRB—a founder of the amnesty movement established for the release of Irish political prisoners—he had no ambition to be a political star and seldom made speeches, preferring to remain a power behind the scenes. One Irish MP described him as "the ablest strategist of the whole campaign, and perhaps, except Davitt, the most resolute and invincible spirit amongst them all."

A Home Rule supporter, Egan had been forced to relinquish his role as Supreme Council treasurer by its chairman, Charles Kickham, an implacable idealist with literary leanings, who believed that constitutionalism would contaminate the group's revolutionary creed. Egan, however, was convinced that IRB support for Home Rule was crucial and continued to attend meetings, managing to straddle both open and insurgent movements. "I am a Land Leaguer and something else when the opportunity presents itself," he declared. He was not alone. Thomas Brennan, secretary of the Land League, was also general secretary of the Supreme Council; and John Walsh was the north of England's Land League organizer as well as Supreme Council representative. All three were part of an inner circle of IRB rebels and influential Land Leaguers who formed the directorate of the new assassination society: the Irish National Invincibles.

*

It was John Walsh, a powerfully built veteran of the Fenian cause, who was sent to Dublin to recruit men for action. His first call was to a Dorset Street pub owned by an extremist named James Mullett. "Mr. Walsh said he had a little mission for me," Mullett recalled. "The Land League had determined to carry out the No Rent manifesto with a vengeance and to establish a new society to wipe out tyrants and harass the Government by the use of dynamite on public buildings. I said that was very dangerous ground and told him that Mr. Kickham would not have anything to do with it. He said that Kickham was an old fogey and too fond of poetry." Mullett, who shared Kickham's opposition to Home Rule, was uneasy about abandoning his principles, but after Walsh reassured him that the project had Egan's support, he agreed to allow parcels to be left at his house and to relay important messages.

A short while afterward, Mullett heard that Patrick Sheridan wanted to see him. Sheridan was someone else whose affiliation to the Land League had overlapped with that of the Supreme Council, until Kickham deposed him for distributing IRB rifles for Land War agitation. The proprietor of a small hotel in the West of Ireland, Sheridan had been heavily involved in arms importation, but his recent arrest and internment in Kilmainham was because he was suspected of organizing intimidation to prevent payment of rent. Released on parole in October, as his alcoholic wife was gravely ill, he had fled to Paris to join Egan and had now covertly returned to Ireland with dispatches for the Invincibles.

When Mullett went to the Midland Hotel to meet Sheridan, he found him in the guise of a priest. "Father Murphy" said that he was sorry to hear he was holding to "Mr. Kickham's old-fashioned notions of sunburstry and honourable business," which was all humbug, and that it was imperative to wipe out tyrants such as "Buckshot" [Forster] and the big landlords. The Land League had devoted £10,000 (over $1 million today) for the purpose, Sheridan said, and there would be generous compensation for anyone carrying out Invincibles orders.

This was a major departure from the IRB, whose members subscribed what they could afford—often no more than a few pence a week—as the Invincibles would actually be given a fee. A few days later, Sheridan came to Dorset Street, where he was introduced to Mullett's wife as "a clergyman from the country," telling the publican that he hoped he would see fit to join them. Sheridan pulled out a little parcel from his pocket containing fifty gold sovereigns. And then he asked Mullett to go and fetch James Carey.

*

A thickset, bearded, middle-aged Dubliner, James Carey gave every impression of being an exemplary citizen. A devout Catholic and doting family man, he was a successful building contractor who had come to be recognized as the spokesman for his trade. His father and brother were bricklayers, but he was self-educated, with a canny flair for business and ambitious plans for his future. A committed nationalist from the age of sixteen, Carey had joined the IRB in 1861. "My object was to assist in separating Ireland from England," he said. "It was not from personal ambition. It was not to make money; it was for the good of Ireland."

In March 1877, Carey had resigned from his post as IRB treasurer and rented rooms in Peter Street for the purpose of drilling recruits—fifty to sixty men who could be called on for insurgent action. A founding member of the Mooney Volunteers, Carey had a violent disposition, once threatening the life of a Supreme Council official who refused to reveal the whereabouts of a meeting. He was responsible for arranging the execution of anyone found to be a traitor to the IRB, and he was said to be guilty of the cold-blooded murder of a colleague who refused to join it.

Superintendent Mallon had been told of the circumstances. Carey and several co-extremists had met the young man, a bricklayer named Behan, on his return from an Easter weekend with his family in the country and tried hard to enlist him for extremist activities. Having recently taken Communion in his native church—"The young fellow's religion was very fast upon him," as Mallon put it—he refused to get involved. Carey must have thought that he had given away too much, and as the two walked side by side along the quay toward Carlisle (now O'Connell) Bridge, he let the others go ahead, drew a stonemason's hammer from his pocket, struck Behan with a fatal blow on the temple, and threw him into the Liffey. Mallon later found out that it was Carey who reported the youth's absence to the police, and when his floating corpse was recovered, Carey managed to get himself appointed foreman of the coroner's jury investigating the case. A verdict of drowning was returned, the wound said to have been caused after death by collision with a passing boat. "Facts came to my knowledge that made me suspect he had been personally responsible," said Mallon. "But I only had an informer's evidence and we could not obtain corroboration."

In May 1881, Carey left the building firm that had employed him for eight years and started up on his own—a move that caused some surprise. "It could not come by his honest day's work," remarked a Fenian acquaintance, Patrick Delaney, who soon learned from the boastful Carey that his new venture had been funded by Patrick Egan with Land League money. That was not all. Egan had also undertaken to back Carey as a nationalist candidate for Dublin's town council. "Pat Egan urged him on, and had sent letters from Paris that he would pay all expenses," Delaney said—a claim confirmed by a note to Carey dated November 9, 1881.

Normandy Hotel, rue de l'Echelle

My dear James,

I have only to say that there is no one of my acquaintances whom I would sooner see in any position in which it were desirable that sterling worth and true Nationalism should be represented than yourself. . . . Should you be selected I will send £30 towards the expense of the contest. . . .

Don't say much in reply, as my letters are liable to be opened, and don't give your address or name in your letter, only your initial "J."

Sincerely yours,
P. Egan

Egan's reason for courting Carey, Delaney declared, was because he was determined that an Invincible should become lord mayor of Dublin. John Walsh called on Carey later that month and, appealing to his sense of self-importance, said that his name was one of four submitted to be the Dublin leaders of a society that would "make history." After explaining its purpose, asking Carey's opinion of possible members, and finding out whether he was willing to join—"I said I was"—Walsh proceeded to administer an arcane initiation ritual.

Any new candidate to the IRB was subjected to an elaborate induction ceremony and minutely cross-examined before being blindfolded and led by guardians into the president's lodge. There he was addressed by their leader, testified to his belief in the Deity, and finally took the brotherhood oath. The Invincibles' version, by contrast, was accelerated and secular: instead of swearing on the Bible (which, as Mallon remarked, "might have aroused their consciences"), the recruit was instructed to hold a knife and recite from a written text. "It was an ordinary penknife," said Carey. "And I held it in my right hand, [Walsh] holding it in his right hand at the same time. I read the words myself: 'That I, of my own free will and without mental reservation whatsoever, will obey all orders transmitted to me by the Irish Invincibles, nor to seek nor to ask more than what is necessary in carrying out such orders, violation of which shall be death.' There were a great deal more words than that, but I forget them. I destroyed that paper."

A few days later, Walsh returned to Carey's house accompanied by James Mullett and two other leading Fenians, whom he said had been chosen to head the Invincibles' Dublin directory. Edward McCaffrey was an old-timer who had served six months in jail for his activities; Daniel Curley, a romantically handsome thirty-two-year-old carpenter, had given over his youth to his country, importing rifles for the Supreme Council and becoming a "center" (commander) of the city's advanced nationalists. Mullett was selected by the men as their chairman and given charge of another fifty gold sovereigns—further proof of the promised resources. "I never saw anything at all like that coming into the [IRB] organization," exclaimed Carey. "We were always in debt. . . . Mullett, Curley and I often talked among ourselves as to whence the money came. I expressed the opinion that it came from America; some of the others said, 'Perhaps we are getting some of this from the Land League.'"

*

On November 24, George Talbot received another Mallon report:

> Egan is now Dictator, he has directed all his friends and adherents here to oppose the Home Rule Program. It will be remembered that this man's antecedents from the commencement of his reckless career are Fenian and extreme Nationalist, to these principles he has steadfastly adhered.

Mallon strongly suspected Egan of using Land League money to fund terrorist activity, and yet he could not help admiring him. Son of a smallholder in County Longford, at fourteen years old Egan had been employed by a local flour mill and then worked his way up to become general manager of the firm. In Dublin, he had opened his own bakery and milling company and was now extremely wealthy. "A very remarkable man," said Mallon. "He fought hard luck and humble beginnings in a very plucky fashion."

With his weak, rounded shoulders, receding hair, and mild manner, Egan was an innocuous-looking figure, but those who knew him well recognized the "storm signals" that prefigured an explosion of fury. During a Land League meeting at the Hotel Brighton in Paris, William O'Brien had looked at Egan, a staunch Catholic, when one of the executives began a coarse attack on priests and nuns. Egan listened in silence, the tips of his ears reddening and a bright scarlet stain appearing in the center of each cheek. "Suddenly '. . . he flamed forth: 'You filthy dog. . . . If you utter one word more against my religion in my hearing, by God Almighty I'll smash your pig's head into a pudding.'" Mallon heard that Egan had so alarmed the "querulous bully who mocked his religion" that the man quit the Land League and Irish politics altogether.

In Paris that spring, an Englishman meeting Egan for the first time saw right through the silken glove to the hand of iron. This was Thomas Beach, better known under his pseudonym, Henri Le Caron, "the prince of spies." Posing as a Frenchman and practicing as a doctor in a small town near Chicago, Le Caron had penetrated the very heart of the Clan na Gael, the American sister to the IRB, keeping England's Home Office supplied with information about its workings in the United States. Egan's warm handshake, smiling eyes, and cheery, lilting voice had disconcerted Le Caron—"He was the last person in the world you would take for a deep conspirator and a constructor of murder"—but over the coming weeks he was able to form a true picture of a ruthless man. The two were constantly in each other's company, frequenting only the best cafés and restaurants, where Egan always insisted on paying the bill. Le Caron found himself thinking of "the poor dupes in America and Ireland who subscribed the funds over which he was then presiding," especially as Egan admitted siphoning off Land League money for purposes other than agrarian resistance: "You remember the committee of Dutch officers from Amsterdam who were sent down to South Africa in the Boer affair? I defrayed the expenses of those gentlemen out of the funds of the League. That is an affair that would never do to come to light." It later appeared that between £70,000 and £100,000 ($6 and $10 million) of Land League funds had been disbursed in various ways throughout 1881.

Egan talked earnestly about the need to break the barriers between constitutional and advanced movements and discussed with Le Caron fundraising efforts by the clan's revolutionary directory to carry out dynamite attacks on Britain. But it was not until six months later, in October 1881, that Egan virtually went public about a plan of vengeance much closer to his heart. Replying to a question by a *New York Herald* correspondent about "the exact nature" of an important new movement he had mentioned, Egan said, "I cannot tell you exactly, but there will be such a movement. . . . By declaring the League illegal the English Government has cut the constitutional ground for agitation from under our feet. We shall now be compelled to have recourse to other action."

With Parnell and the other leaders still in Kilmainham, Egan had the field to himself, and after writing his own inflammatory declaration, known as the No Rent Manifesto, he began organizing its distribution on posters and flyers.

TO THE PEOPLE OF IRELAND

The Government of England has declared war against the Irish people. The organization that protected them against the ravages of landlordism has been declared "unlawful and criminal." A reign of terror has commenced. Meet the action of the English Government with a determined passive resistance. The No Rent banner has been raised . . .

NO RENT, AVOID THE LAND COURT

Your brethren in America have risen to the crisis, and are ready to supply you with unlimited funds, provided you maintain your attitude of passive resistance and

PAY NO RENT

The person who does should be visited with the severest sentence of social ostracism.

Signed by order,
Patrick Egan, Treasurer

Behind him was one of the most formidable political forces in America—Patrick Ford's *Irish World*. With 125,000 subscribers, the journal accrued enormous sums from reader donations, allowing Egan to reward tenants for standing by the No Rent agreement. The *Irish World* was Ford's megaphone to promote social justice—in his radical, moralistic prose purpled with Old Testament rhetoric. Like Egan, Ford was a small, modest man, shy of public speaking and intensely religious; only the eyes blazing beneath heavy brows gave sign of the patriotic passions he vented in print. To some he was a committed humanitarian, to others an unscrupulous fanatic, a "loud-tongued apostle" of dynamite, who advocated group and individual terrorism. Ford legitimized his extremism as a response to colonial warfare by Britain, which, to protect its empire, had killed civilians and destroyed property. He had no hesitation about publishing the rantings of his European correspondent, Thomas Mooney, who had told Ford of a chemist he knew who could provide a compound that could be carried in a small bag and was capable of blowing English public buildings to atoms.

On October 21, two days after the suppression of the Land League, Ford made a searing appeal for even more funds. (His plea was also published in full in the *New York Times*.)

Brothers, English despotism has outlawed the Land League, but the spirit of the organization is indestructible. . . . America is an unassailable base of operation. In truth the war has just commenced in downright earnest. England and Ireland are now face to face. . . .

Now is the time for you to show your strength. . . . Hold public meetings. Increase the members of your branches. Send out collectors into wards and parishes. Promptly forward to us all moneys—the sinews of war—which the *Irish World* will flash, by cable, to Mr. Egan in Paris. Do these things and you will give new hope to the people of Ireland.

God defend the right!
Patrick Ford

Ford's thunderous endorsement and financial support of the Land League was troubling the head of the Clan na Gael. Not only had the Land War diverted attention away from the fight for Irish independence, but it was fast depleting American funds. Early in 1882, a sleek Chicago lawyer, Alexander Sullivan, then the clan's president, went to Paris to see Egan and urge a fair division of *Irish World* contributions. Sullivan demanded that the Land League turn over half its capital—£20,000 immediately and 50 percent of all future receipts—a suggestion to which Egan expressed sympathy, while haggling "like an Irish farmer selling a pig at a fair." Sullivan achieved his aim (Land League cash was invested in US bonds "to be used at some future time for a far nobler and better purpose"), and yet he still felt threatened by the Egan-Ford alliance, writing to John Devoy, the former Clan na Gael executive, to urge a breaking of ties.

> We can't continue to be the tail to this Ford Kite—which will lead to God knows where. It seems to me a duty to steer clear of this danger ahead—a danger which must be manifest to all observers and which cannot be averted if Egan and Ford are to be permitted to run things as they please. . . . I can see now that he and Mr. Egan have entered into a mutual admiration society each one to be the head at his side of the pond.

Mallon knew this. "The game is being played solely at present by Egan and his special retainers, and Ford of the New York *Irish World*," he told Talbot:

> The Miller [Egan's business partner James Rourke] has stated to the informant this morning that Egan was going too far, that he was a rabid revolutionist to be blamed for all that has occurred. . . . He said if Egan was to have his own way, the whole thing is bound to come to pieces. The farmers are not subscribing or abiding by the manifesto of the League, but they mean to try and coerce them.

Three weeks later it was made clear just what this coercion entailed. "It is also understood," Mallon reported, "that tenants who have paid their rents, and laborers who work for boycotted farmers are to be assassinated." Already, as a direct result of the No Rent Manifesto, a young man in County Galway had been shot dead at night by a band of armed men; in mid-November, in County Leitrim, three boys were maimed for life because their father was a bailiff; in December, a process server in Queen's County was battered to death by a party of men, and a farm laborer in County Roscommon was fatally shot because his brother had paid rent; the New Year saw an eighty-year-old land steward from County Clare shot for refusing to leave the employer he had served for fifty years; in County Galway, two men, a bailiff and his seventeen-year-old nephew, were found dead in a lake. In late February, in County Mayo, a young man was dragged out of his bed by a gang shouting for the "traitor who had paid his rent." Badly beaten outside his house, he managed to escape inside but was forced out again and shot dead.

*

One of the No Rent flyers had found its way into the hands of Queen Victoria, then in residence at Osborne House on the Isle of Wight. Alarmed by Ireland's spiraling anarchy, she wrote immediately to Gladstone.

[The Queen] has *today* seen the copy of a manifesto signed Patrick Egan, stating that the tenants are at war with the Government and ordering them to pay no rent. The Queen hopes that greater efforts may be made to arrest the agitators who have created this state of affairs. . . . If there are not sufficient soldiers to perform the duties required of them, let more regiments be sent. If the law is powerless to punish wrongdoers, let increased powers be sought for and at any rate let no effort be spared for putting an end to a state of affairs which is a *disgrace* to *any civilized* country.

It was the last day of 1881, and Queen Victoria had spent much of it grimly reflecting on the "horrors and sorrows" of the old year: the assassination of the Russian czar, Alexander II, in March; the "Irish Atrocities"; the recent conflagration of Vienna's Ringtheater, in which some 449 operagoers had burned alive; the death of her beloved Disraeli, an "*overwhelming*" personal loss.

With the connivance of her faithful servant John Brown, Victoria and Disraeli had kept up their spirited correspondence—"an unguarded exchange between sovereign and subject, ranging the gamut from formal to friendly, from grave to gossipy." But Disraeli's health had fast deteriorated over the last eighteen months, and by Easter, with snow blanketing London, he was bedridden. The queen sent primroses from Osborne and talked of a visit to Disraeli's Mayfair house, but he asked that she be dissuaded. "It is better not," he said, adding with a flicker of the old wit: "She would only ask me to take a message to Albert." On April 19, 1881, a tearful John Brown came to tell Victoria what she had long been dreading.

Gladstone had written her a formal, carefully phrased note of condolence, paying tribute to "the extraordinary powers of the deceased Statesman," while not attempting to seek favor by burying their differences. But the queen and her current prime minister had grown no closer. Disraeli had invariably complied with her decisions, whereas Gladstone made a debate of them, tediously driving home his point when convinced he was right, and exasperating, often humiliating her with his high-mindedness. Even his wife, Catherine, was said to have exclaimed, "Oh William dear, if you weren't such a great man you would be a terrible bore!"

Recently, Catherine had been urging him to soften his attitude toward Victoria—"Do pet the Queen," she said—but this would never happen now; their distant civility had stiffened into what Gladstone perceived as a terminal rift. "The repellent power which she knows so well how to use has been put into action against me for the first time," he told Lord Granville. "I have found myself on a new and different footing with her." And in his diary, he bleakly noted: "I am always outside an iron ring: and without any desire, had I the power, to break it through."

Gladstone was seriously considering resigning. He believed that his return to office had been "accidental, conditional, and temporary," that he had resumed leadership only to fulfill certain purposes—most pressingly to bring an end to Disraeli's profligacy and imperial wars. Now, with the withdrawal of British troops from Afghanistan, the signing of a peace treaty in the Transvaal, and the country's finances restored to a satisfactory footing, Gladstone felt that he had carried out much of what he had undertaken to do. Ireland, of course, still required his care, but he had convinced himself that things would improve by Easter of 1882 and felt that if he did not retire at that point, there was no moment in the foreseeable future when it would become possible.

Gladstone had confided all this and more to Cavendish during a week Frederick and Lucy had spent at Hawarden at the beginning of November 1881. Cavendish dismissed outright Gladstone's hope that the Irish situation could be settled within four months and later discussed their conversation with Lucy. She was well aware that her uncle was finding his position toward the queen "intolerable," but agreed with Frederick that it would be wrong for him to leave the helm with politics in its present state. "Nor can the moment be foreseen when it would be right. . . . *While he retained his full powers* the country would not let him resign and nobody else could lead."

A week later, however, Gladstone was talking even more persistently of disentangling himself from office, only to find that he had no support. It was out of the question, Lord Granville declared, after conferring with Gladstone's doctor, who confirmed the prime minister's exceptional strength, reckoned he had a good chance of living to be a hundred, and compared his physical flawlessness to a Greek statue of the ideal man. "It may seem unfriendly to you," wrote Granville, "but I cannot aid or abet you in striking such a blow on the Liberal party, and one which they would so deeply deplore and I fear resent."

*

Forster was also yearning to retire—or rather, withdraw permanently from Ireland. The physical strain for a man in his sixties had become increasingly hard to endure. Over the last two years he had made the taxing sea crossing and train journey from Dublin to London more than thirty times, given at least fifteen hundred speeches in the House of Commons, and been responsible for helping the Irish to understand Parliament and—far more challenging—Parliament to understand the Irish. "Seriously," he told his daughter Florence as they walked through Phoenix Park, "I think the best thing would be for me to give up altogether." Cabinet support was rapidly waning, and Forster openly admitted in the House that his policy had failed. He had underestimated the forces with which he was contending; intimidation and murders were on the increase, despite the thirty thousand troops and constabulary that had been sent to Ireland and the hundreds of suspects imprisoned. He felt exhausted, disillusioned, and so unconfident and erratic in his decisions that colleagues had begun calling him "the Pendulum." Deciding to tell Gladstone that he wanted to leave Ireland as soon as possible, Forster wrote suggesting that he be replaced "by someone not tarred by the coercion brush."

*

Queen Victoria was most concerned about her chief secretary, suspecting that the Irish troubles were affecting his health ("his handwriting showed this")—an observation that a meeting at Osborne House only confirmed.

> He looks ill, & seems much out of spirits. He says the state of affairs is as bad as possible, & the insecurity of everything, dreadful. The necessity for strong measures, becomes more & more imperative. . . . He gave some horrible instances of murders, all, connected with land. . . . He

would, he said, give anything, to get out of the whole thing, but he cannot desert his post.

The British press was portraying Forster as a victim of his paramilitary policing, publishing illustrations of the Chief Secretary's Lodge with three constables posted outside its drawing room window, and picturing him traveling in an open carriage surrounded by a mounted escort, with a regiment of guards in Dublin Castle's courtyard and a large cannon in the foreground. Slipping through the security net, however, was a letter sent to Forster at the beginning of February 1882, oozing a suspicious liquid. This turned out to be iodide of nitrogen, dampened so as not to go off in transit, but which when dry would have exploded with enough violence to injure seriously, if not kill.

*

The Invincibles conspirators were strengthening forces to effect Forster's "removal." James Carey had sworn in a laborer turned cabdriver, James Fitzharris, a convivial, elderly man well known to Dublin's underworld as "Skin-the-Goat" (he was supposed to have sold the hide of his pet goat to pay off drinking debts). Among James Mullett's recruits was Joe Brady, "a giant in stature and a boar in strength," one of twenty-five siblings brought up in the tenements of Dublin's North Anne Street. With his huge block of a face, tight lips, and shock of black hair, Brady embodied the primal, brute strength necessary to act on orders without thought or scruple. His best friend, Tim Kelly, also a new Invincible, was the physical opposite, a slim, delicate nineteen-year-old, who hero-worshipped Brady and sang with him in the choir of Dublin's Franciscan church. It was this incongruous pair that had been selected by the Invincibles directorate to carry out the actual murder.

The Invincibles' gatherings were usually held in the Bricklayers' Club, of which James Carey was secretary, or in Dublin taverns—Wrenn's in Dame Street or Little's in North King Street—where they huddled around the fireplace, knowing that nobody would dare intrude. One afternoon, Carey and Dan Curley went together to Phoenix Park to try to identify the chief secretary. They learned about Forster's movements from newspaper reports or telegrams sent from London— "Mr. Forster was referred to in racing phraseology"—but they were not yet capable of recognizing him. Later that day, Carey went to the Angel Hotel to meet Patrick Sheridan, still in the disguise of a priest. They talked about the weapons needed for their mission, and Sheridan, who was on his way to London, promised to speed up their arrival.

New to the Invincibles' directorship was the infamous Captain John McCafferty, an American guerrilla officer and wealthy miner, whose death sentence for planning the 1867 raid on Chester Castle had been commuted to deportation. Violating the conditions of his parole, McCafferty had returned to England; in the police "Wanted" poster, he was described as forty-four years old, five foot eight, with a tattooed left hand; small, dark, sunken eyes; and a sallow "scowling visage." McCafferty was known to be in London in October 1881, almost certainly one of the Americans who attended the first Invincibles planning meeting, and he called on Carey at his Dublin house four or five months later, handing over twenty-five more gold sovereigns. Arms were again discussed, and McCafferty, said to have coined the phrase "the gun is mightier than the sword," suggested rifles for work at long range, but Carey, having asked Sheridan to provide daggers, continued to press for these. Blades make no sound.

*

The Invincibles executive responsible for securing weapons and transporting them to Dublin was Frank Byrne, secretary of the British branch of the Land League, a tall, fair, well-educated thirty-five-year-old, highly respected by his colleagues. A doctor friend, who was an advanced nationalist living in London, had volunteered to purchase surgical knives from a reputable medical supplier. Soon afterward, a Supreme Council man went to the Land League's Westminster headquarters, where Byrne, after speaking authoritatively about a certain design of handgun, opened a drawer containing a brown-paper parcel. "The doctor has been buying some surgical instruments," he said, pulling out a knife from a corner where the paper had torn. It was an amputating blade, about ten inches long, beautifully finished and bearing its maker's name: Swiss & Son, 62 Strand, London. "I was somewhat surprised to see such a thing in the League rooms," remarked the visitor. "It was an extraordinary thing, but I thought no more of it." McCafferty had asked for some kind of handgrip to be made, so the instruments were then taken to a Fenian cobbler in London's East End, fitted with short handles of black horn, covered with leather sheaths, and returned to Westminster's Palace Chambers.

Sometime in February, at around eight o'clock in the morning, James Carey was visited at his house in Denzille Street by a woman he did not know. This was almost certainly Byrne's wife, Mary Ann, an impassioned nationalist with a mannish face and large, dark-circled eyes. Conspicuously pregnant, she was wearing a voluminous, fur-lined black cape, under which, tied to a string around her neck, hung a Winchester rifle. She had also brought two handguns, a box holding some of the knives, and a large quantity of ammunition wrapped in a parcel. After about week, she arrived again at Denzille Street with a second consignment for Carey to distribute.

*

On a bitterly raw evening at the beginning of March 1882, about a dozen Invincibles were stationed at intervals along Dublin's quays, each knowing how they were going to make their attack: as soon as Forster's carriage crossed over Victoria Bridge, the horses were to be shot, along with anyone who passed by or interfered. Tim Kelly and Joe Brady would then move in to "do the remainder."

As it happened, Forster was not even in town at the time. He had decided to see for himself the places most badly afflicted by the winter's violence, determined to dispense with any barrier of police protection and come face-to-face with the people. Whether on a train, on a steamboat, or in a foreign restaurant, he had always found it easy to talk to strangers, making new acquaintances who warmed to his sympathetic, witty manner. The Irish, he felt sure, could also be won over. "You see," Jane Forster told their daughter, "he *likes* them."

Traveling first to County Clare, Forster called on a boycotted landlord and visited the workhouse, where he was appalled by the plight of one of its inmates, a victim of a vicious nocturnal attack. As a result of paying his rent, Michael Moroney had been dragged from his bed in front of his wife and children and taken into the yard, where shots were fired at his leg by a gang of Moonlighters. The limb had been amputated, but the damage was so severe that Moroney would soon die.

After visiting "the worst part of Galway," Forster went to Tullamore, in the center of Ireland, where he intended to address the town's inhabitants. Nothing had been done to advertise his appearance, so Forster did this himself, walking without an escort through the town, speaking to groups of farmers, laborers, and factory workers. A Land Leaguer who owned the hotel where Forster lunched suggested that he make his speech from one of the windows, which he came back to do, talking to a waiting crowd of about three hundred. His aim, he told them, was to prevent honest, hardworking men from being terrorized, and he described what he had just seen and heard at Moroney's bedside, asking why they did not unite to stop such outrages. "Let out the suspects!" someone shouted in reply. Expecting to be blamed for the detention of Parnell, Dillon, and O'Kelly, Forster said that the prisoners would be released as soon as the murders and intimidation had stopped.

There was only a trickle of applause at the end of the speech, and later Forster would be mocked by Parnellites for haranguing an audience they claimed was hired extras. In Parliament, the renegade Joseph Biggar went much further, accusing Forster of seeking out suffering as he had during the Great Famine, as if this were some kind of perversion. On the whole, though, Forster was admired for the Tullamore speech, impressing even some of his bitterest detractors with his courage, approachability, and self-deprecation. Edward Hamilton spoke for many when he said, "Why did he not do this months and months ago?"

*

The failure of the Invincibles to carry out their mission had infuriated the London directorate, which would have been angrier still had it known details of the would-be assassins' ineptitude. Crassly obvious in their surveillance, they had parked their vehicle on consecutive evenings in a copse near the Chief Secretary's Lodge, and a Dublin Castle employee, while driving through the city with Forster, had caught sight of two men, "leaning forward and peering into the carriage as if to make sure who was inside." Clearly, the Dublin men needed someone to take control.

Frank Byrne had decided to enlist a close friend and neighbor who, unlike Walsh, Sheridan, and McCafferty, was unknown to the police. Ostensibly, Patrick Tynan was an insignificant figure, a commercial traveler, who also kept a bookshop and lending library in Kingstown, Dublin's ferry port—his itinerant working routine perfectly suited to coming and going on Invincibles matters without causing suspicion. Although a participant in the 1867 Fenian Rising, he now kept his nationalism hidden under a facade of the British establishment: his friends were mostly conventional, nonpolitical businessmen, and he was a member of a volunteer rifle regiment, the Queen's Westminsters, one of the most elite in the country. He took pride in being a soldier; in a studio photograph, dressed ready for action in braided, gold-buttoned military regalia, he is a stocky, faintly ludicrous figure with pince-nez, a theatrical beard, and white-gloved hands grasping a musket almost his own height. A regular visitor to the Land League's office, Tynan claimed to have been "staggered and astonished" by Byrne's offer, coming as it did from a prominent Parnellite official, "in the very chamber where Parliamentary members sat to consult and arrange 'Legal and Constitutional Agitation.'" But the prospect of commanding an actual armed combat excited and flattered Tynan, who had no hesitation about accepting Byrne's proposal, provided he was given complete charge of operations.

*

In early March, Joe Brady, wearing his Sunday best, seemed to be expecting an important visitor. Tynan had arranged a meeting with Brady, Carey, and Dan Curley, although the three men would never discover his name. "If he left a note it would be signed with the figure I," Carey said. And so the Invincibles began referring to Tynan as "Number One."

Tynan's first question was, how many members had been enlisted, and when told there were twenty-two, he asked for "a few more good men to be got." He wanted to know if they had any complaints. They needed funds, Brady said, at which point Tynan put thirty sovereigns on the table, declaring that there was no limit to money—even a thousand pounds if necessary. And then they got to the main reason for the meeting: the planning of Forster's assassination.

Unlike the Invincibles, Tynan was able to identify the chief secretary with certainty. After a recent visit to the House of Commons' public gallery, he had come across Forster while walking along the passage to the members' entrance. In Tynan's version of their encounter, Forster had felt threatened by Tynan's proximity, his face draining of color as he clutched the dispatch box he was carrying as if trying to shield himself. "How easily this tyrant could at that very moment be shot!" Tynan thought, deciding to tail him at a distance. But when

Forster emerged into the forecourt, he was surrounded within seconds by several plainclothes policemen. Dublin presented an even greater challenge for close access. Tynan decided to carry out his own reconnaissance, and after driving down by the quays near Phoenix Park, he selected the narrowest point of a street in a Fenian neighborhood as the ideal site for an ambush.

Information about Forster's movements was unreliable, but the Invincibles got news that he would leave home at about eleven a.m. on Monday, March 27, and drive down the quays on his way to the castle. The man chosen to ensure that he had left the lodge was James Carey, instructed to sit on the box seat in a cab alongside the driver and follow Forster's carriage, giving the signal to the first sentry, who would then pass it along the line to the others. But at a meeting of the Dublin directorate the night before, Carey had begged Tynan to spare him from such a dangerous position, citing his family of six children as the reason. Brady and Curley exchanged withering glances. "Carey suffered in their estimation," said Tynan, who was also taken aback by such a display of weakness in an Invincible officer.

The next morning, a substitute was sitting beside Skin-the-Goat, the cabdriver, and Carey was stationed near the park gates. Next in line, near Kingsbridge, was Peter Doyle, and next to him, in Queen Street, was the elderly Harry Rowles; Brady, Kelly, and Curley were positioned at the Esplanade Tavern, opposite the Guinness factory. As soon as Carey saw Forster set off, he gave the signal down to Doyle before running across Kingsbridge and jumping onto a moving tram. Rowles was leaning against the quay wall, waiting to get the signal from Carey, whom he expected to see next to Skin-the-Goat. Forster's carriage was rapidly approaching, and on the opposite side Doyle made the prearranged gesture, drawing a white handkerchief across his face. Rowles failed to notice. Returning in a cab from a business appointment, Tynan had seen Forster's speeding carriage, closely followed by the Invincibles' vehicle, and every second he expected to hear the sound of firing. The carriage passed the appointed place, and nothing happened. Carey, meanwhile, had got off the tram and crossed over to where a vexed Curley was standing. When they realized that Rowles was responsible for the blunder, they violently threatened him, but Tynan took his side, pointing out that he "should have been made to repeat the order back again to make certain it was intelligible. . . . Had the signal been properly taken up, Forster would have been 'suppressed.'"

*

The recess of Parliament over Easter gave the Invincibles the opportunity to increase their efforts. On one occasion a police escort prevented the Invincibles from taking action; on another they looked into Forster's carriage to see only his wife and daughter inside. Security precautions were tighter than ever, and much resented by Forster: "What are those confounded fellows here for again—I shall have this stopped—I shouldn't mind if I was shot—everything over here is so disgusting." It did in fact seem that Forster was going out of his way to court danger, taking advantage of a fine spell of spring weather to stroll with Jane and their dog around Phoenix Park's Circular Walk, and on Easter Sunday, after the family had been to church and he had caught up on work at the castle, walking back alone through the park.

He spent that afternoon, March 27, in his study. He had not yet had the courage to mention to Jane—"She would think it so dreadful," Florence wrote in her journal—that he had suggested to Gladstone he be appointed lord lieutenant, otherwise known as "viceroy." Currently occupying the position was Lord Cowper, who, although wellborn, with a beautiful wife and all the social graces required by the viceregal court, was just a cipher—something Cowper knew only too well: "I go into the Castle nearly every day. . . . But I feel all the time that everything would go on just as well if I were not here." Forster's view exactly. He had made sure that he alone governed Ireland, consolidating his power by his presence in Parliament and close bond with Gladstone—and Francis Cowper had capitulated.

Forster's Sunday seclusion was interrupted by the delivery of a telegram. It was from Parnell in Kilmainham Gaol, and it prompted "a sudden Council of War" at Cowper's residence, the Viceregal Lodge. "Have just heard of the death by typhus of my sister's only child," Parnell had written. "Wish to attend funeral in Paris. Will undertake not to take part in any political matters while absent."

SEVEN

Coercion-in-Cottonwool

THE TELEGRAM was a genuine plea by Parnell. For many years his eldest sister, Delia, had been locked in a miserable marriage to a pathologically jealous man, their son Henry, a twenty-one-year-old gifted musician, her only joy. Parnell considered it his duty to try to comfort her, but at the same time he felt compelled to be with Katharine, who had just informed him that their baby girl, born in February, was critically ill.

The couple had been corresponding two or three times a week, Parnell giving one of his regular visitors envelopes addressed to a "Mrs. Carpenter" at a London address and writing between the letters' visible lines in "secret ink." Drawing on knowledge he had acquired as an amateur scientist, Parnell gave Katharine instructions that were pedantically exact: to reveal the hidden words, she had to brush the letter with a unique formula and in her reply use a different solution, pressing very lightly with a pen nib on special, unglazed paper.

Do not crowd what you write in ordinary ink into one little space in the middle of the sheet. After the solution has dried if you rub over the letters with an ink eraser it will remove all the glistening and appearance of letters. I wonder they have never opened any of them, but they may do it at any time. It would not hurt me in any way as I do not use it for any other purpose. Unless, indeed, they sent it to a certain person.

This of course was William O'Shea. Since his discovery of Katharine's pregnancy, the captain had virtually moved into Wonersh Lodge, hoping, she said, that the baby's birth would seal a reconciliation. It was out of the question, and yet O'Shea, regarding himself as the father and proprietorial about his marital rights, was exhausting Katharine with his overactive libido. Rather astonishingly, she complained of this to Parnell, who wrote asking, "Has he left yet? It is frightful that you should be exposed to such daily torture"; and repeating two months later, "I do trust you have been now relieved for a time by his departure, and that you are getting a little sleep." Confident of his hold on Katharine, Parnell displayed no sign of jealousy, only deep concern for her well-being—"really the only reason why I wish for a change."

His incarceration in Kilmainham had not been an ordeal—in fact, he described the experience as "inexpressibly consoling." Spared any kind of responsibility, he had been given the best accommodation in the jail, a spacious room, which, with its elegant furnishings, provided by the Ladies' Land League, could have been the cigar lounge of a gentlemen's club in London's St. James. "Coercion-in-cottonwool," one observer called it. Parnell knew when he arrived that he and his two fellow MPs had been let off lightly, telling Katharine that they had fully expected to be split up and housed in different jails but instead were allowed to associate freely. They would congregate in Kilmainham's magnificent, glass-roofed central hall, which had a long central table strewn with newspapers, magazines, books, game boards, and packs of cards; Parnell often seen absorbed in a chess match or outside in the courtyard playing handball with James O'Kelly. Another prisoner assigned to look after him served as butler-cum-barista:

He makes me a soda and lemon in the morning, and then gives me my breakfast. At dinner he takes care that I get all the nicest bits and concocts the most perfect black coffee in a "Kaffee Kanne" out of berries which he roasts and grinds each day. Finally, in the evening . . . he brews me a steaming tumbler of hot whiskey. He has marked all my clothes for me also and sees that the washerwoman does not rob me. Don't you begin to feel jealous?

This sybaritic picture could have been exaggerated to reassure Katharine, were it not confirmed by the account of the journalist and politician T. P. O'Connor, to whom Parnell declared he had never felt better: "He himself told me that the time passed very pleasantly, that he had not been so happy for years." For Katharine, on the other hand, the long separation was "surely killing" her, and in December she had begged Parnell to negotiate for his release. "I could not very well make any arrangement or enter into any undertaking with Government unless I retired altogether from politics," he firmly replied.

The final stages of the pregnancy had been stressful for them both. Katharine felt compelled to deceive O'Shea, who expected the baby to be born in late March or early April—nine months after their resumption of sexual relations—and Parnell was distraught that she might also have misled her doctors about the due date. By the end of December, he was pleading, "*Tell one of them the right time*, so that he may be on hand, otherwise you may not have one at all. It will never do to run this risk"; a fortnight later, he urged, "You must tell the doctor and never mind about ———."

Receiving no word from Katharine, Parnell grew frantic, and when two short messages arrived on February 14, Valentine's Day, he broke down in tears. A day later she safely delivered their child, and learning of this, Parnell was overjoyed, dismissing her disappointment for him that the baby was not a boy. "I shall love her very much better than if it had been a son; indeed my darling, I love her very much already." The captain registered the birth of "Claude O'Shea" (named after an old friend of Katharine's), and Parnell suggested a middle name of Sophie (in memory of his sister Sophia, who had died in 1875), although aware "it might make suspicions." With her father's brown eyes and a golden tint to her hair—a curl of which Parnell had put in a locket with one of Katharine's own—she was a placid baby who rarely cried and lay watching her mother with solemn eyes.

Feeling "very much like a father," Parnell had now begun contriving a way to free himself. He was devoting his time to drafting clauses to the 1881 Land Act that would provide legislation to help the smaller tenants with arrears on their rents. He was convinced that this would immediately help to restore peace in Ireland and, consequently, give him an opportunity to come to some arrangement with Gladstone.

Claude Sophie, meanwhile, was growing increasingly frail. In her fifth week, doctors told Katharine that the baby did not have long to live, and there was nothing they could do. "My pain was the greater in that I feared her father would never see her."

*

Parnell left Kilmainham at six a.m. on Monday, April 10, and by the evening, the Irish mail train was approaching London. A large crowd of protestors had assembled at Euston Station to meet the Irish leader, but when the train stopped at the railway hub Willesden Junction, in west London, a group of Land League executives came on board, aiming to assist Parnell to honor the conditions of his parole by diverting him away from the Euston demonstration. The first to enter the compartment was Invincibles leader Frank Byrne.

Parnell, who knew the affable Byrne slightly and had a good opinion of him (unaware, he later insisted, of his murderous conspiracy), shook his hand genially. They spoke of Parnell's treatment in prison and his immediate plan, which was to go to the Jermyn Street house of his trusted colleague Justin McCarthy, with whom he wanted to discuss the No Rent Manifesto, now "practically withdrawn," together with his suggestions for an arrears act. Parnell would later claim that he was obliged to spend the night in London because the train's late arrival had made him miss his connection to Paris, but of course his priority was to visit Katharine. In the early hours of Tuesday morning, he arrived at Wonersh Lodge, where the couple had "the unspeakable comfort" of a reunion, and Katharine was able to lift the fading Claude Sophie into her father's arms.

*

The following day, before catching the Dover railway to Paris, Parnell dined with William O'Shea in London. He wished, Katharine said, "to conciliate Willie as much as possible" and encouraged the continuation of a correspondence the captain had begun with Gladstone. Its main purpose was to convey Parnell's new attitude of goodwill toward the government, but O'Shea seized the chance to promote himself as a go-between. In a letter to Gladstone dated April 13, he boasted of his influence over the Irish leader and took credit for having "brought Mr. Parnell within the sphere of moderate counsel." Gladstone knew nothing about Captain O'Shea, but sensing that the Irish were disposed to make terms, he decided to make his response cautious but encouragingly positive.

Buoyed up by the prime minister's letter, O'Shea now approached the MP Joseph Chamberlain, leader of the Liberal's left-wing faction. With his monocle, cigar, and orchid boutonniere, Chamberlain cultivated the appearance of an aristocratic dandy, but his beginnings were humble and had influenced his loathing of coercion and his sympathy for "the unfortunate tenants, who had been racked and robbed for so many years." His reply was noncommittal, but O'Shea was undeterred and wrote again, attempting to impress the Birmingham industrialist with his continental sophistication. "What the French call the psychological moment ought not to be lost," urged O'Shea. "I have heard from Mr. Parnell this morning. He says in confidence that he hopes 'something may come out of the correspondence.'"

Gripped by the possibility of a new understanding with the Irish, and subsequently learning from O'Shea that Parnell "was sick of prison and in a most conciliatory frame of mind," Chamberlain wrote to Gladstone, offering himself as an intermediary. "I had hitherto refrained from speaking to any of this section for fear of embarrassing Mr. Forster, but if desired I would see Messrs O'Shea and others, without committing the Government, and would find out what humor they were."

*

Forster had got wind of Chamberlain's negotiations and suggested to Gladstone that he should have a private meeting with Justin McCarthy, who was acting as leader in Parnell's absence. It was vital for Forster, and Forster alone, to take control of Irish matters now that he had set his sights on the top job. On April 19, before leaving for London, he walked over to the Viceregal Lodge and, after discussing various matters, suddenly launched into his "astonishing proposal," suggesting to Lord Cowper that he take indefinite leave. "Instead of feeling inclined to kick him out of the room I was really almost amused," Lord Cowper recounted. "It was like a clumsy blundering brute who keeps treading upon one's toes with the best intention. . . . I don't know whether to be more angry with him for the manner in which he grasped the whole management from the first . . . or at my own easiness in allowing it."

Writing immediately to Gladstone about the conversation, Cowper was reassured by the prime minister that the scheme was "purely and exclusively" Forster's own. Learning of it, Edward Hamilton wrote, incredulously, "Old 'Buckshot' actually suggested the idea that he should be made Lord Lieutenant! . . . This of course Mr. Gladstone cannot hear of."

*

Forster's departure from Dublin that day had been publicly announced, and the Invincibles seized their chance. Carey, who had actually brushed Forster's arm early that day when the chief secretary passed him on the way to the post office, was stationed at the castle gates. When Tynan arrived, he saw Carey standing outside a tavern in Dame Street, smoking a cigar, with the cab driver waiting nearby.

"He said that from what he was told, Forster was inside the Castle and would soon leave." By the afternoon, however, Forster had still not appeared, and Tynan, thinking he must have got away unnoticed, ordered the men to concentrate on Westland Row railroad terminus; Forster was almost certain to leave by train for Kingstown, sleeping on board the steamer, as he so often did, during the crossing to the Welsh port of Holyhead. Shortly before the 6:45 train was due to depart, the Invincibles rushed along the platform, searching every carriage. "He was to be shot with the occupants," Carey said. "Anyone who interfered was to be disabled." But this train left without Forster, as did later ones, and after the last departure at 11:45, the sentinels gave up and went home, grateful to be sheltering from the night's wild winds and rain.

As it happened, Forster was already on board the mail steamer. His private secretary, Henry Jephson, had suggested they take an earlier train than planned so they could relax at the Royal St. George Yacht Club, a few hundred yards from the ferry berth. "We left by the quarter to six-o'clock train for Kingstown, dined at the club there, and walked on board the steamer where we met Mrs. Forster and her daughter, little knowing at the time how dreadful a tragedy had been avoided."

*

On April 19, Parnell was making his way back to Kilmainham. He was prone to hypochondria and anxiety about his health had kept him in Paris two days longer than he had intended. He had a slight cold—"I think I caught it from leaving off a flannel jacket which I used to wear when asleep in prison"—and even when fully recovered remained indoors because of an icy north wind. On arriving in England, he went straight to Eltham. Claude Sophie had only hours left to live, but he and Katharine had little time to comfort each other—O'Shea was expected at any moment. To explain his presence at Wonersh Lodge, Parnell had asked the captain to collaborate on the truce he was planning with the government, a decision he must have regretted, as the emotional strain on him and Katharine was scarcely bearable. The two men sat up in the dining room until the early hours working out terms of a treaty; "Willie wanted me to join them," Katharine said, "but I would not leave my baby." Eight-week-old Claude Sophie died at dawn on April 21. After a few hours' sleep, relieved to escape the "wretched state of the house," O'Shea went to the House of Commons, leaving his grieving wife alone with Parnell.

*

At a cabinet meeting on April 22, it was agreed by a majority that Joseph Chamberlain should be allowed to enter into a dialogue with the Irish leader through O'Shea, the venture "to be disavowed if he failed." O'Shea then sent a message to Eltham, asking Parnell to come to his Victoria apartment that afternoon—a request Parnell ignored. By providing him with close access to Katharine, O'Shea had served his purpose, and wanting someone more dependable as a broker, Parnell called on Justin McCarthy that afternoon. By the evening of May 24, Parnell was back in Kilmainham.

O'Shea was beside himself. These negotiations were the greatest event of his political life, the kind of opportunity he sought in having "pimped [Katharine] to the Irish party leader." The letter he immediately sent Parnell seemed to crave a repudiation of McCarthy and a declaration of faith in his own involvement. "What do you think I had best say to it?" Parnell appealed to Katharine. "I told my friend in Jermyn Street [McCarthy] what steps to take, so that the matter referred to in enclosed will probably go on all right without, or with, the further participation of the writer."

*

On April 26, John Redmond, another of Parnell's devotees, introduced the new arrears bill, the author of which was widely assumed to be their leader. Not only amounting to a recognition of the Land

Act, with certain modifications, it was a covert admission that the Irish were now prepared to cooperate. Forster, however, was unconvinced: the government needed a written guarantee, not just a promise that outrages and lawlessness would cease. "Parnell and Co must publish their pledges," he insisted.

O'Shea saw his opportunity. After telling Katharine that Parnell was "so shifty" he could not be trusted to carry out any pact that was not on paper, he approached Forster, asking for his help with an exchange of correspondence—"two private letters each way." Forster disliked the conceited, devious O'Shea and doubted that he had the sway over Parnell that he claimed, but he was so anxious to involve himself in the current negotiations that he went out of his way to ensure that the letters were not opened.

Having kept his conciliatory advances to the government a secret from his two fellow "suspects," James O'Kelly and John Dillon, Parnell was dismayed by the prospect of O'Shea turning up at the jail. "If you come to Ireland I think you had best not see me, for reasons I will explain hereafter," he had written on April 27, but in vain, as two days later, O'Shea duly appeared. For six hours, closeted together in Parnell's room, the two men discussed and drafted a settlement that became known as the Kilmainham Treaty—a document that proposed a curbing of rural violence in return for an arrears settlement. Parnell was pressing for the release of Michael Davitt and also wanted to enlist the help of Patrick Sheridan, who, as an organizer of insurrection in the West of Ireland, "knew everybody." He told O'Shea that it was equally important to get Patrick Egan back from Paris so that he could explain the advantages of the new policy, saying he was confident that if he saw Davitt, Egan, and Sheridan in person, he could win their support—if he got what he called "the first run at them."

The document O'Shea took away with him was little different from the terms in a letter that Parnell had written to Justin McCarthy after their meeting, except for one crucial addition—a long sentence offering a détente with Gladstone's government.

The accomplishment of the program I have sketched would, in my judgment, be regarded by the country as a practical settlement of the land question, and would, I feel sure, enable us to co-operate cordially for the future with the Liberal party in forwarding Liberal principles; so that the Government, at the end of the session would, from the state of the country, feel themselves thoroughly justified in dispensing with further coercive measures.

Parnell may have added this compromising overture on the basis that only Chamberlain, who hoped for an alliance with the Irish, would see the text, but it has also been suggested that O'Shea, wanting to take credit for an important pledge not in the McCarthy letter, had prized it out of Parnell by threatening to expose the relationship with his wife. This is unlikely. Parnell had told Katharine on March 30 that he would be damaged only if their letters fell into the captain's hands, and writing a month later, he says nothing about a blackmail attempt: "He came over to see me, so I thought it best to give him a letter, as he would have been dreadfully mortified if he had had nothing to show."

*

On Sunday, April 30, the Forster family breakfast in London's Eccleston Square was interrupted by the arrival of O'Shea. Taking him into the library and reading through the document the captain had eagerly thrust into his hands, Forster seemed disappointed by its content. "Is that all, do you think that Parnell would be inclined to say . . . that upon our doing certain things he will help us to prevent outrages?" O'Shea was crushed. "What more do you want?" he demanded. "Doubtless I could supplement it. . . . Well there may be faults of expression, but the thing is done. If these words will not do I must get others." And then Forster was stunned to hear O'Shea suggest adding a line of his own: "That the conspiracy which has been used to get up boycotting and outrages will now be used to put them down." It could be achieved, he said, if Parnell enlisted the help of Patrick Sheridan.

Knowing Sheridan to be a notorious Fenian agent—"a very dangerous troublesome fellow"—Forster considered this to be a virtual admission that the Land League was behind agrarian crime, an indirect confirmation that if Parnell had not actually instigated the conspiracy of violence he had almost certainly connived in it. Choosing not to reveal his opinion, "which might be interpreted to be that of the Cabinet," Forster told O'Shea that he would send the letter to Gladstone right away. That evening, as he sat with Florence in the library, Forster repeated much of the conversation, saying that it was a deal O'Shea considered as good as settled.

"But is Mr. Gladstone impressed with this?"

"Oh Gladstone is delighted—he only thinks it's too good to be true."

*

It had been with a heavy heart that Gladstone read Forster's memorandum warning him that the result of O'Shea's talk with Parnell had been far from satisfactory. Reaching the end of the Kilmainham Treaty itself, however, Gladstone felt overwhelmed with relief. He paid little heed to the sentence about a future cooperation with the Liberals—"an *hors d'oeuvre* which we had no right to expect, and, I think have at present no right to accept"—and told Forster that he could not understand his skepticism: Parnell's proposals, he declared, were "the most extraordinary I ever read." He then wrote jubilantly to Lord Granville:

> It would hardly be possible to describe the amazement with which after reading Forster's note I perused Parnell's letter. The promise seems to me if anything wider than we wanted—and the sole condition is the settlement of the arrears. The only question perhaps for tomorrow is the release of the three [Parnell, Dillon, and O'Kelly]: about which, as at present advised, I see no remaining room for doubt.

Now, though, a difficult question presented itself: How were the liberals to meet the Parnellites halfway without laying themselves open to the charge of surrender? "It seems that Mr. Gladstone does not realize the bad effect it would have on the Government if the letter of Mr. Parnell were to come out," observed Florence, "Still more if Mr. O'Shea's offers on his behalf and with his sanction should become known." But Gladstone had no intention of broadcasting what was happening behind the scenes. He wrote to the queen, telling her that the Irish would no longer be encouraging agrarian outrages and saying that he believed the release of Parnell and his two colleagues would lead to peace. He added disingenuously, "He need hardly assure your Majesty that there has been nothing in the nature of a bargain or negotiations with this party."

*

On Tuesday, May 2, a telegram from Gladstone arrived at Windsor Castle alerting Queen Victoria to the fact that Lord Granville would soon be arriving to request an immediate audience. Noting how agitated he was and clearly pressed for time, she agreed to see him before luncheon, and Granville, having brought with him a box containing cabinet notes, came straight to the point: all the ministers, with the exception of Forster, had voted to release the three political suspects. Victoria had not been consulted about Parnell's parole, learning from newspaper reports that he had been "*let out* to attend his nephew's funeral at Paris," and had written irritably to Forster, "Surely this ought not to have been allowed just now." This latest capitulation disturbed her even more. Writing in her journal, she said:

> I *very reluctantly* had to give my consent but it was a great mistake and would be a triumph for the Parnellites, which Lord Granville denied. I pointed out that the result of this decision might be failure, and what would they do then? "Oh!" answered Lord Granville, "we must then

be effaced!" Alas! I cannot cease regretting this consent, which I ought never to have been asked to give in such a hurry.

*

At two o'clock that afternoon Florence and her mother went to the House of Commons, calling on the way at the Irish office, only to find that Forster was not there. The previous evening, during a long talk with Jane, he admitted that he had virtually resigned but said that nothing would be settled until the next cabinet meeting. Not wishing to see anyone during this uncertainty, Jane stayed in their carriage as Florence ran upstairs to check who was in the Ladies' Gallery. On the way down to say that it was empty, she was given a sealed envelope addressed to her mother. "He has resigned," Jane told her, saying that no statement would be made until Lord Granville's return from Windsor.

*

When question time in the House was over, Forster picked up his red box of papers and left his front bench seat by Gladstone's side for the last time. Wanting to hear the prime minister's statement but not be observed, Forster took refuge in the Ladies' Gallery. He sat next to Mary Gladstone, who was there with her mother, and "growled out now and then to know more exactly what was being said." Forster then went to his club, the Athenaeum, where, in a sad and yet celebratory state of mind, he remarked to members, "Well, I think you might all drink the health of the Right Hon. Gentleman the Member for Bradford, as Gladstone called me!" Ireland's former chief secretary was now just another Liberal MP.

*

Queen Victoria much regretted the loss of Forster, "who must know the state of Ireland better than anyone," but was glad that John Poyntz Spencer, a former viceroy in Dublin, was to be given a second tenure.

She had a soft spot for Francis Cowper, whose handsome, noble features may have reminded her of her mentor Lord Melbourne, a youthful infatuation, but she knew that Lord Spencer's previous experience, combined with his cabinet position, made him far more able to cope with Irish problems. Her grave concern, as she told Gladstone, was his decision to release the three MPs:

> She cannot conceal from him that she considers it a very hazardous one. . . . The Queen cannot but feel that it will have the effect of a triumph to Home Rule and of great weakness. She trusts she may be mistaken as to the results of this course but she much dreads they will not be favourable to the maintenance of authority and respect of law and order.

*

That same day, disregarding the queen's misgivings, Gladstone sent Lord Cowper a telegram requesting him to authorize the liberation of the three prisoners. Cowper had meekly accepted his replacement by "a better man," but this radical move—a total surprise—had alarmed and angered him. Cabling back that he would prefer his successor to carry out Gladstone's orders, he followed this up with a letter protesting that the men had been incarcerated "for a gross violation of the law." Gladstone was implacable, insisting that Cowper sign the release, and on May 3, the three politicians, Parnell, O'Kelly, and Dillon, left Kilmainham as free men.

*

Accompanied by O'Kelly, Parnell went straight to Avondale, where all the servants rushed out to see him. One old woman, seizing his hand, kissing it, and covering it with tears, cried, "Oh Master Charley, are you back to us again?" Observing this, O'Kelly felt his own eyes welling up, but Parnell remained impassive. "I thought he was the most callous fellow I had ever met," said O'Kelly. "He was like a statue. He made some casual remark as if he had been out for a morning walk."

It was impossible for Parnell to feel euphoric. Quite apart from the shame of having employed his mistress's husband as an interme- diary, this peacemaking departure—a reversal of the Land League's policy of angry resistance—had been embarked on without con- sulting his closest followers and was certain to infuriate the extrem- ists. To the press he now resorted to lying, denying rumors of talks with a government agent during his parole; there had been no nego- tiation, he told the *Irish World*. "Not the slightest. There have been no communications whatever between us, nor has there been any understanding."

Gladstone was convinced that Parnell had left prison a different man, but in fact, the Irish leader's change of attitude had preceded his arrest. He told Katharine that he had been "dragged into" mak- ing the anti–Land Act/Gladstone speech in October, confiding, "I cannot describe to you the disgust I always felt with those meetings, knowing as I did how hollow and wanting in solidity everything con- nected with the movement was." During their few days together in April, Katharine had used all her strength to persuade Parnell that a conciliatory treaty was for the greater good for Ireland and likely to result in immediate peace. "I was very anxious that he should 'reign' by constitutional means, establishing such amicable communications between him and the Government as would lead to that end."

But the inevitable outcome, as Parnell knew, would be a with- drawal of American financial aid. Anxious to prevent this, and to win over his left wing, he may have taken matters to an extreme. A story has come to light that a day or so after his release, Parnell returned to Dublin and came across Patrick Sheridan in the street. Intending to research land valuation, Parnell was on his way to Trinity College; the two are said to have sat talking quietly in a corner of the library. Many years later, Sheridan told the Irish MP T. J. Quinn that Parnell had asked him to administer there and then the IRB oath—a vow of allegiance to the organization under penalty of death—making him swear that he would never make this public during Parnell's lifetime. "For myself, I believe that statement," said Quinn, "as I did not think Sheridan would make such a deliberate statement if it were untrue."

*

On Thursday, May 4, the House of Commons, abuzz with anticipation for the return of Parnell to the House, and for Forster's resignation speech, was filled to overflowing: members stood in double rows; the Ladies' Gallery was packed with eminent spectators, Catherine Gladstone, Lady Spencer, and Lady Harcourt among them; and in the prime position above the clock were the Prince of Wales and the crown prince of Denmark. Raising his binoculars to scan the room, Forster spotted the familiar ashen face of John Dillon, who was sitting among the packed Irish ranks with the stout, soldierly James O'Kelly, but there was no sign of their newly released leader. Just after five o'clock, Forster rose and said, in a low, gravelly voice, "Mr. Speaker, I have received Her Majesty's gracious permission to make a statement." An outburst of cheers gave way to silence as all eyes fixed on the visibly aged man, his brow now deeply furrowed, his hair turned to white. Forster's voice did not falter, except once, when he spoke of Gladstone, whose support and friendship he could no longer count on. Reaching the middle of his speech, he began explaining the reasons for the arrest of "the hon. Member for the City of Cork," when, as if right on cue, and to a deafening ovation from the Irish benches, Parnell entered the House.

Like Forster, Gladstone held Parnell responsible for instigating rural unrest with its punishing system of boycotting and intimidation. "Nothing can be more clear than that he has used lawlessness for his ends," he remarked. Now, however, he regarded Parnell as a restraining force. "I locked him up in '81 because I thought he was in the wrong," he told Lucy Cavendish. "I act with him now because

I think he is in the right. I should lock him up again tomorrow if I thought he deserved it." The man Gladstone had once believed to be "the evil genius of Ireland" could help to bring about peace—a possibility confirmed that evening in Parnell's speech.

"His words are so important that Mr. Gladstone is unwilling to cite them from memory," the prime minister reported to Queen Victoria. "But they distinctly enough asserted that outrage was to be utterly condemned, and that with the arrears duly settled, their desire was unequivocally to labor for putting it down." The ending of rural violence would be a triumph of statesmanship on both sides, a victory that Gladstone convinced himself had been achieved without the impropriety of a bargain. "There has been *no* negotiation," he avowed in his diary. "But we have obtained information. The moment is golden."

EIGHT
Mayday

Two days earlier, on Tuesday, May 2, Frederick Cavendish had warned Lucy that his name was among those being considered to take Forster's place. "He was much disturbed and I was very much vexed, hating his being taken out of what he was doing so well," she wrote. She wished it could be his elder brother, Lord Hartington, who had been chief secretary a decade earlier, with Lord Spencer in the role of viceroy. But this was out of the question. Gladstone had Hartington in mind to replace him as prime minister and felt that an interim posting in Ireland—"almost inevitably one of odium and failure"—might jeopardize Hartington's political future.

The following morning, in a state of rising panic, Cavendish called on Lord Granville, wanting to stress his unsuitability for such a crucial appointment: "I told him I had no tact, no real knowledge of Ireland, no powers of speaking"—all of which Granville dismissed. True, Cavendish was a poor orator, lacking in charisma and self-confidence, but he was widely respected for his integrity, and Gladstone had come to rely on his judgment and financial skills. (In his two years at the Treasury, Cavendish had undertaken almost all the practical duties of the chancellor of the exchequer, allowing the prime minister to focus on politics.) After the "almost unmixed mischief" resulting from Forster's reign in Ireland, Gladstone wanted a representative he could trust to act on his behalf, someone reliable, responsible, and closely in sympathy with himself.

By Wednesday afternoon, the matter was settled as far as Gladstone was concerned, but Cavendish was still profoundly disturbed. Craving reassurance from his peers, he asked a Treasury colleague if he thought he was strong enough for the post. "I told him I considered him strong enough for anything," said Sir Ralph Lingen. "Indeed, I had long thought that his brother and he had the future of England in their hands." Cavendish then went to consult Lord Spencer, a distant relative and good friend, unaware that Spencer had already been given a letter from Gladstone submitting Cavendish's name to the queen. Known as "the Red Earl" on account of his startlingly red beard, whiskers, and shaggy eyebrows, Spencer did all he could to encourage Cavendish; as the scion of a great family he would be completely at ease among the splendors of the viceregal court, and Spencer believed that they would work comfortably and constructively together in Dublin, each equally convinced about the urgent need for change. Carrying the box with Gladstone's letter (to be given to Victoria on receipt of a telegram), Spencer was driven from Whitehall to Paddington Station in time to catch the six thirty train to Windsor. Cavendish accompanied him as far as Constitution Hill, where he left the phaeton to go to see his father, the Duke of Devonshire.

William Cavendish, when briefly a member of Parliament, had been appalled that England should impose its own religion on a predominantly Catholic country and vigorously supported Gladstone's 1869 bill for disestablishing the Anglican Irish Church. But now, as an Irish landlord himself, proprietor of County Waterford's Lismore Castle, whose estates and rents had been badly hit by Land War agitation, he resolutely opposed Home Rule and condemned Gladstone's "very rash course of action" in siding with Parnell. On learning that his son was almost certainly being forced to accept the thankless role of chief secretary, the duke was filled with foreboding. "F. seems to have nearly made his mind up to accept," he wrote in his diary. "I should have been against it if I had known of the proposal before matters had advanced so far."

Above all, it was the prospect of Freddy's absence that he dreaded—especially from Holker Hall, which of all the Devonshire properties was the one the Cavendish family considered home. After the death of his young wife, Blanche, William had brought up his three small sons and daughter at Holker, personally supervising their education, as he did not wish to inflict on his boys the kind of bullying he had endured at Eton. This had instilled an unusual closeness between an aristocratic Victorian patriarch and his children—especially in the case of Frederick, who was much like Devonshire himself, a committed Christian, with his father's moral earnestness, reserved manner, and hesitant way of speaking. Surrounded by Lancashire's exquisite Lake District and filled with portraits of the siblings as children, the house was a favorite sanctuary of Frederick and Lucy, who planned to settle there one day. And while both knew that a move to Ireland would upset the duke, they had not realized how deeply. "F. is much disturbed . . . ," Lucy noted. "[He] told me on Friday that he cd. hardly have taken it if he had known beforehand how strongly his father wd object."

When asked what Lucy herself thought of the posting, Cavendish replied, "O, she is as brave as possible, and has confidence in her husband." The couple's childlessness had been an early grief in their marriage, but they had reached middle age—Lucy noticing her first wrinkles, Frederick's hair "sprinkling itself with grey"—and their life was serenely happy, their partnership modern in its equality. Referring to Cavendish throughout her diary as "my Fred," she felt maternally protective toward him, once surreptitiously holding his hand while he struggled through a speech. "If only he could learn less ungainliness and fierceness of manner," wrote Lucy, who had been urged to persuade her husband to have elocution lessons, but she knew "his defective 'r' and 'th' could not be cured." She told him that if he truly believed he was unfit for the job then he must refuse it, but if not, it was his duty to accept. "I felt half afraid when he paused, lest he really should feel he was incompetent . . . [but] he answered 'Well, as to that, I must let the others judge for me.'"

*

When Parliament met on Thursday, May 4, the announcement of Frederick Cavendish's appointment was received with howls of derision. "By the God of Heaven we will tear him in pieces within a fortnight," exclaimed Irish MP Tim Healy. Nepotism was suspected—"I suppose it is all the result of Lady Frederick being Mrs. Gladstone's niece," reflected one observer—while the *Freeman's Journal* voiced the opinion of most by writing, "Never was so small a politician appointed to so great a post at a crisis so important."

It had been widely expected that Joseph Chamberlain would take Forster's place; as the Liberal's most vocal opponent of coercion, he had played a key role in the Kilmainham Treaty, was pressing for Davitt's release, and had even anticipated Parnell in arguing for an arrears amendment to the Land Act. While waiting to be offered the post, Chamberlain admitted to having "the greatest horror of it," fearing that it might destroy him politically as it had done Forster. By Wednesday night, he had decided to accept as a matter of duty and went after dinner to a party at 10 Downing Street, fully anticipating congratulations, only to discover that he had been bypassed. Gladstone claimed to have had no idea of Chamberlain's expectation. "Had I known . . . I should not have set it aside without consideration and counsel," he said some years later. But it was Gladstone's nature to be blind to what he did not want to see.

*

In Dublin, Patrick Tynan was waiting for orders. There had been no communication from the London directory since Forster's departure, and he was anxious to know whether his superiors were behind what appeared to be a "disgraceful surrender to the enemy." He had sent an urgent inquiry to Frank Byrne and at last received a dispatch in reply. Nothing had changed; the active policy was to continue.

The Invincibles had been enraged by "the old tyrant escaping," and one was desperate to follow Forster to England, but Tynan dissuaded him: they were not at war with individuals, he said, and the former chief secretary was now politically dead as far as Ireland was concerned. Their next target was to be the undersecretary, Thomas Burke.

A conscientious civil servant, the son of an English mother and Catholic gentleman farmer from County Galway, Burke was a bachelor in his early fifties with a refined, almost feminine face, clean-shaven, with long white sideburns. He was something of an ascetic, living with his devoted sister Alice, who kept house for him and his brother in an elegant lodge in Phoenix Park. Employed at the castle since the age of eighteen, Burke had worked his way up from a clerk and private secretary to his current position through sheer diligence and efficiency. Laboring away seven days a week and refusing to take a holiday, he had carried out most government business during the Land War, passing on police reports of outrages and letters from individuals describing their lives under threat of murder.

Forster, although fearing that his Dublin colleague would literally work himself to death, counted on Burke's knowledge of local intelligence and appreciated his fair-minded opinions, noting, "Over and over again, he has pointed out to me the other side of the question, the question from the tenants' point of view." To republicans, however, the undersecretary, by advocating coercive measures, employing informers, and imprisoning people of his own nationality, was nothing less than an incarnation of England's oppressive regime. Tynan gave Dan Curley orders to have the men ready by Friday to "suppress" Thomas Burke on his way home through the park.

*

A massive stretch of pastoral land west of the city center, carved in two by a long, straight carriageway, Phoenix Park had been donated to Dubliners as their playground by an eighteenth-century lord lieu-tenant and, with its zoo, bandstand, and cricket, football, and polo grounds, remains a recreational space to this day. Out of bounds to the public are the three residences built for the rulers of Ireland: the Viceregal Lodge (now the residence of the president of Ireland), a long, white, Ionic-columned mansion, which used to be the lord lieutenant's summer home; and the more modest lodges of the chief secretary (where the current American ambassador lives) and of the undersecretary, both half-hidden behind trees on either side of the main thoroughfare.

On the morning of May 5, while several Invincibles were posted at Park Gate, and others loitered in the vicinity of Thomas Burke's lodge, Joe Brady brazenly went across to its gatehouse to ask the woman on duty about the undersecretary's movements. "[Brady] told us Mr. Burke had gone to town," said Carey. "He must have gone in through the Lord Lieutenant's and on to the polo ground. . . . We were watching his gate." Tynan arrived some hours later, bringing word that there would be a state entry into Dublin of Lords Spencer and Cavendish—the new invaders. He also gave an account of a violent conflict that had taken place in Ballina, County Mayo, earlier in the day, when a parade held in celebration of Parnell's release had got out of hand. A number of boys, marching to tin whistles and drums, had thrown stones at policemen, one of whom had had his teeth broken; in retaliation, the force fired a volley of buckshot, which killed a twelve-year-old and wounded several others. The national press portrayed the tragedy as "a massacre," while the Invincibles viewed it as a spur for immediate revenge. "We must see," Tynan vowed, "that this hideous deed of blood is answered back by the destruction of the responsible tyrant whose official hands are already stained with our children's gore."

*

Frederick Cavendish remained in his office, winding up Treasury busi-ness, until late on Friday evening, Spencer having persuaded him to travel to Dublin in time for Saturday's official entry and swearing-in ceremony. Leaving Euston Station around eight thirty, they shared a sleeper compartment to Holyhead, the Welsh ferry port with regular crossings to and from Dublin. "We talked a while but we were both tired & I believe we slept most of the way," Spencer recalled. "We separated on board & I did not see him until we got up in the morning." Unusually, it was a smooth journey across the Irish Sea, but Cavendish was a poor sailor and grateful for the chilly breeze when he joined Spencer on the upper deck at around seven a.m. As the mail steamer glided toward Kingstown harbor in County Dublin, the Hill of Howth looming in the mist, the sun broke through, lighting up the bay and its emerald surroundings with the brilliant beauty of an Irish spring.

While the pair walked up and down, talking over their prospects, they were observed by a sixteen-year-old girl returning to Ireland after seven years in a French convent. "It was a magical country that morning, a mystic isle," remarked Elizabeth Burke, whose father had drawn her attention to the two Englishmen at the far end of the deck. "There was a tall man with a vivid red beard that stood out from his face. . . . He looked cold and tired, almost a little dour at that early hour." Her father said that they were bringing with them a message of peace and conciliation for Ireland. "It is in my memory of that morning, the feeling of hope, of a fair prospect for the country that lay shimmering so peacefully before us."

*

Saturday, May 6, was a glorious day on Dorset's Isle of Portland, where Michael Davitt was enjoying the sunshine in the prison yard. He was well liked by Portland's Governor and his staff and had been made unusually comfortable, given a cell in the infirmary, a nourishing diet, and special permission to work in the garden—an activity for which he had developed a passion. Davitt was growing a profusion of cottage flowers—columbine, wild eglantine, sweet-scented stock, and mignonette; he prided himself on having rooted in English soil a shamrock sent by Irish friends on St. Patrick's Day, and was cultivating runner beans alongside a variety of pea with an intriguing history. A friend of Governor Clifton, exploring an Egyptian catacomb, had found a few dried peas and grains in the hands of a mummy and gave two of the peas to Clifton. Amazingly, "after their singular mode of preservation during a period of some 2,000 years," they flourished, and Clifton had passed on eight of the seeds to Davitt. "In spite of my prowling enemies, the snails, I have secured a few hundred to take with me to Ireland, should I live to regain my liberty again."

He did not have long to wait. That morning a smiling Clifton came up to him in the yard, bringing news that he was to be released in the afternoon. Clifton was carrying a letter from Parnell, a short note addressed to "My dear Sir," announcing that he and John Dillon would shortly be coming to collect Davitt and accompany him to London. "We were ourselves released from Kilmainham only on Tuesday last, Mr. Forster having resigned, and further legislation on the land question promised. We shall arrive at Portland about two o'clock." Knowing that Davitt would have received no political communication since his detention fifteen months earlier, Parnell felt that it was vital to explain the Kilmainham negotiations himself. As it was, the cold formality of the leader's note had put Davitt on guard: Was there a fuller story of some compromise with which he was expected to comply?

*

Shortly before noon, having arrived at Westland Row Station in a festooned special train, the viceregal party, which also included the new lord lieutenant's two private secretaries, was met by the lord mayor of Dublin, who presented Spencer with the keys to the city. A commanding figure in his black frock coat, the Order of the Garter, Britain's most prestigious chivalric medal, pinned to his breast, Spencer was the obvious choice to be the queen's representative in Ireland.

Before becoming a politician he had served as a courtier (groom of the stole to Prince Albert and then to the Prince of Wales), while his wife, Charlotte, a fair English beauty, was the perfect hostess, accustomed to act as chatelaine at Althorp, home to the Spencers since the fifteenth century, and Spencer House, the family mansion in St. James.

The couple would be moving into Viceregal Lodge in Phoenix Park and spending the winter in Dublin Castle, which has none of the romantic features its name suggests—no turrets, moats, drawbridges, or dungeons—but is more like a fortress, built in the thirteenth century as part of the city's defenses. They would furnish their sumptuous quarters to their taste, bringing from England their own antiques, paintings, and objets d'art. During the summer season, they would be expected to preside over Dublin Castle levees and balls held in palatial St. Patrick's Hall, its central chandelier of Waterford glass throwing light on the empaneled ceiling painted with historical and allegorical scenes. Dinners would be for at least one hundred guests, all seated at long, damask-covered tables arranged in the shape of the St. Patrick's cross, who would then dance to Strauss waltzes as their excellencies watched from their thrones. Charlotte would be wearing court dress and a coronet, Spencer a coat emblazoned with a diamond star and orders, his gartered knee breeches exposing thin, silk-stockinged legs. By the end of the evening, his flaming beard would be white with the powder of all the debutantes it was customary for him to kiss.

The splendor of castle seasons would draw the Dublin poor to Dame Street, a ragged crowd waiting to see the carriages spilling out the nobility from Fitzwilliam and Merrion Squares, brightly uniformed soldiers, colonels, and country squires, pretty young women in their crinolines and furs. The expressions of the onlookers were more starstruck than resentful—much like those of today's spectators at film premieres and royal appearances—but during the Spencers' last tenure, the disparity of their existences had troubled Charlotte: "The atmosphere seems tainted with the breath of injustice," she wrote to her sister. Nevertheless, the Spencers' Dublin existence would be no less opulent than before; while rural Ireland was subsisting on its daily diet of potatoes, the viceregal party would be sitting down to a banquet served on tableware of solid gold.

*

A born equestrian, never happier than when on horseback, Spencer led the May 6 state procession, top hat in hand, which he waved at the cheering Dubliners. Behind him in a landau sat Frederick Cavendish with the private secretaries, Courtenay Boyle and Edward Jenkinson. At one point, when their carriage slowed to a stop, a man came up and asked which of them was the new chief secretary. "Jenkinson would not reply," said Spencer, "and after a time Freddy said 'I am.' The man then left." The cavalcade's crowded route was lined with troops, the streets strung with bunting and "Welcome to Erin" banners; brass bands, posted at intervals, played the English national anthem as the procession passed. "Certainly the best reception I ever got in Ireland," Spencer told Charlotte, the enthusiasm reflecting his former popularity, when he had proved to be a firm supporter of the tenants' proprietorship of land.

There were reports of "an occasional faint hiss" and of the practical joke by students of Trinity College, who threw bags of flour at the mayor's carriage as it made its way down Nassau Street. The party, however, was unaware of the sinister remark made by one spectator, "a respectable, earnest-looking man," who with his eyes fixed on Spencer, muttered, "My fine fellow, I am in good hopes that you will be shot like a thrush."

Having reached Dublin Castle, the government's headquarters, the party crossed Upper Castle Yard to the Viceregal State Apartments, where Spencer and Cavendish were formally received by the lords justices, and then proceeded to the Privy Council Chamber to be sworn in. A rocket announced the completion of the ceremony, and a salute of fifty guns was fired in Phoenix Park. Directly after luncheon, the new arrivals set to work. In his office, one of a gloomy warren of rooms off Lower Castle Yard, Cavendish spent nearly three hours with Thomas Burke and a law adviser, discussing the different provisions that were to replace the Coercion Act. Although arguing for them to be as moderate as possible, Cavendish listened attentively to everything Burke had to say. "No-one is of the slightest use except Tom Burke and if he is knocked up and fell ill we should be done for," Lord Cowper told Spencer before his departure; indeed, in the opinion of many, the undersecretary, self-effacing, yet capable of acting on his own initiative, was the real ruler of Ireland.

That afternoon, Burke urged Spencer to free two political suspects about whom there was considerable feeling in Dublin, but the new viceroy wanted more time to consider their case. He told Lucy Cavendish, "I thought that, although they must be released, it would . . . produce the effect of my being in a hurry to do an act which might appear to be simply for the sake of popularity."

Immediately after the meeting, Spencer rode to Phoenix Park, where he called on Alice Burke, wanting to pay his respects and congratulate her on the fact that her brother was so well liked.

*

At ten to five that day, James Carey, driven by Skin-the-Goat, crossed the river at Kingsbridge and entered the park. He was accompanied by an Invincible named Joseph Hanlon, as well as by a castle workman, Joe Smith, who had been enlisted for the day, as he alone was able to identify Thomas Burke. They stopped by the polo ground, parking on the main road, which was deserted except for a couple of tricycles and a second stationary jaunting car, whose pony was nibbling at the turf. Sitting waiting on the dickey was its driver, Michael Kavanagh, a hard-drinking young man, who had transported four other men, including Joe Brady, now standing by the car. There were clusters of Invincibles lying on the grass so close to the raised path that a woman walking with her husband had to lift her skirts to get past.

Superintendent Mallon walked through Park Gate about an hour later. He had left his office in Lower Castle Yard earlier than usual, as he had arranged to meet an informer behind Viceregal Lodge. One of the constables from his division saluted him and asked in which direction he was thinking of going.

"There are some of the 'boys' in the Park this evening, and I don't know what they may be up to."

"*Whom* have you seen?"

"Well, there is James Carey, sir, and Brady, and that little man Delaney, and two or three others. They came in some while ago and went over towards the polo ground, and I have not seen them since."

Mallon's new boots were pinching him, and grateful for an excuse to go home, he told himself that the informer's news could keep for a day or so and decided to turn back. As he made his way past the zoological gardens toward North Circular Road, where he lived with his wife and family in a modest terraced house, the constable came hurrying after him, insisting that he take his gun.

*

On the afternoon train journey accompanying Davitt from Portland to London it was Parnell who did most of the talking. The No Rent Manifesto had failed, he said; Ireland was in a state of anarchy, but just in the last few days, Gladstone had not only thrown over Forster and coercion, but he had promised to legislate further on the land issue. Davitt later recalled:

> How bright the future looked on that day. . . . I from imprisonment to liberty—*all* of us from defeat to apparent victory. How we talked of the "new policy" of Gladstone, the good it was likely to perform for the country, the rest from political turmoil it would insure to us and

our friends! I believe we actually "fixed" the personnel of the Home Rule ministry that was to be!

When asking how this change had come about, Davitt noticed Parnell's unease, but he was promised that everything would be fully explained the following day. "I see no reason why we should not soon obtain all we are looking for," Parnell assured him, and Davitt was too elated by the triumph of the Land League to harbor any suspicion.

News of the release of the four prisoners had inspired joy throughout Ireland. Tar barrels blazed on hillsides; windows were brilliantly illuminated by pyramids of candles; banners hung with pictures of the political heroes and the mottoes "Ireland a Nation" and "Down with Coercion"; processions marched through the streets while people danced and sang, stirring "every chord in the Celtic heart." In Gortin, County Tyrone, an effigy representing the former chief secretary was hoisted on a pitchfork and slowly consumed by flames to the booing of spectators; in Dublin, a goat's head was held up on a stick with a fake gun in its mouth and a torch lighting the words "R.I.P.—Buckshot."

*

Jane Forster was exhausted by the emotional strain of her husband's resignation. It felt like being at her own funeral, with everyone coming up and speaking with deep feeling—"half condoling, half congratulating." She found herself pitying Lucy Cavendish, who could have no idea of the ordeal in store, and wrote suggesting that they meet.

> It is selfish to find any pleasure in a friend's acceptance of such a burden, but we must hope & trust that you may fall on better times than we did—and at any rate my daughter & I cannot help being glad that it is you who are to follow us at the Lodge and who will enjoy the lovely view of the mountains which was my greatest consolation there.

Soon after six o' clock on Saturday, May 6, Lucy went to the Forsters' house in Eccleston Square, glad to talk over the practicalities of moving to the Chief Secretary's Lodge, where only basic necessities were provided. She too was drained by the stress of the last days, still feeling injured by "the shower of contemptuous comments," "the unanimous scolding of all the press," and she responded gratefully to Jane Forster's friendly words. But despite the assurance of how much Tom Burke would help them, and an affectionate account of his sister, the impression Jane gave of a sad and dark outlook was disturbing.

Lady Cowper had been even more discouraging when she met Lucy at Spencer House. "I cannot congratulate you," she said, giving a chilling description of their life in Dublin—"the cold-shouldering of the gentry, the isolation." Early on Saturday afternoon, while passing Westminster Abbey, Lucy had gone inside to pray. It was the end of a service, and the hymn being sung, first by a single voice, then a second, then a third, resonated deeply—the lovely, simple harmony of Wesley's "Thou shalt keep him in perfect peace whose mind is stayed on Thee."

> I thought "O, these are the very words for my Fred"; during the final chorus I knelt down and prayed for him with my whole heart, but not that he might be saved from peril (a mere idle thought crossed me once—what if the steamer shd. go down on the passage?) that I never thought of—but that he might have wisdom and strength and help.

Cavendish was due back in London the following evening, but even so, Lucy went to the Treasury to write him a note, which would be delivered to Dublin in the castle pouch.

*

After a light shower, it had turned into a beautiful evening. In Phoenix Park the hawthorn was in snowy blossom, the trees in their freshest, lime-green leaf, while in the distance rose the smoky blue Wicklow

Mountains. Faint sounds of a brass band mingled with the gentle *tock* of leather on willow and the rumbling of galloping hooves; a cricket match was being played, and on the polo field directly opposite, turf flew as ten riders in breeches, rolled-up shirtsleeves, and cloth caps frantically converged on a ball. Lord Spencer, on horseback himself, had stopped to watch. He was president of a London polo regiment and interested to see how the game, which was relatively new to Ireland, differed in technique and speed (Europe's first polo fatality had occurred in Phoenix Park).

*

Observing the match close by was James Carey. In a Browningesque monologue entitled "At the Polo Ground, 6th May 1882," the nineteenth-century Irish poet Samuel Ferguson gives voice to Carey's thoughts as he waits for Burke to arrive.

> Here I am
> Beside the hurdles fencing off the ground
> They've taken from us who have the right to it,
> For these select young gentry and their sport.
> Curse them! I would they all might break their necks!
> Young fops and lordlings of the garrison
> Kept up by England here to keep us down . . .
> And doubtless, as they dash along, regard
> Us who stand outside as a beggarly crew.
> 'Tis half-past six. Not yet. No, that's not he.
> Well, but 'tis pretty, sure, to see them stoop
> And take the ball, full gallop . . .

Polo was still dominated by British cavalry officers, and the stretch called Nine Acres was seen by militant nationalists to be an offensive appropriation of public land—a little enclave of England—as was the cricket ground. Phoenix Park's statues—the robed figure in

the People's Garden commemorating an earlier lord lieutenant, the
Seventh Earl of Carlisle, as well as the bronze equestrian memorial
of the war hero Lord Gough—were further reminders of British
rule (both demolished by twentieth-century nationalists). Ferguson's
verses, however, express more than national resentment. The poet,
later to be worshipped by the young W. B. Yeats, cannot have known
about Patrick Egan's plan for James Carey, and yet, with remarkable
insight, he reveals it: "Lord Mayor for life—why not?" Carey muses,
visualizing himself riding in a state carriage in green and gold livery,
the sheriff's chain about his neck. In the countdown to the Invincibles' ambush, Ferguson suggests that Carey's personal aspirations
have made him ambivalent about the mission and detects his tendency
to leave dangerous action to others.

> 'Tis twenty minutes now to seven o'clock.
> What if he should not come at all? 'Twere then
> Another—oh—fiasco as they call it.
> Not pleasant to repeat to Number One,
> But, for myself, perhaps not wholly bad.
> For, if he comes, there will be consequences
> Will make a stir; and in that stir my name
> May come in play—well, one must run some risk
> Who takes a lead and keeps and thrives by it
> As I have done. But sure the risk is small.
> I know those cut-throats on the pathway there
> May be relied on. . . .

✻

Soon after six p.m., prepared for another shower, Frederick Cavendish
took his umbrella and set off for his new residence. He had declined
Spencer's offer of a drive in his private secretary's carriage, as he loved
a walk after working hard, "so deeply and tranquilly" relishing good
weather. Visits to his brother a decade earlier had familiarized him

with the streets of Dublin, and from Lower Castle Yard he crossed cobbled Dame Street into Parliament Street, passing Trulock Brothers, the gunmakers, and numerous solicitors' offices before heading toward the river. Flowing from west to east between walls of dirty granite, the River Liffey, then busy with the traffic of paddle steamers and cargo and Guinness barges, divides Dublin into two almost equal parts. Turning left along its south bank, Cavendish was approaching the Law Courts on the opposite side when he met one of Spencer's aides-de-camp riding down the quays. Greeting him with the remark "Fine evening," Cavendish crossed one of the bridges and continued west along the north bank. There were squalid tenements in the streets behind and scowling clusters of men lounging at the corners, but walking along the open quays posed no threat. After about twenty-five minutes, Cavendish entered Phoenix Park by its main gates and had almost reached the Gough statue, when he heard himself hailed. It was Tom Burke, sitting in the sidecar of a hackney cab.

*

Thomas Burke also enjoyed being outdoors at the end of the day, regularly walking the three-mile distance from the castle to his lodge—a splendidly erect, military-looking figure, with his cane carried sword-fashion against his right shoulder, his gray gloves elegantly matching his gray tweed suit. In the last weeks, however, he had changed his habit, going only as far as Parkgate Street, where he would summon a cab to take him the rest of the way. Although warned by Superintendent Mallon of preparations for the "removal" of "the Castle Rat," Burke had declined all offers of police protection, and when Mallon came to him a few days earlier, begging him to carry a handgun, Burke exploded, saying, "I will not carry arms to protect myself against my own countrymen, to whom, rather, I feel that I am entitled to look for protection." As a compromise, he had stopped walking through the park, and on this particular evening, was driven by a man he had hired many times.

Spotting Cavendish on the footpath near the Viceregal Lodge, Burke paid the jarvey and jumped down from the cab to join his new colleague. "Those are Castle swells," one young clerk remarked to another as they passed, and both caught the words, "Forster's policy." Walking arm in arm as they talked, Burke and Cavendish made their way toward their respective lodges. "Two men dressed the same, looking the same," James Joyce would later write in *Ulysses*. "Two by two."

*

Shortly before seven o'clock, Dan Curley came over to reprimand Carey for allowing himself to be distracted by the polo match.

"What are you doing here?"

"Looking at this; I never saw it before."

"Come back. We don't know when he may arrive."

Carey went over to where Joe Smith was waiting on the park bench to identify Burke, and when a builder for whom he had once worked passed by, they chatted for some time. By now it was a few minutes past seven, and Smith was getting agitated. "He's not coming," he said, getting up and walking away but stopping after a few yards, exclaiming, "Here he is!" They rushed toward Kavanagh's cab, which Curley had arranged to be standing by, and just as Carey was putting his foot on the mount, he saw two men approaching. "Hurry up, hurry up," he urged Kavanagh, who was taking the nosebag off the horse. They made their way toward the Gough statue, stopping on the right-hand side, where Skin-the-Goat's cab was parked, Carey signaling the seven Invincibles scattered on the footpath with the white handkerchief he had taken out of his pocket. Brady and Curley came over.

"Well is he coming?"

"Yes, the man in the grey suit."

Pointing to Smith, still sitting on the car, Carey asked, "What about this man?"

"Tell him to go off to hell out of it," Brady replied. Carey went over and instructed Smith to go home, and then asked Brady what he himself should do. "You may go. . . . You are not wanted here." Before heading on foot for the Island Bridge exit, Carey said, "Mind be sure. The man in the grey suit."

*

Three Invincibles began walking abreast toward Burke and Cavendish, followed twelve feet behind by Tim Kelly and Joe Brady, with another two men six feet farther away. A hackney cab passed with a passenger sitting beside the driver; Brady stooped as if to tie his shoe, and the gang did nothing, allowing the pair to pass through. Glancing back, Carey thought it was another failure, but after a few more steps looked around again: "I saw two men in the rear getting to the front and closing on the two gentlemen. . . . Joe Brady raised his left hand and struck the man facing him. . . . It was 17 minutes past 7 o'clock."

As Burke sank to his knees, Brady stooped over him, repeatedly thrusting the knife at his chest and neck, shredding his victim's gloves as he tried feebly to ward off the blows. With a cry of "Ah, you villain!" Cavendish darted forward, attempting to defend Burke with his umbrella. Enraged by the insult, Brady went after Cavendish and, when the chief secretary protectively put up his arm, struck it so violently that he cut right through the bone. Stabbing him again and again, Brady looked around to see Kelly "at Mr. Burke" and came over to finish the job, drawing the long blade across Burke's throat. Before leaping up onto the waiting cab, he coolly wiped his bloody weapon on the grass.

*

Lieutenant Greatrix of the Royal Dragoons was walking his dogs when saw what he thought was a drunken altercation. Going over to the man he had watched being followed into the road and struck to the ground, he found him lying in a puddle of blood, his right cheek buried in the earth, his hat and umbrella beside him. The man's eyes were half-open, and he appeared to be breathing, but a second man, spread-eagle on the footpath, blood leaking from his open mouth, showed no sign of life. "I was so startled that I candidly confess I did not know what to do. The person in the road was so dirty and looked such a ruffian as he lay there that I thought he was one of the men who attacked the gentlemen." A passerby came rushing up. "This looks like murder," he cried, and they both went off to fetch help. There were two uniformed policemen sitting on a park bench, but they refused to get involved, saying that it was no business of theirs. "No-one that I told paid the slightest attention to me," Greatrix recalled.

Two young friends, Patrick Maguire and Thomas Foley, were riding their tricycles, when Foley, who had the faster bike, came across a body in the middle of the road. "Halloa," he shouted behind him. "There has been a murder, or suicide, or something of the kind." Telling Foley to stay on the spot, he pedaled furiously toward Island Bridge, passing the pair from the Royal Irish Constabulary, who once again said that they were not on duty. He had almost reached Park Gate when he spotted another constable. "He did not get excited at the news, and told me that they got many such messages." Meanwhile, a clerk named Alfred Walters, who worked for the Inland Revenue, had heard Maguire's shouts and gone over to the prostrate figure on the footpath. He recognized him immediately as Thomas Burke and ran toward the Viceregal Lodge, vaulting over its fence.

Lord Spencer was in an upstairs room when he heard a wild cry—"a shriek which I shall never forget. . . . It is always in my ears." He looked out of the window, from which he saw a man sprinting toward the lodge, waving his hands and shouting, "Murder, murder!" He was about to go investigate but was stopped by a member of his staff, who said that it could be a ruse, that someone could be lying in wait for him outside. Colonel Caulfield, controller of the viceregal household, and the two private secretaries followed Alfred Walters to the place where he claimed Burke had been stabbed. When he pointed out the body lying nearby on the road, they assumed that it was Burke's murderer, until Courtenay Boyle, kneeling over him, exclaimed in horror, "Good God, it's Lord Frederick!"

*

Conor Maguire, a medical student studying for his final exams at the Royal University, was sitting reading with his two roommates when their landlord came in to say that a couple of men had been murdered in the park, and their bodies taken to Steevens Hospital. It was a short walk from their lodgings to the Royal Military Infirmary, and when they arrived, they discovered a crowd outside and police guarding the gates. They said that they were doctors attached to the hospital but were refused admittance until a surgeon recognized them and took them into the room where the dead men had been laid out on two candlelit tables. Maguire found himself staring at Cavendish's shoeless feet. "I noticed that Lord Frederick's socks had been most perfectly darned, and I thought to myself . . . a poor devil like me need not be ashamed to wear darned socks."

On opening Cavendish's blood-soaked vest, eight wounds were revealed, the fatal one having severed the large artery under the armpit and caused death by rapid bleeding. A deep transverse cut on the middle of his left forearm, "inflicted by a man of Herculean strength," had slashed through the muscles, fracturing one of the bones and slicing off a small portion of another. Although covered in dirt, with a slight abrasion on one cheekbone, Cavendish lay as if asleep; Burke, on the other hand, appeared to have died in agony. His neck, chest, and hands bore the gashes of a violent, protracted encounter; his refined face was scarcely recognizable through the mask of dried blood. When the coroner arrived, he pronounced that Burke's death had resulted from either the stab wound near his shoulder, which had pierced the pericardium and heart, or the cut, three inches deep, that had severed the jugular vein. "The clean edges of the wounds were remarkable," Dr. Porter, surgeon-in-ordinary to the queen, was later to say. "The weapon must have been very clean and well-tempered."

*

After meeting Joe Smith at Cody's tavern, near Kilmainham Gaol, James Carey had gone to Clery's in Grafton Street, deliberately making himself conspicuous to the publican, Mr. Clery, shaking his hand and chatting for about half an hour. At around nine p.m., he returned to his Denzille Street house, where Dan Curley was waiting.

"Is it true what I hear that Lord Frederick Cavendish and Mr. Burke are killed?"

"It is. So I believe. I cannot tell whether they are killed or not of course."

Curley and two Invincibles had made their escape in the cab driven by Skin-the-Goat, who had been flicking his horse with a whip so as to be ready to hurtle off. Curley described how they had passed two tricyclists near the Gough statue and covered them with their handguns until they were out of sight. When the Invincibles had left the park and were sure they were not being followed, they stopped at a pub in Upper Leeson Street, where the two other men stayed drinking and talking while Curley went to the *Express* newspaper office. The card he put in its mailbox (and those of the *Irish Times*, the *Irishman*, and the *Freeman's Journal* the following day), claimed responsibility for the murders. It read: "Executed by order of the Irish Invincibles."

*

Viceregal Lodge was kept fully illuminated all night, and Spencer was advised to sleep in a different room than he usually did. He could not dismiss from his mind the thought that if only he had acted on his first impulse, cantering along the grass with his aide-de-camp and groom, rather than taking a shortcut to the lodge by the zoological gardens, he would have passed the murderers within a couple of minutes of Cavendish and Burke reaching them. "The whole thing would have been stopped for they must have dispersed in the presence of three mounted men." In a barely legible note to Lord Hartington, he claimed that his brother had been "quite conscious" when found, relating how Cavendish had insisted on walking from the castle that evening. "He well knew that he had never done a stroke of work to harm a single Irishman."

Spencer sent cables to Henry Ponsonby, Queen Victoria's private secretary, and to the home secretary, Sir William Harcourt; he was determined to stay in control, but in his message to his wife Charlotte his shock is palpable in its disjointed scrawl:

> We are in God's hands. Do not be filled with alarm and fear. I was alone and have no apprehension. God knows how I feel—this fearful tragedy—two such men at such a time.
>
> I dare not dwell on the horror for I feel I must be unmanned.
>
> I am very calm.
>
> Do not, loved one, come unless you feel more unhappy in London than here.
>
> There is no danger really whatever.
>
> See dear Lucy if you can tell her that I am not made of ice but I dare not face what has occurred.

*

Harcourt was dining at the Austrian embassy when Spencer's telegram was put into his hand: his first thought was how to tell the Gladstones, who were also dining at the embassy, but he decided that they must learn of the tragedy in their own home. Waiting until the meal had ended, Harcourt went to 10 Downing Street, where he entrusted Edward Hamilton to break the news on the couple's return. "I must go in search of Hartington," he said, heading for an Admiralty party, where both Lord Hartington and his sister, Louisa, were among the guests.

*

William Forster arrived at the Admiralty with Florence at around eleven p.m., and they had barely taken off their coats when Harcourt came up and took Forster aside. "Put your things on—we must go," Forster said brusquely to Florence on his return; but only when they were sitting in a hansom cab returning to Eccleston Square did he tell his frightened daughter what had happened. "I shall go tomorrow and ask if they'll take me back as Irish Secretary. They'll find out now the sort of people they have to deal with." Surprised to see them home so early, Jane Forster had cried pitifully on learning the reason, while Forster spent the next hour standing grimly by the fire, his head leaning on his hand. "I feel it most about Burke," he murmured.

*

In Downing Street, Mary Gladstone was sitting miserably in a corner of Edward Hamilton's room, having rushed there after hearing "someone stammer 'bad news'" and thinking it concerned her father. At eleven thirty, Hamilton sent a cable to Queen Victoria's lady-in-waiting, the Marchioness of Ely:

> Mr. and Mrs. Gladstone have not yet returned from dinner and I am still waiting to break the awful news to them. All is over with Lord F and I do not yet know whether the terrible intelligence has been conveyed to Lady F.

*

Catherine Gladstone had arrived alone at the Admiralty party, her husband having decided to give it a miss and walk home. When the host, Lord Northbrook, hurried out to meet her, saying that she must go at once to Downing Street, while assuring her that it was "nothing about Mr. Gladstone," she left under the impression that the queen must have been shot. Entering the hall of Number 10, she cried out to Hamilton that she must know the worst at once. "I briefly told her the news; & no sooner had I done this than in came Mr. G. There was no chance of breaking it to him by degrees." The Gladstones both fell on their knees to pray, and as soon as they had partially recovered, hurried off to see Lucy.

٭

Queen Victoria had spent the day in Epping Forest, which was being opened to the public for perpetuity. She had been nervous about security arrangements during the ceremonial procession through the woods, but the police and army presence was conspicuous, and everything passed off smoothly. With a blue and white sky and balmy breeze, the weather was perfect, and as the reclusive queen was driven between the crowds, dressed in black, a white ostrich feather in her bonnet, she seemed visibly touched by her people's display of warmth. "Was ever such a May-day, was ever such a Queen!" proclaimed a banner along the route, and the cheering that greeted her short speech delighted her even more. "Nothing but loyal expressions & kind faces did I hear & see it was most gratifying."

It had been a long, tiring day, but the queen was bright and animated during dinner with her ladies-in-waiting, and Ponsonby decided to wait until she had finished before sending a note with the news. Victoria responded instantly:

This is awful—terrible! But it is only what the Queen dreaded from this [fatal occurrence?]. *Poor* Mr. Burke! how dreadful & poor Ld Frederic[k] Cavendish—& *no one* taken! It is an awful blow for Mr Gladstone— disapp[ointment] & distress & remorse at sending Lord Fred: & loss of his favourite nephew!—& for Mrs. Gladstone—a most terrible shock & poor dear Ly Frederic[k], for whom the Queen's heart bleeds—is her niece! The Queen hardly knows how they will bear it. The Queen had no conception that they let so many of those people out of Kilmainham Gaol! (RAVIC/ADDA12/719.)

When she had seen Forster, two days earlier, he told her that he believed the release of the three politicians would be an encouragement to crime, and now his words seemed prophetic. Railing at Lord Granville, she said that she considered the murders to be "the *direct result* of what was a most fatal and hazardous step."

At midnight, Janie Ely had come in saying, "All is over with Lord Frederick," and after telegraphing to inquire about Lucy and letting her children know what had happened, Victoria retired to bed, her mind reeling with anxiety.

[I] could think of nothing else. How could Mr. Gladstone and his violent radical advisors proceed with such a policy which inevitably has led to all this? Surely his eyes must be opened now.

*

At Waterloo Station on Saturday, May 6, Michael Davitt and John Dillon had been met by a throng of friends, Parnell having made an excuse that allowed him to return to Katharine in Eltham. Believing, as their chief did, that the government's conciliatory measures could well be the beginning of Home Rule, they drove in buoyant spirits to Westminster Palace Hotel, the Irish MPs' off-duty headquarters. At about half past eleven, sitting together in the dining room, they were talking about recent political changes and still feeling euphoric that their land agitation had not been in vain, when a journalist from the Central News Agency burst in with a telegram. "Oh, come . . . ," Davitt said on hearing about the Dublin murders. "This is a patent bogus outrage for tomorrow's Sunday papers." He and Dillon went upstairs to bed, both refusing to accept that "so dire a calamity" could dash the day's hopes to the ground.

NINE

Falling Soft

A T MIDNIGHT Lucy Cavendish was alone in their house on Carlton House Terrace, having spent a cheerful evening with her favorite brother, Alfred, her sister Meriel, and her sister-in-law Louisa Egerton. Now that the painful decision about Ireland had been made, it felt as if the worst were over, and all that remained was to face the difficulties ahead with courage and faith. Lucy had been invited to the Admiralty party but had forgotten all about it, and when the others went off there, she sat at her desk to write a few letters and unwrap a parcel sent earlier in the day by Gladstone. "Please to ask Freddy to give these little volumes a place in his library, in memory of the last two years," her uncle had written in his note, asking her not to resent the appointment and to try hard to be patient. She was just starting to reply when the door opened, and Louisa came back in.

No thought of fear struck me at first; I knew she wished for a talk, and I only thought that on her way home from the Admiralty she had looked in so as to find me alone. But as soon as I saw her face, the terror seized me, and I knew something must have happened to my darling. She had the dreadful telegram in her hand—but it said "dangerously wounded" and I clung to the hope he would get over it.

When Meriel returned from the party, Lucy was saying to Louisa, "Oh I know he will pull through, if I can only go to him at once; he is in such fine health just now, I know he will get through it . . ." But then she saw her sister's expression. "Tell me everything, tell me the whole," she cried, and the two women watched her plunge from hope to utter desolation. "[He] was all I had," she whispered. "I have no-one else. . . . I don't think they could have done it if they had known about me." She sank to the floor, leaning against Louisa, gently moaning, "It is cruel, so cruel," and then saying urgently, "Don't let them hate them, don't let them be angry with them; Freddy wouldn't like it."

In the middle of her black confusion, Lucy's thoughts turned to Gladstone, terrified that the knowledge might kill him, and minutes later, he and Catherine walked into the room. "I saw his face, pale, sorrow-stricken but like a prophet's in its look of faith and strength. He came up and almost took me in his arms, and his first words were, 'Father, forgive them, for they know not what they do.'" Gladstone was quoting Luke's account of the words Christ had spoken from the cross, and when he added, "Be assured it will not be in vain," the meaning struck Lucy in an epiphany. "Across all my agony there fell a bright ray of hope and I saw in a vision Ireland at peace, and my darling's life-blood accepted as a sacrifice for Christ's sake, to help to bring this to pass."

By now, the house was full of people. Scotland Yard's Howard Vincent was there, trying to arrange an immediate Dublin trip for Lucy, asking the commander of its Metropolitan Police if Cavendish's features were recognizable and whether he saw any objection to the widow coming over. Lord Granville had arrived half in tears; Mary Gladstone was still sitting hunched up in a chair; Lord Hartington was weeping uncontrollably. Meriel heard Lucy begging her brother-in-law to make the Duke of Devonshire feel that it was fitting that Frederick should have gone to Ireland, something she repeated to

Gladstone as he was leaving, imploring him not to blame himself. "Oh no," he replied. "There can be no question of that. I don't repent sending him; I was *right* to do it."

Shored up by her uncle—"like an oak to lean against"—Lucy allowed herself to be taken upstairs, where she undressed and got into bed. Lying beside her, Meriel let her cry and listened as she voiced thoughts and feelings that were remarkably composed. "She never seemed bewildered, or to lose her balance. . . . We spoke a great deal of Freddy's tenderness, and their ways together, how they were just like lovers always." Once, overwhelmed by the injustice, Lucy cried out, "How *could* they do it—it was cruel. He only wanted to help them. He never said one bitter word against Ireland. He always thought if the right remedy could but be found they would behave well." Almost brightly, she described the comfort she was drawing from the analogy of Christ's sacrifice, how his crucifixion had seemed a tragedy, the collapse of his work and of his followers' hopes, and yet his death had been a sublime victory. "Freddy's will be like that; it will do more good than his life."

Observing her sister during those first hours of her great sorrow, Meriel felt she was seeing "a marvelous manifestation of the power of religion," the blessedness given to those with unwavering faith. Some years later, Lucy recalled:

All through the long awful night I was saved, I know not how, from nervous agony such as would seem inevitable under such a blow. All the reviving hopes for Ireland . . . and the fear of what would come next. All seemed wrecked in the darkness. Then came from Heaven into my soul the thought of the greater darkness [of Christ's death]. . . . So GOD carried me in His arms though the first terrible hours. He soothed me, even by the very exhaustion of grief, so that I could sleep.

*

On Sunday morning, intending to meet Davitt and Dillon in London, Parnell drove with Katharine to Blackheath Station, where she asked him to buy her a copy of the *Observer*. Waiting in the carriage, she saw him glance at the front page and then stand absolutely still. "King, what is it?" she said, going up to him and taking his hand. Parnell pointed to the headline, gripping her fingers so hard that her rings cut and bruised them. He would have to abandon politics, he told her, but when Katharine heard the train approach, she rushed Parnell into a compartment, and as she ran along the platform beside the moving train, she declared, "No, you are not a coward."

More shaken than ever before, Parnell felt that he had been "stabbed in the back"; he had won a major victory by drawing the prime minister to his side, but now all his work had been undone by the act "of a few hare-brained fanatics." The murders would discredit his leadership, wreck his policy by negating the promised concessions, and bring disgrace to his country. "I regarded them as the greatest possible calamity that could have befallen Ireland and the future of our movement at that time or any other time." Arriving in London, Parnell went straight to see William O'Shea, asking him to deliver his offer of resignation to Gladstone.

*

Michael Davitt had been woken at five o'clock on Sunday morning by Henry George, the American journalist and reformist, who handed him a telegram, remarking, "One of the worst things that has been done for Ireland for fifty years, old fellow." Davitt felt exactly the same.

> One act of hellish vengeance by unknown hands has undone the labor of the Land League and left it *the victim* of the crime—the National character of Ireland—and helpless, defenseless before the fury of England and perhaps the alienated sympathy of the whole civilized world.

When Parnell arrived, he flung himself into the room's only chair, avowing to have nothing more to do with Irish politics; what was the point, he said bitterly, if they were to be struck at in this way by irresponsible men? "He was wild," Davitt recalled. "Talk of the calm and callous Parnell. There was not much calmness or callousness about him that morning. . . . It required all my influence to prevent him from carrying out his resolution. I told him that he was called upon then more than ever to remain at the head of the Irish people in order to prevent those who had perpetrated this deed from carrying out some other atrocity."

When John Dillon joined them, the expression of horror on his cadaverous face told the full extent of the catastrophe, mirroring the distress felt by all the Irish MPs about the damage to their movement. "The murder has ruined us practically as politicians and I have, like many others, been thinking of giving up Parliament," Tim Healy wrote to his brother. "However, we will struggle on a while longer, I suppose." Taking command, Davitt suggested that they compose a manifesto to calm the minds of the English people. Rapidly written in pencil on a couple of sheets of foolscap, it called upon the Irish people to make every effort to bring the murderers to justice.

> We feel that no act that has ever been perpetrated in our country during the exciting struggles of the last fifty years has so stained Ireland as this cowardly and unprovoked assassination of a friendly stranger, and that until the murders of Cavendish and Burke are brought to justice that stain will sully our country's name.

The manifesto was wired to America and to Dublin for mass printing and posted in every Irish town and village the following morning.

*

Although deathly pale, Gladstone had faced what he called "this dark Sunday" with studied calm. He was having lunch in Downing

Street when O'Shea arrived with Parnell's offer of resignation, a gesture that touched him—"He wrote evidently under strong emotion" —but one that he had no intention of accepting. Parnell's retirement from public life would do far more damage than good; he would be replaced by harder men, and the scale of violence would escalate. "The conviction was borne in upon the Grand Old Man . . . that here was a leader who could govern Ireland, and that no one else could do it," Winston Churchill would later write. "Here was a man who could inaugurate the new system in a manner which would not be insupportable to the old."

> Dear Mr. O'Shea,
> My duty does not permit me for a moment to entertain M Parnell's proposal, just conveyed to me by you, that he should if I think it needful resign his seat; but I am deeply sensible of the honorable motives by which it has been prompted.

*

On May 7, both houses of Parliament were adjourned as a mark of respect for a fellow MP's murder, but a cabinet meeting was held that saw Harcourt "flaming for reprisals." Defiantly refusing to punish "the *people* of Ireland" with crushing coercive powers, Gladstone argued that the government should wait before issuing a new protection bill; he had heard about the manifesto drafted by Parnell, Davitt, and Dillon, and attached great importance to it. By denouncing the assassins, and exhorting the Irish people to give them up, it promised to quell English anger and make desperate measures unnecessary. "Even in this black crime & terrible calamity, there may I hope be a seed of good," Gladstone remarked. "This may be a turning point in the history of Ireland—the pure & noble life may be a great peace-offering."

*

Later on Sunday, sick with anxiety, Katharine sent a telegram to
O'Shea asking him to bring Parnell to dinner at Eltham. She had
spent the day brooding about the murders' impact on Parnell's future,
terrified that he would be arrested for a second time under the Coercion Act. Parnell, on his part, was afraid for his life—"They will
strike at me next," he had said in a meeting earlier that day with
Joseph Chamberlain. Arriving ashen-faced at Wonersh Lodge, he had
to greet Katharine as if seeing her for the first time since his release,
and throughout dinner he sat staring stonily ahead. Unaware that his
wife already knew of Parnell's determination to resign, O'Shea urged
Katharine to use her influence.

"He must show that it simply does not touch him politically in
any way."

"I do absolutely agree with Willie about it, Mr. Parnell."

"Well, I will write to the G.O.M. and offer to reign and abide by
his decision; [but] the thing makes me feel hopeless of doing any
good."

As the parlor maid who had brought in their coffee turned to
leave the room, a picture hanging behind Parnell crashed to the floor,
bringing all three to their feet in alarm. "There goes Home Rule,
Parnell!" O'Shea said, laughing, and bent down to help the girl pick
up the shards of glass. Parnell remained standing, gripping the back
of his chair and staring at the engraving—a group portrait of the
1880 House of Commons, with Parnell and O'Shea among its newly
elected Irish MPs. Later, alone with Parnell, Katharine said, "You
did not really mind about that picture, did you? It was only a rotten
wire!" To Parnell, however, it was a malign omen—"But for whom?
Willie or me?"

*

When Patrick Tynan saw Joe Brady and Dan Curley on Sunday, he
grasped their hands with a charge of pleasure: thanks to this heroic
young lieutenant and their captain's "sacred band," "the glorious 6th of

May" had become the historical event the directory had planned. The assassination of Frederick Cavendish was an unexpected bonus—"a thousand times greater in its results and its magnitude to Ireland than that of 'suppressing' the Under-Secretary alone"—although Brady admitted that he had not known the Englishman's identity. "Only for himself he would not be the way he is now," he said brusquely, explaining how he had killed Cavendish in a fit of anger. "[When] the strange gentleman struck me with his umbrella and called me a ruffian I got annoyed and excited and I struck him in the arm, and then followed him out into the road and settled him there." Once Tynan had heard the details, he told the two men that after this meeting, all discussion of the incident must cease; any member who mentioned the names of those involved would be found guilty of treason—a verdict bringing certain death. Tynan transmitted an order to the Invincible soldiers, "impressing upon them the necessity for the most rigid silence on recent events, and directing each man to quietly resume his normal peaceful duties" for the present.

∗

That evening in Paris, Patrick Egan strolled from his home on the avenue de Villers to the Madeleine tram station, where he intended to buy the Sunday papers. There had been no news in early editions about Michael Davitt's release, and Egan was anxious to know whether the Ballina incident might have prevented the government from carrying out its promise to free him. As he left the kiosk with his paper and sat down on a nearby bench, he was observed by the Paris correspondent of the London *Daily News*, who knew him by sight, as they were neighbors. "When [Egan] opened and looked at it the paper fell from his hand, and he became quite corpse-like," wrote the journalist, describing how he had feared that the Irishman was having a seizure and had rushed up to help. "For perhaps five minutes he could not speak, and kept staring in a fixed way. I questioned him at last and he pointed to the paper, *La France*, and said, 'Look at that. . . . What an awful calamity; Cavendish was the best of the whole lot. Poor Cavendish; poor Lord Frederick.'"

Tynan's account confirms that the Invincibles executives had indeed been astounded by the news: "They knew nothing of [my] plans, or the manner by which the Dublin men were to carry out their orders"; it had been Frank Byrne, not Egan, who had sent the dispatch sanctioning action despite the government's concessions. And while scathing comments made by Egan suggest that he would have condoned the assassination of Burke—"an old Castle official, and one of the clique who misguided Mr. Forster"—he was appalled by Cavendish's unmerited murder. "Lord Frederick Cavendish had only been in the country a few hours, and came as a messenger of peace," Egan remarked in a London *Daily News* interview, adding that Cavendish's appointment had boded well for Ireland. "He had been so long a time the Premier's secretary that he would doubtless have carried out faithfully his instructions, and not been influenced by the Castle clique, like Mr. Forster and every other Chief Secretary."

Egan's description of the assassination as "stupid as well as atrocious" exactly anticipated the opinion of an American Land League president over a decade later, who declared: "None but the most stupid ass and blunderer would have murdered Lord Frederick Cavendish, the man whom Gladstone selected as his messenger to introduce in Ireland the policy of peace. The acts of Tynan and his fellow assassins were nearly the death blow of the whole movement for Irish Home-Rule." The twenty-one-year-old Irish poet and novelist Katharine Tynan declared, "The most anti-English of us had a sick sense of guilt in those days. We felt the blood was on our hands"; and even the fanatical Thomas Mooney described the murders as "abhorrent to every true friend of Ireland." In New York, a veteran Fenian was heard to remark, "What harm if it was only Burke? But to kill the strange gentleman who did nothing to us!"; while another Irish extremist claimed to have been so disillusioned by the Phoenix Park murders that he left his home country shortly afterward. "[That was what] first disgusted me with what was going on. . . . Lord Frederick Cavendish was a tip-top man."

*

On Monday morning, the Invincibles were outraged to see the Irish leaders' proclamation of "allegiance to the enemy" posted alongside Spencer's offer of an enormous reward, of £10,000 (more than $1 million today), for their capture. "Was this hypocrisy . . . spurred on by nervous fear of personal consequences?" spluttered Tynan, and his indignation was shared by Egan, who had made a point of distancing the Irish movement from the murders. "You surely do not think that public opinion will regard us as accomplices?" he remarked in the London *Daily News* interview; and yet, here were Parnell, Davitt, and Dillon appearing to accept some kind of responsibility. When a letter to the *Freeman's Journal* proposed that $5,000 from the Land League funds should be added to the offer of a reward, Egan wired the paper in protest. Egan declared that he would at once resign the treasureship if a penny were used for that purpose. To the editor of the *Mail*, he drafted the following lines:

> I yield to no man in honest sincere abhorrence and condemnation of the Phoenix Park crime but at the same time I differ from some of my friends as to the policy of elevating the informer . . . into a popular hero in Ireland.

*

From all over the world, hundreds of telegrams and letters of condolence arrived at 10 Downing Street, the reaction in the international press as shocked as it had been by the assassination of the czar by Russian nihilists a year earlier. The majority of European papers suggested that the murders had endangered the government; Madrid's papers expressed surprise at the Gladstone cabinet remaining in office "after the signal failure of its Irish policy"; France's *Le Clarion* stated, "If there is another outrage committed, all England will turn against the Ministry which has made terms with Mr. Parnell. . . . It is not impossible that this evening may bring us news of the resignation of Mr. Gladstone"; *République Française* announced, "Mr. Forster is proved to be right. Probably Mr. Gladstone's authority will receive from this a fatal blow. [It remains to be seen] whether he retains power a short time longer or whether he is immediately overthrown."

It was also the view of Edward Hamilton, who, for all his loyalty to Gladstone, was convinced that this was the death knell for his government.

> Even Mr. Gladstone's bitterest enemies show I think that they are sensible of the terrible loss he has incurred, though some may regard it more in the light of a deserved punishment. . . . If the state of the country does not improve and improve rapidly, I expect that in the autumn there will be a general outcry for a dissolution which would be certain to mean the total and complete rout of the Liberal party.

*

On May 8 it seemed that all London had converged on Westminster, and police struggled to clear a passage for MPs entering the building and to control the crowd roaring its anger whenever an Irish politician was recognized. The House inside was unusually hushed, every member dressed in mourning. Political assassination was new to Britain, and this was seen to be a national catastrophe. Burke's death, like one more report of a brutal agrarian outrage, would have caused little reaction; it was the slaughter of a respected Englishman, carrying a symbolic olive branch, that had provoked a mixture of horror and great sorrow. Hearing of his colleague's murder, Sir Ralph Lingen, a cantankerous "dry man of figures," had cried like a child.

Although reluctant to attend the day's session, Gladstone had forced himself to appear, sitting on the Treasury bench with his face buried in his hands. When he stood up to speak, leaning heavily on the dispatch box, his head bowed, it was in a low, broken tone. The silence in the House was so profound that Florence Forster, too far away to see the prime minister, could plainly hear his every word. Gladstone had feared that he might "give way and make a scene," but he managed to hold his nerve, although he could not bring himself to mention Cavendish by name.

The hand of the assassin has come nearer home; and though I feel it difficult to say a word, yet I must say that one of the very noblest hearts in England has ceased to beat, and has ceased at that very moment when it was just devoted to the service of Ireland, full of love for that country, full of hope for her future, full of capacity to render her service.

There were sobs from women in the upstairs gallery, and when Gladstone sat down, Catherine was heard to whisper, "I am so thankful it's over."

But there were many skeptics. It was only now, one pointed out, when "the Prime Minister's face and hands are sprinkled with the pure and innocent blood of his own relative and friend," that he had become truly aware of the horrors taking place in Ireland. There had been no outcry about the aged bailiff and his young grandchild thrust, either dead or alive, into sacks and thrown into Lough Mask; nor about the shooting of an innocent, elderly woman on her way back from church on Palm Sunday. The bullets had been intended for her brother-in-law, the magistrate Barlow Smythe, who was sitting beside her when a gang hiding in a clump of trees ambushed their carriage and blew her head to pieces. Soon after this incident, Gladstone had received an angry letter from Smythe, denouncing the weak policy that had allowed the "assassin guerrillas" of the Land League to flourish: "I lay the guilt of the deed of blood at your door, in the face of the whole country," he wrote. Mindful of such accusations, and yielding to the insistence of colleagues, Gladstone again felt compelled to abandon his principles and concede to a policy of coercion. He ended his tribute by announcing that new measures would be introduced for the repression of crime in Ireland.

When Parnell rose, a strange, fierce murmur ran around the house, a sound described by his colleague John Redmond as not exactly a growl but one charged with savage hatred:

What had this man to say? This man, the indirect if not the actual cause of the murder? What right had he to speak—What right had he to be here at all? His very presence was an outrage! Never as long as I live, shall I forget the looks of fierce detestation turned upon Mr. Parnell at that moment. We, his friends, tried to counteract all this by a cheer, but so chilled were we by the scene that it died away unuttered on our lips. Mr. Parnell, however, did not falter. In a few simple words, expressed without any outward sign of the influence of the scene upon him, he expressed his horror at the crime and sat down the most hated, distrusted, and feared man in England.

Forster was next to take the floor, moving the House with his tribute to Thomas Burke, who had never wanted praise, Forster said, let alone any kind of formal acknowledgment or decoration. "He was satisfied with the respect of those who worked under him and with the confidence of those above him, and he entirely forbade my asking for it. . . . I think I never met with a man so completely without prejudice —so completely and absolutely fair, and so determined to do justice to all classes, and that in a country where it is sometimes difficult."

*

That night, after dinner, Gladstone sank into a deep sleep on the sofa. One MP had been shocked by the change in him in twenty-four hours; another remarked that he had never seen "a more utterly crushed being." Only a few days earlier, Gladstone had spoken of the restoration of order soon to occur in Ireland, saying he was convinced that in three months' time the country would be more peaceful and more prosperous than ever before. Now, in the view of his great friend and counselor, Lord Acton, it was crucial that Gladstone did not abandon his optimism. "Do not let him lose confidence in himself," Acton appealed to Mary.

> I apprehend a violent burst of passion in the country and I fear that [the cabinet] will either forsake him or urge him to forsake his own ideal lines. . . . Still I see great opportunities of recovery, and I know in what spirit I hope that he has had the strength to receive the blow aimed through Freddy Cavendish at himself.

*

A Peak District valley in Derbyshire, where a steep, rocky hill descends through woods to lush grazing land and a wide, winding river, is the arcadian setting of Chatsworth House, home of the Duke of Devonshire. The mansion itself, with its pilasters, decorative moldings, and gold-leaf window frames, is a sublime example of English baroque. But on that Sunday in May, for all its beauty, Chatsworth was a place of inconceivable gloom. "It is impossible to describe the desolation in this home," Queen Victoria was told by Emma Cavendish, who was staying there with her husband, Edward, the youngest of the three brothers. It was he who broke the news to their father that morning, watching in anguish as the old duke fell to his knees, piteously whimpering, "My Freddy."

On Monday, May 8, arriving at Chatsworth with Louisa and Alfred, Lucy went directly to the duke's room. She had always felt awkward in the presence of her "papa-in-law" and "horribly shy, [with] such a painful conviction that he must think me a fool and a bore." On Louisa's wedding day, more of a wake for the duke, who

was losing his daughter, Lucy could not help going up to him standing forlornly in a corridor to kiss him and squeeze his hand. Now,
however, she felt it appropriate to be formal, repeating how much
she hoped that he would never think it had been wrong for Frederick
to go to Ireland. Adopting the stiff upper lip of his class, the duke
replied that he was comforted in some measure by knowing that his
son had fallen in the discharge of his duty. But he touched her by saying, "He was the best son, and I do believe the best man."

The coffin containing Frederick Cavendish's body arrived at day-
break on Tuesday, after having been wheeled on a gun carriage through
the streets of Dublin, escorted by cavalry officers with muskets and
drawn sabers. At Chatsworth it was placed in the private chapel under
the guardianship of the old housekeeper who had nursed Freddy
as a child. The coffin was open, but there was no catafalque, drap-
ery, or anything else to suggest a death chamber, and the chapel's
tranquility—the dim light from stained-glass windows, the scent of
cedarwood—helped prepare the family to see Cavendish for the last
time. For the duke, the sight of "this dear dear face," its expression
calm, with no trace of suffering, had alleviated some of the horror.
It had helped strengthen Lucy too, the consolation she had found in
Cavendish's "sacrifice for Christ's sake" fortified by the sight of her
husband lying in the chapel, surrounded by murals of the life of Jesus
and the Ascension. "His face beautiful and serene and pure, like sleep
only more tranquil: the lines smoothed away. No sign of hurt except
a little scratch on the bridge of the nose."

Now able to believe that Cavendish's pain cannot have lasted long,
she felt a rush of pity for Tom Burke's sister, who would not have had
this consolation, and she wrote asking Spencer to send her a message:
"I have never seen her but she will not wonder at the earnest sympathy
for her which fills my heart. . . . I sadly fear this must be crushing her;
for I have had such soothing in the heavenly peace on my Freddy's face."

Alice Burke had been unable to shed a tear on learning of the death
of her brother, "the pride and center of her life." It was only when she

was led into the room at the Chief Secretary's Lodge to which the two corpses had been moved, and saw the appalling mutilation of Burke's noble features, that her pent-up anguish was unleashed, and she threw herself on his body. Throughout the following day, Alice had sat staring, with a vacant expression, speaking to no one.

Although Lucy had amazed those around her with her composure, she had not yet fully taken in the tragedy. Waking alone in the early dawn, vividly conscious of what had happened, she was saved only by her belief in what she described as an impalpable sense of something guarding and enfolding her, "as if I was indeed falling down a precipice of grief, but with the feeling of *falling soft.*" When a wreath arrived from Queen Victoria, Lucy once again voiced her hope for a positive outcome in Ireland as a result of the murder: "If by God's Almighty power such an end can be brought to pass through his cruel death, rather than by his life, I must never dare to grudge the sacrifice. Nor would he have grudged it." And yet, spiritual solace was not enough. Lucy found herself craving concrete details, begging Spencer to help her to visualize her husband's final hours.

*

Queen Victoria was also clamoring for details. She had been "most painfully interested" in an account given the previous night by a young Irish Catholic guardsman, Lieutenant Ross of Bladensburgh, who provided her with a blow-by-blow scenario, a tutorial on secret societies, and his own view of the identity of the murderers, deducing from the bowie knives believed to have been used that they must have been Irish Americans hired by the Fenian brotherhood. He had heard it said that the extremists were furious at the so-called agreement among the Parnellites, and he agreed wholeheartedly with the queen's condemnation of Gladstone's "fatal policy."

Not content with Ross's account of the "dreadful details of this horrible crime," Victoria instructed Henry Ponsonby to keep her minutely informed of new developments. A patient, intelligent man, with a liberal outlook unusual in a courtier, Ponsonby understood the queen's foibles and knew when it was important to indulge them. Somewhat embarrassed by the prurience of his undertaking but aware of its necessity, he enlisted the help of Courtenay Boyle.

> Every detail is of interest here [and] I do not want to trouble the Viceroy more than necessary, so please telegraph fully and cypher if necessary. H.M. has been told today on good authority that Lord Spencer had seen the scuffle—not knowing what it was—but you very distinctly deny that. Indeed from my recollection of the grounds I scarcely understand how he could.

Ponsonby was then told to find out more about the tricyclists—"Why they gave no arms or pursuit is extraordinary"—and to try to obtain photographs of the Viceregal Lodge and of the actual spot where the murders had been committed. Victoria could "think of nothing, nothing else." She wrote again to "poor dear Lucy," and asked Gladstone to tell her that she felt that a cross should be erected at the murder site. She requested a pension for "poor Miss Burke" and sent her a personal note of condolence, waiving royal protocol and adopting the informal first-person pronoun.

Preoccupying her most was her own sense of guilt at having consented too easily to the release of Parnell and the two other suspects. "She ought never to have been asked in such a way but she ought to have asked for time to reflect upon conditions," she told Ponsonby, and in a letter to Spencer, she insisted on the need for uncompromising new proceedings.

> The barbarity & daring of these diabolical murders as it were almost under the walls of the Vice Regal Lodge which she knows so well—makes ones blood run cold! The Queen *feels most* anxious that the very strongest & most energetic measure should be taken & that the Lord Lieutenant should insist on the Cabinet giving him all the powers that

he asks for, which alas! Were so often not granted to poor Mr. Forster.
We *must strike* terror into these ruffians & make some strong examples for
else anarchy will reign triumphant & murderers go about unpunished.

"One person is solely responsible for all this," the queen's son
Prince Leopold remarked, and she also believed that it was Gladstone
alone who deserved the brunt of the blame.

*

Writing spontaneously on the day after the murders, Gladstone had
sent what Victoria considered "a very strange" letter, citing lines of
poetry, "which best compresses his thought." Ponsonby had warned
her that the shock might derail a man of his temperament, and she
held back from expressing her views while "he was still stunned by the
terrible blow." By Monday, however, she was demanding that Gladstone make no further concessions "to those whose actions, speeches
and writings have produced the present state of affairs in Ireland,"
saying that what she considered to be the government's weak, vacillat-
ing action would encourage them to make further demands.

"She will never be happy till she has hounded me out of office,"
Gladstone complained to Catherine, but he was determined not to
be cowed. The queen's admission that she had felt "an indescribable thrill of horror" when learning lurid details of the murders was
distasteful, and he gave short shrift to her suggestion that he would
profit from an interview with the "very intelligent" Lieutenant Ross.
Staunchly defending the Kilmainham Treaty, he intimated that the
private communications with Parnell had been invaluable, adding, "A
minister of the Crown has no right to refuse information tendered
to him by a Member of Parliament." So unwavering was Gladstone's
conviction, in fact, that Ponsonby told the queen that her prime minister believed that "if the Government have judged wrongly they
ought to lose their office."

*

It was a cold, rainy Dublin morning when a long cortege of carriages, passing shuttered shops, crepe-hung doorways, and silent onlookers, their hats respectfully removed, made its way toward Glasnevin Cemetery, where Thomas Burke was to be buried in a vault beside his father. Today, it is the final resting place of some of the most illustrious names in Irish history, but in 1882, the only tomb of note was that of Daniel O'Connell, the great Catholic campaigner, much of the ground containing the unmarked mass graves of cholera victims and the multitude felled by the Great Famine. Although announced as private, Burke's funeral was attended by many sympathizers, Mallon among them, but there were no grandees, Lord Spencer having decided to send a representative. "Better not to draw more crowd than was necessary."

Frederick Cavendish's funeral, on the other hand, was on the scale of a state ceremony. At 9:40 a.m., on Thursday, May 11, a special train left London's St. Pancras Station, transporting most of the House of Parliament to Chatsworth (the Irish MPs conspicuous in their absence); the tenantry arrived from the Devonshire estates of Bolton Abbey, Hardwick, Lismore, and Holker; and the numbers in the park swelled to at least thirty thousand. An early thunderstorm had blown over, leaving the most perfect May day, and as the politicians walked up toward the great house, its golden window frames glinting in the sun, some were stopped in their tracks by the sheer glory and stateliness of the place.

At half past two, the procession left Chatsworth for St. Peter's Church in the picturesque model village of Edensor, about a mile away. The Duke of Devonshire at first walked alone behind the hearse, the people standing hushed, with hats off, as he passed. Seeing their father falter, Lord Hartington and Edward Cavendish went to support him, and as they approached the church they were joined by Lucy and Louisa. After the service, they proceeded to the family graveyard, Lucy leaning on the duke's arm and standing by his side. "I never saw anything so like an angel as her face," remarked Forster.

"She was looking up with a sort of rapt expression." She put a wreath on the coffin and quietly turned away. Hartington took a posy of flowers from his pocket and dropped it into the grave. As the first clods of earth hit the wood, the duke broke down completely, but Lucy remained calm, supporting them all by her fortitude. "Her faith never failed her for one instant," said her sister Meriel.

It was *there*, ready to her hand. She had not to look for it, but only to lean heavily upon it, and she was enabled to be patient and trustful, and absolutely without one thought of bitterness, much less of revenge on those who had shattered her earthly happiness in one instant.

TEN

Mallon's Manhunt

THE GLADSTONES had decided to drive back from the church to Chatsworth to avoid attracting attention, but a number of people spotting the Grand Old Man had broken away to run alongside his carriage. The crowd's sympathy was palpable and had deeply touched Gladstone. "It is a great occasion," he wrote in his diary. "Another tie snapped and 'reversed our nature's kindlier doom.'" He was quoting the end of the epitaph that a previous prime minister, George Canning, had written for his son, who had died at the age of nineteen, and that night, lines of Gladstone's own "forced their way" into his head. This was almost certainly the germ of a poetic tribute to Frederick Cavendish—his "dearly loved son"—and he wrote a few verses down at an early hour. At ten thirty that morning, he and Catherine left Chatsworth for Downing Street, and half an hour after their arrival, Gladstone went to Buckingham Palace for an audience with the queen.

Shocked by how pale and distraught he looked, Victoria broke convention by insisting on his sitting down. After talking about the funeral, she could not resist bringing up the "dreadful murder," sharply criticizing Gladstone's decision to release the three suspects. "He defended himself, but when I said I knew Mr. Burke had been of the same opinion and greatly deprecated it, it seemed to shake him and he said the catastrophe had certainly followed very rapidly." She had already written to Gladstone about the necessity for far harsher legislation—"The whole country cries out for it"—and she had rejoiced to hear that new measures had been introduced in the Commons by William Harcourt the day before.

The Prevention of Crimes (Ireland) Bill made Forster's infamous Protection of Person and Property (Ireland) Act seem mild. Trial by jury would be abolished and replaced by a hearing conducted by Dublin Castle–chosen judges; police would be free to invade people's houses night or day without a warrant; newspapers were liable to be seized if the lord lieutenant objected to their content; resident magistrates would be empowered to send any citizen to prison for six months hard labor without trial. *United Ireland*'s editor, William O'Brien, furiously denounced it as a savage declaration of war on human liberty, and even the Conservatives were taken aback by its severity, the MP Lord Henry Lennox telling Henry Ponsonby that it was "little, if any, short of martial law."

The key player in the Kilmainham negotiations, Joseph Chamberlain, was the first to admit defeat. Conciliation had been made impossible by the murders, and once more the Liberals were forced to adopt the policy of repression from which they had hoped to free themselves. To Lord Spencer he wrote, "We have committed ourselves to a whole code of Draconian Laws which will place every Irishman's public and private life at the mercy of an official and administrative class. . . . A few days ago we had the game in our hands—now we have lost it beyond recall."

As if reading Chamberlain's mind, John Dillon remarked in his Commons speech on May 11, "You will be simply playing the game into their hands . . . if you pass this Bill"—his enraged outcry making the point that one object of the Invincibles' conspiracy had been to ruin the chance of constitutional rule by forcing the government to adopt a course of brutal opposition. This in itself, Dillon said, was an invitation for the extremists to take over.

We have posted placards in every village in Ireland calling upon the Irish people to aid the Government in discovering the criminals. If the English people refused the proffered weapon . . . there will be no option left to men who hold my views but to give up Irish politics for the present in despair. There will be no public platform left for us; and as I am not prepared to ally myself with assassins, I shall have no choice but to retire from political life.

Other Home Rulers were more rancorous, Tim Healy opportunistically turning his violent denouncement of the new bill into an implicit attack on Parnell for "handing over the Irish Party to the Liberal Government." And while Michael Davitt appeared to pity their leader—"The whole public burden of a deed which wrecks his prospects, and is abhorrent to his soul, falls upon his shoulders"—he too blamed Parnell for selling out; the Kilmainham Treaty should be better defined, he said, as "the Capitulation of the Land League."

Parnell now found himself poised between Irish radicals disillusioned by his accord with Gladstone and English parliamentarians who held him "directly or indirectly" responsible for the murders. Deliberately tempering his opposition to the Prevention of Crimes Bill, he said that he understood why the government had felt itself compelled "to take some step or other," sounding so moderate that Davitt believed that he actually favored it. "But *we all lost our heads*," he later admitted.

Davitt was referring to his own double game. He had approached Scotland Yard's Howard Vincent, disavowing his former Fenian allegiances and offering to work hard to restore peace in Ireland. "Davitt will do anything I want and give every assistance that is possible," Vincent told William Harcourt. But so inflammatory was a Manchester speech Davitt made soon afterward that Queen Victoria angrily cabled Harcourt, "Have you seen how Davitt profits by his release? Is this language to be tolerated with impunity?" It was no more than insolent swagger, Harcourt assured Ponsonby, an attempt to impress Irish nationalists and save his own skin (convinced his life was in

danger, Davitt had decided not to travel to Dublin). "If he does mischief he will be shut up again," Harcourt continued, "but I believe at
this moment his influence is being used to stop outrages and this is
Spencer's view also."

*

Having made little impact during his earlier Irish tenure, Lord Spencer was now emerging as a major political figure, exercising far more
authority than Gladstone had intended and acting as a moderating
buffer between the prime minister and the despotic Harcourt. Spencer's calm handling of the Dublin crisis had amazed his London
colleagues but not his wife, Charlotte, who told Lucy Cavendish that
the more harassed he was by day, the sounder he slept at night. Work
was his way of banishing dark thoughts from his mind—the reason
he was able to keep going, she said. "It was from being so entirely
absorbed. . . . He never looked forward; but put his whole heart into
what had to be done from hour to hour."

Charlotte had wanted to leave for Dublin immediately after learning of the murders, but Spencer begged her to stay in London, saying that her presence in the Viceregal Lodge would only add to his
anxiety. Four days later, however, she arrived on the early mail boat,
afterward describing the incongruously tranquil scene in Phoenix
Park to Queen Victoria.

> Everything looked so fair and peaceful . . . the fresh green of the early
> spring and the beautiful outline of the Wicklow Hills, with the soft lights
> & shadows resting on them—that it seemed impossible to believe that
> a deed of such horror could have been committed so near at hand. As
> I told your Majesty . . . one cannot see the actual spot from the win-
> dows as it is sheltered by some trees. . . . People pass and repass all day
> long. . . . Bicycles, cars, cabs, carriages & horses pass from time to time
> just as they must have done that day, & one wonders more and more how
> such a thing could have happened without anyone going to their rescue.

In the grounds of the three English lodges, sentry boxes had been erected in flowerbeds; soldiers and police marched up and down the gravel paths and skulked behind bushes. Charlotte could go for walks only in a gloomy enclosure at the back of the castle known as the Pound, where a few straggly lilac and laurel bushes surrounded a plot of dirty grass. Nevertheless, she was glad to have come. "I do not in the least care how dull or quiet or prison-like the life is," she told Spencer, and she meant it. When the viceroy rode to and from the castle, he carried pistols on his saddle and was preceded by two soldiers with carbines at the ready; on his right was a captain, on his left an aide-de-camp—both of them armed—while his groom followed behind with five mounted soldiers, each provided with a sword and a handgun. "He purposefully rides very fast, and the clatter made by his escort is wonderful," an observer remarked.

The two men most in danger after Spencer were Robert Hamilton, who had filled Burke's place as undersecretary, and Cavendish's replacement, George Trevelyan. Although not Gladstone's first choice, Trevelyan was "a capital fellow," who had been wholeheartedly behind the government's conciliatory policy, believing that the only way for the British to govern Ireland was "by justice & *sympathy*." The ordeal he would face, however, was foreshadowed by a chilling portent on his first visit to the Chief Secretary's Lodge: going to the window to look at the view, he pushed aside the curtain and saw lying under its folds the bloodstained coat of Frederick Cavendish, which had not been removed from the room into which his body had been brought.

*

In the first days after the murders there was much conjecture about who was responsible, the crime having shown exceptional ambition and organization. Until then, Dublin assassinations had targeted informers not officials, but these latest murders appeared to be the work of a revolutionary organization at war with England, and the consensus of opinion was that it was American. The Home Office consulted Henri Le Caron, the spy who had infiltrated the Clan na Gael, and after a long conversation with one of its veteran leaders and several others "in a position to know," Le Caron was certain that the clan had not been involved in the Invincibles' conspiracy. Reporting to his chief in London, Sir Robert Anderson, he said,

> From no nationalist here do I hear sympathy—on the contrary. . . . The scheme was got up and carried out by individuals in Dublin, doubtless connected with the org [sic] there. Morally the org here may be responsible for the funds that support the org at home; [they] are being freely sent from here and without money nothing could be done.

Le Caron suggested that nationalist contempt for the Kilmainham Treaty may have led some militants within the cause to take action—an impression also held by Spencer, who told Harcourt that the extremists had plotted "this foul deed" to antagonize England and prevent further conciliation with Ireland.

All kinds of other theories were circulating: there were tip-offs about where the weapons might have been disposed; a report by a London informant who ascribed the murders to the shooting at the Ballina rioters; a rumor that Dublin Fenians had got hold of umbrellas with sword-stick handles transported from Paris by Patrick Egan. The "utter incompetence" of the Dublin police was condemned by the press, one English journal questioning why clearly defined wheel tracks of the assassins' cab had not been followed.

The criticism sparked a flurry of arrests throughout England as well as Ireland, but most of those held were released without charge. They included "two rough-looking Irishmen whose appearance corresponded in every particular with the advertised description of two of the murderers"; and a poor psychotic in London's Whitechapel whom two policemen saw wringing his hands and talking to himself. Spencer optimistically cabled Queen Victoria about the arrest of a man seen wearing bloodstained trousers in Preston, in the north of

England, who admitted that he had been in Phoenix Park on Saturday afternoon and had traveled to Liverpool that night. But this proved to be another false lead.

Aware of the necessity for combined action between the Irish police and forces in England, the United States, and Europe, Spencer had just appointed someone to take charge. This was Colonel Henry Brackenbury, a wax-mustached, quintessential military type, who had commanded troops in India, reorganized the colonial police in Cyprus, and most recently served as military attaché to the British embassy in Paris. Informing Queen Victoria, Ponsonby wrote, "No force could have behaved better than the Constabulary as soldiers, but as detective police they are useless. Whether they can be made effective in this line is he supposes what Colonel Brackenbury will have to try."

*

What nobody had taken into account was the formidable expertise of Superintendent Mallon. Eighteen months earlier, Mallon had not only warned of the formation in Dublin of an assassination society; he had named its leading members as "Carey, a bricklayer of Denzille Street, Daniel Curley, a coach builder, and James Mullett." Two days after the Phoenix Park murders, Mallon had identified the driver of the escape vehicle as Michael Kavanagh, providing a description of the man, his cab, and the horse. A week later, "failing assistance from the persons who were in the Park . . . and working on private information," he had singled out the five key Invincibles:

James Carey
Daniel Curley
Patrick [sic] Brady
Edward McCaffrey and
_____ Kelly were the assassins

A jealous colleague at the castle would later accuse Mallon of having invented the story of his pinching shoes to conceal his failure to observe the suspects who had assembled in the park that evening. But if this small indulgence was a lapse, it was soon put right. Half an hour after the bodies were discovered, Mallon had been on the spot gathering "meager details" from the main witnesses. The contradictions in their evidence did not bode well: the color of the car was described by one bystander as "red paneled," by a second as "olive green picked out with white," and by someone else as "brown or chocolate color." To one observer, its driver "looked of the middle age with bloated red face"; to another, he was "young and fresh." Undeterred, Mallon went to the castle, where he sent cables ensuring that every British seaport and Irish rail station was on high alert. He arranged that telegraph offices would stay open on Sunday, and he obtained Spencer's authorization to read all messages, in case of a reference to the murder or to the procuring of the knives.

On Tuesday, May 9, a dozen coast guards arrived in Dublin with appliances for dragging the River Liffey between Phoenix Park and the village of Chapelizod, in the hope of finding a weapon. The city's licensed cabdrivers—around two thousand of them—were ordered to pass in front of witnesses standing in Lower Castle Yard, even though Mallon had actually detained Michael Kavanagh that day. "I had examined the whole of the car drivers of the city, but all could account for their movements on the day of the murder except Kavanagh, who said he was drinking."

Mallon was sure that Dublin Fenians were not behind the deed— "They are sufficiently wicked but they have not sufficient brains or money"—and, since the very beginning of the investigation, he suspected Patrick Egan of being the organizer. Writing in his sloping hand beneath the date (15 May) of his first report to the chief commissioner of the Dublin Metropolitan Police, Mallon had added:

P Egan
Phoenix Park Murders

To him, the involvement of the Land League treasurer was obvious: Egan had the funds, he lived outside of Ireland and so ran less risk of detection, he was trusted by "the low desperadoes in Dublin," and he had the motive.

All this makes me incline to the belief that Egan supplied the sinews of war for the late outrage. . . . What is now known as "The Kilmainham Treaty" had occurred and he was compelled to take some desperate step. It was besides no new idea of his, as it was mooted in December 80 and repeatedly since that period, that if all failed he would make some desperate coup.

An anonymous letter Mallon received gave weight to his conviction. Its author claimed that two years earlier, around the time of the formation of the Land League, he had heard Egan advocating the assassination of the viceroy and chief secretary in Phoenix Park, even suggesting knives or daggers as "the most noiseless weapons."

The writer who was for nearly 20 years most intimate with Patrick Egan had to break off his acquaintance owing to the murderous doctrines he preached in private and knowing him to be a Communist of the most sanguinary type. His father was a plebeian and a marksman and Patsy, his son (as he was called when only an errand boy), always entertained a spirit of the most atrocious hatred to all that had a decent parentage on their side. . . . The writer heard him often say if he had the command of money he would rid the world of aristocrats and public officials. . . . Egan has thousands at his command & the writer has every suspicion that he supplied the sinews of war to compass the Phoenix Park Murders. Don't treat this lightly. *Verbum Datis Est.*

Mallon had no idea whose account it was but commented, "This is a remarkable letter," adding at a later date: "Of course I was said to be demented for concurring with the writer." There was further incriminating correspondence. On May 13, Spencer wrote to Harcourt about a document found among Thomas Burke's possessions. "There seems to be proof that Egan is at the bottom of this atrocity. If he can be watched in Paris it would be very desirable."

*

Parnell also appears to have suspected Patrick Egan of involvement in the Phoenix Park murders, even though he had always regarded him as a political mentor. Now, however, Parnell had become wary, and later admitted to having "made inquiries of Mr. Egan." Over the next few months, "at daggers drawn with Egan," Parnell went out of his way to end the Land League treasurer's control of expenditure.

Michael Davitt was someone else who seemed to suspect Egan's participation, and on May 17 traveled to Paris to question him. "Anything but welcome visitor," he noted in his diary. "Am evidently *de trop*. Land League movement has been betrayed all along the line. Could throw no light upon outrage. Visit altogether unsatisfactory."

With no intention of admitting collusion to the league leaders, Egan was adopting a position of indignant self-righteousness. Writing the following day to John Dillon, he emphatically denied any sinister connection with Sheridan—an "atrocious accusation" made by Forster in the Commons on May 15—saying that he had used Sheridan only to investigate the exorbitant expenditure of the Ladies' Land League. This in itself was questionable. It was Egan who had provided the massive total of £72,000 (more than $7 million today) to fund the Ladies' extremist efforts to sustain the No Rent campaign. Did the Ladies' League also provide a cover for funding the Invincibles? Egan's payments were sent from his private account at the Paris bank of Messrs. Monroe and Co.; no exact audit of expenditure was ever made, and Egan's cashbooks have never been found.

*

The May 15 parliamentary debate saw what many believed to be the most deficient performance of Parnell's political career. Opposition ministers were demanding documentary evidence connected to the suspects' release (one would insolently accuse the government of having "negotiated in secret with treason"), and although Gladstone had tried to deflect the request, Parnell volunteered to read "the letter in question." This was of course the Kilmainham Treaty, which the Irish leader described to the House as a private and confidential letter that he had written to William O'Shea while still in prison. He had reached the end, saying that only his signature followed, when Forster, "his furrowed brow and gleaming eyes portending trouble," rose to speak.

"Might I be allowed to ask the Hon. Member for the City of Cork, did he read the whole of the letter?" Visibly flinching, Parnell answered that it was possible that a paragraph may have been omitted in the copy he had been given by his "Hon. Friend the Member for Clare." Seeing this as a cue to come to the rescue, O'Shea took over.

> "I think the best plan would be that I should take the earliest opportunity of explaining every detail in connection with this matter. . . . [*Cries of 'Read, read!'*] I have not the document with me, and am, therefore, unable to read it." He sat down, and Forster thrust a paper towards him. O'Shea stood up again. "A copy of the letter in question has been put in my hands. . . . [*Cries of 'Read!'*] I do not think it is fair. . . ."

Florence Forster had been convinced that her father would never make the Kilmainham negotiations public—"As long as the matter is in [his] keeping the Government is quite safe," she wrote in her diary. But she was mistaken. The opportunity to vindicate himself and expose the credulity of Gladstone and Chamberlain was too tempting for Forster to resist. "Read the last paragraph," he said coldly.

This time the House heard Parnell's written promise of full cooperation with the Liberal Party—a misjudgment on his part that horrified the Irish MPs. "We felt that the Chief had lowered the flag, and had tried to deceive alike his countrymen and the British," Tim Healy said. "His attempt to suppress what Gladstone styled the '*hors d'oeuvre*' filled us with disgust."

According to Katharine, it had been during an Eltham weekend that Parnell and O'Shea agreed between them to make available a version of the treaty in which the closing lines were omitted. Now, however, O'Shea was claiming all responsibility, saying that because Forster had not liked the wording, he had taken it upon himself to delete the last passage. At one in the morning, he launched into an elaborate account of the Eccleston Square meeting on Sunday, April 30, while Forster, not content with what Chamberlain called his "blow below the belt," went on to provide further damning revelations. Reading from his transcription of the conversation, he quoted O'Shea's rash words, "That the conspiracy which has been used to get up boycotting and outrages will now be used to put them down," telling of Parnell's plan to make use of "a certain person [*cries of 'Name!'*]" to carry this out.

Both Parnell and O'Shea denied knowing that Patrick Sheridan had disguised himself to elude the police, "coming backwards and forwards from Egan to the outragemongers in the West" (Forster's words). But the Irish leader's hope of employing a suspected terrorist shocked many people, as did the furtive *realpolitik* of the government's deal with him. Parnell bitterly blamed O'Shea for making confidential pledges to Forster that linked him to advanced nationalists and at the start of the captain's long, pompous account was heard to mutter, "This damned fellow will make a mess of it, as usual!" William O'Shea's days as a government intermediary were over.

*

A week later, Gladstone received a letter from Katharine, asking him to meet Parnell in private and suggesting her Eltham house as a possible location. "I am writing in perfect confidence that you will not mention the subject of this letter to *anyone*," she said. "I have not, and shall not, even to Captain O'Shea."

What can Gladstone have thought? How was Parnell able to authorize an Irish MP's wife to represent him behind her husband's back? Untruthfully, he told Katharine that only he knew of her letter, whereas in fact he had decided to seek the advice of Lord Granville before sending his answer. "She is said to be his mistress," Granville confided, but Gladstone, who despised scandal and Commons gossip, paid no heed. He badly wanted to reopen confidential communications with the Irish leader, who, since the murders, had treated him with compassion and understanding. Gladstone's fear was that Parnell had already been too badly compromised to exert his influence in bringing peace to Ireland, and if word got out of a secret meeting, he would be rendered completely useless.

Telling Gladstone she was "inexpressibly sorry" that he had declined to meet Parnell, Katharine begged him to talk to her instead. When Edward Hamilton found out that Mrs. O'Shea had "actually inveigled Mr. G. into seeing her," he was seriously alarmed. He too had heard that she was Parnell's mistress, and there were rumors enough about the prime minister's new acquaintance with the actress Lillie Langtry, who had eagerly adopted the practice Gladstone had suggested of using a double envelope so that their "intimacy on paper" remained private. "I took the occasion of putting in a word and cautioning him against the wiles of [Langtry], whose reputation is in such bad odour that . . . nobody will receive her in their houses," said Hamilton, who was just as dismayed to learn that Gladstone had resumed his habit of nocturnal wanderings, engaging prostitutes in conversation in an attempt to convert them. "It is a terribly unfortunate craze of his, and the only wonder is that his enemies have not made more capital of it. It is quite an unpardonable indiscretion for a man in his position."

Now there was the threat of Katharine O'Shea. To Hamilton, the sensible option would have been "for Mr. G. to decline point blank to

see her or communicate with her," but Gladstone was entirely at ease
with women of precarious virtue and rather looked forward to meeting this influential, if unorthodox, intermediary. Punctually, at three
o'clock on Friday, June 2, he arrived at Thomas's Hotel.

With perfect courtesy, Katharine led Gladstone to know—"what
I desired that he should know"—that the only reason for her interest in Irish politics was her emotional involvement with their leader.
They talked at length about the change in Parnell's attitude toward
Gladstone and his party—the new amity that Katharine was confident he wished to continue. By the end of their meeting, Gladstone
had no reservations about participating in an arrangement: "It might
be advantageous to the Irish leader and myself," he said, "if you,
Mrs. O'Shea, would accept the thankless office of go-between, as
you suggest."

*

Gladstone had now completed his elegy "on F.C.'s noble end," which
takes its form and inspiration from Tennyson's *In Memoriam*, a tribute
to their beloved mutual friend Arthur Hallam, who died at the age of
twenty-two. This "noble monument" to Hallam is among the great
literary works of the age, and if "May 6 1882" is mawkish and for-
mulaic by comparison, the impulse behind it is equally heartfelt. The
paradox of Cavendish's death as a new beginning was Gladstone's
only consolation:

> On Reconcilement's altar laid
> This high peace-offering may avail
> The work of angel-hosts to aid,
> And turn to joy a nation's wail. . . .

To the Irish leaders, however, such pious belief would have
seemed delusional: May 6, 1882, was "the blackest [day] that was
perhaps ever dawned for Ireland" (Davitt's words). Even the loyal

Lucy Cavendish was struggling to draw comfort from the concept of sacrifice—"which still abides with me, though so often I can but feebly cling to it"; the guilt she felt at not embracing her husband's death meant that she could not allow herself to mourn. It was a cruel coincidence that she had received a copy of the poem on June 7—eighteen years to the day since she had married Frederick in Westminster Abbey—although her note of thanks gave Gladstone no hint of her inner conflict: "All my darkened life ought indeed to be a thank-offering for what has been in the blessed past."

Gladstone had been heartened to hear of the immense impact of Lucy's own noble sentiment expressed in the letter she wrote Spencer immediately after the murders. She had asked him to let it be known to the Irish, "so that it may have some good effect," that she did not resent Cavendish's death, "if only it leads to the putting down of this frightful spirit of evil in the land. *He* would never have grudged it, if he could have hoped that his death could do more than his life." When a Connemara priest read the lines from the altar, the whole congregation fell to its knees.

*

In Dublin, the newly appointed secret service head, Colonel Brackenbury, was driving a hard bargain. "Money—plenty of money—is absolutely essential to success," he declared, requesting £20,000 (over $2.5 million today) for the current year—more than four times the existing budget for Ireland. "Should I be able to show that it has been satisfactorily expended & that more is needed, more shall be given." Then there were his conditions. Insisting on total control, he called for the right to employ his own agents in his own way without questions or reports: he and his men would need free access to prisoners; his informers must be granted state protection for all acts committed to order—even if these acts were illegal.

This demand for sole authority and control of financing was not unreasonable, Brackenbury insisted, but the prerogative of any general commanding an expedition. The reason the undertaking required an enormous amount of money was also justifiable because of its scale; concerted action would be essential, not only in Ireland and England but also in America and France.

> I venture to think that to grapple with & overthrow Irish secret Societies is of quite as great importance to the Nation at this time, as have been many of the small wars, which have cost hundreds of thousands of pounds. To combat them there must be a secret organization formed. . . . Informers must be bought, & men must be paid to enter these societies, work into the confidence of their leaders & betray them. Two things are required for this—money & men—such an organization should, *must* be entirely independent of the existing Police organization.

Urging Gladstone to accept Brackenbury's proposal, Spencer pointed out how important it was for the government to extend its intelligence network to Paris and America, suggesting that an initial figure of £5,000 (over $650,000 today) be made immediately available to the colonel: "The sum asked for is large but the forces to which we are opposed are very powerful." Gladstone agreed that the money must somehow be found but remained cautious; anticipating skeptical queries in the House about the powers of this new recruit, he warned Spencer that it was a delicate political question and one that should be introduced to the cabinet. Nevertheless, Brackenbury was immediately offered the £5,000, with further sums dependent on his success. This he rejected outright. He would probably spend £5,000 in a few months without visible result, he said, and he had no intention of attempting the task without a formal pledge of £25,000 (over $3 million today) to follow, and up to £50,000 (over $6.5 million today) for the next two years. "I very urgently pressed that Brackenbury's full demand should be promised to him," Spencer told Harcourt. "He will resign if it is not made. . . . It is a case of 'Trust me all in all or trust me not at all.'

As we have chosen him for the police the words of the song should be followed."

*

The Home Office had placed great importance on a tip-off Brackenbury received from an acquaintance in the Irish branch of Brown Shipley, an American banking house. It concerned one General J. D. McAdaras, who had asked Brown Shipley for an enormous remittance and wanted the bank to confirm with a Dublin estate agency that he had the funds for an expensive rental in the city. The banker, who knew of "a most dynamitic speech" that McAdaras had made in Paris, felt obliged to send a warning:

> If he is taking a house in Dublin he means no good to the Queen's government you may be sure & should be watched. Being a man of independent means, a "General" & living in a good house, the attention of the authorities would not be attracted towards him but he is a dangerous man all the more for that & has decided ability & audacity too.

On July 26, McAdaras arrived in Dublin from Paris, and Mallon was instructed to watch his movements discreetly and report anything that would justify his detention. Several weeks later, Mallon reported that nothing suspicious had been observed, and that McAdaras was in his view, no more than a filibuster with "a great deal of swagger about him."

Having poured scorn on the utter inability of the Irish police to penetrate their country's secret societies, the profligate Colonel Brackenbury was yet to come up with anything that Superintendent Mallon—"for a five pound note"—did not already know. Convinced that the assassination society was on Dublin's doorstep, Mallon had secured as an informer Harry Rowles—the Invincible whose failure to spot the white handkerchief signal had aborted one of the many Forster ambushes. Protected by the alias "Bernard,"

Rowles had named fourteen members of the conspiracy, including James Carey, Daniel Curley, and Edward McCaffrey, whom Mallon described as its organizers and three of the most dangerous men in Dublin. "The informant says he has no doubt whatever that Land League money was freely spent in committing crime. I certainly feel bound to believe him."

*

Parnell was working hard to freeze Land League funds. Patrick Egan had received an enormous total, of $1,230,000 (around $28 million today), mostly contributions from America, but there had been no detailed audit of expenditures, and £108,000 (close to $4 million today) remained unaccounted for. The system, Parnell admitted, had been extremely defective, and at the beginning of June he opened a Hibernian Bank account in his own name along with those of two other league leaders. "I was anxious that the payment of money should be under my own control," said Parnell, going out of his way to inform Gladstone through a Liberal intermediary, Henry Labouchère, that he had laid an embargo on Land League money. Labouchère's letter contained a sobering warning.

> Parnell wants Mr. Gladstone to know facts. He says that there are two sections in the Land League. The funds of the League are at Paris, where a large sum is invested in securities. Egan wishes to trench on these securities, but Parnell and Davitt have been able to stop this, and at present nothing is expended but the weekly contributions. Egan and his section of the League are furious at the idea of the League being converted into a moderate tenant right Association, with its headquarters in Dublin. This [Parnell] desires. . . . If the Bill is to be passed in its present shape, he declares that neither he nor his friends can have anything to do with a moderate policy, and, as they absolutely decline to associate themselves with Egan and his desperate courses, they must withdraw. The result, he says, will be that the Fenians will be masters

of the situation, and that they will have funds, and that there will be assassinations and outrages all over Ireland. So soon as he withdraws, he considers that his own life will not be worth a day's purchase. . . . He wishes most sincerely to fight with the Government against all outrages.

In her own communications with Gladstone over the coming weeks, Katharine also made clear that Parnell was distancing himself from Egan and the extremist section, although she pointed out that he could not control money sent through the *Irish World*.

The main reason for their exchange was to discuss various amendments suggested by Parnell to the new Coercion Act, Katharine taking credit for having persuaded him to do all he could to facilitate its passing. As Parnell's vicarious voice, she was enabling the Irish leader to say in private what would be impolitic, even life-threatening, to be made public. Liberal colleagues feared that their prime minister had allowed himself to be hoodwinked (Spencer had heard it said, "Parnell has put his finger in the Old Man's eye"), but Gladstone was in complete control. When Katharine wrote proposing another meeting in Thomas's Hotel, he politely but firmly refused. Signing herself "Katie," she wrote again, teasing, "I beg you will not 'boycott' me altogether," but Gladstone would not budge. Disturbed by a recent escalation of violence in the West of Ireland, he replied:

The news of another double murder in Galway again darkens the horizon. This exacerbation of the Fenian passion is terrible. I do not doubt that your friend does all he can, & I observe that what we may call ordinary outrage declines. . . . But these savage murders exhibit an open unstaunched source of mischief which goes far to destroy all confidence.

*

At the end of June, Mallon had an important breakthrough: the original Invincibles leader, James Mullett—"the person subsidized by Egan to get outrages committed in Dublin"—had agreed to tell what he knew about the Phoenix Park conspiracy. Since early March, when he was arrested as a suspect for the murder of an informer, Mullett had been detained in Dundalk Gaol, but he had decided to obtain his release by offering to provide the authorities with information.

The publican's Dorset Street premises had served for years as a revolutionary center, and hearing of his return, about a hundred people gathered there to welcome him back. Slipping in unobserved, Mallon was able to speak to Mullett and arrange a secret encounter. On July 5, after they had met in Botanic Road, Glasnevin, Mallon reported to Colonel Brackenbury that Mullett was "open to temptation." He was badly in debt, beleaguered by creditors, and Mallon believed that he would work for money. To Mullett, he wrote, "Business is very bad. Do what our team wish, but do it thoroughly and they will act generously."

Immediately after his release, "E," as Mallon referred to him, moved from Dorset Street to the Dublin suburb of Terenure, where he was visited one evening by James Carey and a man he did not know, introduced by Carey as "a friend of Brennan." This was Patrick Tynan, who, having learned that Mullett had been talking in prison about Sheridan's involvement in the affair, had come to threaten him. "He said that if I mentioned anything of the kind again I would be certainly killed," recalled Mullett, who did not take the warning lightly; Henry Jury, the proprietor of Jury's Hotel, had died in late May, and there was talk that he had been slowly poisoned by Carey and "that man he called No 1." The hotel, on Dame Street, was where Tynan stayed in Dublin, and it was alleged that Jury had inadvertently opened a letter to him from France containing English banknotes and documents, including "directions as to the working of some secret organization." Fearing the consequences, Jury got rid of the papers. "But the fact of his having received the letter reached Tynan's ear and it was then resolved to destroy him."

The menacing Terenure experience, combined with fear that his dealings with Mallon would be discovered, might have been enough to silence Mullett, but his debts gave him no choice: he confirmed that James Carey and Dan Curley were the Dublin leaders of the assassination society, and on July 6, both men were arrested and detained in Kilmainham Gaol, along with several other Invincibles. Writing to Brackenbury the following day, Mallon said, "I feel morally satisfied Carey was implicated in the Phoenix Park Murders."

ELEVEN

Concocting and "Peaching"

ARLY IN July, a letter arrived in Downing Street from Chicago, addressed to "Right Hon William E. Gladstone, Prime Minister of England, London, England." It was headed "The Pinkerton National Detective Agency," with its trademark logo of an unblinking eye and motto "We Never Sleep," and signed by Allan Pinkerton himself. Raised in the notoriously rough Gorbals district of Glasgow and trained as a deputy sheriff in Chicago, Pinkerton was America's first and most famous private eye. The agency he started in 1850, offering intelligence, counterintelligence, and law enforcement to private business and government, had hunted down such legendary outlaws as Butch Cassidy and the Sundance Kid and would become the model for the FBI (among Pinkerton's innovations was the use of photography, leading to the "Ten Most Wanted" mug shots). Historically, the agency's most significant case was that of the Molly Maguires, a covert organization of Irish coal miners in Pennsylvania, whose violent response to appalling working conditions had escalated into arson, bombings, and murder. An agency detective, James McParlan planted himself among the men for over two years, securing enough evidence to convict more than sixty members of the group, nineteen of whom were hanged for murder.

It was Pinkerton's pride in this victory over Irish terrorism that had led him to write a letter of advice to Gladstone. He was convinced that Irish emigrants in America, banded together in secret societies, were responsible for the troubles in Ireland.

> My plan would be as follows: Scatter your well drilled force through all the larger cities of the United States. Have them gain admittance to and become members of the "Ancient Order of Hibernians"; the "Fenians"; the "Land League" and the other secret societies, and by that means the hidden mysteries of these unlawful conclaves will be fully divulged. The cry of these men is "Free Ireland" and I believe that a war with Great Britain would be gratefully hailed. . . . Of course this plan would require time and patience to execute properly—but once attempted I am satisfied that the revelations thus obtained would be startling and convincing.

Infiltration on an international level was precisely what Brackenbury had in mind, but Pinkerton would have been appalled by the scheme he proposed of highly paid informers; his agency's "shadows" were forbidden to accept rewards and were known to the American underworld as incorruptible.

Although not volunteering to direct proceedings himself (age sixty-two, Pinkerton had been the victim of a stroke and would die in 1884), he nevertheless provided two referees, one a prominent New York attorney and the other Franklin B. Gowen, president of the Philadelphia and Reading Railroad and the man who had overseen the Molly Maguire operation. Gladstone seems to have been more impressed by Gowen than by Pinkerton; he had read "with great interest and profit," F. P. Dewees's 1877 book *The Molly Maguires*, astonished by the compelling narrative of the Irish miners, whose radicalism had been triggered by the despotism of English landlords back home, and whose outrages were prefaced by threatening notes identical to the Moonlighters' crude sketches of coffins, skulls, and firing handguns. On July 21, Gladstone wrote Spencer, telling of his discovery, suggesting that the Foreign Office inquire "what advice or suggestions might be obtained from a man like Mr. Gowan [*sic*] if disposed to give aid." Spencer, however, had pinned all his hopes on Brackenbury, who had just met Harcourt in London, where they discussed "all sorts of prospective arrangements as to action in America." But as they were all about to discover, Brackenbury was conducting undercover business of his own.

*

Egypt that summer had eclipsed Ireland in the British public's interest. The nationalist leader Ahmed Urabi had become a virtual dictator, reducing Khedive Tewfik Pasha to a cipher and launching a military revolt. An anti-Christian uprising in Alexandria on June 11 had left fifty foreigners dead, and the remaining European residents had fled. Of greatest importance to the British was the recently acquired Suez Canal, and Gladstone, overcoming his loathing of imperialist wars, reassured the queen, "Should it be endangered, instant action would take place." Exactly a month later, a force of over forty thousand soldiers invaded the Suez Canal Zone, and bombardment began. "The news from Alexandria is bad," Edward Hamilton noted on July 13. "Arabi has apparently withdrawn . . . and left it to the prey of fanatic Bedouins and released convicts, who have looted and nearly destroyed the city, and have also massacred the Europeans who were still left behind."

Colonel Brackenbury, who considered himself "above all things a soldier," felt duty bound to be there. His mentor was the empire's chief troubleshooter, Adjutant-General Sir Garnet Wolseley, under whose command Brackenbury had served in the 1879 Boer war. Now Wolseley had been chosen to suppress Arabi's revolt, and yearning for active service, Brackenbury wrote to Spencer asking to be released from the Irish project—"I could hand over my work to such a man as [Edward] Jenkinson. . . . [Robert] Anderson knows all I am doing." His request was greeted with fury. Gladstone was "shocked at Brackenbury's behavior," while Harcourt, recalling their recent discussion about espionage action in America, was even more outraged. "He has behaved quite infamously," he exploded to Spencer. "I have strongly urged Childers that *on no condition shall he be employed at present in any port of distinction.*" A "very angry" Queen Victoria was equally determined to thwart Brackenbury's military ambitions. "If his appointment to any post in the Expeditionary army depended on her," remarked Ponsonby, "it would be long before he got it. . . . With one eye on the pyramids he never would have been heartily in his work in Ireland."

At the beginning of August, Spencer promoted his private secretary Edward Jenkinson to the role of assistant undersecretary for police and crime in Ireland. "I wish he had been a bit better known, or an Irishman," he told Trevelyan. "But there was no man of that kind or a better man that I could have appointed." Jenkinson was to establish a new secret service department, a permanent criminal investigation section that was the forerunner of today's Special Branch. He would control the intelligence network working against the Fenians, assist Scotland Yard with crime detention, cooperate with the cabinet and leaders of the army, and coordinate the intelligence work of the Royal Irish Constabulary and the Dublin Metropolitan Police. In essence, the ambitious, egotistic Jenkinson was to be the first British spymaster, his prominence proving to be a humiliating threat to Superintendent Mallon.

*

Two and a half months had elapsed since the murders, and although the main perpetrators were behind bars, Mallon was finding it impossible to obtain the independent testimony necessary to convince a jury of their guilt.

> I confess I was more than anxious. . . . We had the evidence of two informers, and might have had more of the same class. But they were both confessed accomplices and the law is clear, and rightly so . . . no man may be convicted on the unconfirmed evidence of an informer. Moreover, we had not found the weapons.

The amputating knives had been destroyed in May on Patrick Tynan's orders, "broken up into little bits and the handles burnt to ashes, and the dust produced to No I." This had come as a disappointment to James Carey, who was so buoyed up by their "historical" deed that he wanted to preserve the weapons as patriotic relics, half-seriously proposing they be sent for exhibit in Dublin's forthcoming national exhibition of Irish industries and arts. He must have decided to keep other of the Invincibles' weapons as mementos, for it was this cache that was found by one of his tenants. At the end of July, after a torrential rainstorm, the man had gone onto the roof to investigate a leak and found two long knives and a Winchester rifle hidden under the tiles. He reported his discovery to the police.

*

August 15 had been declared a public holiday in Dublin for the unveiling of a monument to Daniel O'Connell, the legendary political leader who had campaigned for the right for Catholics to sit at Westminster. Parnell gave a speech, responding to loud cheers by saying that their most enduring tribute to the great liberator must be to gain the national independence to which he had devoted his life.

The other Dublin celebration that day was the opening of the national exhibition. One of the largest displays ever witnessed of Irish products and trades, it drew hordes of spectators and corporate representatives from all over the country, delegates from England and America, and the key Irish MPs. Also in town were members of the Invincibles executive, including Patrick Egan, who had moved back to Dublin from Paris and subscribed £500 toward funding the exhibition. Patrick Tynan visited the fair with his friend Patrick Kinsella, Blackrock's stationmaster and a minor player in the murder conspiracy. As they reached the top of Sackville (now O'Connell) Street, they saw Lord Spencer on horseback, followed by his entourage of cavalry. Outraged that he had received no orders "to assail this tyrant and his red-coated escort," Tynan arranged that evening to see Dan

Curley and Joe Brady and told them of his resolve. He had been asking the executive to supply the Invincibles with hand grenades, but it was agreed that the attack on Spencer "must come off at once, even without the shells."

After attending the Dublin exhibition, Frank Byrne had called his own meeting of Invincibles, with several new recruits present. The next assassination victim was discussed, and when a judge named Lawson was proposed, Brady said that he "would sooner go in for Spencer." He mentioned other possibilities, to which Byrne, realizing they were intending to act independently, replied that nothing could be done without orders: "Egan would have to be acquainted." Byrne told them that he was looking into their finances—"[He] made some complaint about the enormous lot of money that was spent"—but there was a pile of gold and notes on the table, and Byrne said they would not be restrained for lack of funds.

*

Parnell was also overseeing finances in Dublin. In six months, the Ladies' Land League had spent nearly £22,000 (more than $2 million) providing for imprisoned suspects alone. Since July, when the drafts Egan sent them had ceased, their account had become overdrawn to the sum of £5,000, and Michael Davitt had appealed to Parnell to pay off their debts. "No," he replied. "Not a shilling. They have squandered the money given them, and I shall take care that they get no more." Davitt was deeply shocked. Parnell's sister Fanny had founded the Ladies' Land League in New York (their mother, Delia, was its president); Anna Parnell had headed the Irish Ladies with admirable practical ability and understanding of parliamentary procedure—and yet this family connection seemed to count for nothing. Storming off, Davitt ignored all overtures from Parnell until the following day, when the leader handed over a check for £500, saying that the women must make the best of it. "They will get no more money from me, and let the League be dissolved at once."

"Parnell never made a greater mistake or a more mischievous blunder than in suppressing the Ladies in the manner he did," Davitt told John Dillon, but Parnell had his reasons. To Katharine, he wrote:

The two Ds have quarreled with me because I won't allow any further expenditure by the ladies and because I have made arrangements to make the payments myself for the future. They were in hopes of creating a party against me in the country by distributing the funds amongst their own creatures and are proportionately disappointed.

Parnell's callousness and breach with the two league leaders made Katharine even more concerned for his safety. Lately, he had begun carrying a handgun in his pocket, even though she withheld at least half of the threatening letters that were sent to him. Driving back to Eltham after a late-night session in the House, she always took the outside seat of the hansom cab, hoping to conceal to some degree the fact that Parnell was sitting beside her.

Once, to my horror . . . I saw a man rise from the ditch and the glint of steel in the moonlight. The man driving saw it, too, and, with a lurch that threw us forward in the cab, he lashed his horse into a gallop. I could just see that the man threw up his arms as he staggered backwards into the ditch and a shot rang out.

Parnell had refused the police protection he had been offered, suspecting that it was the government's way of testing the extent of his influence over the extremists, and certain that it would be interpreted by the Irish as a betrayal. "If I turn to the Government I turn away from them," he told Katharine. "And then?"

*

At the end of August, Katharine had her second encounter with Gladstone, meeting this time in his study at 10 Downing Street, a large, homely room overlooking Horse Guards Parade. Rising from his desk to greet her and solemnly handing her a chair, Gladstone headed for the double doors leading to Catherine's sitting room and firmly pushed them shut. Wanting to impress on Gladstone Parnell's resolve "to confine himself with bonds of legality," Katharine reported that he had just broken up the Ladies' Land League and stopped their funds; laid hold of league money amounting to £60,000; and fallen out with Davitt and Dillon, both of whom she clearly disliked. What she most wanted Gladstone to consider, however, was William O'Shea's wish to be made undersecretary for Ireland. The idea that the husband of the Irish leader's mistress could be given this crucial position was absurd (Spencer dismissed it outright—"I can hardly think of a man more unfitted for the place"), but Gladstone appears to have considered it. "Mr. G. thinks the Government is under *some* obligation to O'Shea," wrote Edward Hamilton.

The prime minister's close advisers were urging him to end his dealings with "that bothersome woman," as Hamilton called her. Appealing to Spencer for help, he wrote, "I can't say how greatly open to objection these continued communications from Mrs. O'Shea (whom rumor reports to be no better than she ought to be) appear to me to be; and I feel pretty sure you will agree with me in this." Spencer needed no persuading. He had been involved with a request made by Katharine on Parnell's behalf for the reprieve of a Galway man due to be executed for killing a policeman. There was no evidence that he actually fired the shot, but he was known to have ordered the murders of a father and son simply because they herded cattle on a particular farm. Spencer told Gladstone that he had been "unpleasantly struck" by Parnell's claim that were it not for his restraining influence there would be many more such murders.

Hamilton had asked him to hint to Gladstone how damaging the contact with Katharine O'Shea might prove, but Spencer could not have been more frank. "How I wish she would not write to you," he said. "I quite dread the fact of her communications leaking out."

Gladstone's reply was firm and unapologetic: "Some time ago I signified to Mrs. O'Shea that we had better not meet again. Her letters I cannot control but do not encourage. I think she has been of some use in keeping Parnell on the lines of moderation: and I imagine he prefers the wife to the husband."

*

In late September, James Carey, newly released from Kilmainham after the expiry of the three-month term decreed by Forster's Coercion Act, met Patrick Tynan. Confessing that the Invincibles' arms had disappeared from South Cumberland Street, he said that his wife, brother, and eldest son had turned up there with Joe Brady to fetch them from the roof and failed to find them. "A letter came to me from my son, and I heard something about Mr. Mallon or the police—that they had them."

This Tynan already knew. Sternly rebuking Carey, he said that while his obligations to the Invincibles would continue as long as the organization existed, he would now be relieved of all duty. "Carey promised obedience, but looked very sad." In fact, Carey was delighted. For some time now he had been wanting "to get out of the affair but was not allowed and could not do so"; he was eager to consolidate his reputation as a respectable businessman and to focus on his political aspirations. After placing a small ad in *Flag of Ireland* ("James Carey: Builder and Contractor 15, 17 and 19A Denzille Street. Estimates Free. All kinds of repairs executed with Promptitude"), he began to work on getting himself elected as a candidate for town councilor in November's municipal elections. His line was that he was entering not on political principles but only for the good of the working man; he would fight to support home manufacture and prevent the infiltration of foreign contractors and materials "from Welsh stone to an English brick." Already popular as a vociferous nationalist, Carey intended to capitalize on his detention without trial: as a victim of English coercion, he would attract the sympathy and votes of all good Irishmen.

*

In October, Patrick Ford cabled Egan a cash transfer of $17,424 (nearly $500,000 today) and announced in the *Irish World*, "with a keen sense of pain," that he would no longer use its columns to raise funds for the Land League; the Kilmainham Treaty, he explained, had sabotaged its aims: "A quietus was put on the land agitation, the No-Rent Manifesto was withdrawn, public meetings were discountenanced, and finally the Ladies' Land League—the 'best men in the whole movement' as someone said—was disbanded. Thus repression has actively co-operated with coercion."

October 17—a year to the day since the banning of the Land League—saw the establishment of the Irish National League, a more national, political, and law-driven organization than its violent, agrarian forerunner. To Michael Davitt, it was something of a betrayal— "the complete eclipse by a purely parliamentary substitute of what had been a semi-revolutionary organization"; while Egan conveyed his contempt by using the Dublin inauguration to announce his resignation as treasurer. Concerned about whether the new league would be constitutional enough, Parnell showed some hesitation before agreeing to endorse it; through Katharine, he promised to keep Gladstone closely informed of its resolutions and even forwarded a draft of his speech, with the offer to remove any points with which the prime minister did not agree. Parnell, Katharine stressed, was determined to "shake himself free of the set by which he was surrounded."

And yet, Parnell still maintained a degree of loyalty to Egan. In a memo to Gladstone, Katharine wrote, "He is anxious to be in a position as soon as possible to inform Mr. Egan that if he resigns the Treasureship and returns to Ireland, *no* proceedings against him under the new act are contemplated by the Government." Egan, however, had no intention of showing gratitude to Parnell by moderating his aims.

*

A "mysterious cheque" signed by Egan had come to Mallon's notice—a moderate sum of forty pounds, which he learned was to be shared between Dan Curley and his fellow Invincible Edward McCaffrey. "Mallon could not for the life of him discover what business relations existed between McCaffrey and Egan to justify the passing of such a sum of money from the one to the other," writes Mallon's friend and first biographer Frederick Bussy. It would soon become clear. Mallon was told of several meetings attended by leading Invincibles and had alerted his new superior. "They are, I am sure, concocting something," Edward Jenkinson wrote in his report. "I wish we had them safely locked up. From information I have received today I am sure Judge Lawson's life is in great danger. However, the men are closely watched and for the present I can do no more."

Justice Lawson, who had sentenced a Catholic republican to death on thin evidence before a jury of twelve Protestants, had become a hated figure among Irish militants, and his assassination had indeed been ordered by the executive. He was known to be well protected at both his city and country residences, but the Invincibles planned to create a diversion by holding up a Donnybrook tramcar at the moment of the attack.

Shortly after five p.m. on November 7, the judge left his house in Fitzwilliam Square, and as he approached Kildare Street, the small, ferrety figure of Patrick Delaney was seen moving rapidly toward him, the butt of a handgun clearly visible in his breast pocket. One of the guards wrestled Delaney to the ground, while two policemen rushed up to help. Tynan claimed that Delaney had been posted as a sentinel to signal Lawson's departure but was "so stupid and blundering" that he decided to carry out the murder himself. (Later, it was thought that Delaney may have "feigned the attack *in order* to be arrested"—his only way of breaking free from the organization.)

Another attempt on Lawson's life was thought to be unwise, and so a double assassination of two jurors was plotted instead—the idea being that their deaths would act as a warning to future jurymen who might be ill-disposed toward nationalist violence. One man happened to be out of town, but the other, Denis Field, the foreman at a recent murder trial, was attacked outside his front door on the night of November 27. Joe Brady, Tim Kelly, and a backup of several other Invincibles, had waited in Kavanagh's cab at the corner of Hardwick Street until they were given the white handkerchief signal that Field had left his office. At a few minutes to six, he had walked along Sackville Street to his house in North Frederick Street. Surprised by a hand on his shoulder, he looked up to see two men in front of him and two more nearby. He heard a mumbled curse of "Ah, you villain!" as he was knocked to the ground and felt the thrusts of what seemed like a sword aimed at his heart, some of which he parried with his umbrella. When he lifted his arm in self-defense, the long blade penetrated right through it, and another slash pierced his cheek and sliced his tongue. He decided to lie as if dead and saw his assailants staring down at him before they ran off down the street. He was badly mutilated and yet managed to stagger to his feet as passersby began gathering around.

It had been almost a carbon copy of the attack on Frederick Cavendish, although this time it was Brady who, remembering his victim's affront, softly echoed "Ah, you villain!" All criminals, Pinkerton once pointed out, have a marked personal technique that gives them away, and the Field assault, by exposing Phoenix Park tactics, provided the police with what they needed—confirmation that the murderers were still in the city.

*

Early that summer, Spencer had remarked to Harcourt: "We depend in Dublin on one man, Mallon; were he to die or be killed we have no one worth a row of pins." Now, however, with still no arrests for the Phoenix Park murders, Spencer and Jenkinson had decided to put the case into new hands. Feeling powerless, Mallon confessed that he was "ashamed and vexed"; he had three informers in his confidence,

"Bernard," "Andrew," and "Charles," all giving virtually the same account of the conspiracy—but he had lost hope of finding a witness willing to provide corroborative proof while the perpetrators were still at large. A seventeen-year-old girl had seen the Field attack and recognized Joe Brady and Tim Kelly as the assailants, but Brady had come to her house to threaten her into silence.

In desperation, Mallon appealed to London's chief commissioner of police to allow the interrogation of people who had not actually been charged with the crime—a process reviled by Irish nationalists, who dubbed it the Star Chamber Enquiry, referring to the English practice used since medieval times to enforce laws not remedied by ordinary courts.

It was decided that Mallon would produce the suspects, and an Irish magistrate, John Adye Curran, would cross-examine them—a formidable team of two that began working together at the beginning of December in a room in Lower Castle Yard with a view of Wrenn's public house—the Invincibles' favorite meeting place.

Denis Field had recovered enough to recount his experience in detail, and when he described his attacker's words, "Ah, you villain!" Curran remembered the phrase in Mallon's report and instantly made the connection. He interviewed most of the Invincibles, taking the precaution of holding a handgun at full cock in a jacket pocket, his finger on the trigger. Unsurprisingly, the men denied all knowledge of the murders, Joe Brady sullenly replying, "I disremember" to every question. "He could have beaten them, he was that strong!" his mother would later boast, but no assassination attempt was made on the two interlocutors during these examinations, although word reached them of serious intention.

Several days later, Mallon and Curran had obtained a statement from an Invincible who had been in Phoenix Park on May 6 and had turned informer. Robert Farrell had been sullenly taciturn at first, but Mallon succeeded in getting him to talk. He had chosen to begin the examination straight after Farrell, "a better Catholic than he was

a conspirator," had returned from Mass, and because he was afraid
to be seen entering or leaving Dublin Castle, Mallon took him to
Curran's house. After midnight on January 11, 1883, Farrell signed a
deposition, which allowed warrants to be issued for Mallon to seize
all the suspects.

> I had the whole of our men who were to be engaged brought together
> without any intimation of the kind of purpose for which they were sum-
> moned. Then I gave to each pair the warrant they were to act on, and
> instructed them to execute it at eleven o clock at night, not a minute before,
> and to tell none of their colleagues what their work for the evening was.

Not one Invincible attempted to resist arrest or asked what the
charge against him was, and by the morning of January 13, almost all
had been detained in Kilmainham. In a "most secret" memo, Spencer
told Harcourt:

> We took a very decided step last night. The Attorney General con-
> sidered there was a firm case against about 22 men for conspiracy to
> murder. . . . We have got all the leading tools, very probably 2 of the
> Council. . . . The question was should we wait. . . . We have not yet got
> up to the top of The Conspiracy. We are very near it however.

                              *

The first day's hearing at Green Street Court on Saturday, January 20,
was devoted almost entirely to Robert Farrell's evidence—the outcome, Spencer told Queen Victoria, proving most satisfactory.

> The witness bore himself with courage & gave clear & distinct evi-
> dence. It was a great relief to Lord Spencer as he feared that a witness
> confronted with his brother conspirators might have broken down.
>   The secret as to who was going to give evidence was admirably kept.
> Farrell was brought in as a Prisoner last of the lot and was quietly

moved on one side to the witness box. The effect on the other men was said to be most extraordinary. Their faces showed the utmost astonishment & no-one who watched them could doubt the alarm which his appearance created.

There are two or three other witnesses who will corroborate Farrell & his evidence is substantiated by independent evidence. . . . It is of course a very critical affair, for moral certainty of the guilt of individuals is not always the same as legal proof. This however it is hoped has been obtained. . . . The probabilities are that the conspirators not trusting each other will now make further disclosures.

Intent on keeping the informer safe, Mallon had arranged for a local publican's wife to supply Farrell with food as a precaution against poisoning, and wrote to Jenkinson to request that he be exempted from attending Mass with the other prisoners: "Farrell cannot be seen, spoken to or sneered at, or in any way intimidated."

This first betrayal had greatly perturbed the Invincibles: if one of their number had already testified in court to their guilt, it was more than likely that another might try to save his own skin by "peaching." They were being kept in separate cells so that no strength could emerge from a sense of unity, and suspicions of treachery would be likely to get them to implicate each other. And yet, as the judge sternly pointed out, no amount of corroboration by an informer carried any weight unless his evidence was confirmed by a witness beyond suspicion.

Finding independent observers to place the Invincibles in the park on the evening of May 6 became imperative, and Curran went to enormous lengths to track them down. There was a servant girl who had been on her way to visit a friend on the staff of the Viceregal household and had witnessed a scuffle that frightened her into turning back. It was discovered that she now worked as a lady's maid in Scotland, and she was hastily brought to Dublin. Emma Jones had not forgotten the handsome face of one of the men who walked away from the fight in Phoenix Park and, on identifying him, was willing to swear in court that he was Daniel Curley. Curran then heard of a spectator at the polo match who had started a conversation with a stranger, telling him that Lord Spencer had allowed him to skate on the viceregal pond the previous winter. This in itself was unimportant, but he had crossed over to the main road and spoken to one of two men who were sitting on a bench. "Wanted" advertisements for the skater were placed in the press, and not long afterward, Mallon produced a letter from a man in Carlow saying that he remembered the incident. His name was Michael Glynn, and he was the builder to whom James Carey had chatted minutes before the murders.

Battering rams used by police to destroy homes of evicted
families in Ireland, taken by Robert French, leading
photographer of Dublin's renowned Lawrence Studio.

COURTESY OF THE NATIONAL LIBRARY OF IRELAND,
LAWRENCE COLLECTION.

Gweedore's priest, Father James
MacFadden, head of the local Land
League, a ferociously commanding figure,
who was both feared and idolized
by his parishioners.

COURTESY OF HAMILTON THOMPSON,
HOLYHILL, STRABANE.

Uniformed guards protecting the County Mayo residence of landowner
Captain Boycott, whose victimization by Land League activists gave
the new weapon of social ostracism its name.

COURTESY OF THE BOARD OF TRINITY COLLEGE DUBLIN,
MICHAEL DAVITT COLLECTION.

Robert French's portrait of evicted tenants,
a father and son.

Michael Davitt, whose boyhood experience
of eviction marked him for life, and was
the driving force behind his revolutionary
campaign for tenants' rights.

By the Derry photographer James Glass, whose album of Gweedore scenes taken during the
1880-1881 Land War captured the bleakness and poverty of the region. This image of rural
dwellings and what appears to be a mounded potato crop is in Meenlaragh, near Meenacladdy.
The "New Cuts" division of land in the vicinity was a major cause of landlord/tenant strife.

Gladstone in 1877 at Hawarden Castle,
his Cheshire country estate, taking a break
from his favorite hobby of tree-felling.

PUBLIC DOMAIN, REPRODUCED COURTESY OF
THE NATIONAL LIBRARY OF WALES.

Queen Victoria, pictured here ca. 1880.

PHOTO BY POPPERFOTO.
REPRODUCED COURTESY OF GETTY IMAGES.

London's Houses of Parliament.

COURTESY OF PUMP PARK VINTAGE PHOTOGRAPHY / ALAMY STOCK PHOTO.

Mr. Forster.

John Poyntz Spencer, Liberal MP and viceroy of Ireland, known as "The Red Earl" on account of his fiery beard. Spencer's calm authority in the wake of the Murders greatly impressed the British establishment, and intensified his political power.

PHOTOGRAPH BY J. RUSSELL AND SONS, PUBLISHED IN BUSSY, *IRISH CONSPIRACIES*, 73.

Ireland's Chief Secretary, William Forster, the instigator of a brutal coercion policy that made him the Invincibles' first assassination target.

COURTESY OF THE BOARD OF TRINITY COLLEGE DUBLIN, MICHAEL DAVITT COLLECTION.

Dublin Castle, the bastion of British rule in Ireland.

COURTESY OF THE NATIONAL LIBRARY OF IRELAND, LAWRENCE COLLECTION.

PICCADILLY PORTRAIT

MRS PARNELL.

Katharine O'Shea, Parnell's mistress and
(briefly) his wife—an English woman
demonized for causing his downfall.

COURTESY OF THE NATIONAL LIBRARY OF IRELAND.

Charles Stewart Parnell,
Ireland's inspiring leader.

COURTESY OF THE LIBRARY OF CONGRESS.

Captain William O'Shea, the
Irish MP, and husband of
Katharine, who engineered
her liaison with Parnell so
that he could further
his own ambitions.

PUBLIC DOMAIN.

Kilmainham Gaol, Dublin, where Parnell was imprisoned
in October 1881, and where, seven months later,
he and O'Shea forged the secret treaty with
the government that secured his release.

COURTESY OF THE NATIONAL LIBRARY OF IRELAND, LAWRENCE COLLECTION.

Irish businessman Patrick Egan,
who masterminded the assassination
conspiracy and secured its funding.

FROM LE CARON, *TWENTY-FIVE YEARS*, 161.

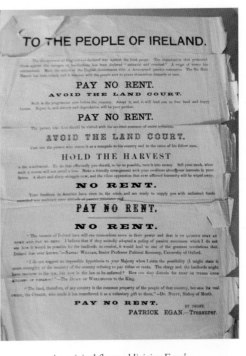

An original flyer publicizing Egan's
"No Rent Manifesto."

COURTESY OF THE NATIONAL ARCHIVES OF IRELAND [INL/BOX 9].

Patrick Ford, editor of the *Irish World*,
the New York-based journal that
almost certainly helped finance
the Phoenix Park Murders.

COURTESY OF THE BOARD OF TRINITY COLLEGE
DUBLIN, MICHAEL DAVITT COLLECTION.

Lucy and Frederick Cavendish, surrogate daughter and son of Gladstone and his wife, Catherine, who was Lucy's aunt. The political affinity of their marriage was way ahead of its time.

ROYAL HOUSEHOLD PORTRAITS.

Irish undersecretary Thomas Burke, a conscientious, kindly bureaucrat, whose behind-the-scenes power at Dublin Castle caused him to be nicknamed "the Castle Rat."

COURTESY OF THE BOARD OF TRINITY COLLEGE DUBLIN, MICHAEL DAVITT COLLECTION.

Diagram of the murder scene.

ILLUSTRATED LONDON NEWS, MAY 13, 1882.
REPRODUCED COURTESY OF
THE BRITISH LIBRARY NEWSROOM.

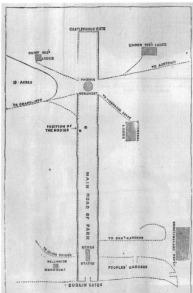

John Foley's equestrian statue of Lord Gough,
a British commander-in-chief, whose commemoration
in Phoenix Park was blown up by the IRA in July 1957.

COURTESY OF THE NATIONAL LIBRARY OF IRELAND,
LAWRENCE COLLECTION.

One of the Phoenix Park Murder witnesses, Thomas Foley, who came across the
two victims' bodies while riding his tricycle in Phoenix Park with a friend.

COURTESY OF LANMAS / ALAMY STOCK PHOTO.

The funeral of Frederick Cavendish at St. Peter's Church, Edensor ["Ensor"], the picturesque model village in Chatsworth Park. Lucy Cavendish is seen holding a wreath.

Superintendent John Mallon, whose sleuthing genius earned him the reputation as Ireland's Sherlock Holmes.

Patrick J. Tynan, the Dublin leader of the Invincibles, a delusional, would-be military hero, who relished his infamy as "Number One."

Courtroom sketches of the twenty-three Invincibles, with the informer
James Carey pictured in the witness chair.

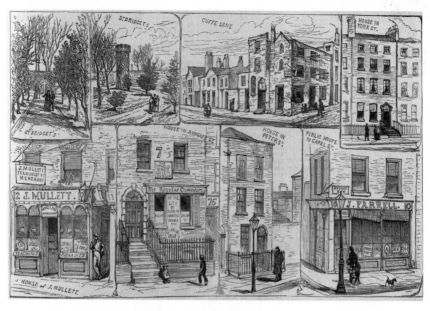

Several Dublin haunts of the conspirators, including James Mullett's public house
[bottom left], a center of radical nationalism.

ILLUSTRATED LONDON NEWS, FEBRUARY 16, 1883. COURTESY OF THE BRITISH LIBRARY NEWSROOM.

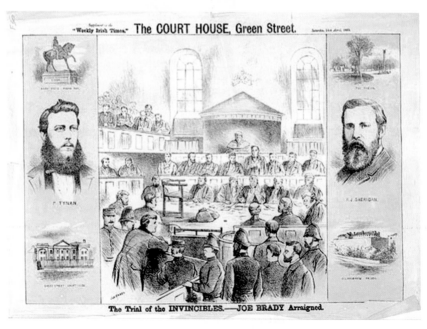

An *Irish Times* sketch of Green House Courtroom with Joe Brady in the dock.
The thumbnail portraits are of two ringleaders, left, Patrick Tynan, and right, P.J. Sheridan,
who recruited James Carey as an Invincible while disguised as a priest.

COURTESY OF THE NATIONAL LIBRARY OF IRELAND.

The Irish newspaper's portrait and sketches that unmasked James Carey to his fellow passengers on their steamship's arrival in Cape Town. [Supplement to the *Weekly Freeman*, May 5, 1883.]

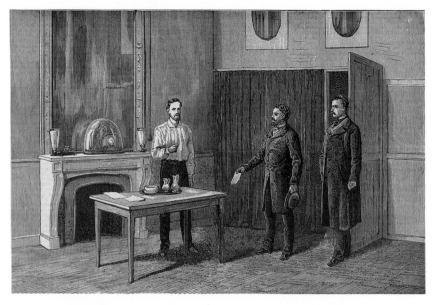

The arrest by French police of the fugitive London ringleader, Frank Byrne,
in his hotel room in Paris's rue St-Honoré.

THE *GRAPHIC*, MARCH 10 1883. REPRODUCED COURTESY OF THE BRITISH LIBRARY NEWSROOM.

Headshots of the two assailants Joe Brady and Tim Kelly, equally passionate
in their devotion to Ireland.

COURTESY OF THE NATIONAL LIBRARY OF IRELAND.

Patrick O'Donnell, assassin or
legendary Irish hero?

PUBLIC DOMAIN, REPRODUCED COURTESY OF
THE LIBRARY OF CONGRESS.

Eighteen-year-old Susan Gallagher, who posed as
O'Donnell's wife on the voyage to Cape Town.

COURTESY OF THE NATIONAL LIBRARY OF IRELAND.

The *Kinfauns Castle*, the steamship that transported the Carey family,
along with Mr. and "Mrs." O'Donnell from Southampton to Cape Town.

COURTESY OF THE NATIONAL MARITIME MUSEUM, GREENWICH, LONDON, GOULD COLLECTION.

The colonial town of Port Elizabeth, in South Africa,
where the Natal-bound streamship the *Melrose* was forced to berth.

PHOTOGRAPH BY ROBERT HARRIS, ALAMY.

O'DONNELL LEAVING THE PRISON FOR THE COURT-HOUSE

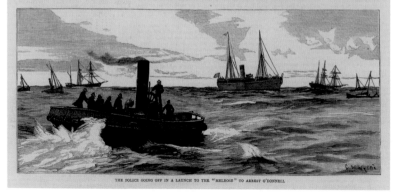

THE POLICE GOING OFF IN A LAUNCH TO THE "MELROSE" TO ARREST O'DONNELL

Top: O'Donnell leaving Port Elizabeth prison for the court; bottom: police
setting off in a launch bound for the *Melrose* to arrest O'Donnell.

THE *GRAPHIC*, SEPTEMBER 8, 1883. REPRODUCED COURTESY OF THE BRITISH LIBRARY NEWSROOM.

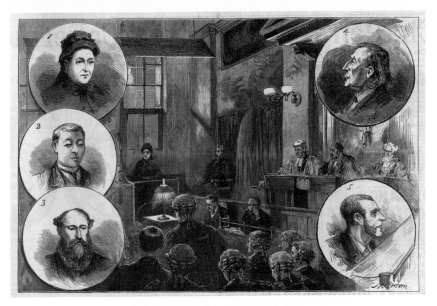

The cross-examination of Maggie Carey at O'Donnell's Old Bailey trial.
Left hand cameos, top to bottom: Maggie Carey, her son Tom, and Nathan Marks,
the Cape Town cab driver who was the only defense witness. Right hand cameos,
top: General Pryor of the American Bar, below: Patrick O'Donnell.

O'Donnell's defense lawyer, A. M. Sullivan,
the Irish MP and editor of the *Nation*.

O'Donnell's death certificate.

TWELVE

Who Is Number One?

AT HAWARDEN Castle, Gladstone was suffering from acute insomnia. This was so unusual for him, and so distressing, that he told his daughter Mary he was "totally unfitted for the Premiership." The situation worsened in London, where there was a night that he lay dreading every ponderous toll of Big Ben, not sleeping for even five minutes. His wan, anxious demeanor alarmed everyone around him. "We have had great difficulty to prevent his bolting," Harcourt told Ponsonby, but to Granville he remarked that the queen and her private secretary had "much to answer for."

Staying at Osborne, Harcourt was able to observe Victoria's reaction to what she called Gladstone's "somewhat sudden breakdown." Harcourt was struck by her chatty, relaxed manner, and felt that the Grand Old Man's indisposition had touched her. Indeed, she did appear uncharacteristically solicitous, telling Gladstone, "He must be really quiet and not occupy himself at all with affairs and not write long letters like the one he did yesterday." Harcourt, however, did not appear to realize that the cause of the queen's high spirits was almost certainly relief that Gladstone's term as prime minister was coming to an end. Gladstone's personal physician, Dr. Clark, had ordered him abroad, and although he said he would be back in Parliament in a fortnight, Victoria was determined that it should not be so. "He ought to be persuaded to take a longer rest," she told Lord Granville, "and even then the Queen greatly doubts his being able to go on lead-ing the House of Commons."

                                        *

Gladstone had decided to go to Cannes, the favorite winter resort of the English since Lord Brougham discovered it, as a small fish-ing village, in 1834. His host was to be the politician, banker, and philanthropist George Glyn, Second Baron Wolverton, a confidant and ardent supporter. On January 18, the Gladstones were met at the station by Lord Wolverton and driven up twisty roads to his Riviera property, Château Scott, an enormous, neo-Gothic villa in landscaped subtropical gardens high above the sea. To Gladstone, it acted as an instant tonic. "I am stunned by this wonderful place, and so vast a change at a moment's notice in the conditions of life." He went early to bed that night and woke eight and a half hours later. "P.M. a changed man," Mary remarked.

The following day was spent with the man Gladstone revered more than any other, the historian and moralist John Dalberg Acton. Resembling "an ecclesiastical statesman" by Titian, with a spacious forehead, stern eyes, and a magnificent chest-length beard, Lord Acton was Gladstone's main reason for coming to Cannes. Mary Gladstone, who had established an intellectual intimacy of her own with Acton, understood better than anyone the bond between him and her father. "In three things they believed with all their strength: liberty, truth and the moral law." Unlike most Italian citizens, Acton was in favor of national independence, and he fiercely defended liberty against absolutism in church and state (coining the aphorism "power tends to corrupt and absolute power corrupts absolutely"). The Victorian poet Matthew Arnold once said, "Gladstone influences all around him but Acton. It is Acton who influences Gladstone." Mary argued, however, that this was not the case: "In truth, they acted and reacted on one another."

Five years earlier, Gladstone had poured out his soul in a speech about liberty, but now it was a belief that parliamentary pressure had begun to erode; Acton would help to consolidate it.

Gladstone found himself reinvigorated by the force of Acton's conversation, his command of metaphysics, his range of knowledge, and above all, his uncompromising moralism. "We have no thread through the enormous intricacy of politics," Acton had written, "except the idea of progress towards more perfect freedom and the divine right of free men."

Every day they talked while taking long walks together. A short distance away were the woods of the Maure, their soft paths covered with reddish sand of powdered *greiss*; there was a footpath leading to the hermitage of St-Cassien, and one to the village of La Napoule at the foot of the Esterel mountains, whose peaks and porphyritic rocks resembled Gothic ruins. One day they drove over the Antibes peninsula and on another took a steamboat to the island of St-Marguerite. From the little pier they walked to Fort Monterey, where the so-called Man in the Iron Mask had been imprisoned, and from its battlements had a clear view of the rugged Esterel mountains and distant snowy peaks of the Alpes Maritimes. Below, bathed in sunshine and backed by pine forests and hazy olive groves, Cannes formed a white semicircle around the bay. These were blissful days, and in the evenings, Gladstone read steadily—Homer, Dante, Shakespeare—or played whist with his hosts. "We fell in with the foreign hours, the snack early, dejeuner at noon, dinner at seven, break-up at ten."

The idea of returning in a fortnight was out of the question, and Lord Granville, Acton's stepfather, undertook to convey this to the queen: "Dr. Clark thinks it possible that Mr. Gladstone may return quite fit for work at the time proposed, but believes it to be expedient and desirable that he should remain till after Easter. . . . In my opinion he would do much better for a long rest."

*

Staying in a nearby hotel was Superintendent Mallon's journalist friend Frederick Bussy, who wrote for a London news agency and had traveled with Gladstone to the South of France. Soon afterward, Bussy received a telegram from Frank Byrne, who occasionally worked as a reporter, contributing articles to the agency. "Am coming to Cannes to watch Gladstone, as you have been doing." A letter from the office shortly followed to explain that Byrne would be taking over, as he needed to be in a temperate climate for health reasons. Bussy set off for London and stopped on his way in Paris, where he was met at the Gare de Lyon by Byrne and a man he introduced as a close friend—a "Mr. Tisdale." This was Patrick Tynan.

They all dined together and ended the evening at 8 rue de Bac, where two Paris-based Irish revolutionaries kept an open house for people of "our way of thinking." Patrick Casey was a former gunrunner, and his brother, Joseph, was a hard-drinking, voluble extremist who frequently entertained visiting journalists in Reynold's Irish American bar on the rue Royale. They were joined by twenty-five-year-old Eugene Davis, who, at Egan's request, had edited an underground Parisian version of *United Ireland*. Byrne then followed in Bussy's wake to Nice, checking into a hotel Bussy had recommended as "the most decent place near Lord Wolverton's home, Château Scott."

*

Five more Invincibles had joined their comrades in Kilmainham, including the two drivers, Skin-the-Goat (James Fitzharris) and Michael Kavanagh—the latter having been seen at the time of the Field attack by a servant girl who agreed to testify against him. Soon after Fitzharris was arrested, Mallon led him into the exercise yard where Kavanagh was walking, and while talking in a conspiratorial manner, took out a notepad and pretended to be interviewing him. This baffled Fitzharris but had the desired effect on Kavanagh, who interpreted it as, "Skin giving Mallon information which would hang [me] and the rest." An hour later, in Kavanagh's cell, Mallon declared that all the detainees had volunteered to give queen's evidence—a plea deal—to save their lives.

There was some truth in the deception, as one by one, the Invincibles were beginning to crack. Before a medical examination of Kavanagh and James Carey's brother Peter in the prison surgery, Mallon had replaced an oak panel with a ventilation grill and eavesdropped on their conversation. He was able to confirm that James had been in the park that evening, and he learned the names of four other members of the gang, so that when Kavanagh lied during the subsequent interrogation, Mallon was able to challenge him. "Sure, Mr. Mallon, there's nothing at all you don't know," said the defeated Kavanagh, who was then taken out of prison, seated in a cab beside the detective, and made to reenact his whole escape route. "This quickened his memory," wrote Mallon, "and he was able to clear up matters that were still somewhat obscure to me."

On February 10, in the tightly packed little courthouse adjoining Kilmainham, when the order "Bring up Michael Kavanagh" was heard, the faces in the dock turned livid with fright. Courtenay Boyle sent Henry Ponsonby more details.

The prisoners looked wonderfully cowed, Brady especially. . . . Skin-the-Goat, a most repulsive villain, also looked bold. Young Kelly the boy of nineteen or thereabouts tried to look defiant and occasionally tried to sneer, but it was a feeble effort, and there was a hectic spot on each pale cheek. The effect of this will be great and the flow of evidence and information not only in this but in other cases will be stimulated. . . . The evidence was firm and was very credible.

Turning himself away from his fellow conspirators, the pale young witness named Brady and Kelly as his two passengers in Phoenix Park and claimed that there were two others that he did not know. "One of them is there," he said, pointing to Patrick Delaney, sitting in the front row. After Kavanagh recounted how Brady had given him a pound on May 6 and another two pounds the following day and had engaged him for the Field attack in November, Brady uttered a growl of fury and then buried his face in his hands.

Looking like a battered pugilist, with half-closed eyes and a flattened nose, Skin-the-Goat scowled and shouted, "You scorpion!" and "You're a liar!" to Kavanagh, the rival jarvey he already despised. When it was Skin's turn to testify, he singled out James Carey as the passenger he had driven toward the group of waiting men and as the one who had raised a white handkerchief to instigate the murder. To Mallon, this was the clinching moment of the whole trial.

*

In his solitary quarters in Kilmainham, Carey heard the tread of several pairs of feet in the corridor. The footsteps stopped outside the adjoining cell, and with a jangling of keys, the door was opened. The passage was in semidarkness, but by peering through the chink, Carey could make out the shadowy forms of three men. One was Superintendent Mallon, who called for "a small table, a chair, some pens, ink and foolscap paper," clearly intending to transcribe an interview.

Carey slept little that night, brooding about Kavanagh's damning evidence and the identity of the "peacher" next door. In the morning, the warder arrived—a detective planted by Mallon to win the prisoner's confidence—who had hinted to Carey that he sympathized with his advanced nationalism and had conveyed notes to and from Carey's wife, Maggie, recovering from the birth of their seventh child. Now, however, the man would reveal nothing, murmuring only before locking the door, "There's black business going on."

Later that evening, there was a repetition of the previous visit, with Mallon accompanied this time by a tall, thin man with a long white beard: George Bolton, the Crown solicitor. The warder was more confiding the next day and hesitantly whispered a name: "Daniel Curley."

Carey flinched. "Tell Mr. Mallon I want to see him," he said flatly. The ruse had worked: Mallon had staged a convincing little tableau in a cell that had been empty all along.

The idea of turning informer was as repellent to James Carey as it was to most Irishmen. After the murder of one of Mallon's informers (John Kenny, the man the superintendent had been due to meet in the park on May 6), Carey was heard to say, "It is not so much the loss of life as the stain and degradation on your memory, and then think of the infamous name which would be attached to your children and their posterity. It is too horrible to think of." But he loved his wife and family too much to allow himself to be hanged; he would volunteer evidence to save his life, he decided, but give only facts of which Mallon was already aware, adding nothing that would lead to a new arrest.

"He commenced to tell me all about the Invincibles and their meetings and so on. . . . ," wrote Mallon.

So I said to him sharply, "Carey all this you are telling me is ancient history. . . . Your statement is worth nothing." And I tore it up before him and flung the pieces into the fireplace in his presence.

That was on Wednesday May 14 and on the Thursday he was placed in the dock with the others, who would have strangled him if they had known that only twelve hours before he had made even a part confession. He was in a tremendous state of excitement, his features working, and his face grey and anxious. He besought me at the close of the proceedings to see him again.

Mallon despised Carey—"about as bad a lot, in most ways, as ever breathed the breath of Heaven"—deploring his hypocrisy in attending Mass with his family the Sunday after the murders and profaning the Holy Sacrament. And yet, he knew that Carey was the only conspirator articulate enough to speak persuasively in court—a man "who could in any degree be considered a platform political spouter."

The other Invincibles were laborers and artisans—carpenters, brick-layers, shoemakers, tailors, van drivers. They were small fry, whereas Carey had achieved new significance by getting himself elected as a town councilor for Dublin's Trinity Ward, supported by its burgess, William O'Brien, who had published a letter in his favor. To John Dillon's wife, Elizabeth, Carey was "the only well dressed & fairly educated man amongst the prisoners—a highly respectable master mason—highly prosperous and made Town Councillor," while *United Ireland* hailed Carey's victory over his rival candidate—a wealthy, esteemed Liberal, whom he defeated by 124 votes to 93—as an "extraordinary triumph . . . the highest water-mark of democracy yet touched in Ireland." This experience, Mallon realized, had given Carey "a very useful kind of platform courage for such an occasion as this"; Carey knew—and must be made to reveal—the identities of the instigators of the conspiracy, and Mallon was determined to break him. "See here, Carey," he said. "If you want to make a statement I am willing to take it from you. But I warn you that I have known the Fenian organisations longer than you, and perhaps better than you, although I am not a member of either, and it is no good you trying to mislead me." Carey did then open up, recounting the formation of the Invincibles, supplying names, and giving a minutely detailed account of the Park murders. But would his evidence be accepted?

*

Spencer wrote urgently to Harcourt to help him come to a decision about whether to allow Carey to "turn approver"—that is, strike a plea bargain—or to inflict the punishment he deserved.

> James Carey the Town Councilor has offered to make a clean breast of his knowledge of the conspiracy & Phoenix Park Murders. . . . He has said that Kavanagh's evidence is quite true, that he Carey was present at the Murders etc. . . . I confess that I hesitate before saving his life.

His criminality is as great nay even greater in some degree than the man who slaughtered the murdered men. He led the attack, superintended it & as he seems to be the leader of the gang, he deserves, if convicted, to hang if any man ever did. On the other hand he probably can tell us more of the conspiracy than any one we yet have in custody. He will most probably be able to show who are at the head of it. It is of the utmost importance that we should get at the whole history.

Spencer went on to say that although Carey's brother Peter had also turned informer and given the same account of the murder, his version had come from an eyewitness, and he would not be able to identify the prime movers. They had a perfect case against James Carey, but he wanted Harcourt's view on whether the general public might be enraged if the key perpetrator of the Phoenix Park murders escaped punishment. The two options were clear: a hanging would elevate Carey to martyr status among the Fenian underworld, whereas a betrayal of his comrades would ensure that "he & his family will be damned & execrated for all time."

Harcourt responded immediately with a ciphered telegram telling Spencer that he and Cavendish's replacement, George Trevelyan, both agreed that Carey should be allowed to turn queen's evidence. A follow-up letter explained why:

The great importance of getting a man in his position to avow publicly his own villainy in the face of the world and betray those he has seduced will have so great an effect in sowing alarm and distrust throughout the whole conspiracy, in which no man will feel safe hereafter, that it is worth almost any sacrifice to obtain it. The existence of informers is the best method of intimidation we possess against these villains. This is a chance not to be lost.

*

On Saturday, February 17, in a back room of the Kilmainham court-house, Mallon was alone with his star witness. Carey had dressed that day with considerable care: he wore a yellowish tweed suit, with matching yellow cloth on the uppers of his boots and a gold watch-chain looping from his pocket; his wavy hair was middle-parted and slicked down, his beard neatly trimmed. Beneath the dapper appearance, however, he was petrified, shaking so violently that he could barely walk. Mallon gave him a few spoonfuls of brandy to steady him, but it was not enough; he drank some more and as the spirit took effect said, "I am ready now." He had almost to be pushed through the door into the court, and as he walked past the waiting prisoners, Tim Kelly, hissing an expletive, struck the front rail with his fist, while Joe Brady lunged forward as if to grab him by the throat. But Carey addressed only Dan Curley, his widely reported remark mystifying everyone except Mallon: "I was before ye's after all, Dan!" Once seated at the table, he gradually gathered courage, never hesitating before answering questions in a quiet, measured voice. Courtenay Boyle recounted what he had observed for Ponsonby to tell the queen.

> His evidence was given with great coolness and determination. When he talked about "removing"—with a lift of his eyebrows—Mr. Forster and Mr. Burke, when he described the scene as he saw it and as Brady told him of it . . . when he described the notice sent to the papers, and when he identified his own brother, his sangfroid and unconcern were the most disgusting things I ever saw. He was perfectly self-possessed, repudiated being an informer as he had never had anyone arrested, and told his vile story as I should recount a day's ride. Brady was driven out of his boldness and bravado and hung his head in sullen gloom. Only the young ruffian Kelly kept up any pretense of audacity and he was really feeble. It was a wonderful scene.

*

"Evidence tomorrow will make men concerned fly," Spencer had warned, and Lord Hartington was not alone in wondering why Carey had appeared in court before "the more important scoundrels" had been captured. The government's prize informer had given no hint of Patrick Egan's involvement nor been able to identify the man who was known as "Number One," but he had implicated all the other ringleaders, whose extradition was urgently called for. Patrick Sheridan was known to be reachable through the Press Club in New York, although Spencer told Harcourt that this would require the cooperation of the Foreign Office, as well as depositions to support a charge of accessory before the fact to murder. "Will you do all you can to get [John] Walsh & [Captain John] McCafferty," he cabled, adding, "I hope every exertion is being made to arrest Frank Byrne and wife in France and prevent escape to America." Steps had been taken to secure Byrne long before Carey's appearance, Spencer claimed, "but the stupidity of the police spoilt our game."

*

It was at the end of January, when Mallon learned from Carey of Frank Byrne's acquisition of the knives, that the Byrnes' house in Peckham Rye, London, was put under police surveillance. Byrne himself was absent—"There is no doubt he is in Paris, not here," Edward Jenkinson reported—but the constable on duty spotted a middle-aged woman emerging from a cab and heard her speak to the maid in an Irish accent. Having traced the driver, the police questioned him and learned that the woman had arrived at Euston Station on the Holyhead boat train; Mallon identified her from the description as Frank Byrne's sister. She had brought letters from Dublin and £200 in cash "to enable the wanted parties to get out of the country," and it was when she was delivering the package to Tynan's wife, Polly, who lived several doors away in Avondale Road, that she had been observed. The Home Office believed that Mrs. Tynan had been entrusted to take the money to Paris and discovered that she would be getting the first train in the morning to meet her husband at the Gare du Nord. Scotland Yard men were responsible for following her—and at this point, things went badly wrong. "Whether she had left before the watch began or whether she is still there, I am powerless to say," reported an exasperated Robert Anderson. "The police [are] utterly unfit for work of this kind."

But if Polly Tynan had failed to provide the police with a route to Byrne, a new lead had suddenly emerged. On February 18—the day after Carey gave evidence—Harcourt cabled Spencer:

> I will tell you a very extraordinary thing. Herbert Gladstone came in here just now saying that [Irish MPs] Justin McCarthy and [John] Barry had been to him in great terror assuring him that F. Byrne . . . went to Cannes a fortnight ago on the grounds of ill-health, and imploring Herbert to take precautions for his father's life against their own secretary. . . . Unfortunately Byrne left Cannes when we traced him on Tuesday last. We are trying to find him in Paris but I am sorry to say we have not yet got him.

They had, however, arrested two women at 4 Gothic Villas, Avondale Road, both defiantly answering to the name of Mrs. Frank Byrne. (When the police placed them side by side and said, "Please step forward, Mrs. Byrne," the elder of the two did so.) Byrne's sister was discharged, and his wife, Mary Ann, was arrested and dispatched to Dublin on February 19, where she spent the night at King Street police station. In the morning, she was driven to Kilmainham Gaol and taken into a small room, where a prison official entered with a brawny man dressed in a light tweed suit. "He came in sideways, so to speak, and did not seem to look at me very much." But Carey refused to name Mrs. Byrne, even though he had promised John Curran that he would be able to identify her. "You must remember that I shall not always be here, but expect to go out once more a free man," he told the magistrate. "So I had to do something to soften the people outside, who feel resentment against me, and who are sore at my having given evidence."

*

Queen Victoria had written to Spencer saying how "most painfully interested" she was in the Dublin examinations.

> They are quite thrilling. Will the *not* finding of the knives (which she fears is likely) cause any difficulty in condemning these monsters? She *trusts not*. What has struck & shocked her, she must say, is the evidence of that gentleman who described (in May) having seen people wrestling—but no more—proving *now* that he actually *saw all & yet never gave the details* before. Surely it is very wrong that he did *not* do so sooner.

A few days later, she impatiently quizzed Harcourt, "Is there any further news? The Queen sees that Mrs. Byrne (who must be a worthy mate of such a Husband), was taken on Sunday."

Both men had reported at length their reasons for accepting Carey's evidence, and Victoria acknowledged that they were right, although she wanted him punished nevertheless. "She was anxious he should not get off altogether," Harcourt told Spencer, "but I explained to her that was impossible." He had been quick to draw the queen's attention to the complicity in the Phoenix Park murders of key Land League figures named by Carey, gloating that it would "shut the mouths" of critics of his coercion measures. "The public will at last know what Sir William has long been aware of and has over and over again declared in Parliament during the last two years, viz: that the Land-League, Fenianism and the Assassination Societies, though distinct in name and profession, are in reality one and the same concern." Victoria agreed that the connection was "*appalling*," but said that at least the eyes of many Irish sympathizers would now have been opened. "Will not Mr. Gladstone be dreadfully shaken by all these disclosures, as he never would believe in any connection between the Land League and the Fenians?" she asked Harcourt, noting in her journal: "Sir William believes Ireland could not be governed for the next 20 years without the Crimes Act. Mr. Gladstone & others were under a complete delusion. The feeling of the Irish against England, has never been more bitter."

*

The strain of the daily court disclosures was affecting Lucy Cavendish badly. She had inherited a tendency for depression from her father, who had killed himself in 1876, and she admitted, "It is my nature too to see everything on the dark side." She had written to the Dublin doctor who assisted on her husband's postmortem requesting more information about the fatal wounds and was obsessing over tiny details—wondering whether, for instance, it was a stick or an umbrella that her husband had taken with him. She had thought that her sorrow was so constantly present that sensational new facts could not affect her, but she had found Carey's starkly graphic evidence almost too painful to bear.

She and the duke were staying at Holker Hall so as to be surrounded by family during the trials, but as Edward Cavendish's wife, Emma, wrote to Hartington, it had been a "terrible week":

> I went down earlyish this morning to see the papers in case there was anything I thought would be particularly trying to Lucy and found Lou [Cavendish's sister, Louisa] already down doing the same . . . so we read the papers together then your father took them to read in his room. . . . [Lucy] has had great floods of grief but has been very calm generally. Your father seems well, Lou says he reads everything but of course he never alludes to it.

Alice Burke, on the other hand, now living in London with her other brother, had been strangely galvanized by the press coverage. When a letter arrived from Lucy, she wrote back immediately:

My dear Lady Frederick,

I was so glad to hear from you. I had been thinking so much of you all these dreadful days wondering how you were bearing up—longing to say some words of heartfelt thanks to you for the help given by him you have lost to my darling. Do you know that Friday morning when they lay in wait for him he & I walked into Dublin together but did not go by the road. If only. I know it is wrong to say it—God knows what is best—but it is hard to stifle the regret that the awful deed was not done then. Your husband would be alive, he & I would not be parted.

You ask about my health. Considering how ill I was only a month ago, my strength is wonderful. I think the very excitement of daily expectation helped to keep me up—but the strain is terrific, is it not? If only I could share your hope that good will come in the end out of all this evil & blood. To me the future of my poor country seems so dark, so full of gloom—it is as if the minds of the people were perverted & they no longer could distinguish right from wrong. God grant that light may come at last.

Affectionately yours,
Alice Burke

In fact, the ideological significance of Cavendish's death was no longer redemptive for Lucy, who was now settling for a humbler consolation. She had learned from the evidence that Cavendish could have run off at the moment that Burke was attacked but had deprived himself of the chance by striking out at Brady. "How content I was with the words 'In attempting to save the life of his friend, sacrificing his own,'" Lucy told Spencer, echoing this to Hartington. "It makes his death noble, as well as so innocent," she said.

She was writing to her brother-in-law to allay his fear about her well-being, reiterating what she had said to others: "There can be no reopening of a wound that has never closed." Her letter is as admirably stoical as always—except for one telling line: "I can't help hoping you will get Mr. Gladstone home." Lucy craved the company of both Gladstones—missing the motherly support of Catherine, who had written from Cannes, "Oh, I have yearned to be at your side during this fresh revelation"; and above all, the strength she needed to draw from her uncle's indomitable faith. "I hope Mr. Gladstone will come back," she repeated plaintively to Spencer.

*

"Mr. G's plans are still undecided," Edward Hamilton wrote in his journal on February 23. "But there seems to be a growing consensus of opinion that he is hardly justified in remaining abroad much longer. He is so happy with his Homer & his theology that he seems averse to turning his head homewards to resume fighting in the H of C." Catherine and Mary, "bored to death," had begun to despair. "The P.M. is only too content to sit still in this spot as long as they can get on without him," Mary told a friend. "It is too funny the way people imagine he is panting to return and that it is we who are restraining him by force. It is exactly the contrary." In an effort to entertain Gladstone's women, Lord Acton had arranged a trip to the tumbledown perfume-making town of Grasse, where the winter air was heady with the scent of orange and lemon blossom; they ate luncheon in an olive grove and visited the medieval village of Gourdon in the foothills of the Alpes Maritimes. Now, however, the weather had broken; an expedition in a hired steamer in torrential rain had been a miserable failure, and their days were further darkened by anxiety about Lucy. "Everybody's minds and thoughts are with her and for her," remarked Mary. "Carey's evidence is making people's hair stand on end."

Gladstone had laid aside *The Iliad* to read "the long and harrowing particulars" of Saturday's evidence, answering Spencer's letter about his dilemma in accepting Carey by comparing it to the decision he had been forced to make about Parnell's release. "There could not be any doubt (in our view) as to the right thing, but it was not quite pleasant to do." To Lord Granville, he added:

> About Carey, the spectacle is indeed [a] loathsome one, but I cannot doubt that the Irish Government are distinctly *right*. In accepting an approver, you do not incite him to do what is in itself wrong: only his own bad mind can make it wrong to him. The Government looks for the truth—approvers are I suppose for the most part base, but I do not see how you could act on a distinction of degree between them. Still one would have heard the hiss from the dock with sympathy.

"In a pouring Scotch rain," Gladstone and Acton went on an eight-mile walk, hardly stopping to rest, except occasionally to take in the view. They spoke mostly about Ireland, both certain of the necessity of Home Rule and believing that the crimes and bloodshed were the direct outcome of injustice and oppression. When Gladstone met the radical politician Georges Clemenceau at Château Scott, he had talked optimistically about the country's future, saying, "We have disestablished the Church, relieved the tenant class of many grievances, we are now trying to produce a state of things which will make the humblest Irishman realize that he is a governing agency, and that the Government is to be carried on for him, and by him."

To Acton, though, he was convincing himself of a successful pacification of Ireland so that he could soon retire "without detriment to anybody." Gladstone's ill health was no longer an excuse for further absence: his sleep was as good as it could get; he had energetically felled a tree on the site of an Englishman's villa and had completed the marathon walk. "Part of it was much more precipitous than what he shrank from a fortnight ago," Acton told Granville, who had heard from Gladstone himself of his fine physical shape. "It has got better and better as I have stayed on, and is now, I think, on a higher level than for a long time past." Parliament had just resumed, and while Catherine and Mary were "sitting tight for a messenger with accounts of the opening," the prime minister had loftier things on his mind: "There is a noise at Westminster & I hear it not!"

*

The "noise" had been made by William Forster, who had been emboldened by Carey's disclosures to discredit Parnell. "It is not that he himself directly planned or perpetrated outrages or murders; but that he either connived at them or when warned . . ."—"It is a lie," Parnell cried out—but Forster went on: "Those miserable wretches who planned the murders in Dublin, they took not, indeed, the letter of the Hon. Member's advice, but what seemed to them its spirit." When he sat down, everyone expected Parnell to spring up and repel the charges, but he calmly kept his seat; only on his return home to Eltham did he show what Katharine called "a fierce joy." This attack had given him exactly what he needed to restore his ascendancy—a total repudiation of charges made by the advanced nationalists that he had pandered to the English government. Before he left for the House the next morning, Parnell told Katharine that he would not deign to defend himself, but his party insisted that he must. "We had to force him," said Justin McCarthy.

On February 23, with every seat in the House filled and a palpable charge of expectancy in the air, Parnell impassively waited to be summoned by the Speaker to resume the debate. He could not have denied many of Forster's statements, and he did not intend to; there would be no explanation or apology, only a contemptuous dismissal of the right to be judged by a discredited English politician. He said that he held himself responsible to his countrymen alone and compared Forster's revelation of cabinet secrets relating to the Kilmainham Treaty to the treachery of James Carey. "He has not even the pretext of that remarkable informer whose proceeds we have lately heard of. He had not even the pretext of that miserable man that he was attempting to save his own life." Mercilessly persisting, Parnell poured scorn on Forster's repudiation by his own party, his imprisonment of political opponents, and the ignominious failure of his Irish administration—the defeated policy of despotism and rage that had bred the Invincibles who sought his life and that was directly responsible for the present condition of the country.

> Call him back to his post! Send him to help Lord Spencer in his congenial work of the gallows in Ireland! Send him to look after the Secret Inquisitions of Dublin Castle! Send him to superintend the payment of blood money! Send him to distribute the taxes which an unfortunate and starving peasantry have to pay for crimes not committed by them! . . . Push forward the task of misgoverning Ireland! For my part I am confident as to the future of Ireland. . . . I believe that our people will survive the present oppression as we have survived many and worse ones.

To Michel Davitt, it was the greatest and most dignified speech ever made by an Irishman in an English Parliament—splendidly defiant in its assertion of their country's independence. "It struck a note which reverberated through every Irish nationalist heart everywhere; a note of Irish self-reliance; a key-note of nationhood . . . which set the Irish frantic with enthusiasm from one side of the world to the other."

*

Aware of the presence of detectives outside his hotel on the rue St-Honoré, Frank Byrne had attempted to throw them off the scent by taking a cab and zigzagging around Paris. When he returned several hours later, it was to leave his rooms and move into an apartment farther along the street, where Patrick Tynan was staying. Byrne had also been tracked down by reporters and agreed to give a couple of interviews; asked by the *Freeman's Journal* about the object of his visit to France, he replied, "I have been for some time suffering from congestion of the lungs, and was recommended by my medical attendant to go to the south of Europe."

After Carey's court appearance, Byrne said, he had judged it necessary to come to Paris in order to acquire the latest information from England, and his wife had joined him; they were about to return to London when he learned through a friend that he would be arrested on arrival. Carey's evidence, he vowed, contained not one word of truth: Byrne had never belonged to any secret Irish organization, and it was a gross falsehood to have suggested that Mary Ann had delivered arms to Dublin; her health was extremely delicate, and during the early part of the previous year, she had been confined to their house in Peckham.

The London *Daily News* was expecting to interview both Mr. and Mrs. Byrne at their new quarters on the rue St-Honoré, but when Frank Byrne came forward to receive its reporter and introduce a second person in the room, it was a man—a Mr. "Lisdale" [sic] (Tynan). Speaking in a low tone, Byrne said that his wife was too ill and tired to participate, suffering from great nervous tension as a result of her arrest. "There she is," he whispered, pointing to what the reporter had thought was a bundle of clothing on a low armchair. Looking more closely, he saw the outline of a human form, covered with a mantle and white knitted shawl. "We had talked for perhaps an hour when the coiled up lady moved and, throwing off the shawl, rubbed her eyes, rose a little and gazed round." Flushed as if with fever, it was the face of a woman with consumption; the hand she held out was skeletal, and the figure she revealed as she raised herself up was also emaciated.

"Does she look like a conspiring woman?"

"Certainly not like one who could take 4,000 rounds of ammunition and knives into Carey's office . . ."

Byrne came across as a quiet, affable man; he was smartly dressed, well-educated, and there was a touch of good-natured humour in his response to questions.

"On what terms were you with Carey?"

"No terms whatever. Since 1868 or 1869 I never had any political relations with him. My relations were entirely social. I saw him about three or four times."

"How did he impress you?"

"We were both young then, and youth is not the time at which to gauge the moral qualities of a man; but I thought him an earnest patriot and a good sort of person. . . . He is evidently fond of money, has gone on making it, and has clearly set his heart on getting rich . . ."

"Who was, do you think, 'Number One'?"

Mr. Byrne had not the least idea. The notion had flashed across his mind that he was a myth of Carey's creation.

*

"*Who* is N° 1?" Queen Victoria was also demanding to know. Spencer told her that he was "supposed with good reason to be an American Irish soldier of fortune who was suspected of planning the abortive Fenian raid on Chester Castle" (Captain John McCafferty). The London *Times*, however, had just published a description of another Irish American contender.

During the last year and a half he was in the habit of visiting Dublin at frequent intervals. He always signed himself "No 1" and was designated by the members of the organization "General." This man had apparently unlimited money at his disposal, and an inquiry addressed by a large business establishment in Dublin, with which he had some financial transactions, to a large banking firm in Paris, which he gave as a reference, was replied to in the following manner: "The gentleman in question has seemingly unlimited means, derived from large drafts in his favour from America. 'General' is a man about 50 years of age, five feet ten and a half inches in height, full face, clean shaved, except a long, fair moustache which is inclined to be reddish. He has a military bearing and is slightly lame from the effect of a wound he received during the Franco-Prussian war. . . . His last appearance in

Dublin was about two months ago, and since then all trace has been lost of him. The police . . . are diligently endeavouring to get on his track. . . . They are confident of obtaining sufficient information to trace his whereabouts on the Continent, or in America, where they believe him to be."

Clearly, this was Mallon's "filibuster," General McAdaras, who, moving between Paris and Dublin, was still being closely watched. Suddenly, however, he had ceased to be of interest to Her Majesty's Government.

✻

In Dublin, Mallon had just identified Patrick Tynan. An album of photographs found by London police in Frank Byrne's house included a small, oval sepia portrait of a man sporting a heavy, spade-shaped beard, his hair forming an odd little topknot. Believing it to be Byrne, Edward Jenkinson sent for Mallon, who showed the picture to James Mullett and Patrick Delaney: Mullett recognized the visitor who had turned up with Carey in Terenure and "used very serious threats"; Delaney said that he was "one of the head men" and that he often stayed at Jury's Hotel. Mrs. Jury was able to name him. He was a Mr. Tynan, representative of a London stationery line, who took show rooms at their hotel. He had last been there about three months earlier. In a "most secret" Home Office memorandum dated February 21, Sir Robert Anderson released the news:

> The photograph is the likeness of Tynan who is "No I" if my infor-
> mation be correct. His name never has come up before. He is a very
> intimate friend of Byrne's. He served with him in the Franco-German
> war, and has lately been his neighbor at Peckham. He visited Dublin last
> year. I can learn very little about him, but I conjecture he is a Protestant.
> As soon as the arrests were made in Dublin, he bolted, and has not
> been heard of since by my Inspectors until now; but now they hear it

whispered that he is in Paris with Byrne. . . . I have great confidence in
the information I give and I have no doubt Tynan is No I.

When Carey saw the picture he too confirmed that it was the
man he knew as "Number One," and only Mallon remained unconvinced: Tynan, "a needy and seedy commercial traveller," did not
have the sophistication to have masterminded the conspiracy. "He
was regarded by myself and my colleagues as a very 'bumptious' sort
of fellow talking very big, and frequenting the grill-room at Jury's
Hotel. . . . He was never known to us as one of the 'dangerous men.'"

*

The real Number One was en route to New York, where he arrived in
early March. "Mr. Egan's flight to America is very significant," Spencer told Queen Victoria. "There was not enough evidence against him
to issue a warrant for his arrest, but the police on purpose watched
him somewhat ostentatiously. He pretended he was kept at home long
after he had left, butchers & tradesmen being told from the house in
the hearing of the police that he would see them at a particular hour
while all the time he had left."

Egan had been under surveillance since the beginning of February;
the window blinds of his house were kept down, and he was said to
be ill, but within twenty minutes of receiving a tip-off that Carey
was turning queen's evidence, he had made his escape. In Henri Le
Caron's account, Egan had been in his office when he heard the news
and rushed to his house to pack a satchel of documents and burn a
number of others. "Some of them appertaining to the IRB during his
connection with the Brotherhood, also some letters of James Carey.
He destroyed all letters tending to incriminate him." A Scottish business acquaintance met Egan with a suitcase and traveling rug at Dublin's northern terminus minutes before a train left for Belfast. Finding
there was no boat leaving that night, Egan checked into a hotel and
in the morning purchased a return ticket to Leeds, in the north of

England. In case he was being watched, he traveled as far as Manchester, where he purchased another ticket, to Hull. From the Hull docks, he took the steamer to Rotterdam, "and thus got out of the country."

In fact, Carey had gone out of his way to safeguard Egan—both in court and during pretrial interrogations. "He volunteered no definite information as to the source of the money," Mallon recalled. "So I put the question to him bluntly. . . . And at last he gave me the name of a leading member [of] the organization, a telegram from whom I had intercepted almost immediately after the murder. I never managed to get sufficient evidence to connect him with the conspiracy." Mallon does not identify the man in question but calls him a teetotaler and a close friend of Mullett (both of which Egan was). It was later alleged by a colleague investigating the Invincibles executive that Mallon had actually stopped Carey from proving that Egan had financed the Invincibles and concealed evidence of checks he had issued. William Joyce, a district officer, was convinced that Egan was not only the controlling force behind the conspiracy; he was also one of Mallon's key sources. Joyce hinted that it was Mallon who had helped Egan to get away in time—a belief shared by the detective's biographer Donal McCracken. "He certainly gave Egan the nod."

The two were on first-name terms, and although Mallon had long known of Egan's involvement in the murder conspiracy, he could not help admiring the way he had overcome his lowly background. More to the point, Mallon owed Egan his life. At a Prince's Street public house gathering of Invincibles, Joe Brady had remarked that it was "all up with [Mallon]," and there was only one thing to be done. Egan would have none of it. "I believe I would have been assassinated only for No I," Mallon recounted in a newspaper memoir, and when he repeated the story on another occasion, he named his savior as Egan.

It was Parnell, however, who provided the most likely explanation of what might have caused Mallon's switch of loyalty. In a House of Commons speech late that summer, he declared:

Now, it was perfectly well known that neither Mr. Jenkinson nor any other member of the Executive Government had anything in the world to do with the discovery of the Invincibles; but that, in fact, the proceedings of that Organization were brought to light by a detective officer named Mallow [*sic*], an Irish police officer, whose name was studiously kept in the background in order that of Mr. Jenkinson might be put in the front. Mr. Jenkinson, Lord Spencer and the right hon. Gentleman the Chief Secretary [Trevelyan] himself, were pushed to the front, and got all the credit for an achievement with which they had nothing whatever to do.

If Mallon was indeed the castle mole responsible for Egan's flight, then the British establishment had only itself to blame.

*

In Cannes, Gladstone had far outstayed his welcome; Lady Wolverton was said to be exhausted, and even Lord Acton had become irritated by his idol's serene neglect of his duties. Telling Lord Granville how deeply Gladstone had plunged into studies far removed from politics, he went on: "I contemplate with alarm the figure he will present when you let him go. The world will exchange a man of genius and power for a tiresome homilist quite unable to see the weakness of his own traditional argument, and not very apt to understand the force of the adversary's case." The response of a bright seven-year-old who met Gladstone at this time was impeccable: told by her mother, Lady Queensberry, that the elderly gentleman was the head of the government, she asked, "But how can he govern England, if he is drinking tea here with me?"

Gladstone had made up his mind to remain in Cannes until Easter, when he received Granville's "immediate summons" to return. Catherine and Mary were delighted, but it was with a heavy heart that Gladstone left the Riviera, exchanging sunshine, exotic surroundings, and splendid views for foggy Paris, where the ambassador had invited them to stay. By March 2, feeling "like a boy going back to school," he returned to Downing Street.

✻

By now, French detectives had arrested Frank Byrne. The British had encountered nothing but surly resistance and red tape when attempting to track him down, so the French government had agreed to act. Showing no surprise, Byrne allowed himself to be escorted to the Prefecture of Police, where he remained perfectly calm and expressed his confidence in French justice—with good reason. His detention infuriated left-wing newspapers that played up his role in *la Compagnie Irlandaise* fighting for France against the Prussian invasion. "This foreigner," wrote *L'Intransigeant*, "who having generously offered his blood for France, is more French than many Frenchmen, is actually arrested and handed over to those who, in defiance of all justice, are preparing the gallows for him." Their attitude, Harcourt warned the queen, was likely to deter the French government from giving up Byrne—as indeed it did. When the prisoner was about to retire to his cell, two warders asked him to follow them to a room, where he was informed that he was free to go. Stepping into a cab, he went to the rue St-Honoré to meet Mary Ann, and then the couple made their way to Le Havre. Soon afterward, they set sail aboard *L'Amerique*, their passage having had been paid by the wealthy Irish nationalist Thomas Quinn.

John Walsh had also been arrested in France. "Man believed to be Walsh is at Havre. Send necessary depositions without fail today," Anderson cabled Jenkinson on February 26. Mallon was instructed to leave immediately for Normandy and asked the veteran Fenian John Lucas to accompany him in order to help to identify Walsh. "Your Majesty will remember that this is the man spoken of by Carey as having come to Dublin & organized the 'Invincibles' & who told them to 'make history,'" wrote Harcourt. "He is the recognized agent and organizer of the Land League, and if the case can be proved against him we shall have made a great advance in the proof against the real authors of these detestable crimes."

Passing under the name Stephen Hyland, Walsh was staying at the Hotel d'Albion when French police took him into custody, waiting, with £100 in cash, to embark on a ship bound for New York. This was incontrovertibly the wanted man, and the case against him was stronger than that against Byrne, and yet the British were not optimistic that he would be surrendered. They had little more to convict him than the claims in Carey's testimony, and it was highly unlikely that new evidence could be found in time. "Will the French admit that an accessory before the fact is the same as an actual murderer?" Spencer asked Harcourt. But it turned out that French law required an accessory to have been on or near the scene of the murder when it was committed. "So they let Walsh go," writes Bussy, "and he slipped off to America, where another of the chief organisers of the Invincible murder society had preceded him, leaving their tools to be hung or sent to gaol."

*

"The Invincible Directory threw up the sponge, and the brave imprisoned manhood were left to feel they were deserted. O God, what base ingratitude! What infamous cowardice!" trumpeted the hypocritical Patrick Tynan, who was following hot on their heels. He was wanted not only for the Phoenix Park conspiracy but also for the murder of Henry Jury, the hotel keeper, even though the inquiry had not yet been fully investigated. "The case against No I is probably strongest of all," Spencer declared, while Jenkinson urgently instructed: "Request French Government to arrest No I at once. Warrant and depositions go by post." A detective's search of the American steamer at Ireland's Queenstown Harbor had proved futile. "Is there any use his going back to search each steamer?" inquired Jenkinson. "Or would it be better for him to go to London to search there?" A week later, March 10, a frustrated Anderson wrote: "See no prospect of getting information of Tynan's movements; friends have no doubt that he is in America or on his way there."

The government's scheme for sparing James Carey had totally misfired. "If [he] had been silent and been executed we had no means of getting any further into the secret of who were the real instigators and paymasters of these crimes," Harcourt had told the queen. But the men Carey had betrayed were awaiting their punishment, while every one of those who had issued orders was free. Mallon may have tipped off the prime mover, but he knew—just as he had known from the start of this conspiracy—who the hard men really were. "I have no doubt whatever," he said, "That as long as Egan, Walsh & Co are at large we cannot afford to sleep."

THIRTEEN
Marwooded

MICHAEL DAVITT was back in prison. He had learned of the return of horrific famine conditions in West Donegal and, in late November 1882, delivered a speech warning that if the government failed to act he would incite the starving peasantry to rise up against the landlords and claim back their ancestors' grazing rights. Prosecuted for sedition, he refused to find bail and, in February 1883, was sent to jail for six months.

This time, held in Dublin's Richmond Bridewell, a penal institution for petty criminals, Davitt received VIP treatment: he was allowed visitors; he could brighten his cell with rugs; and he had access to writing materials, books, and newspapers. When the Invincibles trials resumed in April, he started a diary recording the progress of each case, expressing his views and including snippets of inside information.

Have heard that car man & informer Kavanagh got blind drunk on evening of 6th of May & confessed aloud to a publican that he had driven to & from the park the men who perpetrated the assassination. Heard also that said publican was summoned before Curran at the Castle and succeeded so well in acting the part of a "stupid" that he was let off unsuspected of having any knowledge of the murder. The prisoners are supported in prison by funds supplied from some mysterious source. Their meals are furnished from Cody's public house, where Carey stopped to take a drink on his way from the scene of the murder, and a strange gentleman, whose name is not known, calls regularly every week to pay the bill. . . . It has been said that Carey was in a state of mortal terror lest his testimony might not be accepted—that he went upon his knees to Mallon beseeching to be taken as a Crown witness, and that his wife did otherwise.

Davitt considered the castle's "Star Chamber" preexamination of witnesses to have been scandalously unjust and, still scarred by his own experience of British injustice, was shocked by the "persistent envenomed howling" for lives of men who had not yet been placed in the dock. The assassinations had been "purposeless and hideously inopportune," the perpetrators "a contemptible gang" that Ireland was well rid of, but he nevertheless took exception to the prisoners being treated as if their guilt were already established. Links between leaders of the land movement and the Invincibles had been extremely unsettling (he heard a rumor that Carey's testimony had been accepted in the expectation that he would expose Land League complicity in the murders), but Davitt was confident that nothing damaging had yet been disclosed.

I fancy the Castle has been to some extent outwitted by this damnable ruffian. . . . The Fenian organisation, as such, had no more to do with the acts of Number I and Co than the Carlton Club would have with the doings of a member who might be concerned in some city swindle or other crime.

*

Anticipating intense curiosity in the Phoenix Park trials, Madame Tussaud's wax museum in London was advertising its display of models of Cavendish, Burke, and Carey, as well as their escape vehicle— "The identical car now also on view"; and on sale in Dublin, penny ballad sheets were lamenting the informer's betrayal of his comrades. Diverting popular interest, however, was the Irish American dynamite campaign: in March there had been an explosion at a Whitehall government office; a device was found at the premises of the *Times*; and on April 5 a nitroglycerin factory was discovered in Birmingham, where the plotters were all arrested. Knowing that this was a crusade being funded by Irish republicans in the United States, William Harcourt insisted on immediate legislation. On April 9—the day the Invincibles trials began at Dublin's Green Street Courthouse—the Explosive Substances Bill was rushed through both Houses of Parliament in a matter of hours (making any detonation endangering people or property a crime punishable by penal servitude for life). At Windsor, waiting to learn more from Harcourt "about those dreadful explosions," Queen Victoria gave the royal assent. "Mr. Gladstone is a good deal alarmed," she noted in her journal. "But still does not realize the hatred of the Irish to the British Rule."

*

The queen was again in mourning. At the end of March, her beloved factotum John Brown—"my dearest best friend to whom I could speak quite openly . . . the one who since 1864 had helped to cheer me, to smooth, ease and facilitate everything for my daily comfort"— had died without warning. Brown's gruff, manly presence and disregard of courtly obsequiousness delighted the queen, who had come to depend on his frank counsel and strong, steady arm. "There is no rebound left to recover from it," she wrote to her eldest daughter, the crown princess of Prussia. "Now all, all is gone in this world and all seems unhinged again in thousands of ways."

And yet, for all her misery, Victoria's inquisitiveness about the Phoenix Park conspiracy had not dimmed. After dinner she would ask her lady-in-waiting to read the day's press coverage, finding the account of Joe Brady's qualities as a dutiful son and loyal friend "very curious." She was particularly interested in the boy killer Tim Kelly, whose trial had ended with the jury disagreeing over evidence of his presence in the park. A second trial followed a few days later, but two jurors still held out against passing the death sentence. "The failure in Kelly's case is most unfortunate & the Queen feels very suspicious about it," she cabled Spencer, who answered her by saying that the unsatisfactory result had not come as a surprise. His long account advised her that the initial display of support shown by the crowd watching the prisoners arrive in court had now ceased, although there were many "among the lower classes" who, Spencer said, manifestly sympathized with the accused. "They no doubt take the dangerous view, which the informer Carey glories in stating, that these murders are acts of political warfare & are not murders"—a view that can only have riled the queen.

*

By mid-April all the Invincibles ringleaders had gathered in New York, and no progress had been made by the British authorities to secure their return for trial. Only a warrant for actual murder could activate the Anglo-American Extradition Treaty, and depositions sent to New York had been insufficiently damning to justify the men's arrest. "Conspiracy to murder is not enough," said Harcourt, who had come to the conclusion that nothing further could be done. "Their keeping out of the way is probably a stronger proof of their guilt than any you would be able to produce in court," he told Spencer.

Patrick Egan had been the first to arrive, spending most of his time with Patrick Ford and Patrick Sheridan, now working as a journalist at the *Irish World*. The Byrnes landed on April 4, and Sheridan met them at the docks, returning a fortnight later to greet John Walsh. Thomas Brennan followed next, dropping in immediately to the *Irish World*'s Park Place office, which had become a kind of headquarters, and going to Ford's house in Brooklyn for the evening to meet Egan, Sheridan, and Byrne. Although not one of the *Irish World* clique, Patrick Tynan had also renewed Invincibles ties in New York, staying on his arrival with Hamilton Williams, the doctor who had procured the surgical knives.

When Sheridan and Egan gave press interviews, they both denied any involvement in the assassinations: Sheridan claimed never to have known James Carey, declaring that the informer's every word had been a lie; while Egan, telling the *New York Times* that he had come to the United States for commercial reasons, said that he had first heard of the conspiracy when he read about it in the newspapers: "I don't know 'Number One,' or where he is. I never wrote Carey a letter sympathizing with the work of the Invincibles. I wrote him two business notes; no others."

A week or so later, in Chicago, Egan was the guest of Alexander Sullivan, president of the Clan na Gael, who confided to the British agent Henri Le Caron that although he had never doubted Egan's commitment to the Irish cause, he was now "more than satisfied." Le Caron had seen Egan soon after his arrival, renewing the friendly relations they had in Paris and discussing a continuation of "active work." Le Caron had been adamant that the clan had played no part in the Phoenix Park murders, but an entry in Davitt's diary, dated April 23, implies that Sullivan may have been a controlling force behind Egan: "He has evidently used P the Little [Patrick Egan] for his purpose—P the Little will regret having allowed himself to be thus made a tool of."

The pair was certainly in collusion over what was caustically described by one Fenian leader as "Messrs. Sullivan and Egan's big machine." This was a major convention, to be held in Philadelphia on April 25 and 26, to launch a restructured Land League—the Irish National League of America. Egan sent invitations by special delivery to "a conference (informal) of a few friends" to take place in the Continental Hotel the day before, its purpose being to discuss a program that, he told Le Caron, "would give full satisfaction in America." Addressing a small audience of about sixty people, Egan remarked, "I have been reading up the records of the Italian banditti, and from them I have come to believe in this rule: Let us meet our enemies with smiling faces, and with a warm grasp of the hand having daggers up our sleeves ready to stab them to the heart."

With five thousand spectators and around twelve hundred delegates, among them Egan and Brennan (the Byrnes having been given prime seats on the platform), the convention was an impressive assembly of Irish American voices. It was evident that the Clan na Gael was firmly in control, but although secret discussions had endorsed what Le Caron called "nitro-glycerine methods of procedure," care was being taken at the conference that the clan should not be publicly identified with violence, and that the new league should be seen to endorse the constitutional line laid down by Parnell.

*

From prison in Dublin, Davitt closely followed reports of proceedings in Philadelphia, anxious that the new organization should not be taken over by the militants. He deplored the Americans' dynamite campaign, believing it to be counterproductive: while bombs might kill individuals or wreck buildings, they did not harm oppressive institutions but only provoked harsher coercion measures.

Parnell had promised to attend the convention but then changed his mind. His Commons annihilation of Forster had regained him the allegiance of key extremists, who postponed the Philadelphia date to accommodate him. The likely militant connection with the league made it imperative for Parnell to disassociate himself, but wanting to encourage a continuation of Irish American financial support, he sent a carefully worded telegram: "I would advise that a platform so be framed as to enable us to continue to accept help from America, and to avoid offering any pretext to the British Government for entirely suppressing the national movement in Ireland."

The necessity to remain in England, Parnell explained, was to oppose a criminal law bill, which he believed would permanently enforce unacceptable coercive measures. But there was a private reason too.

On March 4, 1883, the *Times* announced the birth of a daughter to "The wife of William Henry O'Shea Esq, MP," but Clare was Parnell's child. With memories still raw of Katharine's previous post-natal infirmity (she had been bedridden for a month) and of Claude Sophie's tragic decline, Parnell was determined to be close at hand. Katharine had moved with the children and new baby to a rented house in Brighton, to which he had his own key; a maid remembered O'Shea visiting "sometimes, but not often," and a gentleman, whose name she did not know, coming almost every day. The couple had their favorite Brighton haunts—a secondhand bookshop and a shop selling pebbles and crystals, where Parnell, still a keen mineralogist, liked to watch the cutting and polishing process. Most of all, they loved to drive out to the South Downs, climbing to the crest of the hills and returning as night fell, Katharine's hair "all flying."

During the spring it became known that Parnell was experiencing financial difficulties, unable pay off a huge mortgage that had accrued on Avondale. As a tribute to the Irish leader, a national collection was launched; small contributions began trickling in from tenant farmers and shopkeepers, together with more substantial sums from the National League and from a number of priests and bishops. When the Vatican expressed disapproval, there was an outburst of public indignation, and the fund more than doubled within a few months. At the end of the year, at a banquet in Dublin, the lord mayor formally presented Parnell with £38,000 in the name of the Irish people— a massive sum for any country but quite extraordinary for poverty-stricken Ireland. "There must be a powerful sentiment at the bottom of this incongruous liberality," commented a snide editorial writer in the *Times*—but he was right: Parnell had come to embody the over-whelming anti-English feeling in almost every Irish heart. It was the main source of his popularity and the secret of his power.

*

The Invincibles trials began at Green Street Courthouse in Dublin on April 9, 1883. There were no further revelations, but Lucy Cavendish, staying once again with her relatives in Holker Hall, became increasingly dismayed by the absence of remorse in the convicted men. She had heard, however, that Joe Brady had been disturbed to discover that one of the men he had murdered was Frederick Cavendish—the only thing he regretted, he told Mallon—and she sent him a letter of forgiveness, enclosing an ivory crucifix.

Lucy learned that a cousin of Thomas Burke's, a Sister of Mercy named Mother Magdalene Kirwan, had also wanted Brady to know that she bore him no grudge. The nun made regular visits to Kilmainham, spending most time with the man who had struck the fatal blow but also working with the other Invincibles in an effort to persuade them to repent. She found each to be a fanatic, defending what he had done as "obeying orders" or being "for Ireland." When she asked what good they hoped would come of it, "They did not seem to have thought of that." Queen Victoria had been fascinated to hear of "this relation of poor Mr. Burkes, a most courageous, excellent person," who with gentle persistence had achieved more with the men than the prison priest. "She had the greatest difficulty in getting them to forgive Carey."

*

Two Invincibles had now pleaded guilty, not out of compunction but as a way of saving their lives. Edward McCaffrey and Pat Delaney were both in the car that had carried the actual murderers, and the queen was eager to know whether this meant that their testimony could now be accepted against Tim Kelly. Spencer replied at length, telling her that it was a question much on his mind, one he had discussed in detail with the attorney general and William Harcourt. Already sentenced to death for the Judge Lawson assassination attempt, Delaney was a tainted witness, likely to give false evidence more readily than an informer who testifies before he is convicted. From a legal point of view, the case against Kelly was strong enough without Delaney, but if the jury once again disagreed, the government would be blamed for not having used him.

James Mullett's guilty plea of conspiracy to murder caused far more of a stir, and rumors reached Davitt that he was about to turn queen's evidence.

> It was even said that the Crown would go through the form of try-ing Mullett in order to create the belief that he had not supplied the government with information, hoping, it was alleged, that a ruse of this kind might entice certain people back to Ireland who had fled in consequence of the supposed "Careyism" of Mullett.

From America, Egan publicly stated faith in his friend James Mullett—"a man of sound business principles and integrity of character"—and nothing in Justice O'Brien's sentencing speech gave any hint that Mullett had informed. He had not been involved in the murders of Burke and Cavendish, as he was already in custody under suspicion of another crime, and yet, his ten-year jail term was tell-ingly light for someone who had not only been an Invincibles leader but had also planned the attack on juryman Denis Field.

Then came news that twenty-three-year-old Joseph Hanlon, who had been with Carey in Skin-the-Goat's car, had been accepted as an informer. "How many have been *refused* is known only to the Crown," Davitt wrote. "It is nevertheless astonishing that so many poor laboring men . . . should have refrained during the space of eight months from making any effort to obtain the enormous reward of £10,000. . . . Threatened with the consequences of others *supposed* rev-elations they turned to save themselves—Skin, honorably excepted."

Not according to James Carey. In a letter he wrote from Kilmain-ham to Joe Brady's parents, Carey claimed that their son was the only Invincible who had not "told all before I said one word." He goes on to provide names, and Skin's is among them. Tim Kelly is not included on the list, but Mallon revealed that the youth had asked to see him to find out whether making "a clean breast of it to the authorities" might save him from the rope. Mallon told him that he believed his end was inevitable and advised him instead to make a full confession to the prison priest.

*

Kelly's third trial was set for May 9, and anxious to know whether there was justification for subjecting him to yet another ordeal, Spencer sent for Mallon to learn whether he had a reason for believing that the prisoner was guilty.

"I have, my lord."

"And what is it?"

"He told me so himself."

Nevertheless, Spencer could not help hoping for a compassionate verdict for Kelly—"an ardent nationalist, full of patriotic zeal, his mind stored with patriotic poems and songs. . . . He believed absolutely that he had done a brave and a proper act in the direct interests of Ireland." Joseph Hanlon's evidence would corroborate the fact that Kelly had been one of the two assassins, and an independent witness had come forward to confirm his presence in Phoenix Park. Thomas Huxley, a young English gardener on the neighboring Guinness estate of Farmleigh, had cut across the park for an evening in town, passing close enough to a loitering group to be able to identify Tim Kelly. Under cross-examination, Huxley admitted to have been given "£7 and then £8" by Superintendent Mallon, which, it was suggested, might have been payments for false evidence but in fact were to cover travel expenses to England (it had been thought wise for him to leave Ireland for his own protection). The Crown's case was indisputably strong, but Kelly's extreme youthfulness, his chin covered in golden down, had touched a public nerve. "Putting aside the alibi, Huxley the Englishman at

Farmleigh," Parnell was heard to comment, "I fail to see how the jury could convict the boy at the bar." The note from an anonymous young woman, who wrote to Kelly in Kilmainham, was one more expression of this universal sympathy.

Dear Mr. Kelly,

Please forgive the liberty I'm taking in writing to you, but I want to say how sorry I am for you. You are so young, and you have such a nice kind face in your pictures, I don't believe you could have committed such a horrid crime. I hope you will be reprieved. I took more interest in you from the first than any of the others, being a country woman of yours and about your age. Goodbye dear Mr. Kelly. God help you and comfort your poor mother.

JL

Playing to the court's emotions, Kelly's lawyer emphasized how unlikely it was that the Invincibles' ringleaders would have selected as their murder instrument this "lad of nineteen, the epileptic, the boy suffering from St Vitus's Dance [the neurological condition Sydenham's chorea], the youth whose health necessitated his frequent attendance at the hospital." When the jury retired, and Kelly stood waiting at the bar, he was heard to say, "I'll bet you a bob this lot hangs me!" Sure enough, the verdict was "guilty," and it brought tears to the eyes of counsel and spectators alike. Determined not to show any agitation, Kelly had smiled cheerfully as he headed toward the cells, blowing a kiss to someone he knew in the gallery. Then, with a sweeping motion indicating a circle around his neck, he thrust his fist upward, as if yanking a cord, and jerked his thumb over his shoulder toward the jury box. It was a characteristic display of cocky bravado, but it masked pure terror. Before Mass one day, Kelly and Brady had discussed their likely execution, which would be carried out by Kilmainham's hangman William Marwood, who had developed a technique known as "the long drop." It was said to be a more humane method that broke the prisoner's neck instantly, rather than a slow death by strangulation caused by a short drop. But it can have been of little solace to Kelly. "Marwood will have a terrible job on me; the weight of my body will never break my neck," he said, adding to the massive Brady, "You're all right, Joe."

*

Joe Brady's execution was scheduled for May 14, which fell on the religious holiday of Whitmonday, and demonstrations were expected against its insensitive timing. By seven a.m., Kilmainham was encircled by armed police and guardsmen, and the gathering throng had swelled to several thousand by the time the black flag was hoisted—at eight a.m. precisely.

Later that morning, Mallon was spotted hurrying toward a waiting car, clutching a parcel tied up in a white table napkin. It was Brady's head. The Royal College of Surgeons would be performing a postmortem dissection of the brain—a routine method of nineteenth-century psychiatry—in an effort to determine what might have caused an upright youth to commit such a brutally calculated murder.

Commenting on Brady's character, Parnell described him as "a brave self-sacrificing misguided man," who had acted not through any base or mercenary motives but through his passionate allegiance to Ireland. As unshakable as the Invincibles' patriotism was a religious faith that enabled them to embrace their end, a blessing Parnell could not help envying. "The Catholic Church is the only one that can make a man die with any real hope," he remarked while reading about the executions.

After Curley was hanged later that week, Patrick Egan was quoted in *United Ireland* comparing this "work of ruling Ireland" to the massacre by the British Crown of captured rebels after the 1798 uprising. "The hangman has had a busy time in Dublin. . . . Two more of our countrymen have died on the scaffold. One of them—poor Daniel

Curley—I knew long and well, and I can say with truth that a more sterling patriot never died for Ireland."

Next to be "marwooded" was Michael Fagan, who had played a minor role in the Phoenix Park conspiracy but was suspected of complicity in other political murders. Davitt's journal entry for May 28 reads:

The third life which has been taken by the law in atonement for those of Lord Cavendish and Mr. Burke. Is justice not satisfied at this expiation? The intrepid spirit exhibited by all three while undergoing the most awful ordeal which human flesh could be subject to is about the only redeeming feature of the whole "Invincible" chapter of Irish history. There has been no whining, no begging for mercy, no manifestation of fear, no regrets, and, above all, no "theatrical" show of bravado. Each and all have shown the possession of the finest qualities of fortitude & courage when face to face with death, forcing the conviction upon reflective minds that such men under other circumstances would have been equal to the highest efforts of self-sacrifice heroism & devotion in a higher and a nobler cause. May this be the last life of its kind that will be offered up to the vengeance of the law for that accursed tragedy of the 6th of May. Amen.

FOURTEEN
An Abyss of Infamy

A NARROW path winds up and down through a birch wood, where brambles run riot over clumps of heather and ferns, stopping at a hollowed-out rock face, where a crude stone Celtic cross has been erected. This is the Carraig an Duin shrine, a prayer site during the year of the Penal Laws, 1695–1741, when Catholic services were forbidden, and people were forced to keep their faith alive at Mass rocks in the wilderness, the priests officiating under threat of death.

A few minutes' walk away is the holy well of Doon, filled by a spring whose water is said to have been blessed by a sixth-century Columban missionary and is believed to this day to have miraculous healing powers. Irish emigrants before leaving their homeland came on pilgrimage to the well, where they would recite the Catholic Stations of the Cross with bared feet.

On the hill above, with 360-degree views of forests and distant mountains, is the Rock of Doon, the inauguration site of the ancient O'Donnell chieftains and a sacred place to the O'Donnell clan. This was where, at the beginning of June 1883, Patrick O'Donnell arrived to "do the stations" and to bid farewell to Donegal.

Virtually nothing had changed in Gweedore since Pat's childhood. The potato crop had failed once more, and an apocalyptic storm, raging along the Bloody Foreland, had swept away cabin roofs and decimated the cottagers' grain and hay supplies. In the angry speech that had landed him in prison, Michael Davitt had called attention to "the sufferings of this wretched district of Donegal"; the *Freeman's Journal* predicted another catastrophe, warning, "The burning memory of the horrors of '46 and '47 is being recalled amongst the poor people of this parish"; while Derrybeg's Father MacFadden declared, "The horror of hunger and the more hated horror of landlordism stare at me from every point. . . . There is not a spot in all Ireland where the supremacy of the landlord is so much felt as here." Emigration remained the only option, and James Tuke's committee had arranged for fifteen thousand people to be relocated—two-thirds of them settling in the United States.

For Pat O'Donnell, however, America was "played out," and when news reached him of the diamond rush to South Africa, he decided to join it. Thousands were traveling to secure even a foot of this valuable soil, some arriving with hardly a cent and leaving six months later with $100,000. The most fertile region was said to be the *koppies* [hills] along the banks of the Vaal River, where gems were to be found in the stony red earth, and the only equipment required was a pair of India rubber boots, a waterproof overcoat, a ground sheet, and a handgun and shot belt. Having worked in gravel diggings near St. Louis and learned out in the American West about the kind of rocks that contained silver, Pat considered that he had experience enough for such a venture. "He often said he would go to the diamond country and make our fortunes," recalled his wife, Margaret.

The couple had been estranged for years, but in May 1883, Pat had arrived in Philadelphia to attempt a reunion. "He said he was going to Ireland, to Dublin maybe, for a little while, and from there to Africa where they find diamonds." He had brought with him $700, some of which he offered to give Margaret if she would either live with him again or agree to a legal separation. She would do neither. As a devout Catholic, she considered divorce out of the question, and she no longer felt herself to be Pat's wife. In his absence, she had grown close to her brother-in-law, Roger McGinley, the owner of a Philadelphia shop selling rosaries, crucifixes, and holy pictures. "I thought it best for us both that I should have nothing to do with my husband and not take up with him after he came back." Crushed, O'Donnell replied, "When I go this time you will never set eyes on me again."

He arrived by steamer in Londonderry, Ireland, on May 27, stopping for a few days at a public house in Bishop Street and talking about his intention of going to South Africa. He then went to Letterkenny, where he had friends, before moving on to the village of Kilmacrennan, because it was close to the Doon holy well. O'Donnell had a tough physique, but a boyhood injury to his elbow, worsened by decades of manual labor, had almost paralyzed his left arm. He traveled with a galvanic machine, as doctors had advised him that regular use of electrical currents could help to restore the wasted muscles, but he was determined to try the healing effects of the water.

Staying at a small lodging house, he spent ten days saying the Stations of the Cross—five "Our Fathers" and five "Hail Marys" for every bucket of water he drew. He was visited by one of his sisters, who had married a local farmer, and he may or may not have gone to Derrybeg, about twenty-five miles away, to see his mother and brother (there are conflicting accounts). What is certain is that he ended his Irish trip in Derry. The manager of the city's branch of Belfast Bank organized a cash transfer to Cape Town, South Africa, and wrote a letter of introduction, dated June 27, to a relative of his who could help O'Donnell find work. Pat was seen in O'Hanlon's, a nationalist public house, having long conversations with Neil McDevitt, a militant known to the Derry police. All talk at the time was about the Invincibles hangings, and patriotic fever was high. O'Donnell, who carried a small, six-chambered revolver, was forthright in his views and passionate in his denunciation of James Carey. "I would not shoot him," he vowed. "I would burn him by inches."

*

Hatred of the informer runs deep in Ireland. "A Corydon, a Nagle, or a Carey. . . . Hell isn't hot enough nor eternity long enough for them!" declared a bitter old Fenian; others described how James Carey— "traitor, decoyer of the innocent, murderer in heart, murderer in effect"—had made their flesh crawl. "It impossible for human power to add one hideous feature to the foul thing he is," declared the *Freeman's Journal*. "He sinks into an abyss of infamy, in comparison to which the pit into which other conspirators are buried is a pinnacle." A memorandum sent by the Bricklayers' Society, after a meeting to discuss Carey's expulsion, makes clear how its former colleague was regarded in the trade.

> We hereby call upon the Government to transfer him from the witness box and place him on the dock to be hanged . . . his body to be skinned and stuffed with briars and hung on the gaol wall as an emblem of nationality and his rotten carcass to be buried in the assassin's grave with a stone over it and this inscription: "The Principal Assassin (and afterwards Informer) of Lord Frederick Cavendish and Mr. Burke, May 6 1882."

There had been something especially loathsome about Carey's jokey banter in court, the arrogance with which he would step out of the prison van smoking a cigar, and the hypocritical flaunting of his religion (a member of the Sodality of the Sacred Heart, he hung the elitist order's medal and ribbon over his prison bed). Davitt observed how his denunciation by the Invincibles' defense counsel had been more crushing than any of the onslaughts on the Fenian informers at the state trials of 1867. Not even the saintly efforts of Mother Magdalene and the prospect of "the hereafter opening slowly before his very eyes" could bring Joe Brady to forgive his betrayer.

Carey told Maggie that had it not been for her and their family, he would "rather have died with Brady and the others," and in a letter instructing her to pack up their furniture and belongings with care, he declares his commitment, vowing that when he joins her they will "never more be parted until death" and sending rows of star kisses to her and their seven children. He had always been a model husband and father, never absent from home, except for his eleven-week sentence as a suspect, and Maggie ardently supported his belief that he was not an informer because he had not caused the arrest of any fellow conspirator. Since the trials, she had paid sixteen shillings a week for him to be blessed during Mass, and although she had been ostracized by former friends and all their neighbors, she was now asking the authorities "most earnestly" if her husband could be allowed to return home.

This was extraordinarily naïve. Their house in Denzille Street was guarded day and night by marines, and a cottage behind it inhabited by constables, yet the windows had been broken, the walls daubed with graffiti. There were chalked messages on Carey's rented tenement buildings warning occupants not to pay rent to the "cursed informer." Learning of this, Carey had threatened his tenants with prosecution and in June began proceedings in the police court. He was conducting business within the walls of Kilmainham as if nothing had changed. He sent instructions for payment for the construction of a mortuary chapel to be forwarded to his brother Francis, who would complete the work, and he wrote to Dublin's town clerk asking for details of the next town council meeting and apologizing for his "unavoidable absence" from corporate duties. In a letter to the lord mayor he remarked, "I might draw your attention to the old and trite saying (nevertheless true) that a certain gentleman is not as black as he is painted. When I give my account to council, my conduct will stand in its true light."

As compensation for having turned queen's evidence, he expected to be provided with a security escort, and he had suggested several new occupations for himself—among them a prison warden. "We are glad to hear that Carey is not to have employment as warden," Ponsonby wrote on behalf of the queen. "He must be a nuisance.

Does he really think himself safe in Dublin!" Word had also reached Michael Davitt that Carey had been seen visiting his Denzille Street house.

> Not improbable. He of course knows to what extent the Government have been enabled by his services as an informer to crush the organization whose members would be likely to "remove" such a gentleman as he, and the fact that he ventures abroad in Dublin streets after his performance of the past six weeks is pretty good proof that the back of the secret movement has been completely broken in this city. . . . Still there is such a thing as unorganized public spirit abroad, and Sodality James had better not presume too far upon the forbearance it is likely to extend to so accomplished a villain.

*

Indeed, not only were assassins supposedly posted at the main ports and stations, a unit of ten Irish Americans, funded by Jeremiah O'Donovan Rossa, leader of the Fenian dynamite campaign, was reported to have been sent to England and Scotland, their purpose being "to find and kill Carey." One was the Irish-born nationalist Captain Thomas Phelan of Kansas City, a Civil War hero and member of the inner circle of the so-called Dynamite Brotherhood, who was known to have arrived on the steamship *Belgravia*. From Glasgow, Phelan went to Hull, where the police were waiting for him and made clear that he was being watched. He stayed at the Salisbury Hotel and chatted openly to its proprietress, Mrs. Edge, telling her that he was an agent of O'Donovan Rossa and making no secret of the fact that he was carrying two handguns and a bowie knife. He spoke of the Phoenix Park murders, denouncing them as "a blunder to Irish brotherhood," and told Mrs. Edge that no matter what the government did to protect Carey, "he would soon be a dead man."

The dynamiter John Kearney, responsible for three explosions in Glasgow in January, visited Phelan at the Salisbury, where they talked at length in his room. According to a newspaper article sourced by a secret dispatch, Kearney believed that Carey was to be a passenger on *The Queen*, a steamer docked in Liverpool, and Kearney had smuggled dynamite in several barrels on board. "He showed me where the acid from the machine which was to explode the dynamite had eaten through the lining of his coat," said Phelan, who learned from Kearney that it would detonate when the ship was at sea and was appalled by the prospect of a reckless waste of hundreds of lives. The officers of the vessel were informed, and the barrels removed in time—all thanks to the fact that Captain Phelan had just been recruited as a British spy. "He came over here in 1883 to assist me solely because he disapproved of dynamite work and wanted to stop it," Spencer was told by Edward Jenkinson, who had been "dreadfully upset" when Phelan's written account of the episode very nearly resulted in his murder.

*

For his last day alive, in nostalgic recognition of their friendship, Tim Kelly asked to be transferred to the late Joe Brady's cell. Describing their closeness, Brady's mother said that her son could have fled during the castle investigations but had refused to leave Dublin, as he was waiting until Tim was "out of his time" (that is, had finished his apprenticeship to a coach maker). Several hours after Brady's execution, Kelly was in the exercise yard when he heard a curious noise; it was "the sods being beaten down over the grave," he was told, and its chilling impact hit home. "From that moment he was altogether changed," said Spencer. "He at once began to think seriously of the matter and he confessed before he died that he had taken part in the murder but that he now believed that the step had been a wrong one."

Throughout the night of June 8, the former choirboy was heard sweetly singing hymns, including "Salve Regina," with the words "Pray for the sinner, pray for me." He rose at five a.m., dressing in his suit and styling his hair with teenage affectation, brushing it forward and forming an angle over each temple. At six thirty, two priests came into the cell and took him to the chapel for the last sacraments. They accompanied him toward the execution yard, stopping when hangman William Marwood stepped forward, holding leather straps. He inserted Kelly's wrists into loops, belted his waist, and took off his shirt collar to bare his neck. Then, with the head warder leading the way, the priests and the prisoner, in Marwood's grasp, walked across the yard to the foot of the scaffold. A rope dangled from two rings on a crossbeam about nine feet above the ground, and Kelly, looking very pale, stared fixedly at it. Marwood guided him onto the drop, pointing out the pencil marks on two boards where his feet needed to be positioned. As Marwood pinioned his legs, Kelly asked, "Won't you let me kiss the crucifix?" and Father O'Reilly held it to his lips. It was now two minutes to eight, and the boy appeared to be praying. Marwood covered his head with the traditional white cap and adjusted the knot on the rope under his chin to the angle of his jaw. Seeing all was ready, he withdrew the safety bolt and stepped aside to pull the lever. Tim Kelly disappeared from view. His death was instantaneous.

*

The following day, June 10, knowing that the last the execution had been carried out, James Carey wrote a letter to the castle authorities.

Sir,

The Trials are over some 3 weeks and I am here yet. I have seen Mr. Mallon to speak to him once since the trials began 10 weeks ago. I have written 5 times to him and he was in Kilmainham 7 times and never called to see me.

Also Sir I have asked him to provide for me a written pardon and if possible a position that would suit me in Cape Town or Natal. I had to make a present of 2 houses to relations as no one would buy anything belonging to me. I am ready to leave in 4 days when I give over those houses to my relations.

As I intend to bring my family I am going a few days before them. . . . And before leaving a private visit as my wife does not know where I am going and 2 warders are present it would not be right to speak in their hearing. If I am required again of course you know where I am. I would wish to spend a few days in London before leaving perhaps forever. I have got some clothes sent to me.

Hoping Sir that you will settle my business soon.

> I beg to remain your most respectfully,
> James Carey. T.C.

He would be made to wait for several more weeks. Frustrated by his confinement and assuming that he was entitled to at least some kind of break, Carey made a request for an excursion to the scenic lochside town of Killarney, with Superintendent Mallon as his escort. Hearing of this, Mallon was furious; he "loathed and shunned" Carey and was filled with disgust at the thought of accompanying him on a pleasure trip. But when he went to see the magistrate John Curran to protest, he was told that the castle had no intention of allowing the outing and had only been "laughing at Carey" by seeming to take him seriously. Nor was the informer to be granted an official pardon—Spencer was implacable about refusing it. In fact, the only concession to Carey's demands was the choice of a South African destination.

*

Patrick O'Donnell was about to embark on his own long journey to Cape Town, and he would not be traveling alone. In Derry, he had met a girl from Gweedore, Susan Gallagher, an eighteen-year-old with a plain face and a tiny waist offset by an ample bosom. O'Donnell was double her age, and one arm was noticeably impaired, the flesh on the hand slightly shrunken, but he was six feet tall and had a fine head of hair, long sideburns, and laughing gray eyes. Carrying himself with aplomb, he dressed dapperly, his felt hat tipped at a jaunty angle, and Susan soon found herself charmed by the worldly O'Donnell and his descriptions of exotic places. When she told him that her employer in the hotel where she worked treated her badly, he begged her to come with him to South Africa; he would pay her fare, and they could get married before they left—it would be a fresh start for them both.

On June 28, Susan left with O'Donnell on the steamer to Liverpool, and the pair then traveled to London, where they stayed in a coffeehouse. They found a priest whom they hoped would marry them, but he had refused, Susan recalled, "on the grounds that O'Donnell was an alien." Nevertheless, she agreed to share Pat's cabin and to travel to Cape Town with him, as "Mr. and Mrs. O'Donnell."

*

At ten p.m. on July 3, when all the prisoners were locked up, and many of the warders had left for the night, Mallon arrived at Kilmainham with an order for James Carey to be handed over. Brought from his cell, Carey—now clean-shaven, his hair cut short and dyed black, the part moved from center to one side—seemed surprised by the suddenness of the summons; he had been told to be ready for his departure but took offense at having no say in its timing or destination. He demanded to know where he was going and where his wife and family were staying; he needed to remain in Dublin, he said, to face the matter out and justify himself, and he insisted on being taken home.

Refusing to provide any information other than that he would be going abroad, Mallon reminded him that he *had* no home: Mrs. Carey and the children had already left, and he would see them on board the steamer. Raging that they had been "kidnapped" and that he had not received a reward or the formal pardon that was due to him, Carey declared that he would go to the castle and wait in the detective's office until the morning, when he would take issue with the higher authorities. There was a cab at the door, Mallon told him, and he would drive there with him, but the detective became so exasperated by the barrage of complaints en route, he ordered the driver to pull up in Parliament Street and flung open the door. "Very well, James. You can go to blazes and take care of yourself as long as you can!"

Mallon had given his charge a handgun that he had taken the precaution of loading with blank cartridges (he had his finger on the trigger of his own gun in his pocket), and he watched Carey put his foot on the step and then slump back onto his seat. The vehicle's abrupt halt had surprised a couple of passersby, who were peering curiously inside, and Carey had been made suddenly aware of the dangers he faced. When they reached the Lower Castle Yard, Mallon gave him a sealed envelope containing his passenger ticket and a check for £100. Another detective drove Carey to Kingstown, where two Scotland Yard plainclothesmen were waiting to escort the informer to London.

Carey slept that night on board the mail boat, and when it departed early the next morning, remained in his cabin throughout the voyage. On the train journey from Holyhead, however, elated by a sense of freedom, he became "most loquacious," chatting to strangers who entered the carriage and generally drawing attention to himself. One press report claimed that he was identified by a passenger at Willesden Junction, its publication prompting Lord Spencer to investigate how the Central News Agency had received its intelligence. "I know how long and carefully Carey's removal was schemed," he wrote. "I doubt if it was known at all how he left, but he probably with his reckless bravado made himself known to someone on the journey, and no-one could guard against that." In a cartoon published on the front page of *United Ireland*, a bushy-bearded rat catcher is recognizably the viceroy, whose pole casts off a raft bearing a huddle of vermin. They are caricatures of the informer and his family, and the caption is: "The Rats Adrift or the Carey Family at Sea."

FIFTEEN

The Assassin's Assassin

T HE STEAM vessel *Kinfauns Castle* set sail from London Docks for Cape Town two days later, July 6, with Maggie Carey and the seven children on board. All went under the name Power, except for thirteen-year-old James, who was given his mother's maiden name, McKenna. Their new identity was printed on their trunks, but Maggie, who could not read, had to be told of it by her eldest son, Tom. There was still no sign of her husband when the steamer departed from London Docks, but as it neared the Nore, a sandbank at the mouth of the Thames Estuary, a small rowboat containing two men drew up alongside it, one clambering up a rope ladder and the other returning to the shore.

James and Maggie Power were to have posed as brother and sister, but it was thought too risky to expect Marie (age three) and little Maggie (five) to maintain the pretense that Carey was their uncle, and the plan was abandoned. As it was, the subterfuge of his arrival had attracted unwanted attention. "There is something suspicious about that man," a third-class steward remarked to one of the passengers, and the two decided to observe him. They noted his attentiveness to the children, whom he tutored himself, crowing that he was instructing them to curse the castle, but thought it odd the way he made the young ones repeat their surname. Even odder was the fact that although Power was beardless, his razors were new, and the steward noticed that he did not seem to know how to use them.

After a few days, shipboard friendships were forming. A passenger from Birmingham wrote to his wife, telling her about two "very companionable fellows," both Irish, whom he made a point of treating as equals—"[I] don't seek to 'come over' them as the 'superior race.'" He particularly liked Mr. Power, as he was genial and well informed, whereas Mr. O'Donnell was rather reserved and did not pay much attention to anyone except a young woman to whom he seemed to be "less than kith and rather more than kin." They were said to be married, but "Mrs. O'Donnell" wore no wedding ring.

When the vessel docked in Madeira to take fuel on board, a shoal of splashing urchins appeared, thrilling the children watching on deck by diving for coins. Most of the passengers disembarked and wandered the cobbled streets, wide-eyed at the island's tropical lushness —the exotic scarlet poinsettia and bright bougainvillea foaming over walls, the traffic of bullock carriages, and tourist shops selling feather flowers, wicker furniture, and walking sticks of palm and guava wood.

Carrying the handgun Mallon had given him in a hip holster, Carey relished his new liberty, joining a group of passengers for a drink and taking the opportunity to post correspondence—a letter to the Dublin authorities (his latest grievance was being made to travel steerage) and another to his brother-in-law. He was unguarded about the voyage, describing passengers and conversations, remarking that when the subject of the Invincibles came up, he had joined in their denouncement of "the miscreant Carey."

There were four or five other Irishmen on board, including a young man from Wexford named Kelly, who flirted with Susan and made O'Donnell jealous. Carey had nicknamed the latter "McDonald" (a misprint on his trunk) and constantly sought his company. "We used to be alone smoking and chatting in nooks and corners on the deck till 11 o clock at night," recalled O'Donnell, who found Power—a stout, affable character—entertaining enough, except for when he was drunk and got "moody and black like." He and Susan both liked Maggie Power, who in her youth must have been decidedly pretty, with black-arched brows and dark, deep-set eyes. She was florid-faced and prematurely gray now, her features blurred with middle age, her shapely figure spread with multiple childbearing, but she was an admirable mother, devotedly tending to the children, dandling the baby on her knee while tidying the rumpled frocks of her two daughters.

The O'Donnell couple had formed quite an attachment to the Power children (one of the girls called Susan "Auntie"). "I got somehow to feel for them. They seemed poor," O'Donnell said, although he disliked the precocious Tom, whom he found too old and deep for his years. The teenage boys slept in the open steerage cabin with their father, who was clearly reluctant to return to its reek and clamor, and "forced himself often" on O'Donnell. There was an evening when they were up late talking or playing cards, and Power was rebuked by one of the stewards for trespassing beyond third class. Offended, he went back to his own quarters, retorting, "I tell you I have been accustomed to sit down with better than the likes o'him."

O'Donnell, however, had impressed Carey. His Californian digger appearance—the weathered face and knuckles hard as barnacles—bore witness to the hardship and hazards of his itinerant life in America; Carey, on the other hand, had always gone out of his way to avoid a physical threat to himself and had never before ventured farther than Ireland. The O'Donnell pedigree was impressive too: quite apart from the chieftain ancestors, Pat's first cousins had been Molly Maguires—Gweedore O'Donnells suspected of involvement in the 1875 assassination of two mine officials; his cousin Mary Ann had been married to Jack Kehoe, king of the Mollies, who was hanged in 1878. Pat himself was rarely unarmed, carrying a handgun—"Where I come from one is used to do so," he once remarked, meaning the mining camps of America. O'Donnell demonstrated his skill as a marksman by firing at flying fish, until ordered by the chief officer to stop.

In one of their many conversations, Carey decided to convince the O'Donnells to change ships when they docked in Cape Town and travel on with his family to Durban. Natal offered far better work opportunities: it was a region rich in produce—sugar, coffee, cotton, and tobacco; O'Donnell could use his herding experience, as the rearing of cattle and sheep was extensive; but more importantly, it was much easier and quicker to travel from there to the diamond fields—the roads were good, the rivers bridged, mule- and oxen-driven wagons (the main method of transport) considerably cheaper. There was an abundance of water and grass for the animals, whereas on the Cape, water had to be purchased from reservoirs owned by roadside farmers. Before they had reached Cape Town, O'Donnell had paid the seven guineas required for a second-class berth to Natal; Carey was delighted, remarking to a fellow passenger, "O'Donnell has taken a fancy to me and he is going up country with me."

*

The *Kinfauns Castle* arrived in Table Bay before dawn on Friday, July 27, and at around six o'clock the first rays of sun began to throw into relief the panorama of mountains forming a stunning backdrop to the sea—the smooth folds of Devil's Peak, nudging up against Table Mountain with its cloth of white cloud, and sloping down and up again to conical Lion's Head. There was a cluster of hansom cabs and horse-drawn hackney carriages on the docks waiting for a fare—one shilling and six pence to any part of town.

O'Donnell and Susan went ashore for the day with the Powers and their older children; he was happy to discover that Kelly had departed for good, and Susan was immensely grateful to be walking on steady land (she had been seasick since crossing the equator, when pounding gales had made the passage terrifying). They had decided to go to a theater, only to find that it was closed, and so the women and children wandered off to window-shop, while the men went into the City Hotel on Waterkant Street for a drink.

They were joined by one of the passengers, an upholsterer named John Williams, and a forecabin steward, Robert "Scotty" Burns, and taking advantage of escaping the watchful eye of Maggie, who knew how alcohol affected him, Carey became increasingly bombastic. When the subject of Irish politics came up, he began ranting against the English and the Scottish—a people too base to live, he declared, and if he had his way, he would exterminate every one of them. When Scotty Burns protested, Carey flew into a rage and, grabbing the man's throat, would have throttled him had it not been for the intervention of Williams. Taking over, O'Donnell steered Power out of the bar and into the street, propping him up as they made their way back to the *Kinfauns Castle*. "'Twas pitch dark and no lamps and I had trouble enough helping him along for he had something taken."

When they had gone, the barman, convinced that he had seen one of the Irishmen before, pulled out an old newspaper spread—the weekend supplement to the nationalist broadsheet the *Freeman's Journal*. The issue of May 5, 1883, contained a large tinted lithograph of James Carey with insets of four cartoons depicting his role in the Phoenix Park murders and trials. With his pomaded black hair and slick, roué's mustache, the irate customer bore little resemblance to this portrait of the informer, his shaggy beard and crinkly hair tinted gingery brown, but what could not be disguised was the low hairline on his wrinkled forehead, the prominent ears, beady blue eyes, and ruddy, ale-seasoned complexion. The man was James Carey: there was no doubt about it.

*

On the morning of Saturday, July 28, a notice appeared in the gossip column of the *Cape Argus*:

I am told that Carey, the informer, has done us the honour of coming out to South Africa by the mail, travelling of course, under some other name than his own. He was, however, recognized on board by his fellow passengers. . . . They say he is going along the coast but his destination is not generally known. . . . When it was announced that Carey would not be sent to any part of the British dominions, I said to myself, "That means South Africa"; and here he is.

Word soon reached the *Kinfauns Castle*. Trying not to show his alarm, Carey asked John Williams if he could borrow his copy of the *Argus* and skimmed through it until he came to the Saturday Sallies column. For several minutes after reading it, he sat with his hand covering his eyes, and then asked if he could take the paper to his wife. In the forecabin, while reading the *Argus*, Scotty Burns remarked to the passenger who had lent him the paper:

"Did you see this about Carey, the informer?"

"No," he said. "What's that?"

Burns read the passage aloud, noticing that Pat O'Donnell, who was listening close by, had become "awfully excited."

"If I had known he was on board ship I would have swung for him!" the Irishman declared, but to Burns it sounded more like banter than a threat.

Sometime on Saturday, O'Donnell was shown the *Weekly Freeman* illustrations. A man named Robert Cubitt, who had disembarked in Cape Town, had been given the spread by the barman. "I recognized that likeness as James Power the man on board," said Cubitt. He went with his brother to the docks, where the steamship *Melrose* was about to sail to Durban, Natal. Spotting O'Donnell, he asked, "Have you seen the portrait of Carey?"

Looking at it closely, O'Donnell exclaimed, "I will shoot that man!" Again, his tone was flippant, and Cubitt did not take him seriously. O'Donnell asked if he could keep the paper and, after folding it up and putting it in his pocket, went on board the *Melrose*.

*

That night a storm rolled in, with vast black breakers thrashing the ship's rib timbers and flooding its heaving decks. The *Melrose* was rearing up and plunging down so violently that few passengers dared venture out from their cabins. Carey, sitting in the second-class saloon with O'Donnell, asked if he would accompany him back to steerage: he was frightened of being swept overboard, he said, but in truth, his fear of assassination was greater. He and his son Tom had been standing on deck as the ship left the quay, when he glanced at a group of men below and realized that he was the focus of their attention. "I will go to the other end," he had said to Tom. "You stop and see if it is me they are pointing at." Now, stumbling along the rain-lashed deck with O'Donnell, he realized how easily he could be shot and thrown overboard at night without anyone witnessing it.

In the safety of his own cabin, O'Donnell's mind kept churning. Could Power, a loving family man and devout Catholic, really be Carey the informer—"the greatest monster on earth"? It had not occurred to him before, although he had noticed a couple of things that had led him to think that Power must either be a detective or a fugitive from the law. "But then I used to say to myself, 'twas dreaming I was against the man." They had discussed Irish politics—"or rather *he* did"—and once or twice the Phoenix Park murders were mentioned, "but somehow we got away from it." O'Donnell had seen the gun Power carried, but then he too carried a weapon as a matter of course. He vowed that he would not believe the rumors until he had found proof. And yet, the possibility that he had been "chumming" with James Carey filled him with self-loathing.

The Gweedore emigrant Jack Curran later heard talk of a meeting of local Fenians in a house in Allentown, Pennsylvania, sometime in May 1883. He describes how it was decided that straws should be drawn to decide who among the group should be sent to pursue and shoot the informer.

The man who drew the short straw had a wife and family. Paddy Michael Art [O'Donnell] got up and stood in the centre of the house and said that they couldn't possibly send that man to shoot Carey. "I'll go and I'll shoot him myself and there's nothing I'd like better." Everyone was ecstatic when they heard what Paddy Michael Art said and they all gathered together and they sent Paddy off in pursuit of Carey.

Curran claimed that O'Donnell had come to see his mother the next morning, carrying two bags, a smart blue suit, and gold-topped cane. He said to her:

"Keep this here until my return, and if I don't return it is yours to keep forever."

"Where in God's name are you going?"

"It doesn't make any difference to you. I won't be long gone at all before I return."

But it had all been bluster and big talk, because finding himself in a position where he might have an opportunity to kill Carey was a responsibility that terrified O'Donnell: "I'd rather have been under the sea or away somehow out of the ship." On Sunday morning, having been awake most of the night, he moved about the *Melrose* with a preoccupied air, undecided about whether Power was or was not Carey. He resolved to have nothing more to do with him until he could be certain of his identity; but how would he achieve that after having been so friendly? He decided that he would pick a quarrel with Power, in the hope it would expose him or else give him the chance to clear his name.

At lunchtime, because Susan was in their cabin feeling too ill to eat, O'Donnell shared a table with a passenger called Charles Schofield, to whom he mentioned his wife's seasickness. When their conversation touched on the Invincibles, O'Donnell said that Carey had been "the worst of the crowd," that it was shameful he had escaped justice. They talked about the possibility that he might be on board in disguise, and O'Donnell, unfolding the *Weekly Freeman* portrait, pointed out the likeness to Power, joshing, "He won't escape long!"

A couple of hours later, O'Donnell was in the second-class saloon, where Susan had joined him, sitting on a sofa, her arm around his neck, her head resting on his shoulder. Tom Carey was standing by the staircase, watching his little sister Maggie play with Thomas Jones, a boatswain, whom she liked to follow around. Their mother was there too and, noticing that Susan was crying, asked what was wrong. "I don't know," O'Donnell replied. "I think she is homesick. Where's Mr. Power?"

Power had asked O'Donnell to go down to the saloon and get drinks for them both, saying that he would soon follow. O'Donnell was a teetotaler, but he had drunk a bottle of stout at lunch and now ordered another, deciding that keeping Power company over a drink would help to draw him out. "Will you take a bottle of ale?" he asked, as the Irishman appeared, but Power wanted a brandy. When it arrived, the two men were seen lifting their glasses, as if toasting each other's health.

Maggie Power, meanwhile, had gone into her cabin, where their sickly baby had woken, and after ten minutes heard what she thought was the pop of a soda bottle cork. Almost immediately came a cry, "Oh Maggie, Maggie, I am shot, O'Donnell has shot me!" and rushing out, she saw James staggering toward her with his arms held out. A gun was fired twice more. As she clasped him in an embrace, he fell, and she fell with him. The officers' servant James Parish, who had seen what had happened, came over and pressed his thumb on the bullet wound in Power's neck to try to stop the spurting blood, while Power's terrified small daughters gathered around, calling out their father's name. An officer, Richard Beecher, went up behind O'Donnell to search for his pistol, but the Irishman voluntarily drew it from his pocket and handed it over. "He said that we need not be frightened, that he was not going to hurt anyone." Raising herself off the floor, Maggie, gruesomely blood-spattered, crossed the saloon toward O'Donnell and demanded to know, "in a grieving, frantic way," why he had shot her husband. The answer was reported differently by each witness, the most likely version being, "Shake hands, Mrs. Carey, I had to do it." Clinging to O'Donnell, Susan was heard by all to remark, in a tone of reassurance mixed with pride, "No matter, O'Donnell, you are no informer."

Dr. Everitt, a passenger who was a surgeon, was summoned, and when he arrived, he found the victim lying on the floor, breathing heavily, his pulse irregular. Carey was lifted onto a table to be examined but died a quarter of an hour later.

The ship's captain had come into the saloon and ordered the gunman to be put in irons. Only now, as O'Donnell was forcibly separated from Susan, did he offer resistance. "He tried to get to his wife, 'his little girl,' he called her," said Beecher, who took him up on deck and locked him in a bathroom. Captain Rose then asked Beecher and another officer to go to O'Donnell's cabin and search through his belongings. His sea trunk was unlocked, and inside they found a large handgun in a leather holster; it was not loaded, but there was a tin of cartridges to fit the Nichol silver pistol he had used to kill Carey. They also found a mahogany case containing "some sort of electric machine." Fearing that it might be a bomb, activated by a clockwork mechanism, Captain Rose put it gingerly to his ear. He heard no sound. This was, of course, the galvanic mechanism O'Donnell used to help restore muscular wastage, but when Dr. Everitt was consulted, he was just as wary. "It was unlike anything I ever saw connected with medical science." It was thought important to retain the suspicious contraption as possible proof of subversive activity, and Rose suggested that it be hoisted to the masthead. Someone pointed out that it might explode, sending the mast blasting through the ship's bottom, and it was decided to tow it astern. The case bobbed behind the *Melrose* for a few nautical miles and then was washed away.

*

The ship had been twenty-three miles south of Cape St. Blaize when the murder took place, and it docked the following day in Port

Elizabeth—a prosperous town, built at the foot of a hill, with handsome English colonial buildings and one wide main street. Adjacent to the harbor was the courthouse, where Captain Rose arrived around two p.m. to report the murder to the resident magistrate and make arrangements to bring the body and the gunman ashore. In the hour it took for a launch to return from the *Melrose*, the news had spread, and the quay was thronged with spectators. O'Donnell, who had been handcuffed to the boat's railings, stepped ashore with a police escort on each side and was marched up Jetty Street, his head held high and his posture regimentally erect. When he heard the cheering of "some roughs" among the crowd, a grim smile crossed his face. The boatmen hoisted up Carey's corpse, enveloped in canvas, which was then carried by convicts to the mortuary. The district surgeon, with Dr. Everitt's assistance, formally identified the body and issued a death certificate. After a short interview with the magistrate, O'Donnell was taken to the *tronk*—the North End Gaol, outside of which, because of rumors of a rescue attempt, an enclosure was being erected for soldiers of Prince Alfred's Guard. Before Monday's late edition of the Port Elizabeth *Herald* was issued, the outer doors of the paper's premises had to be barred against a news-hungry crowd, while hundreds more congregated in Market Square. "We do not remember seeing such excitement," exclaimed the *Herald*'s editorial writer.

*

Queen Victoria had received William Harcourt's telegram about the shipboard murder on the evening of Monday, July 30. "Well deserved, but shocking!" she noted in her journal, adding a few days later: "That shooting of Carey, though he richly deserved it, is not a good thing, as it shows the power of the secret societies to be still very great." She cabled Harcourt, asking him to send further intelligence and adding that she was anxious to know about the reaction in Ireland. "There can be no doubt," he replied, "that the effect produced has been one of extreme exultation amongst the disaffected (unfortunately the greater portion) Irish population. It is to them a triumph, and it is to be feared may have very bad results."

"Last evening and through the night the city was wild with excitement," Mallon told Edward Jenkinson, and all over Ireland, reports of Carey's murder were received with jubilation. Bonfires blazed, public saloons were packed, fife and drum bands played patriotic tunes, and there were mock wakes, effigies ignited, and children begging, "Give me a penny, sir, to burn James Carey!"

The informer's violent death had been half expected—"No man can betray and live, no corner of the earth is too obscure or too far to hide," warned a pamphlet issued by the Clan na Gael—and it had not evoked the slightest pity. "The popular conscience voiced a unanimous verdict of 'Serve him right,'" said Michael Davitt, who found himself analyzing what had caused such abhorrence for Carey: "It was his efforts to retain the character of a 'Nationalist' while playing the part of the traitor . . . that sickened the public mind with so repulsive a picture of human vileness, and which ranked him in pre-eminent infamy above all previous informers."

For the British authorities, the assassination was a damaging embarrassment: no matter how strong their antipathy toward James Carey, it had been their duty to protect him. "The incident certainly reflects on the precautionary arrangements taken by the Irish police & will I fear effectually put a stop to the further supply of Queen's evidence," Edward Hamilton remarked. However, it was not the Irish police who were at fault—Carey's conveyance from Kilmainham had been impeccably handled—but it had been extremely unwise to send Carey on the same ship as his family, as their Christian names and the exact ages of the children were given in the passenger list. Harcourt told the queen that he believed the Careys had been watched en route to London, where their final destination was ascertained. "O'Donnell then seems to have secured his passage and Carey subsequently embarked.

But he ought never to have been sent with his family. They should have joined him abroad."

*

When the district surgeon, Dr. Frederick Ensor, visited Pat O'Donnell in North End Gaol on Monday afternoon, he found a tall, lean, care-worn man, standing "as if he had been under discipline in the army or police force." The muscles of the prisoner's face quivered occasion-ally with suppressed emotion; his pulse was weak; and he told Ensor that he had "partaken of nothing but a small bit of bread and cold water." He had not left his cell since his confinement, and after the sea voyage, felt badly in need of fresh air. The doctor said he would make sure that O'Donnell was properly fed and arrange for him to be allowed into the yard.

"Are you married?"
"Yes, my wife is in Philadelphia."
"Did you travel alone?"
"No. I had my niece with me. She is on board the "Melrose." . . . Her name is Susan MacDonald [sic]; her age is 18 years. We had the same cabin. She was in service but her mistress mistreated her and I brought her away with me, thinking she might do very well out here in South Africa. Finding things bad in Cape Town I brought her on intending to go to Natal."

Ensor promised that he would call on the heads of the Roman Catholic clergy and tell them of his "niece's" circumstances—"They are likely to interest themselves on her behalf." O'Donnell's eyes welled with tears, "Then that is all I care for."

The following morning, he was brought before the resident mag-istrate, Alfred Wylde, who explained that this was a preliminary examination to decide whether there was sufficient evidence to justify committing the prisoner for trial on the charge of willful murder. A defense lawyer had been appointed, but when asked to name witnesses, Thomas O'Brien said that none was required. O'Donnell was pleading "not guilty" and had affixed his mark to a written statement read out in court: "What I did was in self-defense. Mr. Carey pulled the revolver out of his right-hand pocket. I snatched it out of his hand."

Witnesses for the prosecution were then called. Inspector Cherry of the Port Elizabeth police had made a more thorough search of the contents of O'Donnell's trunk and itemized what he had found: a suit of clothing; eleven pounds' worth of gold; an American dollar; a purse containing the *Weekly Freeman* supplement "rolled up tightly"; other newspaper clippings, two dated May 11 and 17, "showing that he was in America at that time"; letters (including the reference from the manager of the Derry branch of Belfast Bank) confirming O'Donnell had been in Ireland in June. There was a certificate of American citizenship; and in a cigar box were photographs of O'Donnell and a woman [his wife Margaret]; a note dated May 11, 1883, from one P. F. Duggan in Allentown [O'Donnell's sister was married to a Donegal farmer named Duggan]; and several envelopes addressed to a Peter McKnight of Button Street, Philadelphia.

The boatswain Thomas Jones recounted how he had been standing in the saloon with his back to Carey and so had not seen the prisoner fire the first shot. The two men had been close together, he said, and were talking in low voices. "I did not hear O'Donnell make use of any threats, nor did I hear any high words between them." James Parish, who had been coming out of his berth to serve tea to the officers, testified to having seen the prisoner draw his gun and fire all three shots. He too heard "no quarrel or high words," but he was not a reliable witness: after having described the pair sitting down together when the first shot was fired, he said when cross-examined by O'Brien that Power had been "standing a couple of yards off."

Charles Schofield, the passenger who had lunched earlier with O'Donnell, told the court that he had gone into his cabin and a few minutes later heard O'Donnell say the name "Carey," followed by the sound of a shot. Like Parish, Carey's son Tom claimed to have seen the first shot fired. He said that the men had been talking and laughing together—"If there had been angry words I must have heard them"—and told how O'Donnell had drawn a handgun from his inside pocket and fired it at his father, who was standing at the corner of the booth. Tom claimed to have then run into his mother's cabin to fetch his father's gun from the bag in which it was kept—"I thought he might want it to defend himself"—and come out in time to see the second and third shots fired. He watched his mother go over to O'Donnell, "who put out his hand and said he didn't do it or he had to do it." Maggie Carey's evidence echoed her son's, except for one important departure—her version of the "shake hands" line gave it a completely different interpretation: "He said, 'Mrs. Carey, don't blame me; I was sent to do it.'"

*

The idea that James Carey had been tracked by a Fenian avenger took hold, and rumors of O'Donnell's activist background were inflated by the press. They claimed that he had been a prime mover in the 1867 Fenian Rising, taking command in the final struggle with Irish constabulary in the village of Tallaght; he was said to have had gone to San Francisco in 1871 as a Clan na Gael agent, reappeared in New York a decade later to take part in the dynamite conspiracy, and acted under the directions of Patrick Tynan, "known to him only as No. 1." One newspaper maintained that he had been one of O'Donovan Rossa's ten men sent from America to kill Carey, his instructions being to watch Plymouth and the channel ports: "It was first suspected that the Government would try to get Carey over to Havre or Rotterdam, and it was mere chance that led O'Donnell to find him on a Cape Town steamer." Another report had him traveling from Dublin to London with Maggie Carey and her children and meeting some Irishmen in a public house at Great Tower Street the night before leaving

London. "He said nothing as to her destination, but intimated that he was going to South Africa on an important mission and that he would be accompanied by another man to see the work was done all right."

Not a word was true. The portraits of O'Donnell as a revolutionary were as apocryphal as the claim that he had been living in Dublin, where he "eked out a livelihood" by selling photographs of celebrated Irish Americans; or that he had acted as "a sort of agent for public lecturers," among them Samuel Clemens, better known as Mark Twain.

And yet, the possibility that Pat O'Donnell was an extremist cannot be ruled out. Jack Curran, whose family knew him well, declared that he had been at the center of an Allentown cell: "There was nothing but Fenians anywhere you would put your foot. . . . Paddy was like a king amongst them and he was their master." And if no evidence has come to light that O'Donnell took part in the 1866–71 Fenian raids in Canada, he was said to have opened a public house on the frontier, as well as invested $2,000 in the Fenian bonds that funded the invasion; the bonds exploited "many simple souls," who handed over their money, believing that when Ireland became a republic, they would be repaid with interest.

An impression of O'Donnell as ardent patriot is also given in an account attributed to the famous Pinkerton detective James McParlan, who had infiltrated the Molly Maguires, an underground group of Irish activists. Coal miners, fighting to improve hazardous working conditions in the anthracite fields of Schuylkill County, Pennsylvania, they were based mainly in Mahoney City, where Patrick O'Donnell is said to have arrived in December 1875. Intending to visit his Molly Maguire cousins, who lived in the nearby town of Wiggans Patch, he supposedly missed by two days a notorious massacre at his widowed aunt's house. A former member of the Royal Irish Constabulary who was then a Philadelphia detective recognized O'Donnell boarding a train and passed word to the Pinkerton agency to watch him. "The mob gathering in Mahanoy City" had already heard about the stranger in the village, and been led to believe—"perhaps deliberately"—that he was an Irish hitman and organizer. McParlan, however, claimed that he already knew "nearly everything" about Patrick O'Donnell.

> I knew when he got to Wiggans Patch and I knew when he left. At first I thought maybe it was me he was after but then I figured if Jack Kehoe [the Molly Maguire kingpin and husband of O'Donnell's first cousin Mary Ann], ever found out who I really was he'd have wanted to do the job himself. . . . As far as Pat O'Donnell was concerned, that boy had one real interest—the freedom of Ireland, and there were few ways he could promote it up in Schuylkill County.

The story would be fascinating were it not for the fact that it comes from an unsourced book authoritatively described as "a peculiarly misleading mixture of speculation, invented dialogue, interviews, and documented, undocumented and mis-documented historical 'facts.'" A genuine McParlan report, dated Christmas Day, 1875—a fortnight after the Wiggans Patch murders—gives a totally different version of "a man named Pat O'Donnell," who had created a stir in Duffy's saloon bar.

> It was reported that he had previously said he would go to Duffy's with a loaded revolver and if he found any M.M.S. [Molly Maguires] there he would shoot them. Duffy accused him of this but the man denied having said it and called for a drink. Duffy refused to give him any and said he was tempted to shoot him on the spot and ordered him to leave.

This Pat O'Donnell came from Ashburton, in Baltimore, and yet another Pat O'Donnell was a member of the Mollies, sentenced for five years in 1877 for second-degree murder of a mine superintendent.

The Pat O'Donnell responsible for Carey's murder remains something of a mystery. Not only unconcerned about being a bigamist, he occasionally acquired suspiciously large sums of money (it was highly unlikely that herding cattle would have earned him the $700 with which he had arrived in Philadelphia in May 1883). But was he a militant Fenian? His name does not appear in letters and memoirs of leading Irish nationalists nor in police reports of known Gweedore activists. O'Donnell himself insisted that he had never been involved in politics, and although Derrybeg's Land War was at its height during the three months he lived with his brother Dan, he had not attended its mass Land League rally, explaining, "I don't mix much in them things, even when maybe I ought." Locals who came to know Pat at the time were convinced that he did not belong to any secret society. "They say he was a quiet, amiable and sober man, and they never saw anything approaching hastiness of temper," wrote the Donegal correspondent for the *Irish Times*. "There is genuine sympathy for him in Gweedore. The idea of his having gone to the Cape specially to kill Carey is ridiculed."

*

On the afternoon of Wednesday, August 1, James Carey was due to be buried in the graveyard behind North End Gaol, but its Irish Catholic priest, the Reverend Farrelly, who was looking after Pat O'Donnell in prison, had refused to officiate at the funeral. A belief existed that the devil would claim informers' bodies after death and that "misfortune and a curse went with them"—but in Farrelly's case, it was more likely that patriotism had erased his Christian compassion.

Dr. Ensor, hearing that no minister would be present, decided to take charge himself. He discovered that there was no coffin and rushed in a cab to the undertaker, where he found one large enough to accommodate Carey, persuading a passing cartman to transport it to the morgue. "It seemed so shocking that the corpse should be buried hugger mugger, like a dead horse." Around three p.m., when he arrived at the jail, Maggie Carey was waiting on the steps with Tom and the baby; the three of them occupied the first cab, followed by Dr. Ensor and the assistant magistrate. Standing in the searing heat on a barren hillside, surrounded by stunted cacti and a few wooden and iron crosses, Ensor addressed the little group. "Friends, I think it only right that a few words should be said over the grave of this poor man," he said, before reading the prayer that he had hastily written down:

> O Thou omnipotent . . . Ruler of the Universe, we restore, as is fit, the mortal remains of this our weak and erring brother to his mother earth. His immortal part, we are certain, is also under thy guidance and control. . . . In mercy, look down on these—the widow and the helpless orphans—as they stand beside this open grave. Grant that Time, the Consoler as well as the Avenger, may throw a thick veil over their past.

The desolation and anonymity of the open ground—the final resting place of the town's paupers, people of color, and executed prisoners—never left Ensor: "What an end. . . . For the future, when I would use a phrase which would best express a miserable, dreary spot, I shall [say], 'As lonely and dreary as James Carey's grave.'"

*

On Thursday, Pat O'Donnell posed in his cell for a Port Elizabeth studio photographer, C. W. Smart. Saying that the portrait was "for the benefit of his niece," O'Donnell took it all very seriously, refusing to sit until he had been allowed a clean shave and time to dress for the occasion, and he spent a restless night, "pacing his cell, whistling and talking to himself." Susan was much on his mind. He had asked, "Can I see the little girl?" and made a special request that she be landed in Port Elizabeth so that she could be provided for. By the weekend he was much calmer. Dr. Ensor had prescribed a sleeping draft, and on Saturday morning, anticipating a visit from Susan, O'Donnell "partook of a hearty breakfast." She had managed to obtain a permit to see him, and while there, wrote a letter on his behalf to Dan, enclosing one of the photographs and describing how he had "wrenched the weapon from [Carey] and fired at him." Clearly, O'Donnell wanted his family to believe that he had killed the informer in self-defense.

*

The resident magistrate was unconvinced. There was nothing in the evidence, Alfred Wylde said, to persuade him that O'Donnell had acted in fear of his own life or killed the deceased by accident. "I therefore am compelled to commit the prisoner for trial for willful murder, leaving it to the Public Prosecutor to direct what steps shall be taken."

It made sense to have Patrick O'Donnell tried in the colony, where he and the witnesses were already in place and where British law was administered. But the fact that the murder was committed at sea meant that the case was out of the ordinary jurisdiction of the South African courts, and the authorities felt compelled to "ascertain the wishes of the Imperial Government."

In London, Edward Jenkinson made himself responsible. After speaking to William Harcourt and consulting Sir Henry James, the Liberal politician whom Gladstone had appointed attorney general. he discovered that statute dictated that a man who had committed an offense on the high seas and been charged in the colony "*must* be tried there." These terms were obligatory, he told Lord Spencer.

> Sir Henry James thinks that it would not be legal to bring O'Donnell to England for trial. If this is so, it is most unfortunate for there seems to be a most decided opinion that the man will be acquitted if tried either at Port Elizabeth or at Cape Town. At the former place there are a good many Irish . . . and there is a feeling of indignation about the dispatch of James Carey to the Cape. It will be monstrous if O'Donnell is acquitted in the face of the strong evidence against him, and of course the reason for his acquittal will be patent to all the world. . . . They were to decide finally about O'Donnell today.

But I hope that no effort will be spared to prevent so great a disaster befalling us as his acquittal.

These were disgraceful remarks by Jenkinson—a direct admission of premeditation, confirming what Irish nationalists would soon suspect: "England wanted to make an example of O'Donnell," declared the author of an anonymous legal pamphlet. "She needs informers to uphold her domination in Ireland." Spencer's response was more measured; he was not against O'Donnell staying in the colony, "if he is likely to be tried properly there." However, for him too, a guilty verdict was a forgone conclusion. "Great advantages will arise from not hanging him [in London]."

*

On August 26, O'Donnell arrived by steamer in Cape Town and was transferred to Roeland Street Jail. There was great sympathy in the Cape for Irish nationalists, not only among its immigrant population but also among Afrikaners, who were just as resentful of British control (Irish nationalists, in turn, had strongly supported the Boer rebels). Several prominent citizens, intending to fight extradition proceedings in the Supreme Court, had started an O'Donnell defense fund. They had employed the eminent Queen's Counsel and leader of the opposition party, Thomas Upington (known as the "Afrikaner from Cork"), but not even his hard fight could persuade the judges to interfere with the Crown's decision. On Monday, August 27, the South African attorney general wrote to the colonial secretary:

The prisoner will leave by the "Athenian" tomorrow in charge of Inspector Cherry of the Port Elizabeth Police and two constables. Mr. Cherry has the prisoner's box and all the revolvers and other exhibits in the case. . . . It will be observed that O'Donnell has no witnesses, and that the woman O'Donnell refuses to go. I do not feel justified in arresting her and forwarding her under escort, though I feel convinced that she can give important evidence against the accused. The evidence of the crime is so clear and direct that her attendance for this purpose at least is not necessary; more especially as her testimony would not be willingly given. Whether she is really the prisoner's wife or not cannot be ascertained. A report is current that she is a man in disguise. I am informed on the positive authority of Captain Rose that there is no foundation for this assertion.

*

At four p.m. on Tuesday, the gangways of the *Athenian* were removed, but a southwesterly wind was blowing so furiously that at nine p.m. the captain made the decision to remain in Table Bay until the following morning. Although confined to his cabin for meals, O'Donnell was given a considerable amount of freedom, spending long periods on deck, walking up and down, smoking cigars or a pipe. Always with him were two constables, Jupe and Cook, and one would sleep in his cabin, which was kept locked. O'Donnell had established an easy rapport with Inspector Cherry and his two men, and when he noticed that there was no knife on the plates they brought him, joked, "I suppose they are afraid I will commit suicide!"

On the whole, his demeanor throughout the voyage was cheerful, although he showed moments of foreboding, complaining to his warders about a newspaper report that falsely connected him with the 1882 explosion at Mansion House, the residence of the lord mayor of London—a bomb planted by an Edward O'Donnell. One passenger with whom he chatted told the press, "O'Donnell does not so much mind standing his trial for the murder of Carey, but he is afraid he may be recognized by the police for other things, and this has preyed on his mind." He had observed how O'Donnell would appear to be in deep thought and then suddenly jump up from his seat and edgily pace the deck. "He states positively that the authorities will not be able to produce witnesses to prove the murder . . . [but] thinks the police may discover things in trying to convict him which will bring other people into trouble."

*

Blaring her foghorn, the *Athenian* entered Plymouth Sound on Monday, September 17, the western shoreline too murky to be visible. Three officers from the Special Branch of the Criminal Investigation Department came on board, men selected for their knowledge of the English dynamite conspiracy and contact with physical-force extremists. Chief Inspector Littlechild and Officers Ahearn and Pope were introduced to the three South African policemen, briefly conferring with them while O'Donnell sat on his sea chest watching, his hands thrust nonchalantly in his pockets. "Have you got Number One this time, then?" he quizzed Inspector Littlechild, whose reply was just as jovial: "Number One is a tall, straight figure. If you had been more rotund we might have taken you for Number Two." Chuckling, O'Donnell said, "There is great talk about me in the Colony!"

With armed guards occupying a compartment on each side of O'Donnell's, the train transporting him to London arrived around noon at Vauxhall Station. After being taken to nearby Millbank Prison, O'Donnell made a three p.m. appearance at Bow Street police court, walking with a spritely air through the police cordon. He was wearing a rusty black suit with a bright yellow-and-pink-striped tie, his black felt hat perched on the back of his head, its wavy brim faded to olive by the sun. The proceedings were merely formal: he was wrongly described as "Michael O'Donnell, puddler of Gadoure," and charged with the willful murder of James Carey within the jurisdiction of the Admiralty of England. There was mention of how the Port Elizabeth magistrate had committed him to be tried in the colony, but that it was "thought it right and proper that the prisoner should be sent to this country." No application was made to provide O'Donnell with a solicitor, and it was agreed to resume the hearing in seven days. "That didn't take long," he remarked, putting his hat back on, and striding out with his customary upright carriage.

*

Maggie Carey left Cape Town with the children on the *Garth Castle* at the end of August, having refused to be on the same steamer as O'Donnell. They were traveling second class, without an escort to protect them, and a *Herald* correspondent had no problem obtaining an interview. Describing the victim's widow as "a tall, quiet, comely woman in black," who quaintly referred to her husband as "himself," he noticed that her remarks were full of contradictions, "so must be received with the greatest caution." Maggie Carey made the claim no other witness had reported, that "a person called his wife" was heard imploring O'Donnell "not to do it"; and she may well have been responsible for the rumor that Susan was a man. ("The so-called Mrs. O'Donnell," she said, was "a person of a very muscular appearance, with hair on the upper lip, a deep voice and masculine gait.") After hearing her repeat the "sent out to do it" remark, the reporter commented, "That seems proof that the crime was deliberate, does it not?"

"Oh, there's proof enough!" Maggie was said to have replied.

On arrival in Southampton, England, where a police tug went alongside the steamer to take the family away, the Careys disappeared for two months. Disguised in the uniform of a female warder, Maggie was detained in Holloway Prison for her safe custody, while the children moved in with a Scotland Yard detective and his family, posing as his nephews and nieces. Informed by his superiors that he was to undertake a duty of the strictest confidence, Sergeant Patrick McIntyre passed himself off as a businessman under an assumed name and rented a house in the East London suburb of Dalston for the Carey siblings, him and his wife, and their own two children. "No one guessed who we were. The only circumstance which attracted attention in the neighborhood was the special appointment of a police constable, who took up his position within a short distance of the house. . . . I was constantly armed with a good six-shooter and had my orders to shoot on sight."

*

Incarcerated in dismal Millbank Prison, and unable to read or write, O'Donnell had never felt more vulnerable and alone. When Dan O'Donnell eventually was allowed to visit Millbank, his brother complained that he was being taunted by prison staff about the desertion of his friends and supporters. "[Pat] also told me the officials used to tamper with him in Millbank, but all their artifices would elicit nothing from him." O'Donnell's easygoing manner had given way to extreme unease and paranoia; he had become suspicious of everyone around him—convinced that the authorities were plotting to control his trial.

> The governor pressed me constantly to secure an American lawyer and to notify the consulate that I was an American citizen. . . . I suspected that Harcourt and the governor were conspiring to . . . make an ostensible connection between my act and the National League in America, and through that the League in Ireland, and finally between the latter and the Invincibles. . . . I told him I wished the Government to let me alone.

O'Donnell was right to be wary of an Invincibles link but wrong to blame the British establishment in this instance. As soon as word spread of his arrest, Irish American radicals began raising money for his defense: the *Irish World* launched an O'Donnell fund, declaring that $100,000 could be subscribed in a week if necessary; and the *Irishman* announced, "In all parts of the world the Irish would contribute their last shilling to save the life of the man who committed the most popular murder since Talbot was shot in Dublin." In Chicago, an O'Donnell defense fund was simultaneously started by John F. Finerty, who had publicly scorned Parnell's abhorrence of the Phoenix Park murders and was described by Henri Le Caron as "the well-known dynamite advocate." In Philadelphia, in a speech about Ireland's faith in nitroglycerin, the new form of warfare, Patrick Sheridan addressed a large meeting, avowing that "there never was a nobler specimen of mankind than O'Donnell. . . . We shall have money enough, not only to defend O'Donnell, but a thousand others who are ready to follow bravely in his footsteps." This opportunism infuriated Michael Davitt, whose letter of protest to the Dublin press was headed, O'DONNELL AND HIS QUESTIONABLE FRIENDS:

> Did it ever occur to Mr. Sheridan that in trotting out the name of O'Donnell for the purpose of raising a cheer, he was virtually putting a rope round the neck of a man whom everybody admits to be a brave man, and for whom an extraordinary amount of sympathy has been excited, even among the masses of the English people? . . . What does Mr. Sheridan's oratory attempt to prove? That O'Donnell was sent expressly for the purpose of executing Carey? He must have known this was not the case. . . . To thus criminally play into the hands of the prosecutors of O'Donnell by indulging in an unwarranted use of his name . . . is a piece of the most wanton and detestable braggadocio. . . . In thorough keeping with this mischievous balderdash from Philadelphia, is the tone of the London press, particularly the *Standard* of the past few days [which sees] his killing of Carey as an expression of the Invincible vendetta.

✳

By early autumn, the O'Donnell defense fund had amassed a total of $55,000, and to represent O'Donnell in court, Patrick Ford had employed a leading member of the American bar, General Roger A. Pryor—"a firm and devoted friend to the cause of Irish independence." Pryor, who had acted for Patrick Tynan on his arrival in New York, in turn recommended a London solicitor to start proceedings, Charles Guy, who was already entrenched in the militant movement, having defended two Americans involved in the dynamite attacks in Britain. But at the second hearing at Bow Street, on October 15, O'Donnell could not have been in safer hands.

He had been taken on by the Irish Catholic politician and lawyer A. M. Sullivan, who was a nationalist and had represented Patrick Egan when the Land League leaders had been unsuccessfully prosecuted for conspiracy but who deplored the tactics of physical force. (Before Henri Le Caron met Sullivan in London, Egan warned him to hide his "revolutionary sentiments whenever Mr. Sullivan was near.") To Sullivan, the Phoenix Park murders had been "an act designed to roil, as it were, a sea of blood between the two nations," and he particularly regretted the death of Frederick Cavendish, expressing his sorrow in a note that he had delivered in person to Lucy the following day.

Most opportune of all, however, was Sullivan's knowledge and love of Gweedore. "There is probably no part of Ireland more self-contained or separate, as it were, from the outer world." It was not only the raw beauty of the land and seascape that had so moved him but also the plight of its inhabitants, whose side he had taken in the bitter conflict over imported Scottish sheep. He had spent time in the district investigating the facts for himself and was appalled by the destitution he witnessed. When news reached him in Dublin of Black Jack Adair's mass eviction of 1861, he felt it as a personal blow: "I am not ashamed to say, even now, that I wept like a child."

Galvanized into angry action, Sullivan helped to form the Australian Donegal Celtic Relief Committee, which subsequently sponsored the emigration of 130 youngsters from Gweedore (one almost certainly being Dan O'Donnell). Sullivan had stood by the side of a young priest during his farewell address to the group in a Dublin restaurant, when, speaking in Irish, his voice full of emotion, the priest reminded the nervous new emigrants that this was their last meal on Irish soil. Arriving in Liverpool to set sail for Australia, their train was met by Sullivan who then accompanied them to the quay and waved them off. Two decades later, he again became involved with the parish of Gweedore, when he helped to raise funds for victims of the 1880 flood in Derrybeg church.

Not only attuned to Pat O'Donnell's background, Sullivan had established an immediate rapport with the man. He was entirely convinced by O'Donnell's claim that he had gone to South Africa as a miner intending to seek employment and had been unaware of Carey's presence on the *Kinfauns Castle*.

The trial was to take place at the Old Bailey, the Central Criminal Court in London, and because of its high profile, Sullivan wanted O'Donnell's defense to be conducted by Charles Russell, an Irish Catholic, considered by the chief justice to be "the biggest advocate of the century." Russell was currently on a long tour of the United States but agreed to take on the case when he returned to London in November. In the meantime, Sullivan sanctioned—and probably organized—the publication of a long interview with O'Donnell distributed through the Central News Agency. As the accused would not be called on to speak in court, the idea was for him to tell the story from his own point of view, and in particular to discredit the idea that he had been an emissary sent to kill James Carey.

INTERVIEWER. Did you not hear him discussed in Ireland?

O'DONNELL. Oh, a hundred times; and I said about him what everyone was saying. I heard so much about him that I knew the Phoenix Park affair was only a small part of the murders he did . . . and I used to say "hanging was too good for him."

INTERVIEWER. It was no idea about him [that] carried you to South Africa?

O'DONNELL. That can be proved; for I had told my friends soon after I came to Ireland this year I would give up America and go to the Cape or Australia. I would not go in one ship with Carey for a hundred thousand dollars sure, if I knew of it. I would expect the ship to sink.

O'Donnell went on to describe a physical altercation between the two men, observed by no witnesses, during which Carey had crushed him down against the end of the table.

> O'DONNELL. Seeing him put his pistol to my face, I made a grab at it and fired. My belief is, though I may be mistaken, that at the moment I snatched or dashed the pistol out of his hand, as I fired; or it may be it fell from him; but it went on to the floor six feet away. He rushed, partly stooping, as if to pick it up, and I fired again, not deliberately, for my life . . .
>
> INTERVIEWER. Was your dispute loud?
>
> O'DONNELL. No; only we were looking black into one another's eyes. . . . We must have made [some noise] in our short scuffle, but not much. 'Twas all in a moment like.

O'Donnell had no memory of anyone except Susan in the saloon at the beginning of their clash; he insisted that Parish had been in his cabin until he heard the first shot, and Jones the boatswain at the top, not the bottom of the stairs. Asked about Tom Carey, he smiled bitterly.

> O'DONNELL. That young chap will come to trouble yet. Do you mean to tell me that anyone could believe the story he told. . . . I tell you his son picked that pistol off the floor afterwards, and there is not one word of truth in his story about getting it out of the bag . . .
>
> INTERVIEWER. Did Mrs. Carey come up to you?
>
> O'DONNELL. I was sorry for her, and I tell you I was sorry for the children. I took her hand and said, "Mrs. Carey, I had to do it *in self-defense*; I didn't do it otherwise."

This was a new variation of the remark, and it does not ring true. If O'Donnell were embroidering his statements, how accurate was everything else he describes in the piece—especially the violent tussle? There were other questions too. South Africa's attorney general had confidently told the colonial secretary that no evidence had been found "to connect the Prisoner with any Secret Society or the Invincibles—or previous threats to take life." But at the Bow Street hearing, Inspector Cherry revealed that among the Dublin newspapers in O'Donnell's trunk was an article entitled "Irish Revolutionists in America." Asked to explain this potentially incriminating evidence, O'Donnell dismissed it, swearing that he had not been in Dublin and had kept no newspapers apart from the Carey spread in the *Weekly Freeman*. "I can't read, and I had nothing except my citizenship papers. If my wife didn't happen to have them, someone put those things in my trunk. It was never locked."

He seemed genuinely optimistic that, provided he was given a fair trial, he would be a free man before long. And he was not alone. "We all hoped and prayed that O'Donnell would not suffer for his act," said the writer Katharine Tynan; while at a meeting in London three days after the shooting, Parnell, speaking "under great emotion," told his audience: "The man who executed Carey is as innocent of a crime as the child unborn."

SIXTEEN

Irresistible Impulse

I N MID-OCTOBER 1883, the sister of Patrick Ford, the *Irish World's* editor, arrived in Dublin to distribute a "Martyr's Fund." A tall, thin bluestocking with grayish hair fastened into a low bun, Ellen Ford and her companion, a Miss Doherty, visited each family of the imprisoned or executed Invincibles (Joe Brady's mother had died in July), dividing $8,000 into equal shares. Superintendent Mallon had instructed men from his division to follow them and reported that the women were also in contact with members of the National League—proof, he said, that the organization was "in sympathy with the assassins." The pair then left for London, where "they will likely be found in communication with the Solicitor for the defense of O'Donnell."

This was General Pryor, who had arrived expecting to act for O'Donnell as an American citizen, only to discover that it was necessary first to ascertain whether O'Donnell's papers were legal. Even if the crumpled certificate found in his sea trunk were genuine, proof was still needed that O'Donnell had lived continuously in the United States for five years before November 1876, when it had been issued. The US secretary of state, Frederick Frelinghuysen, consulted the US ambassador to Great Britain, who passed on the responsibility to a deputy—a man named Hoppin.

From police reports, Hoppin learned some basic facts about O'Donnell:

Born at Gweedore, about 1835

Went to US in 1863

Enlisted in Army, from which he soon deserted

Returned to Ireland c 1870

In Great Britain until 1874/5

Working in Edinburgh in 1879

Went to US c July 1882

If this account was correct, there had been no unbroken five-year residency leading up to the 1876 election. And if O'Donnell had been dishonorably discharged from the US Army, then citizenship was out of the question. Hoppin decided to hear his own account and arranged for Home Office permission to visit O'Donnell in Newgate Prison, where he had been transferred, on October 22.

He found "a quiet, mild-looking, undemonstrative man with a strong Irish accent and possessed of a fair degree of intelligence although quite illiterate." O'Donnell was not certain of his date of birth but told Hoppin that, "as near as he could reckon," he was forty-eight years old. He could not remember exactly when he went to the United States as a child but believed he had been between four and six (in the police account he was nine). He claimed citizenship during his minority through his father's naturalization, backing this up by saying that Michael Art O'Donnell had gone to the States ahead of his wife and children. Hoppin told him that the police maintained they had all emigrated together, but O'Donnell insisted that their reports were "wrong in this and other matters."

The reason that he had taken out naturalization papers at Ironton, Ohio, in 1876, he said, was because he wanted to vote in the presidential election, and his eligibility had been challenged. Two witnesses had signed the certificate—Michael McGinley, an employee of Iron-ton's steel rolling mill, where O'Donnell worked, and Hugh Duggan, a relative of his brother-in-law's. They could be traced, O'Donnell suggested, to confirm his residency in America before 1876 (which he said was seven years, not five). Asked about his army record, he described how he had tried three times to enlist but had been rejected because of his injured arm. Instead, he had been employed as a team-ster in a US government supply train on the plains of Colorado in 1865.

The account he gave Hoppin of his employment in America bore no relation to versions by friends and relatives in the press—no men-tion of herding cattle or sheep, "serving as a butler" or "a navvy," "digging for gold in California," "running a pub on the Canadian frontier" ("a shebeen house in Toronto" in another version)—and yet the details were convincing. He said he had helped build "Hawley rail-road" and a dam in New Haven, Connecticut; worked in the DuPont gunpowder factory in Wilmington, Delaware; on the "town lake" and sewers of Chicago; and in Buck Mountain coal mine in Pennsylva-nia. Hoppin's visit was unannounced, so O'Donnell would not have had time to prepare a false curriculum vitae, and his chronicle came across as "reasonably clear and tolerably connected." Some locations were mispronounced but this was not enough to cast doubt on his having been in the places he mentioned. "I can only state that I was impressed by the apparent truth of O'Donnell's statements," reported Hoppin. "It is of course impossible for me to give an authoritative opinion upon this question of citizenship. . . . [I] must leave the final decision to the superior wisdom of the Department of State."

This was enough for Frelinghuysen to write to US ambassador James Lowell, instructing him that O'Donnell's naturalization, "in the absence of proof to the contrary," had been established and that "he was to be regarded as an American citizen." Frelinghuysen asked Lowell to request "a courteous relaxation" of any rules that might bar counsel from the United States the right to plead in O'Donnell's defense and to provide assurance to the English court of his American advocate's eminence.

*

But what were O'Donnell's wishes? He was clearly counting on the involvement of A. M. Sullivan and Charles Russell, as well as General Pryor, putting his mark on a letter to Pryor, asking him to work with his London counsel. Sullivan himself wrote to Pryor, tactfully saying that should it be more advantageous to the prisoner to have American representation, then he and Russell would "cheerfully withdraw." To Charles Guy, however, Sullivan confided that the participation in court of an American outsider with dangerous connections would be fatal to the case, almost certain to prejudice the prisoner's chances of acquittal—"already not too strong." Realizing that he had to accept this outcome, Pryor told the *New York Times*, "They would have retired if I had not."

*

Of pressing importance to the defense was to gather enough evidence to counter the charge that O'Donnell had traveled to South Africa as a hired assassin. That charge "a matter of sheer impossibility" in the view of Scotland Yard's Patrick McIntyre, who knew that O'Donnell had booked his double berth three weeks before James Carey's destination was known.

> Therefore the Clan-na-Gael did not appoint him as they alleged. Moreover, I will do the Clan-na-Gael the credit of taking for granted that they would have selected a man of more intellect and ability. [In America] he had spent most of his time amongst the uncivilized ranchers of Western States and knew nothing whatever of New York intrigue and conspiracies. . . . If O'Donnell had been a member of any Fenian brotherhood, the fact must have been ascertained by one of the numerous informers and secret servants of the Government.

A police inspector who had arrived in Gweedore to piece together O'Donnell's movements and habits experienced considerable resistance from locals. "The people fear that if they give information they will be brought forward as witnesses & thereby expose themselves to the vengeance of the Invincibles," he reported. Inquiries in Derry were more successful. Officer Newry, sent to investigate O'Donnell's visit in May, found out that he had been seen in company with Thomas O'Hanlon, Neil McDevitt, and "a shot boy" named Black—"all nationalists of this city." But he also spoke to O'Donnell's bank manager, a Mr. Skipton, who confirmed that the branch had made a cash transfer to Cape Town and said he had written a letter of introduction to a relative there on June 27—at least a week before the Crown had arranged Carey's passage to South Africa.

Several Philadelphia friends were brought to London to testify that the accused had not belonged to any Irish secret society. Peter McKnight, a tavern-keeper, said that he had received a letter written on O'Donnell's behalf while he was in Ireland, "keeping his word true about going to Africa"; Margaret O'Donnell, who was traveling to England for the trial with her likely new partner, Roger McGinley, intended to reveal in court that her husband's mind had been "greatly disturbed" over her refusal to live with him again. However, she would also be stressing that when he went to Ireland in May, "it was with plans which had no relation to Carey or any political or secret mission." All this satisfied the defense team that what O'Donnell told them had been the purpose of his travels was true: he had gone to Donegal to make a pilgrimage to the Doon well, and he was emigrating to South Africa to try his fortune in its diamond fields. "Then at the last moment," Sullivan said, "the Crown threw in the sponge after having carried out their own investigations on the same point. They admitted that O'Donnell had no preconceived idea or purpose against the life of Carey."

The determining point of the case now became the informer's pistol. Had Carey's drawing of it caused O'Donnell to fire in self-defense? Susan Gallagher had been sitting next to O'Donnell, and even though he insisted to Sullivan that she had witnessed nothing during the critical moments, if she had seen a pistol in Carey's hand, then it was certain that O'Donnell would be acquitted. Until now, she had refused to give evidence, but the offer of a vast sum of money from the defense fund—possibly as much as $2,000—must have persuaded her to change her mind.

General Pryor was the first to interview Susan on her arrival in England. She was timid to the point of being terrified, and while giving her account, seemed most anxious to establish the propriety of her relations with O'Donnell. They were to have been married "at the altar" when they arrived at their new home, she said, and although they had slept together in a double berth, it was as a "brother and sister alone." When asked whether she knew that Power was Carey, Susan said that O'Donnell had mentioned this possibility to her and that he had been worried about how to shake him off without a row; Power was "a bully and always irritable." She described herself sitting on a bench feeling dazed with seasickness, vaguely aware of his tackling O'Donnell about something, and she did remember a sudden angry outburst, "with some stir of feet," and hearing the words "bloody informer." As a shot rang out above her head, she claimed to have sprung from her seat and rushed in terror to the end of the saloon. (In O'Donnell's version: "When she heard us nagging, she went off round towards our berth; but the minute she heard the first shot she rushed out and threw her arms round my neck, crying in alarm.")

After the interview, Pryor gravely broke the news that Susan would be no use to them as a witness, telling Russell, "I say to you, sir, that this girl is telling God Almighty's truth. . . . She saw no firing at all. . . . Saw nothing." Sullivan, hoping that his attachment to her native Gweedore might help to draw her out, decided to interview Susan himself. He knew her hamlet of Stranabrooey, surrounded by bleak stretches of bog and rock, and he recognized her as the type of "utterly unsophisticated" Donegal girl for whom he had always felt compassion. "She had never been to school and except in the rudiments of her religion had never been instructed in anything." Expressing herself fairly well in English but speaking confidently only in Irish, Susan repeated to Sullivan much of what she had told Pryor, all the time trembling and shedding silent tears.

SULLIVAN. Now, Susan, you heard some angry words between O'Donnell and Carey? . . .

SUSAN. I wasn't much minding them at all, sir; my head was aching from seasickness and I was half drowsy. . . . I heard them talk quick and angry all in a minute, and before I knew anything a shot went off near me and I jumped for my life and ran.

SULLIVAN. Now Susan, tell me nothing but the solemn truth. . . . Did you see anything in Carey's hand?

SUSAN. My back was towards them, sir; oh sir, if I had only turned around!

SULLIVAN. Did you see a pistol either in Carey's hand or on the floor?

SUSAN. I didn't see no pistol, sir. Oh God! Why didn't I look?

But could Susan be persuaded to give false evidence, guaranteeing O'Donnell's freedom by swearing that she had seen Carey with a pistol? She was not as guileless as Sullivan had supposed. Firstly, she was not illiterate: in Cape Town she had posted a letter to her mother, and O'Donnell's account of the murder to his brother Dan was written "in a girl's hand." If the witnesses' evidence was accurate, Susan did not leave O'Donnell's side at any point during the shooting, and the remark she made in response to Maggie Carey's grief—"No matter, O'Donnell, you are no informer!"—was proof of unflinching patriotism. O'Donnell himself hinted in the Central News interview that she held advanced beliefs, suggesting that the "Irish Revolutionists in America" cutting found in his trunk could have been put there by his "wife."

A convincing explanation of why Susan was not called to the witness box was offered by the detective Patrick McIntyre, who knew that she had been medically examined on arrival in London by a prominent nationalist doctor. "The result was not what had been desired, and that may account for her evidence being thought valueless." Was this a euphemistic way of saying that Susan was not a virgin? Or could the consultant have discovered that she was pregnant? If Susan had previously known this to be the case, it could explain why she had agreed so readily to marry a man she had just met. On the other hand, it was just as likely that any child she might have been expecting was O'Donnell's.

＊

Toward the end of November, the police were watching an Irish American sent to London by Patrick Ford. Edward Moran, a short, stout, whiskery County Waterford man, was staying at the Craven Hotel, where General Pryor, Ellen Ford, and Miss Doherty were frequent visitors. His instructions from New York had been to find out why the general, who had been paid the enormous fee of $5,000 (about $130,000 today), was not figuring more prominently in the case. Moran had presented Pryor's card to try to enter the courthouse but had been turned away. Recognizing the officer responsible for tailing him, a Sergeant Redmond, also from County Waterford, Moran warmly shook his hand. They chatted together, and Moran was extremely frank about his reason for being in London: he had been employed by Mr. Ford to take charge of $2,000 to pay the defense witnesses and to make sure that they were well looked after. "He also said if O'Donnell was found guilty and executed that we might look out in England for explosions & blowing up. He said the Americans are taking up O'Donnell's case very hot."

＊

Friday, November 30, the opening day of the Old Bailey trial, was cold, dark, and rainy. Quickly entering the courtroom, O'Donnell keenly scanned all the faces concentrated on him, first crossing his arms, and then adopting a less defiant air by resting one hand on top of the other on the bar. Told that he was at liberty to challenge any members whose names were about to be called, he replied that he would "leave it to his solicitor to do that." O'Donnell's hair was grayer since he had been taken into custody, and he had grown a stubbly beard. He was chewing tobacco and continued to do so as the hours went by; sometimes, as if in nervous response to the evidence, he bit his nails and clasped and unclasped his hands. When Maggie and Tom Carey gave evidence, he seemed almost amused, making it obvious that he took issue with much of what they were saying.

The single defense witness was a Port Elizabeth cabman named Walter Young, who had been engaged to drive Tom and his mother from the courthouse to their lodgings. Chatting to Tom one day, Young had said, "You are a fine fellow; why did you not shoot O'Donnell when he shot your father?" The youth replied that when he went into his parents' cabin to fetch the gun it had been missing, "because my father had it." This was important new evidence, but Young proved to be ineffectual on the stand. Unexpectedly, a stronger case for the prisoner was provided by several prosecution witnesses.

Robert Cubitt, who had shown O'Donnell the *Freeman's* spread of Carey images, described his stunned reaction, confirming that there had been no premeditation on his part. Superintendent Mallon told the court that it was he who had given Carey the handgun and said that he considered the informer to be a highly excitable character who would have gone to any lengths to prevent himself from being unmasked—"a desperate man, and one regardless of human life." A passenger named Nathan Marks, who had witnessed the shooting from a skylight above the salon, had recalled Carey "talking in a very *high* state as if he were laying down the law"—a vital piece of evidence, as it countered the Crown's assertion that there had been no threatening exchange. Charles Schofield (who reported that O'Donnell had said the name "Carey" loudly enough to be heard inside his cabin) could have supported this evidence but did not appear at the Old Bailey.

Leading the prosecution was Britain's attorney general, Sir Henry James. With fine patrician features, he was a handsome man renowned for his gift as a speaker and in court that day made one particularly persuasive point. Even supposing that O'Donnell had fired the first shot in self-defense, he said, why had it been necessary to fire a second time—and even a third, "when Carey was a staggering and a dying man?" James then attempted to associate O'Donnell with extreme patriotism by asking for extracts from the "Irish Revolutionists in America" article to be read. Charles Russell objected. "A man under trial for high treason could not have evidence given that he had books in his library attacking the divine right of kings," he parried, and the request was dropped. The case for the Crown had closed.

On the trial's second and final day, December 1, Russell came into his own. Although modestly admitting his inexperience in criminal trials, he was an imperious personality who dominated everyone, including the judge. He demolished Carey's character, aiming to portray a cruel and treacherous villain, ready at the slightest suspicion to shoot anyone who threatened his life. He dismissed as "idle bravado" O'Donnell's potential threats reported by two passengers and utterly destroyed the credibility of Tom Carey, who was now echoing his mother's allegation that O'Donnell said he had been "sent to do it." Tom faltered under cross-examination, and enough doubt had been planted to draw what Sullivan called, "a conclusion that needed little proof."

When Russell began giving O'Donnell's account of what had happened, Henry James objected, arguing that hearsay was not evidence. Russell replied that he was only following the prisoner's instructions and cited a legal precedent, which Judge Denman accepted. Russell continued, reenacting the confrontation by exclaiming, "You are James Carey, the bloody Irish informer!" and describing how Carey had sprung to his feet and produced a weapon. "O'Donnell was sharper and fired first." He brushed off the second and third shots as "virtually part of the same act following one another in quick succession."

Russell's masterly summing up had lasted three and a half hours, and there was a burst of applause as he slowly sat down, his face gray with exhaustion. Sullivan admiringly grasped his hand, while O'Donnell watched them, his chin resting on his hands folded on the bar, his expression "flushed with gratitude and hope."

Henry James followed Russell and again made one especially discerning point: O'Donnell had mentioned nothing about being forced to act in self-defense to the officer who detained him, to the captain who ordered him to be handcuffed, or to anyone else while at sea. This observation would have been fresh in the minds of the jury as they retired shortly before seven p.m., as would Judge Denman's instruction that if they thought that the act was in self-defense, they must acquit the prisoner, and if they thought it was done in a quarrel "under provocation," they must return a verdict of manslaughter.

After a mere three-quarters of an hour the foreman entered with a hurriedly scrawled note:

> If B has a deadly weapon in his hand and A thinks B is about to use it against him if A in self-defense shoots B would this constitute manslaughter or murder

After reading it, the judge directed the twelve to return to the courtroom. The verdict could be reduced to manslaughter, he explained, if "in the case of a hot quarrel or fight . . . when one is brandishing a pistol against the other," the other is shot. Had this been the situation on the *Melrose*, the prisoner was guilty neither of murder nor manslaughter but of genuine self-defense. "The question I put to you is this," Denman went on: "Where is the evidence of anything amounting to an act done by Carey which would induce the prisoner to think that?" Listening to this suggestion on the judge's part, the defense team was horrified. "That puts the rope around O'Donnell's neck," General Pryor muttered, while Charles Guy told O'Donnell, "It looks blue for you." After the jury left the room, Sullivan rose to speak:

"I understand your lordship to say that the jury must find on the facts proved before them that Carey pointed the pistol at O'Donnell in order to reduce the crime to manslaughter?"

"Oh no, I said nothing of the kind."

"That they must take the facts proven in . . ."

"I certainly told the jury nothing of the kind. I told them nothing as to what they were to find on the facts. It is quite a mistake."

"I was about to submit to your lordship that it is not necessary to prove that and that if they had a reasonable inference they might find justification for manslaughter."

"I did not tell them anything to the contrary. I simply asked where was the evidence of it."

After another three-quarters of an hour, the foreman came in with a second piece of paper. Glancing at it, Denman then ordered the panel back, saying that he was being asked to define the meaning of "malice aforethought." He told the jury that if they thought that the deceased had done something to provoke violent action by the prisoner, they could convict O'Donnell of manslaughter and not murder. However, once again, Denman pointed out that there had been no evidence, only *inferences* of provocation. And not content with one shot, "whatever its origin," the accused had fired two more.

The jury retired again, returning at nine p.m.

THE CLERK OF ARRAIGNS. Gentlemen are you all agreed?

THE FOREMAN. We are.

THE CLERK. Do you find the prisoner guilty or not guilty?

THE FOREMAN. We find the prisoner guilty.

O'Donnell, who had risen from his chair at their entrance, folding his arms and looking unflinchingly in front of him, was asked by the clerk if he had anything to say. He made no attempt to answer but continued staring straight ahead. Silence was called, and Denman put on the black cap, the square of black silk traditionally worn by British judges while passing the death sentence.

When wardens moved in to escort O'Donnell back to his cell, he shook them aside. "Wait a minute, can I speak?" It was too late, Denman told him, even though O'Donnell apparently had not heard the question put to him by the clerk. ("Nobody ten feet away heard," Pryor later recalled.) About to be removed again from the dock, O'Donnell now became violent, wrenching free of his custodians' grasp and shouting, "Three cheers for old Ireland! Hurrah for the United States! To hell with the British Crown!" He was forced down the steps, grappling and shouting furiously, until the doors of the passage beneath were closed and the noise died away.

*

Margaret O'Donnell and Roger McGinley arrived in the Liverpool docks four days later, only to discover that the Old Bailey trial was over. A police sergeant appointed to follow them described Mrs. O'Donnell as "stout, plump face, dark clothing, black bonnet," and her companion as "43–47 years, 5 feet six, dark sallow completion, dark hair & moustache." He made a point of speaking to McGinley, who said that he would have given evidence in favor of the accused, even though he "condemned O'Donnell's morals." The woman, the officer noted, was "buoyant in spirits" and seeming unperturbed by her husband's fate. Margaret later told a Philadelphia journalist that she had come to help O'Donnell if possible, "burying all recollections of the past," but did not want to visit him in prison. "I had no desire to encounter the woman for whom he deserted me," she disingenuously added.

In fact, Susan had just left London for America. "Finding her destitute," Ellen Ford had persuaded her to travel as her maid to

Brooklyn, where there were so many Irish emigrants that she would never be homesick. To give Susan independence, Ford promised that she would open a bank account in Susan's name.

Accompanying the two women on board were General Pryor and Edward Moran. The night before their departure, Pryor had written to Charles Russell, saying that a commutation of the prisoner's sentence would have "a salutary and soothing influence in America"—a view shared wholeheartedly by Michael Davitt. O'Donnell's execution, he believed, would be "a huge blunder" by the government and certain to jeopardize future law and order. An article in the *Chicago Citizen* by the hard-line Irish American congressman John F. Finerty could not have made this clearer.

> The conviction of O'Donnell has ended forever in the Irish mind, all hope of even ordinary justice from Englishmen. We will never again raise a cent to defend any Irishmen before a British court, and never assist or advocate contributions, unless for the purpose of striking terror into England. The result of the trial will be to make party violence henceforth reign supreme in Irish politics. O'Donnell will doubtless hang, but the Irish race will not fail to avenge him. England shows no mercy; let Ireland no longer show any.

Meanwhile, an O'Donnell committee of the Clan na Gael had distributed a circular to the organization's most prominent members urgently calling for a stay of execution.

> The conduct of O'Donnell is regarded as not only justifiable, but meritorious, by hundreds of thousands of American citizens . . . as is proved by their liberal contributions to the fund for his defense. . . . It is acknowledged even by his prosecutors, that not only was he unconnected with any society, but that he was quite ignorant of the identity of his assailant until a very short time before the affray. Therefore, the essential elements of deliberation, premeditation, and malice

aforethought, necessary to establish a charge of murder are totally
wanting. . . .

The question is, simply, whether an American citizen shall, by a
foreign Government, be put to death by illegal and foul means, with
remonstrance, without an effort to save him? . . . The execution of
O'Donnell is fixed for December 17th, one week from next Monday.

*

Drained by the trial, Charles Russell had not stayed in court to hear
the verdict but learned the details in a long letter from A. M. Sullivan. Enclosing the shorthand writer's transcriptions of the judge's
replies to "Papers A and B," Sullivan said that he felt obliged to get
Russell's view on whether he had been right to question Denman's use
of language. He explained that if the judge had not been so emphatic
about the lack of evidence showing that O'Donnell had acted in
self-defense, he felt sure that the jury—or at least, some members of
it—would not have found him guilty of willful murder.

I did think [Denman] had left room for misconception, grave misconcep-
ception by not telling the jury that there need not be express proof
of the circumstances which would reduce homicide from Murder to
Manslaughter or self defense if such circumstances could be reasonably
inferred by them. . . . I entreat your attention to all this, so that if you
think there is anything further I can do I may at once take action. The
unfortunate Prisoner has but ten days more to live.

Russell took this extremely seriously, and although he knew that
judicial mercy was the prerogative of the home secretary alone, he
decided to appeal to Gladstone.

I have long hesitated before coming to the conclusion that I ought to
trouble you with this communication. . . . If justice does not impera-
tively demand that O'Donnell's life be forfeited—I feel strongly that

the interests of peace would best be served by commuting his sentence to penal servitude. I fear his execution would involve injurious consequences.

Russell also wrote the same day to Harcourt, enclosing Sullivan's letter and five handwritten pages of his own, in which he summarized his speech to the jury. Ending by saying, in effect, that Carey got what he deserved, Russell pleaded: "Is not the fearful punishment of Penal Servitude for life fully adequate to the needs of justice? Finally I say let O'Donnell be punished but if, as I strongly urge, punishment short of death will suffice—spare his life."

*

Belief that O'Donnell had been unjustly sentenced was widespread. "The man committed no murder," insisted Michael Davitt. General Pryor, intending to rally the support of the American bar, told the press that the jury had believed that Carey was carrying a pistol and intended to use it, and the fact that their identities had been concealed so that only the British government knew who they were was a virtual admission that they had been specially selected to convict O'Donnell. Pryor also revealed that Denman had brought the black cap into the courtroom before he knew that he would be passing the death sentence. "[He] put it covertly on his desk. There was no longer any doubt as to poor O'Donnell's fate. . . . Judge Denman considered him guilty and meant to see that he was convicted."

Denman certainly admitted that he agreed with the verdict, but he strongly denied directing the jury. Their two notes to him have survived. Paper B—a scribble of blue crayon on a torn scrap—reads: "If we found prisoner guilty of murder without malice aforethought can you take that verdict." It was after seeing these words that the judge left the courtroom to fetch the black cap: he did know what was coming—but it was not until this moment.

In the United States, news of the timing of the sentencing ritual caused a storm. "Judge Denman's wonderfully correct 'anticipation' of the verdict as exhibited by him in the production of the black cap . . . seems to me to prove that this Denman was under instructions to force a verdict of guilty at all hazards. . . . The O'Donnell trial was a murderous farce, and shows that English laws and English courts are enacted and organized for the purpose of registering the will of the British Government" (Honorable Thomas J. Kenna, civil court justice); "He acted like a vindictive Crown prosecutor intent on sending the prisoner to the gallows" (Honorable Francis Nolan); "It is without precedent or parallel in the history of judicial brutality" (Honorable Hamilton Fish); "O'Donnell was murdered" (US congressman Luman Hamlin Weller).

A delegation of fourteen Democratic members of Congress, backed by a resolution of the US House of Representatives, appealed to President Chester A. Arthur personally to intervene. On December 12, Britain's foreign secretary, Lord Granville, received a "pressing" dispatch from Ambassador Lowell: "I am directed by the President to request a delay in the execution of the sentence upon O'Donnell."

✻

William Harcourt had been maddened by the president's intervention. There was no satisfactory proof that O'Donnell was an American citizen, and even if there were, it would make no difference: the accused had been convicted of a murder committed on English territory and was as answerable for it as any Englishman. Above all, Harcourt was determined not to show weakness by conceding to pressure from the United States, telling Gladstone, "The Fenians would believe that they had the Government of the U.S. at their command and that the English Government dare not do justice upon them." It would shatter public confidence in the Courts of Justice, and be an encouragement to murder and crime, both in England and Ireland.

All this was exhaustively stated in a seventeen-page memorandum to Gladstone, in which Harcourt's view that the jury had been "beyond all manner of doubt right" was stressed again and again. If there had been serious disagreement among its members, the prisoner would have been retried with a fresh panel; and if Harcourt himself, as secretary of state, felt there was any need to question the judge's handling of the case, he would have taken the appropriate steps. Not only was there no evidence that Carey had a pistol and had threatened O'Donnell with it, but "there was distinct evidence the other way." No fresh material had been discovered since O'Donnell's conviction, nor would it be supplied were there to be a respite.

> I have come decisively to the opinion there is no error in the verdict or sentence. There is therefore no justifiable pretext or respite in further delay. . . . The execution is fixed for Monday next the 17th. I have written to you at this length in order that you may know my whole mind in it—a mind which I do not conceive anything can alter.

*

Queen Victoria had also been drawn into the negotiations. She had received a letter from Victor Hugo, who had been pressed to "raise his voice" on O'Donnell's behalf. Dated December 14, 1883, and handwritten on flimsy graph paper, it pleads that "the Queen of England will look favourably on the life of the condemned 'O'donnel' [sic] and accept the unanimous and profound gratitude of the civilized world." Victoria had followed press coverage of the trial and, angered by accounts of the prisoner's treasonable outburst, had asked Harcourt for more details. The jury, he replied, had shown "a strange hesitation" in coming to a conclusion on a case that seemed to him clearcut and that had dealt a heavy blow to the Fenian conspiracy. "It is probable that there was some crotchety man on the Jury who perhaps had a great hatred of informers & whose desperation to avoid

a conviction had to be overcome by his fellows." Not entirely convinced, Victoria then asked her lady-in-waiting to write to Gladstone
about the possibility of a reprieve, only to be reminded that this was
the remit of the secretary of state for the Home Department. "But
I must add with regret," replied Gladstone, "That I am aware of no
ground on which a remission or postponement of the sentence could
properly be granted."

*

At the eleventh hour, the New York Times, claiming that the jury had
stood "seven for murder and five for manslaughter," reported that six
of the jurors who convicted O'Donnell had been found.

> Three of these desire that a meeting of the whole twelve should be
> held in order to explain their verdict and arrest the execution of the
> condemned man. It is believed that unless the other jurors are found
> by tomorrow it is scarcely probable that the execution will be stopped.
> The Crown authorities have refused to give the addresses of the jurors
> to O'Donnell's friends. . . . US Minister Lowell states that if any of the
> jury said their verdict was influenced, he is willing to seek a mitigation
> of the sentence; but there is not hope of tracing the remaining jury
> members in time to prevent the execution.

*

O'Donnell spent his last few days in Newgate Prison. He was allowed
to smoke in his cell—"the prison physician says it will have a com-
posing effect"—and he received several visitors, although not Susan,
who was mid-Atlantic, or his wife, Margaret, who said, "When all
hope of saving him was abandoned, we left. I could not bear it." Twice
a day, Newgate's Irish chaplain, Father Fleming, who had taught
O'Donnell to write his own name, came to help with practicalities,
such as making bequests from the defense fund for his relatives. When
Dan arrived, the brothers spoke Irish together and tied up unfinished

business, including the writing of a letter to thank Patrick Ford for his support.

The night before his execution, O'Donnell hardly slept, but only because the warders who stayed with him in the cell—"They're all my friends"—were telling him stories for hours. In the morning, dressed in a navy blue suit, boots, and a scarlet-checked, open-neck shirt, he ate a light breakfast, and when Father Fleming arrived, began to repeat after him the Stations of the Cross. They had reached the Fourth Station when the prison bell started balefully tolling, echoed by St. Sepulchre Church in Holborn—both signaling the imminent execution.

Unable to help himself, Fleming broke down. "Cheer up, Father," O'Donnell said gently. "God bless you. You have been very good to me." The prison's governor and head warden entered, leading O'Donnell away to the pinioning room, where the hangman, Bartholomew Binns, was waiting with a sheriff, three wardens, and the prison doctor.

As Binns was binding O'Donnell's arms, he may have asked whether the thongs were too tight, as O'Donnell smiled and said, "Go on and finish it!" The little procession, with the prisoner at its center, slowly walked to the yard, where the scaffold was erected, the hemp noose suspended from a crossbeam. O'Donnell looked calmly around him. "Father," he said, "I suppose a good many people are praying for me; I feel grand." His composure was reassuring for the priest: "A cooler man I never saw in my life. He was beautifully prepared for death." Precisely as the clock struck eight, Binns drew the lever, and the drop fell with a crash; O'Donnell's neck was cleanly broken, the swaying cord all that remained to show where he had stood. "I would have swung for him," he had remarked in the Cape. And he had been true to his word.

*

In preparation for violent retaliation, London's public buildings including Westminster Abbey, the Mansion House, the Stock Exchange, and the Bank of England were being guarded from cellar to attic; the lord mayor of London had received an anonymous threat to blow up London Bridge and Newgate Prison, and he, along with ministers of state, judges, and other high officials were being kept under surveillance by armed troops. Late on Monday—the day of the execution—a corps of Cheshire police drove to Hawarden Castle to inform the prime minister about rumors of a plot to kill him and to advise him that arrangements had been made for him stay at a nearby Georgian mansion owned by a county magistrate. Attracted by the prospect of a good dinner and night at Soughton Hall, a "very hospitable house," Gladstone was unperturbed. The following morning, he returned to Hawarden, where police remained on guard.

In New York, the *Daily News* reported that 150 "dynamite Irishmen" had gathered at an emotion-charged meeting, where resolutions were passed condemning Judge Denman's conduct and the haste of the execution—an insult by Britain for denying America's request for a respite. One speaker declaimed:

> For every O'Donnell who is murdered, let a hundred British officials die. It is the duty of every Irish citizen of every country to kill the representatives of England wherever found. It is a burning shame that Irishmen should be starving with dynamite only 62 cents a pound. The holiest incense to heaven now would be the smoke of burning London. May God bless the men who killed Burke and Cavendish. Let us give ten thousand dollars to every man who kills a Carey.

Patrick Ford launched an emergency call for funds in the *Irish World* "for warfare against England" and said that what remained of the O'Donnell defense money had been entrusted to his "honor and judgment" to be used for the good of Ireland.

In early February, an Irish American cabinetmaker, who had smuggled a hundred pounds of lignin dynamite through customs, made his way to London. A fortnight later, he left a portmanteau containing a detonating mechanism in the luggage room at Victoria Station, which exploded, but without loss of life. Similar bombs were discovered and defused at Charing Cross, Paddington, and Ludgate Hill Stations. "The origin of these devilish schemes is certain," Harcourt told the queen. "They are planned, subsidized and executed by the assassination societies of American Fenians, who announce their intentions and advertise them openly in newspapers published without the smallest restraint in the United States." O'Donnell's hanging had given new impetus to America's dynamite campaign, and the "active work" was to continue until brought to a halt by the Clan na Gael during the British general election of 1885.

*

Three weeks after O'Donnell's execution, an extraordinary postmortem confession was published in *United Ireland*: "The True Story of the Melrose Tragedy. When O'Donnell Resolved to Kill Carey." Its author was unnamed, described only as "a gentleman" who had been given all the details by the condemned man himself.

At last the truth may be told of the killing of James Carey. It was not to be told so long as a shadow of a chance remained to prevent the sacrifice of a patriot's life. . . . For Patrick O'Donnell did deliberately kill James Carey, and he deliberately killed him because he was James Carey. There was no struggle. Carey made no attack on O'Donnell. . . . Had Judge Denman permitted him to speak before pronouncing sentence, as he was bound by the law to do, O'Donnell would then have told the whole truth and vindicated himself.

O'Donnell did not know Carey on the voyage from England to the Cape. He was not a member of any society. He was merely a rolling stone . . . a Donegal peasant. . . . But he had learned the truth that every peasant in Ireland knows—the truth of the ruin of his native land and degradation of its people by England. . . .

He knew it would not be easy to kill Carey, and he could not afford to make the attempt and fail. . . . Finding himself suddenly alone with Carey and his travelling companion, he could not resist the desire to kill him at once. . . . No human eyes saw the encounter except O'Donnell's companion. . . . He had told her that morning of his determination to kill Carey, and that he would be hanged for it. . . .

Who was responsible for putting up the theory of a struggle and the plea of self-defense? Not O'Donnell. Not his London counsel. . . . [A. M. Sullivan] was determined to defend O'Donnell on the simple theory of irresistible impulse. Sullivan actually believed that he could save O'Donnell by filling the minds of an English jury with the horrible details of the career of the monster who planned and carried out the assassination of Lord Frederick Cavendish, and then betrayed his dupes to save himself. But when the preliminary examination was held, O'Donnell's [South African] friends set up the plea of self-defense and it became part of this legal record of the case. There was no alternative for the London counsel except to make the best of it. Assurances were sent from the Cape that witnesses would be forthcoming who would sustain the plea. . . .

They proved utterly worthless. From the beginning there was scarcely a hope of saving O'Donnell. Whatever hope existed lay in cultivating English public opinion for the prisoner. In this the counsel were thoroughly foiled by the insane folly of some of the Irish in America . . . [who] aroused brutish hatred towards the brave man approaching his trial. . . . Counsel was embarrassed also by the pretended claim of O'Donnell's American citizenship. No authentic record of it was forwarded and O'Donnell himself could not remember when or where he was naturalized. *If he ever was.* President Arthur deemed the fact that he had served in the [Civil] War as sufficient to entitle him to the benefit of citizenship and instructed Lowell to act as if the fact were established. . . . It is certain that no defense would have saved O'Donnell

before an English judge, but it is regretted that the defense of irresistible impulse could not have been set up for the name of O'Donnell
and the truth of history.

*

Four decades earlier, Judge Denman's father, the First Baron Denman, presiding over the 1840 trial of Edward Oxford, a man who
had attempted to assassinate Queen Victoria, had instructed the
jury: "The very important question comes, whether the prisoner
was of unsound mind at the time when the act was done. . . . If
some controlling disease was, in truth, the acting power within
him which he could not resist, then he will not be responsible."
Oxford was acquitted, and the legal concept of irresistible impulse,
or "some controlling disease," could certainly have been argued in
O'Donnell's case.

According to the Cleveland officer under whom he supposedly
served as a substitute in the Civil War, O'Donnell may have been an
alcoholic. He would go on "terrible sprees" with the money he had
earned and was considered to be "the most dissolute and dissipated
fellow in the entire command." Until that Sunday afternoon on the
Melrose, O'Donnell had not touched a drink for what he claimed was
a long time. Tom Carey described him in the saloon as "very drunk,"
and Nathan Marks confirmed that O'Donnell had "looked dazed,
as if he was in liquor." However, what would surely have supported
a plea of diminished responsibility was a remark O'Donnell himself
made to a fellow passenger. The man had asked why he was so abste-
mious, and O'Donnell told him that he had no choice: "If he drank
he did not know what he was doing."

*

A fortnight later, *United Ireland* printed an indignant letter from
Dan O'Donnell, objecting to the "perverted" claims in the paper.
He had twice visited his brother in Newgate after his conviction, he

said, and during their final meeting, Pat had repeated the circumstances that had led to his act of self-defense. "I am sure he told me
the whole truth. . . . I cannot conceive the idea of his telling me a
lie, and on the third morning before his going to appear before his
God." The only people to communicate at length with O'Donnell
in prison, Dan went on, were Father Fleming, his counsel, and Dan
himself. "I am sure the account in question never emanated from
the pen of any of those gentlemen; consequently, then, how can it
be true?"

But the author almost certainly *was* O'Donnell's counsel. A. M. Sullivan, although no longer professionally involved, confided to Michael
Davitt that he had more than one private interview with his former
client in the week leading up to his execution. Both were Catholics,
and the deeply religious Sullivan was determined that O'Donnell—
"for his soul's sake"—should tell him what had really happened.
Finally, Sullivan said, he did. "His story was this: 'When I learned
who he was I resolved to quarrel with him, to give him a chance of
defending himself, and to shoot him if I could. I did so, and I don't
regret it.'"

*

For Davitt, it was the "removal" of the government's prize informer
before he had even reached his distant place of shelter, that gave the
Phoenix Park conspiracy dramatic completeness—"one of the most
marvelous and perfect tragedies which real life has ever contributed
as a contrast to the creations of fiction." Certainly, it was a *coup de
théâtre* vivid enough to spark global interest and capture the popular
imagination. In Ireland, the Invincibles murders and their climac-
tic shipboard ending inspired an unparalleled number of narrative
songs, the momentum of gripping, pictorial scenes crucial to what a
Donegal balladeer called "getting the follow on . . . the path of the
story." "O'Donnell the Avenger," sung to the melody of "The Felons
of Our Land" or "Irish Molloy O" (better known as "Skibbereen")

is one of several existing "broadside ballads" about Donegal's patriot hero and martyr—a classic of the kind still being performed in the Backroom Sessions at Connie Coyle's, the Derrybeg pub once owned by Dan O'Donnell.

> Come all true sons of Erin's Isle
> And listen unto me:
> I'm sure when you have heard my song,
> With me you will agree
> To condemn those English juries
> Who with faces grim and bold,
> Do send all true born Irishmen
> To dungeons dark and cold.
>
> Of that great deed in Phoenix Park,
> No doubt you will have heard;
> When Carey turned informer,
> You remember what occurred:
> To escape a speedy vengeance
> This traitor had to roam,
> And with his ruined family
> He left his native home.
>
> On board the "Melrose Castle"
> As the ship was nearing shore,
> The passengers were all alarmed
> To hear a great uproar:
> They found the traitor Carey,
> With a bullet through his head,
> The rebel, Pat O'Donnell,
> Had avenged the Fenian Dead.

On the last day of November
For that deed he then was tried;
Within the prison dock he stood,
And raised his head with pride;
And over all the great wide world,
The doleful tidings rung,
For this undaunted Irishman
Was sentenced to be hung.

He was a valiant Irishman,
He came from Donegal;
He gave his life for liberty,
At Ireland's noble call;
If every son of Erin's Isle
Had such a heart as he,
They soon would set their native land
Once more at liberty.

After

ON THE scorched hillside behind Port Elizabeth jail, an upright piece of wood was carved with the name "Umfogo-clko," and beside it, a diamond-shaped slab scratched with "Nkalitshaana 1885." Nearby, pebbles marked out the rectangle of a grave, at one end of which, written in penciled scrawl on a large white stone, were the words "J. Carey The Irish Informer." When rain erased the words, someone unknown rewrote them, but as if in response, two rusty strips of corrugated iron were laid on the ground to form a cross. This "rude emblem of salvation" was frequently removed and always replaced—the gesture recalling lines from a poem sent to Dr. Ensor in appreciation of his benevolence at James Carey's funeral:

> When Nero perished by the justest doom
> That e'er the Destroyer yet destroyed,
> Some hands unseen strewed flowers on his tomb.

In 1905, the cemetery's burial remains were removed to make way for a new power station, and an employee who knew the whereabouts of Carey's skeleton reputedly sawed off the top of his skull to use as an ashtray. For many years, well into the twentieth century, it was said that the boiler room in the old Mount Road building in Port Elizabeth was haunted by the informer's ghost.

*

Patrick O'Donnell had been ignobly buried in quicklime in the yard
of Newgate Prison, but in January 1884, a "month's mind"—a mass
celebrated four weeks after death for the repose of the deceased's
soul—was held for him in Derrybeg. This mock funeral was attended
by what the *New York Times* described as "an immense concourse of
peasantry"—inhabitants of the parishes of Gweedore, Cloughaneely,
and the Rosses, who turned out in their thousands, blocking the road
to the church with their carts and horses. Concerned that honoring a
murderer would taint his increasing renown, Father MacFadden had
distanced himself from the event, and the requiem was conducted by
his curate. An empty coffin, draped in black lace and decorated with
a wreath of bright yellow everlastings, was carried by relays of men
to the O'Donnell family burial ground at Magheragallon, where the
mourners, kneeling around the open grave, prayed and recited the
rosary in Irish. After the ceremony, a collection was made to raise
money for a memorial to the local martyr—the thirty-five pounds
donated that day served as the start of a fund to be generously supplemented by contributions from readers of the *Irish World*.

*

Ellen Ford, with the help of a New York women's committee, which
included Mrs. Frank Byrne, had taken charge of raising funds for an
O'Donnell monument and by the summer of 1885 had forwarded
$1,000 "to the patriotic Rev. James MacFadden" for safekeeping.
The plan had been to commemorate "O'Donnell's heroism" with
a Celtic cross in Derrybeg's church grounds, but MacFadden had
refused permission. Instead, to the delight of the American benefac-
tors, an agreement was reached with Dublin's Glasnevin Cemetery—
already something of a "nationalist cemetery" for Ireland's patriot
dead. Eighteen eighty-seven, the year O'Donnell's memorial was
erected, coincided with the twentieth anniversary of the public
hanging of the Manchester Martyrs—a major event in the republican calendar. On a Sunday closest to the men's execution date of

November 23, over a thousand nationalists converged on the Martyrs' cenotaph. They first attended the unveiling of a monument to honor John "Amnesty" Nolan, a forgotten nationalist hero who fought for the release of Fenian prisoners (one being Michael Davitt, who had commissioned it); and then inspected "with manifest pride" the other recent addition to Glasnevin's pantheon of patriots. Although detached from the central area of Irish political graves, the O'Donnell memorial—a Celtic cross on a base of white marble—instates its namesake as a revolutionary icon:

> In loving memory of Patrick O'Donnell
>
> who heroically gave up his life for Ireland,
>
> in London, England, on the 17th December 1882
>
> Not tears but prayers
>
> For the dead who died for Ireland

When an angry reader wrote to the London *Times* holding the Reverend MacFadden responsible for "the monstrous inscription, in flagrant praise of murder, which pollutes the solemnly consecrated soil of her chief Irish cemetery," the priest indignantly replied that he had nothing to do with the project other than act as treasurer. "I loathe the very mention of the murder of Carey. It would be my earnest desire, that its memory should be forever, buried and forgotten."

*

The five executed Invincibles—"noble and fearless men who died for Ireland's liberty"—continued to be lauded by the exiled ringleaders in New York, and the third anniversary of "the victory in Phoenix Park," May 6, 1885, was celebrated at a banquet on Broadway at which Patrick Egan thanked Patrick Ford for his support. At a "Martyrs Meeting" on July 2, Joe Brady was singled out as "a modern Coriolanus"; Frank Byrne spoke of how "two men of the Irish army met and killed two men of the English army"; while his wife, Mary Ann—"a brave little woman whose face is perhaps not known to many, but whose memorable courage . . . [and] sacrifice for the Irish cause is known to us all"—was presented with a well-filled purse as a token of esteem for her delivery of the weapons.

Regarded by his superiors as an attention seeker, "crazy for notoriety" (Ford considered him "somewhat of a crank on the question of 'physical force'"), Patrick Tynan was not among the guests that night. Although just an underling acting on orders, Tynan considered himself to be a major player in the war against England and the leader of the Invincibles' conspiracy, boasting, "One man and one only was entrusted with the full knowledge of every detail." June 1894 saw the simultaneous American and English publication of *The Irish National Invincibles and Their Times*, by "Patrick J. P. Tynan ['Number One']," a rambling, feverishly written tome with a surfeit of footnotes and appendices. Claiming to be an insider's history of nineteenth-century Anglo-Irish tensions, it is essentially a vanity project, in which Tynan—barely disguised as "K"—presents himself as "Captain" of the assassins. (In a long extract in the *New York World*, he describes "the actual scene which he witnessed when the setting sun flashed from the knife uplifted over Lord Cavendish"). But if *The Irish National Invincibles and Their Times* was dismissed as self-promoting sensationalism, it has assumed an importance unimagined by its author. Scholars of James Joyce see it as a source for *Ulysses*—specifically the "Eumaeus" episode, in which Stephen Dedalus and Leopold Bloom stop at a cab shelter kept by Skin-the-Goat. The fragmented, clandestine style, its circumlocutions, and oblique clues, privy only to the initiated, "are all hallmarks of Tynan's voice."

*

Patrick Egan had settled with his wife and eight children in Lincoln, Nebraska, where he speculated in real estate—"Egansville"—and rebuilt his finances by dealing in grain and wool. He was often seen in Chicago with Alexander Sullivan, head of the Clan na Gael, and the British authorities were convinced that both men were directly involved in transatlantic dynamite trafficking; Egan had publicly declared that "dynamite was necessary for the redemption of Ireland" and was accused of having diverted $100,000 of Land League funds to launch the campaign.

For greater operational secrecy, Sullivan had formed a Clan na Gael splinter group named "The Triangle," which the British feared even more than O'Donovan Rossa's bombing teams because "Sullivan's men were more proficient." The August 1884 Convention of the Irish National League of America, held in Boston, was entirely governed by the Sullivanite wing, its secret caucuses presided over by Egan, who was described by one delegate as "that clean-handed, that patriotic, that heroic exile." When Sullivan declined to be reelected as president, he chose Egan as his successor, confident that, as leader of the League, "his worthy *fidus Achates* [faithful friend]" would continue the secret warfare.

Sullivan had stepped down in order to campaign personally for the Republican presidential frontrunner, James Blaine. The influx of Irish emigrants had long been a source of strength to the Democrats, but the Republicans were now actively wooing Irish voters. "I made up my mind that there existed no good grounds by which the Democratic Party should hold any mortgage on my vote because I happened to be an Irishman," remarked Egan, who, along with Patrick Ford, was also supporting Blaine. The Democratic rival, Grover Cleveland, was regarded by them all as the favored candidate of the English press, whereas Blaine, son of an Irish Catholic mother, was a well-known Anglophobe and therefore "the true friend of the Irish." In June 1884, the British ambassador to the United States, Lionel Sackville West, wrote to Lord Granville that Blaine's "pandering to the Irish" was almost certain to carry New York by a sweeping majority. "The dynamite wing of the Irish will go for him because they know he would resist British arrogance and pretention and protect American citizenship abroad."

In fact, with influential voices condemning the attacks on Britain as damaging to America's international prestige, its Irish citizens had become far less willing to donate their dollars for revolutionary purposes. Aware of the mood swing, Sullivan temporarily suspended dynamite operations. (Evidence that militants were taking heed was a notice posted on the door of Chicago's Kessel's Hall, canceling a meeting of the "Joe Brady Club," with the announcement, "All dynamiters who favor the election of James G. Blaine for President of the United States will meet here next Tuesday night.") As it happened, Blaine's questionable dealings in Little Rock Railroad bonds gave rise to damaging press coverage, and Cleveland, a self-declared opponent of corruption, won by a narrow victory.

Four years later, the Republicans were in power. Blaine, who had decided not to run for president and instead endorsed Benjamin Harrison, was appointed secretary of state; Egan, in recognition of his loyalty, was named minister to Chile. At the time, Britain virtually monopolized South American commerce, and Blaine felt compelled to challenge that influence. Who better as his chosen instrument than "an English-hating Irishman"?

*

In Dublin, Superintendent Mallon had become increasingly resentful of the British establishment, blaming his lack of advancement on the castle's cold-shouldering of Catholics. He would complain that "others have earned the credit of my work"—a criticism aimed at Edward Jenkinson, Spencer's former private secretary, who had received a knighthood in 1888 and was now wielding the power in London's Home Office. Mallon's sympathies had always been with his subordinates—he had "a splendid way with young constables"—and his contempt for red tape had earned him little credit with the senior command. Early in 1892, he asked the Irish MP Tim Healy to use his influence to bring about a promotion—an effective plea, as by the end of the year Mallon was appointed assistant commissioner of the Dublin Metropolitan Police.

It was the year *The Adventures of Sherlock Holmes* was first published, and Mallon, regarding himself as something of an institution, was keen to exploit his own notoriety. With Dublin now relatively quiet, however, there was little opportunity for "the DMP's star turn" to exercise his sleuthing genius. He had received word of a mission involving a trip to America by the recently released Skin-the-Goat but gave this short shrift: "Fitzharris could only be used for show, just like a bear. He has no intelligence and is nearly always drunk." He knew of a young political activist who intended "to make herself a nuisance," but not even Mallon's surveillance skills could deter Maud Gonne, a luminous beauty destined to become the muse of W. B. Yeats. Mallon engineered a raid on the offices of the *United Irishman* to suppress the paper for its gloating coverage over the Boer success in South Africa, and he was responsible for security during the April 1900 Dublin visit by Queen Victoria, who felt she should acknowledge the bravery of Irish soldiers in South Africa. Staying at the Viceregal Lodge in Phoenix Park, despite its unhappy associations, the queen had been touched by the warmth of her reception, oblivious to the republican catcalls and the tearing down of Union Jacks in smashed shop windows. "I wish to God she was out of the country!" muttered Mallon.

This was to be his last challenge. A plot was being hatched to reform the hierarchy of the DMP, and both its commissioner and his associate were obliged to take early retirement. In January 1902, Mallon, now a widower with grown children, went home to the family farm in County Armagh, Northern Ireland, where he lived his last thirteen years "in modest but comfortable obscurity."

*

By the end of the 1880s, the Phoenix Park murders would have faded from the public mind had not memories been revived by what Michael Davitt called "an accursed re-echo." On April 18, 1887, a facsimile letter signed "Chas. S. Parnell" and dated May 15, 1882, was published in the London *Times*, clearly implicating the Irish leader in the assassination conspiracy. "No such thunderbolt had fallen in the Irish camp since the deed of May 6, 1882," Davitt exclaimed.

There had been nothing newly damaging in the paper's series of articles, entitled "Parnellism and Crime," which charged Parnell with inciting insurgence (a week after the park murders, he had been depicted in a *Punch* cartoon as Dr. Frankenstein, crouching in terror of the "baneful and blood-stained monster" he had created). But here was written evidence of direct involvement. Parnell could tell at once that the letter was forged—"I did not make an S like that since 1878"—but the effort of proving it was to last another two years.

With the Land League also being held to account by the *Times*, Davitt took it on himself to act as intelligence gatherer. Raising a defense fund of nearly £40,000 and assembling an irregular secret service department of private detectives, defecting agents, and republican insiders, he aimed "to checkmate the most powerful newspaper in the world." The *Times* had at its disposal the Home Office, Scotland Yard, and Dublin Castle, but Davitt's team was able to decipher all code dispatches from the United States and Canada (Gladstone was "Teresa"; Parnell, "John"; Patrick Egan, "George"; Patrick Ford, "Ruby"; Patrick Sheridan, "Bella") and successfully uncovered the truth. Recording his "Notes of an Amateur Detective" in a little black book, Davitt made some astonishing discoveries, the most dramatic being proof of the connivance of the British government in the *Times'* "campaign of systematic calumny against Parnell." And it went right to the top—to the Conservative prime minister, Lord Salisbury.

*

Gladstone's second premiership, "something of a farce and a shambles," had fallen by a small majority in 1885, leaving the prime minister "a good deal mortified by the defeat." Parnell had realized that the Irish could wield the balance of power at the next election—"If we cannot rule ourselves, we can at lease cause them to be ruled as we wish"—and switched allegiance to the Conservatives. The Liberals had done little for Ireland except renew coercion, but he had received a strong hint that a Tory ministry might withdraw the despised act. He knew too that Home Rule stood a better chance if the opposition was in power—a bill proposed by Tory leaders in the House of Commons was almost certain to be accepted by the right-wing House of Lords. On June 9, Gladstone's Liberals, opposed by a united front of Conservatives and Irish nationalists, lost by a margin of fourteen votes.

"The Irish all went against him, and many Liberals too," the queen exclaimed in her journal after receiving Gladstone's resignation telegram. The news had taken her completely by surprise—typical, she complained to Henry Ponsonby, of how the current ministry kept her in the dark. But it was not long before delight set in. She had at last got rid of "these theoretical radicals headed by a wild fanatical old man," and the fact that the Marquess of Salisbury had agreed to form a caretaker government until a general election could be called was further cause for celebration.

Robert Gascoyne-Cecil was a descendant of Sir Robert Cecil, First Earl of Salisbury, who had served as counselor to Elizabeth I. The Third Earl, a true aristocrat, with a dry sense of humor, was not only proud to be "an *illiberal* Tory," but he was a passionate supporter of the empire, the integrity of which, he declared, was "more precious to us than any possession we can have." What appeared to the Irish to be an optimistic sign, however, was his choice of the Earl of Carnarvon as lord lieutenant: Carnarvon let it be known that he believed in Home Rule, and in July announced a noncoercive Irish policy in the House of Lords. It soon became clear, however, that the Irish party had served its purpose and could expect nothing from the Tories.

*

In late 1885, with his mistress, Katharine O'Shea, again acting as intermediary, Parnell reopened negotiations with Gladstone. He was prepared to ask the Irish party to throw out the present government, but first he needed assurance that the Liberals would withdraw coercion and that Home Rule would become a priority. Determined not to be caught again "coquetting with Parnell," Gladstone refused to commit himself, and Herbert Gladstone took it upon himself to bypass his father and force the issue. In a short letter to the *Times*—dubbed "the Hawarden Kite" because it seemed to have been sent out to test Liberal reaction—he wrote, "If five sixths of the Irish people wish to have a Parliament in Dublin for the management of their own local affairs, I say, in the name of justice and wisdom, let them have it."

Herbert's letter, although postmarked Hawarden Castle, had not been authorized by his father, but it reflected his state of mind. Gladstone still yearned for retirement but saw that if he were to make an independent Ireland his own responsibility, it would provide him with a mission—a reason to remain in politics. "I determined on taking any and every legitimate opportunity to remove the existing Government from office."

At the end of January 1886, after Salisbury had presented the Conservatives' own coercion bill, the Irish voted solidly with Gladstone, who won the division by 329 to 250. Clouding any sense of victory, however, was the fact that eighteen Liberals, including Lord Hartington, had sided with the Conservatives.

On the first of February, Gladstone traveled to see the queen at Osborne, his appearance striking her as wan and troubled. Sighing deeply, he admitted that he was weighed down by the seriousness of his Irish undertaking but said that he felt compelled to see it through. He did not explain the high ideals that were driving him on, and if he had, the queen would not have understood. She was blindly prejudiced against any attempt to separate Ireland from England—a "calamitous" outcome that would lead inevitably to the disintegration of her realm.

I told him I feared his proposal of a Central Legislative Assembly in Dublin would never succeed, he would be considered to be acting by

Parnell's advice, & that all the loyal Irish would rise against such a thing, & there would be Civil War! He answered, he might fail, it was 49 to I that he would, but he intended to try.

The queen loathed Parnell, "a really bad & worthless man," and was convinced that Gladstone, without knowing it, was being manipulated by him. Despairing that the prime minister was leading her "great, beloved country to UTTER ruin," she confided her fears to Lord Salisbury when he arrived at Osborne a few days later. In her journal she wrote: "He feels so much for me and for my being alone, so cut off." Before taking his leave, Salisbury assured her that he would do anything in his power to help—an offer the queen intended him to honor. Although it was highly unconstitutional, she began passing on confidential letters and, over the next months, secretly consulted Salisbury about how to ensure the defeat of Gladstone's "reckless" crusade.

*

The Irish controversy was causing a bitterness in English society unequaled by any other political issue—something that Lord Spencer, Gladstone's "great comfort" over Home Rule, knew only too well. Resenting his support for Gladstone, the queen no longer invited him to Windsor Castle; Spencer's friends "actually cut him and won't meet him"; acquaintances taxed him directly ("I trust you are not going to give us all over to the wolves. Our property would all be confiscated, and what would become of us and our children in Ireland, God only knows!"); or berated him behind his back: "We have heard that Lord Spencer, of *all people* is a convert (*pervert* I think I ought to say!)."

Spencer had fallen out with Lord Hartington, who had publicly distanced himself from Gladstone's Irish policy and was leading a Liberal Unionist faction along with Joseph Chamberlain. Gladstone, however, was prepared to proceed without assurance of support from any of his colleagues. "This was one of the great imperial occasions which call for such resolutions," he declared, the historical significance of his stance reflected by the large numbers in the House of Commons on April 8, 1886, when "princes, ambassadors, peers, and distinguished strangers" jostled one another for places to witness the first reading of the bill proposing Irish Home Rule.

Quietly and earnestly, in a voice defined by its "undulating cadences, slight northern accent and hint of retribution," Gladstone began to explain all the factors involved in Home Rule, from the collection of Irish revenue and control of its own constabulary, to changes to the office of viceroy. His speech, a triumph of rhetoric and practical detail—"which I sometimes have thought could never end"—lasted for three hours and twenty-five minutes. It was a tremendous achievement for a man of Gladstone's age, but it was all for nothing. The bill was overthrown by a hostile majority of thirty, a defeat that Gladstone would refer to years later as "the disaster of 1886."

*

"What vast benefit for Britain would have followed from an Irish settlement in the 1880s, thirty years before the Easter Rising," the former home secretary Roy Jenkins memorably remarked in his 1995 Gladstone biography. But what followed instead was the return to power of Lord Salisbury, with a large Conservative/Liberal Unionist majority, and an Irish policy envisaging "twenty years of resolute government." A month after Gladstone's enlightened tour de force, a speech by Lord Salisbury stressed the impossibility of achieving unification in Ireland, describing it—albeit presciently—as "two deeply divided and bitterly antagonistic nations." His great blunder was to let slip his own warped antipathy toward its inhabitants.

> Confidence depends upon the people in whom you are to confide. You would not confide free representative institutions to the Hottentots, for instance. Nor, going higher up the scale, would you confide them to the Oriental nations whom you are governing in India. . . . [Self-government] works admirably well when it is confided to the people

who are of Teutonic race, but it does not work well when people of other races are called upon to join in it.

The furious backlash to his speech forced Salisbury to regret his "stupid calumny," and yet he would soon resort to extraordinary lengths of corruption in his determination to subjugate the Irish.

*

"We have purposely and advisedly abstained from doing anything likely to embarrass them during the crisis of the elections," declared a Clan na Gael secret circular, confirming the organization's suspension of the dynamite campaign. Lord Salisbury, however, presumably following the lead of his Machiavellian ancestor, saw how he could profit by "the powder business."

Historians had recently discovered documents suggesting that the First Earl of Salisbury had been aware of the 1605 Gunpowder Plot masterminded by Guy Fawkes eighteen months in advance. Salisbury had used this knowledge, they believed, for his own political ends. "His lordship, beyond all others, seemed disposed to take advantage of so foul a scandal, in order to root out all memory of the Catholic religion," wrote one chronicler. The discovery of "this plot of powder," not only facilitated the passing of laws against Roman Catholicism, it enhanced Salisbury's prestige, generating "great love and honour from the kingdom . . . [and] at least for a time, a high degree of popularity and power at court."

Some two and a half centuries later, the Third Earl had learned that Irish American militants were preparing "to work with Greek fire" in order to stage a massive act of terrorism. Its purpose was to illuminate "Mrs. Brown's Jubilee celebrations"—the fiftieth anniversary of Queen Victoria's accession to the throne on June 20, 1837. Masterminding the jubilee plot to kill the queen, first from America, and then from Paris, was the Clan na Gael's military expert, General F. F. Millen, an Irish American whom the British had recruited as a spy.

Through an intermediary at the British legation in Mexico, Salisbury had been authorizing huge payments to Millen, an arrangement that began in May 1885, when the general was promised a "renumeration of £2,500 if he carries out engagement details to the satisfaction of H.M. Government." Superintendent Mallon hinted to Frederick Bussy that the jubilee conspiracy was one of several British intelligence efforts aimed at providing "the credit of baffling and entirely preventing the execution of that plot"—a theory fueled by the confession Bussy witnessed from a policeman who admitted planting bombs on a dynamiter, "so that he should be taken 'red-handed.'" The general must have informed on other participants to avoid his own arrest, but Mallon's remark that "Millen humbugged them" suggests that he was less biddable—and therefore more treacherous—than the British had supposed. As it happened, the jubilee celebrations passed without incident; the queen, though "half dead with fatigue," was very much alive, and happily oblivious of the extent to which her cherished prime minister had endangered her life.

*

In July 1888, another letter signed by Parnell was published in the *Times*. Supposedly addressing Patrick Egan, it pointed more emphatically to the two men's involvement in the Phoenix Park murders, although the crudeness of the language made it even less plausible than the first.

> What are these people waiting for? This inaction is inexcuseable [*sic*]. Our best men are in prison and nothing is being done. Let there be an end to this hesitency [*sic*]. Prompt action is called for. You undertook to make it hot for old Forster and Co. Let us have some evidence of your power to do so. My health is good, thanks.
>
> Yours very truly,
> Chas. S. Parnell

Parnell had all along suspected William O'Shea ("always my enemy —my bitter relentless enemy"), but the captain, although increasingly hostile, was not the forger. In August 1888, Egan wrote to Davitt naming a disreputable journalist and newspaper proprietor, Richard Pigott, with whom he had dealt in the past over the sale to the Land League of the *Irishman*. In June 1881, "Dick" Pigott had attempted to blackmail Egan, claiming that he had been offered £500 by "the Castle people" to publish damaging documents. Sending back a sharp refusal and subsequently printing the correspondence, Egan kept the original letters, the handwriting of which bore a striking resemblance to the "Parnell" letters in the *Times*. In one, not only were certain phrases identical, but the word "hesitancy" had been spelled with an *e* in its third syllable. "The only man on earth . . . who could have concocted and forged the letters," Egan told Michael Davitt, "is *Dirty Dick*."

✳

A month later, in September 1888, proceedings began of the special commission to investigate the *Times'* allegations against Parnell and the Land League. Two tons of evidence, including official files, copies of incendiary league speeches, and local police reports of outrages were transported to London, along with hundreds of witnesses: "injured persons, threatened persons, peasants from Mayo, cottiers from Kerry, land-grabbers, bailiffs, land-agents, landlords, resident magistrates, JPs, police officers, convicted murderers released from prison, informers, professional spies, a Catholic priest." Their testimonies ranged in seriousness from accounts of vicious moonlighting acts to "the vaporings of any drunken village babbler," but nothing emerged that was not already known. "It is an old story now; in addition, it is in the main true," remarked the lawyer and writer Richard Barry O'Brien to Charles Russell, O'Donnell's attorney who was now leading the Parnell defense. "The Land League movement was a lawless, a rebellious, a violent movement." Occupying 128 sittings, the commission dragged on until November of the following year, wearying the patience of participants and public alike. "Everyone asked, 'When shall we get to the letter?'" And then, on February 5, 1889, the prosecution presented its star witness.

*

The appearance in court of Henri Le Caron, the English secret agent and infiltrator of the Clan na Gael, came as a shock to the Irish, who had received no warning of it from their network of contacts. They listened as he described how Egan had introduced him to Parnell in the lobby of the House of Commons in April 1881 as "a friend from America" and heard him tell the court of a subsequent conversation in which Parnell declared that only an uprising would succeed in freeing Ireland: "I had heard it before from Mr. Egan, but when I heard it from Mr. Parnell it startled me." An insurgent movement could be formed in Ireland within a year, Parnell had claimed, saying, "[The] Land League will have £100,000 & looks for £200,000 from United States." But was the Irish leader the "revolutionist to the backbone" that Egan claimed, or had this been another instance of his political gamesmanship, of appearing to be "in" with the extremists?

Michael Davitt would dismiss Le Caron's portrayal as a "palpable yarn," and yet he was extremely nervous about what the spy might be holding in reserve. He was conducting his own defense and decided against cross-examining Le Caron, concerned in particular about a document that he had brought to Paris. This turned out to be no more than a letter of introduction—a fact Egan had been able to discover in America. "Have made enquiries about le Caron," he wrote, "*It is all right.*"

Egan and Davitt were in close touch. There was already indignation at the appointment of an Irish agitator as a US minister, and Egan was anxious to play down his militant past. "Now that I am going to Chili [*sic*] I cannot of course be a witness," he told Davitt, and was so apprehensive about the commission's findings that he had decided to withdraw as a stockholder of the nationalist weekly *United Ireland.*

Egan may even have been directing Davitt's evidence from a distance. The discovery that Salisbury was behind the payments for intelligence work to the Clan na Gael's General Millen in Mexico was sensational and could have brought down the government, but Egan instructed, "Don't mention Mexico." His reason remains a mystery.

*

Le Caron had made startlingly incriminating charges, but fortunately for Parnell, the disclosures of his revolutionary intentions were eclipsed a few days later. Next on the stand was Richard Pigott, cross-examined by Charles Russell in what was described as "a marvel of smashing." Barely taking note of Pigott's wheedling account of how he had acquired the published letters, Russell had cut straight to the chase, handing the witness a sheet of paper and quill pen, telling him to write down his name and also that of Patrick Egan. Then, as if it were just an afterthought, he added the word "hesitancy." Looking up from the sheet he had collected with a glint in his eyes after spotting the misspelling, Russell continued his interrogation, relentlessly probing and ultimately destroying Pigott.

Observing the perspiration beading the victim's, face, his bulging veins and rapid breathing, Parnell remarked, "That man will not come into the box again. . . . He will leave the country"—which is exactly what happened. Pigott fled to Madrid, staying at the Hotel des Ambassadeurs under a false name. When the police arrived to arrest him, he asked their permission to fetch his hat, went back into his room, and shot himself in the head.

Vindication over the letters elevated Parnell as never before. Gladstone, believing that Home Rule depended on absolving Parnell of any connection with the Phoenix Park murders, led a standing ovation of Liberals and Irish in the House of Commons; while the Liberal-Nationalist alliance was publicly acknowledged by a formal handshake with Lord Spencer—"the shaking of hands between two nations, the burying of the historic animosities of England." There still remained grave charges against Parnell, but he treated each of these with disdain; his performance on the witness stand was criticized as "little short of ludicrous"—a combination of mock innocence and outright lying, which essentially reflected his contempt for what Davitt called "The Great Inquisition." Charles Russell, responsible for clearing Parnell's name, had been infuriated by his "studied disrespect," his "lordly indifference," but once again, the chief was triumphantly absolved. The judges ruled that he had had no knowledge, either direct or indirect, of the Invincibles' conspiracy, "and we find the same with reference to all the other respondents."

There was another standing ovation in Parliament, and then on December 18, 1889, Parnell was received as an honored guest at Hawarden Castle, "the citadel of Liberalism," where he and Gladstone came close to reaching an agreement over Home Rule. This was, without question, the high point of Parnell's career, but he was standing on a land mine. Five days later, on Christmas Eve, 1889, "someone," in the words of Winston Churchill, "detonated William O'Shea."

*

Toward the end of November, O'Shea and his teenage son, Gerard, had gone to Brighton, where Katharine and Parnell were living in adjoining houses. Gerard had sided with his father against "that awful scoundrel Parnell," and Katharine had promised them both that she and the Irish leader would have no further communication. After "a dreadful scene," during which Gerard threw some of Parnell's belongings out of a window, O'Shea instructed his lawyer to begin divorce proceedings. "Any further hesitation would have given rise to an accusation of complacency under an injury which no honourable man can patiently endure," wrote Joseph Chamberlain, who was in close touch with O'Shea and may well have been the "someone" whom Churchill had in mind.

"The stench of the divorce court" changed Parnell overnight from a proud, enigmatic figurehead into a Feydeau-esque laughingstock, pictured shinnying down a Brighton fire escape to avoid detection. He and Katharine had decided not to challenge O'Shea's petition with proof of his connivance, because legally this would invalidate a divorce and prevent their own chance of marrying. Consequently, because accusations were undisputed by Parnell in court, the defamation and ridicule stuck, generating "a great cry of reprobation" among his admirers. Gladstone's daughter Mary (now Mrs. Harry Drew) felt personally betrayed. She had worshipped Parnell to the point of infatuation and believed that nothing could excuse the years of lying and deceit. "I feel so low, so wretched . . . my own fervent hope is that he will at once retire from the leadership, for no one with soiled hands ought to lead or can lead a noble cause."

At Hawarden, the family waited and watched for Parnell's resignation, Gladstone, who had made the Irish cause his own, the most devastated of all. "For nearly 5 years . . . I have been endeavoring, day by day, to roll the stone up hill. By his own action, Parnell has now driven it to the bottom." If Home Rule were to succeed, Parnell would have to go. The only hope of carrying the bill through the hostile House of Lords was to secure a massive majority at the next general election, and, as William Harcourt had made clear, opinion was unanimous that if Parnell were allowed to remain as leader of his party, all further cooperation between the Irish and English Liberals must end. Gladstone felt that his only option was to repudiate Parnell, not because of the scandalous exposé (he had taken full advantage of Parnell's intimacy with O'Shea's wife), but because it had put an end to their constructive collaboration.

The Irish party, now in splinters, held an emergency meeting to discuss loyalty to Parnell versus adherence to the Liberals, and in what Katharine called a "miserable and most cowardly exhibition of treachery," only twenty-eight MPs were willing to continue their support. Determined to fight on, Parnell composed a manifesto addressed to the people of Ireland, disdaining to mention the divorce and treating the whole matter as an unprovoked attack by "English wolves howling for my destruction." Renouncing the Liberal alliance, which he claimed had destroyed the integrity and independence of the Irish party, Parnell vented his anger at Gladstone by revealing (and misrepresenting) their confidential Home Rule discussions at Hawarden. In a savage editorial, Michael Davitt attacked the leader's "reeking name and blasted reputation," pouring scorn on his manifesto's desperate self-justification and terminating any future rapport with the shocking words, "Mr. Parnell will not succeed in prostituting the Irish cause as easily as he prostituted the wife of his friend."

On the morning that Parnell's "defiant, dastardly, devilish" statement was published—a retraction of his every conciliatory move toward the English—Lucy Cavendish went to see Gladstone; her brother, Spencer Lyttelton, was already in the room.

> [I] found Uncle W so astounded by its "owdacity" & falseness as to be almost amused. . . . He sat down at the study table & went through the manifesto afresh, marking the notable passages in it with very black dashes. As Spencer & I stood opposite him, something in Parnell's words reminded him of something in the *Bride of Lammermoor* [Walter Scott's novel] & he suspended operations for a minute to look up & say to us, "The more I read that book the more extraordinary & admirable I think it."

Gladstone's first words on learning of Parnell's shame, "It'll n'er dae [do]," could have been a line of dialect from *The Bride of Lammermoor*, whose atmosphere of foreboding and crescendo of doom seemed to prefigure the current tragedy. Seven years later, interviewed by Parnell's first biographer, R. Barry O'Brien, Gladstone recalled how let down he had felt by the Irish leader's volte-face, but said that he had never stopped thinking about him—the most remarkable man he had ever met.

> Poor fellow! Poor fellow! A marvellous man, a terrible fall. . . . I think Parnell acted badly. I think he ought to have gone right away. He would

have come back, nothing could have prevented him; he would have been as supreme as ever. There ought to have been a death, but there would have been a resurrection.

*

The decree absolute came through on May 26, and a month later—June 25, 1891—Parnell and Katharine were married in Brighton's registry office. They were dressed in black, the groom in a morning suit, the bride in a silk brocade dress with a lace mantle, her black hat trimmed with pink roses. Katherine held a posy of white roses, their signature flower, to match Parnell's customary boutonniere. Over the summer, at home in Brighton's Walsingham Terrace with his new wife and their two flaxen-haired little girls, Parnell might have felt that it had all been worthwhile—"I can truly say that I am now enjoying greater happiness than I have ever experienced in the whole of my previous life"—were it not for the fact that his idyll was regularly disrupted by his furious fight in Ireland to win back his authority. He tried to conceal the intense rheumatic pain he was suffering and ignored his doctor's advice to cancel an outdoor meeting at the end of September. After speaking without cover under heavy rain, he returned home with a severe chill that grew worse over the following days. Katharine put Parnell to bed and later, in a letter to his mother, described the moments that followed.

> He suffered acute pains in his joints at first, which he bore grandly, and when I was rubbing his dear arm, trying to ease the pain, he said: "My heart aches for the people in Ireland, who suffer so much from rheumatism and have no nursing like this, and perhaps none at all." Then the pain left him, and he seemed to be better, and we were happy and talked of when he would get up and what he would do when he got up. Although very weak he dictated some letters and telegrams to me to send about Irish affairs. Then he said he would try to sleep if I would lie by his side. Then he drank some milk and water and I hoped

he was sleeping for a few minutes. Then he opened his beautiful eyes, and looked at me and smiled.

Katharine was still lying next to Parnell as he slipped out of consciousness. He died of heart failure shortly before midnight on October 6.

A few faithful disciples had traveled to Brighton to pay their respects and were informed by the local doctor of a message their leader had asked him to pass on: "Let my love be given to my colleagues and to the Irish people." The words would have been heartrending had they not been dismissed by Katharine when she learned of them as an "affectation" of which Parnell was incapable. There had been a little catch in his voice when he told her that his much-loved friend James O'Kelly had "gone too." Other than that, he had never displayed emotion toward members of his party. Katharine was the single passion in Parnell's life, the only person who truly understood him and could move him to Wagnerian extremes of emotion. She would always be blamed for his fall, but as Parnell said, it had to be. "I have given, and will give, Ireland what it is in me to give. That I have vowed to her, but my private life shall never belong to any country, but to one woman."

＊

Katharine felt that her own existence had ended with the death of her "glorious King." "It seems so impossible without him," she wrote to Parnell's mother. "You, who know the beauty of his nature will understand the torture of the days and nights that begin and end in nothing—bring no news of him." For nearly twelve years, they had been "all in all to each other," and Katharine had never wanted to see anyone else. "I lived in his hopes, wishes and interests. All that interested him was intensified to me by my love for him. . . . My very life is torn out of me."

Little is known about her widowhood. There were rumors of helplessness, penury, "a taste for the bottle," and even periods in a psychiatric asylum, but a late photograph taken of her in a cab on a Brighton promenade, shows "a sonsy [buxom] comfortable soul not unlike the best type of theatrical landlady." In May 1914, Katharine's life of quiet anonymity was brought to an end by the publication of her memoirs, *Charles Stewart Parnell: His Love Story and Political Life*, in which the world learned about the passion that had disgraced Ireland's leader. Serialized, devoured, and discussed, the book ran to three printings in England but was virtually ignored by the Irish. This "ruinous infatuation" had been the cause of their hero's political mistakes, and "Kitty" (a diminutive given to Victorian prostitutes) O'Shea was demonized in nationalist mythology. What sustained Katharine throughout was the belief that she had been loved as no woman had been loved before, and right up until her death in 1921, she was under "the happy delusion" that she heard Parnell's voice and that he would come to her at night when things were at their worst.

*

Lucy Cavendish, whose grief was "a thing of long, long habit," had no such comfort. "She does not advance an inch," Gladstone's daughter Mary remarked in 1892. "I mean the wound has not begun to heal in the very least—she is still thankful to get from hour to hour and from day to day." But while still devoting herself to charity work, Lucy had developed a keen interest in women's education—surprisingly, for someone who had called female suffrage "odious and ridiculous" and signed a petition against the movement. When asked to become mistress of Girton College in Cambridge, she declined, telling Mary that she had no desire to be "dragged" into a prominent role. "Dear Freddy would wish me rather to be useful in quiet, natural ways."

And yet, behind the Victorian submissiveness was a woman who wielded considerable political power. Lucy's house, 21 Carlton House Terrace, was the Gladstones' London base during the fall of the Liberal government in 1885, and she had used the proximity to constructive effect. "I do, on occasions 'open attack' upon Mr. G. & always with a miserable sense of inadequateness & a longing for Freddy to be in my place," she told Lord Spencer, explaining that she wanted to clarify facts connected with the Crimes Act, which was being used as a weapon against Gladstone's present policy. It was to Lucy that Herbert Gladstone had written to explain the "Hawarden Kite" letter, defending his right to speak "on his own responsibility." Most valuable of all, however, was the support that she gave Gladstone over Home Rule.

With her brother-in-law its most vehement critic, this would have taken some nerve. Even Katharine Parnell was "no longer a whole-hearted Home Ruler," but Lucy, bolstered by her Aunt Catherine, never swerved from her convictions. It was the faith of these two women that encouraged Gladstone to devote the rest of his waning political life to achieving his Irish ambition.

*

When the Grand Old Man returned to office for a fourth term in August 1892, the queen, while voicing her alarm, seemed almost reconciled to having "that dangerous old fanatic thrust down her throat." William Harcourt considered the eighty-two-year-old prime minister "confused and feeble"; Gladstone felt unfit for public life, but his physician saw no sign of mental deterioration, and he resigned himself to abandoning "all hope of anything resembling a brief rest on this side of the grave." He was determined to put Irish self-government at the top of his agenda, although the thought of reintroducing it left him "much troubled & tossed about." Weakened by a sleepless night, he stood before an unenthusiastic cabinet on May 11, 1893, his sight almost gone, his hearing failing, and yet still able to rouse himself into one of the most strenuous sessions on record. "Even among his bitterest opponents," wrote Roy Jenkins, "there was a sense of witnessing a magnificent last performance by a unique creature, the like of whom would never be seen again."

After the Home Rule bill passed its second reading by a majority of forty-three, there followed another marathon Gladstone oration at the third reading, described to Lucy by Catherine as "a never-to-be-forgotten night." But at the end of the week, when the bill reached the House of Lords, it was thrown out by a massive majority of 419 to 41. Exhausted, and probably as bored by the subject as everyone else, Gladstone did not even mention the result in his diary entry that day.

It was not the crushing defeat of the Irish issue, however, that finally forced Gladstone into retirement. In the face of increasingly powerful German and French armed forces, his cabinet was pressing him to boost Britain's naval strength, and sensing jingoism, he refused. It was hoped that a holiday in Biarritz, France, in the company of Lord Acton, might soften the prime minister's resolve, but still he insisted, "I cannot & will not add to the perils & the coming calamities of Europe by an act of militarism which will be found to involve a policy, and which excuses thus the militarism of Germany, France or Russia. England's providential part is to help peace and liberty." His farsightedness would soon be only too evident.

On February 28, Gladstone saw the queen at Buckingham Palace for a half-hour resignation audience, during which they talked mostly about the weather. She did not ask for his advice about a successor (he would have suggested Lord Spencer, but Victoria had already decided to send for the Earl of Rosebery, an ineffectual politician driven to the front by recent Liberal maneuvers). A couple of days later, in a "final, disagreeable but necessary courteous gesture," Victoria invited the Gladstones for dinner and an overnight stay at Windsor. She knew that he would not accept the offer of a peerage —he could hardly sit in the obstructive House of Lords, whose dissolution he longed for—and Catherine had refused an honor in her own right. And yet, this was an opportunity for the queen to thank her former prime minister for his sixty years in Parliament and to say what she genuinely believed—that he was "a good & very religious man," who as a politician "had a wonderful power of speaking and carrying the masses with him." But unable to bring herself to express anything other than formal platitudes, Victoria stood waiting as Gladstone handed her his resignation letter, kissed her hand, and left.

After the visit, Victoria wrote Gladstone what he considered to be an offensively cursory note, which left him brooding about her indifference toward him. It reminded him of his own attitude to a mule that had once served him well—"I could not get up the smallest shred of feeling for the brute. I could neither love nor like it." His own feelings toward the queen were more complex. Two years later, Gladstone appears to have had an erotic dream about Victoria, describing a breakfast together when he experienced "a small perturbation as to the how and where of access" ("access" was the word he had used when alluding to his deflowering of Catherine). In 1897, they met in the South of France, now the queen's favorite escape "from the sunless north," and she shook his hand for the first time in his life. But it was too late for a rapprochement. The Gladstones had aged greatly, Catherine "shaky and much altered," her mind fast disintegrating, and her husband suffering the first excruciating symptoms of the cancer that was about to kill him.

Heavily sedated, with Catherine and his family around the bedside, Gladstone died at Hawarden on May 19, 1898. The colossal outpouring of respect and regret around the world aroused the queen's deepest jealousy, and the loss of "the greatest man of the century" went unmentioned in the Court Circular. Even more ungenerous was her reluctance to write her condolences to Catherine. "I am sorry for Mrs. Gladstone; as for him, I never liked him, & will say nothing about him," she said petulantly, repeating to a friend, "How can I say I am sorry when I am not?" When the Prince of Wales acted as a pallbearer at Westminster Abbey without his mother's permission, she angrily rounded on him for his unconstitutional and unheard-of behavior. His reply to her was that he was "falling in with [the] wishes & feelings of the nation."

Victoria would claim that she had no personal antipathy toward Gladstone and acknowledged the kindness he had always shown her and her family. It was his politics that she loathed. The queen believed that she was born to protect "*all* that *concerns* the *honour, dignity & safety* of the *Vast Empire* confided to her care & wh[ich] she wishes to hand down unimpaired to her children & their children's children." Her prime minister had threatened this with his policies—the most destructive of all, his obsession with separating Ireland from England. "He did at times a good deal of harm—harm which cannot easily be undone."

✻

The Home Rule struggle "must survive me, cannot be survived by me," Gladstone had predicted in 1890—correctly, as it was almost a quarter century before the Government of Ireland Act finally passed into law. Parnell's successor, John Redmond, a loyal follower determined to fight on for the dead leader's principles, was triumphant in obtaining the royal assent for Home Rule in the House of Lords— the first time in history that an English Parliament was allowing a part of the United Kingdom to be entirely responsible for its own legislation.

Friday, September 18, 1914, was a scene of unprecedented emotion in Parliament; at the sound of the ancient Norman phrase *Le Roy le veult* (the king wishes it), cheers broke out, the Irish flag was carried over the heads of the surging crowd, and hundreds of MPs, in defiance of their hallowed surroundings, bellowed out the national anthem. When it ended, there was a cry of "God save Ireland!" and Redmond, stirred with uncharacteristic emotion, called back, "And God save England too"—astonishing words from an Irish leader. Among the spectators was Lucy Cavendish, who, having heard her uncle's long, impassioned plea in 1886, was overcome with relief, exclaiming it to be "one of the happiest days of [her] life." The elation was short-lived. Home Rule would be delayed, first by the embittered opposition of Ulster Unionists and then by the outbreak of the World War I.

By pledging that Ireland would come to England's side in its war, Redmond was hailed as a great imperialist patriot, but Irish nationalists distrusted him as their statesman. Peace-loving and optimistic, he had been blind to the resurrection of militant republicanism, the revolutionary passions being nurtured by the emerging Sinn Féin party. Waiting for an opportunity to blow the old, inept Home Rule policy to ruins was an armed volunteer movement, led by political activist Patrick Pearse, chosen to be president of a new Irish republic. The result was Dublin's six-day insurrection of April 1916—now universally known as the Easter Rising.

A year later, the new prime minister, Lloyd George, offered Redmond the chance to assemble a convention of representative Irishmen to try once again to negotiate a scheme for Irish independence. For seven months, Redmond regularly attended the sittings, his noble character and earnest eloquence winning the respect of the Ulstermen— and yet, still they refused to yield. In late February 1918, stricken with disappointment, his health in ruins, Redmond left Dublin. There was no point in remaining; it was clear that a settlement was impossible, that polarization between Ireland's south and north, its Catholic and Protestant majorities, was irreversible, and that this attempt at a solution would go the way of all the others.

The literary hostess the Countess of Fingall had spoken at the time to the shattered Redmond and had never forgotten his words. "Do not give your heart to Ireland," he had warned her. "For if you do you will die of a broken heart." It was an eerie prophecy. Within days, following an operation in London, Redmond died of cardiac failure. "That is what Ireland gives to those who love her," wrote Elizabeth Fingall. "Some were to be broken by her." She knew it to be true. Because she had been the young girl on deck with Spencer and Cavendish that early morning of May 6, 1882—the dawn of what promised to be a new and peaceful Ireland, a chimera that vanished even before the sun had set.

Author's Note

I T ALL began with a spiral-bound reporter's notebook that I found in a trunk when sorting through my late parents' papers after moving house. My father, Christopher Kavanagh, a South African newspaper editor and novelist, had written "Phoenix Research Book I" on the cover, and inside, on page after page of his neat italic longhand, was a transcription of an Irish assassin's trial in London in 1883.

It told of a murder that had taken place one afternoon in the saloon of a steamship bound for Natal, and finding myself gripped by the details, I decided to search for more. My father's draft letter to potential publishers outlined a book "about the fate of the man who informed on the Phoenix Park Murderers." This was James Carey, alias James Power, who had been sent by the British government, in a witness protection program, to South Africa and had been shot en route by a fellow Irish passenger, Patrick O'Donnell. Also in the trunk, among various family documents, was a scroll of sketches of whiskered men—police portraits of a terrorist gang calling itself the Invincibles, among which was a cabdriver named Kavanagh. A yellowing typescript of the full synopsis revealed that the incident on the high seas was the coda to a riveting earlier narrative—a double stabbing that had occurred in full daylight on May 6, 1882. One victim was an Irish bureaucrat, Thomas Burke, known as "the Castle Rat"; the other was Lord Frederick Cavendish, a gentle aristocrat and much-loved protégé of Prime Minister

William Gladstone. Just that day, Cavendish had arrived in Ireland as England's messenger of peace.

*

I had been vaguely aware, when I was about twelve years old, that my father was working on a book about some Irish murders, but I had just been accepted by the Royal Ballet School, and my every thought was focused on dancing and dancers. Solipsistically, I believed that this was why we had moved from Cape Town to a London suburb in close reach of the school, a former royal hunting lodge in Richmond Park. In fact, as I was discovering over a half century later, my father had "nagged and nagged" for a transfer from the *Cape Argus*, where he was magazine editor, to the newspaper's London bureau in order to pursue his research.

He had grown up with this story. His maternal grandparents had settled in Cape Town in the 1850s after the Great Famine and, coincidentally, shared the informer's (pseudonymous) last name, Power. My great-grandfather was John Power, the owner of a forage store business in Harrington Street, a five-minute walk from Roeland Street Jail, where the assassin Pat O'Donnell was briefly held before being shipped back to England for trial. The whole family would troop up the road to the jail with whiskey and gifts, gathering outside the prisoner's cell window to sing patriotic songs and recite the rosary. As the hero who had "removed" James Carey, responsible for the imprisonment and execution of his comrades, O'Donnell was the darling of the town's large Irish community.

*

In 1964, my father began working as foreign correspondent in the Fleet Street office of the *Argus*, while continuing to research his book. A major breakthrough came in February 1966, when the UK secretary of state allowed him access to papers that had been officially closed to the public until 1985. "Because of what was then considered the explosive political context of the records about the Phoenix Park Murders," my father wrote in his draft letter, "they were embargoed, not for the customary 50, but for 100 years. . . . I said it was not my intention to write political controversy but that I was mainly interested in Carey and a South African aftermath to the Murders."

Patrick O'Donnell was the great mystery. It was essential to know whether the Irishman had traveled on board the *Melrose* with Carey because he was acting on orders or whether he had been a lone avenger. O'Donnell and his counsel claimed that the timing of the trip had been pure chance. My father told the chief archivist of Ireland's National Library that, although he had copied the full account of O'Donnell's trial, he had found out "next to nothing about [the man] and his background."

He spent every free hour in the Reading Room of the British Library or made the long Tube journey to dreary Colindale in North London, where its newspaper collection was then held. Combining this with a full-time job that required frequent spells of night duty was stressful and exhausting. My father was not a healthy man (his wartime heroism as a reconnaissance pilot in the Battle of El Alamein had taken its toll, his hypertension evident in the slight flush of his cheeks). In December 1966, at the age of fifty-two, he died of a heart attack.

*

A year later, as "something in the way of a memorial," my mother, also a journalist, took over the unfinished work, planning to have it published under Christopher Kavanagh's name. Her letter to the Research Department of the New York Public Library shows that she, too, was struggling to throw light on O'Donnell, and the treatment she wrote (not for a book but "a cinema play") focuses only on the Dublin conspiracy. And then the paper trail goes cold.

The most likely reason for that was the publication in 1968 of Tom Corfe's *The Phoenix Park Murders*. Corfe is no storyteller, but his thorough, scholarly book came to be regarded as the classic text on the 1882 assassinations. Drawing on Home Office files, it covers all the political ground that my father had promised to eschew. He appears to have believed that only by undertaking to let the department see his manuscript before publication would he gain access to the classified papers. Clearly, Corfe had faced no such proviso, and so it baffled me that my father had confined himself to portraying "a dramatic historical episode, not so much from the political angle but as an intensely human story." He had spent much of his life as a political correspondent (scooping the world on the overthrow of the Ghanaian leader President Kwame Nkrumah) and must have known that this seismic attack could not be recounted without context. However, in his notebook is a bibliography, a list of books ordered and reordered, many of which suggest that this was indeed the direction he planned to take.

*

If Patrick O'Donnell had been the instigator for my father, so he became for me. I was intrigued by this elusive Irish American; the "next to nothing" I found among my father's notes proving an irresistible challenge. The Internet delivered information within seconds of which a 1960s researcher could only dream, but it was not until I went to O'Donnell's native county of Donegal that I felt I was getting close.

My research took flight. This sliver of history saw the emergence of Charles Parnell, an Irish leader of genius, who had been galvanized by a new fighting spirit in his people; it marked the second term of Gladstone as Liberal prime minister and the souring of his relations with Queen Victoria. And while the Phoenix Park murders would form the core of my text, I found myself exploring how the incident had sent shockwaves into vastly different circles, from Windsor Castle to a cabin in Donegal, where even the nationalist press recorded "the greatest horror and amazement."

I decided to focus on O'Donnell's Gweedore as a microcosm for what was happening in Ireland and to use as my model for the bigger picture the shifting, episodic structure of today's television dramas. Characters would come and go, depending on their importance at a given moment. I extended my cast to a revolutionary Catholic priest, to British establishment figures who had acted as prime movers, and to an "Irish Sherlock Holmes," who weaves his way through the scenario, linking disparate strands. Taking me by surprise were three women in this very male saga: Queen Victoria, whose interest in the murders and manhunt was insatiable; Lucy Cavendish, the widow of one of the victims; and Katharine O'Shea, Parnell's mistress—all of whose political influence, at the time, was extraordinary. The "re-echo" of the murders five years later, combined with England's shocking, clandestine political machinations, could have filled a second volume, but I realized I had to condense it into a postscript, bringing the leading (living) characters back onstage.

Would my father have approved? What had started as an exercise in sleuthing—a fleshing out of the assassin's assassin that I hoped might have impressed the investigative reporter—had evolved into a journey of discovery. Much of the tangled history of my Irish roots was new to me and so was the extent of the queen's spite toward her prime minister and nemesis. My three previous books all deal with cultural subjects, and this undertaking led me into often intimidatingly uncharted territory. But while the book is unquestionably "something in the way of a memorial," the completion of a project close to my father's heart, the fact that I have written about people and places fascinating to *me*, is justification, I hope, for now calling it my own.

Bibliography

Acton, John Emerich. *The Letters of Lord Acton to Mary, Daughter of the Right Hon. W. E. Gladstone.* Edited, with an introductory memoir, by Herbert Paul. London: George Allen, 1904.

Arnold-Forster, Florence. *Florence Arnold-Foster's Irish Journal.* Edited by T. W. Moody and Richard Hawkins, with Margaret Moody. Oxford: Clarendon Press, 1988.

Ball, Stephen, editor. *A Policeman's Ireland: Recollections of Samuel Waters, RIC.* Cork, Ireland: Cork University Press, 1999.

Battiscombe, Georgina. *Mrs. Gladstone: The Portrait of a Marriage.* London: Constable, 1956.

———. *The Spencers of Althorp.* London: Constable, 1984.

Bew, Paul. *Enigma: A New Life of Charles Stewart Parnell.* Dublin: Gill and Macmillan, 2012.

Blunt, Wilfrid Scawen. *The Land War in Ireland.* London: Stephen Swift and Co., 1912.

Brackenbury, Sir Henry. *Some Memories of My Spare Time.* London: W. Blackwood and Sons, 1909.

Buckle, George Earle, editor. *The Letters of Queen Victoria.* Vol. 3, 1879–1885. London: John Murray, 1928.

Bussy, Frederick Moir. *Irish Conspiracies: The Recollections of John Mallon (the Great Irish Detective) and Other Reminiscences.* London: Everett and Co., 1910.

Callanan, Frank. *The Parnell Split, 1890–1891.* Syracuse, NY: Syracuse University Press, 1992.

———. *T. M. Healy.* Cork, Ireland: Cork University Press, 1996.

Campbell, Christy. *Fenian Fire: The British Government Plot to Assassinate Queen Victoria.* London: HarperCollins, 2003.

Canny, Nicholas P. *The Elizabethan Conquest of Ireland: A Pattern Established, 1565–76.* Galway, Ireland: Harvester Press, 1976.

Cashman, D. B. *Life of Michael Davitt.* Glasgow and London: Cameron and Ferguson, n.d. [1881?].

Cavendish, Lady Frederick. *The Diary of Lady Frederick Cavendish.* 2 vols. Edited by John Bailey. London: John Murray, 1927.

Chamberlain, Joseph. *A Political Memoir, 1880–92.* London: Batchworth Press, 1953.

Chapman, Charles. *A Voyage from Southampton to Cape Town in the Union Company's Mail Steamer "Syria."* London: George Berridge and Co., 1872.

Church, Mary C., editor. *Life and Letters of Dean Church.* London: Macmillan and Co., 1894.

Churchill, Winston S. "Charles Stewart Parnell." In *Great Contemporaries.* London: Macmillan and Co., 1942, 26–82.

Cooke, A. B., and J. R. Vincent. "Lord Spencer on the Phoenix Park Murders," *Irish Historical Studies* 18, no. 72: 583–91.

Corfe, Tom: *The Phoenix Park Murders: Conflict, Compromise and Tragedy in Ireland, 1879–1882.* London: Hodder and Stoughton, 1968.

Corrigan, James F., editor. *A History of the Phoenix Park Patriots.* New York: "Number One" Publication Co., 1884.

Cowper, Katrine C. C., Countess. *Earl Cowper, K.G.: A Memoir.* [N.p]: Printed for Private Circulation, 1913.

Curran, John Adye, K. C. *Reminiscences.* London: Edward Arnold, 1915.

Davitt, Michael. *The Fall of Feudalism in Ireland.* London and New York: Harper and Brothers, 1904.

Devoy, John. *Devoy's Post Bag.* Vol. 1, 1871–1880. Vol. 2, 1880–1928. Edited by William O'Brien and Desmond Ryan. Dublin: C. J. Fallon, 1948 and 1953.

————. *Recollections of an Irish Rebel.* Shannon: Irish University Press, 1969.

Dickinson, Emily Monroe. *A Patriot's Mistake: Being Personal Recollections of the Parnell Family by a Daughter of the House.* Dublin: Hodges Figgis and Co.; London: Simpkin, Marshall and Co., 1909.

Drew, Mary. *Acton, Gladstone and Others.* London: Nisbet and Co., 1924.

————. *Mrs. Gladstone.* New York and London: G. P. Putnam's Sons, 1920.

Dungan, Myles. *The Captain and the King: William O'Shea, Parnell and Late Victorian Ireland.* Dublin: New Island, 2009.

Emmet, Thomas Addis. *Ireland under English Rule.* 2 vols. New York and London: G. P. Putnam's Sons, 1903.

Ensor, Frederick. *Gleanings.* London: W. Stewart and Co., c. 1895–1900.

Fair, John D. "Letters of Mourning from Katharine O'Shea Parnell to Delia Tudor Stewart Parnell," *Irish Historical Studies* 31, no. 122: 241–46.

Ferguson, Mary Catharine. *Sir Samuel Ferguson and the Ireland of His Day.* 2 vols. Edinburgh and London: Blackwood and Sons, 1896.

Fingall, Elizabeth, Countess of. *Seventy Years Young.* London: Collins, 1937.

Fitzmaurice, Lord Edmond. *The Life of Granville George Leveson Gower, Second Earl Granville, K.G., 1815–1891.* 2 vols. London: Longmans, Green, and Co., 1905.

Foster, R. F. *Charles Stewart Parnell: The Man and His Family.* Harvester Press, 1976.

————. *The Irish Story: Telling Tales and Making It Up in Ireland.* London and New York: Allen Lane, 2001.

————. *Modern Ireland, 1600–1972.* London: Allen Lane / Penguin Press, 1988.

————. *Paddy and Mr. Punch: Connections in Irish and English History.* London: Allen Lane / Penguin Press, 1993.

Fry, Sir Edward. *James Hack Tuke: A Memoir.* London: Macmillan and Co., 1899.

Gantt, Jonathan. *Irish Terrorism in the Atlantic Community, 1865–1922.* Basingstoke, UK: Palgrave Macmillan, 2010.

Gardiner, A. G. *The Life of William Harcourt.* Vol. 1, 1827–1886. London, Bombay, and Sydney: Constable and Co., 1923.

Garvin, J. L. *The Life of Joseph Chamberlain.* Vol. 1, 1836–1885. London: Macmillan and Co., 1932.

Gladstone, Herbert. *After Thirty Years.* London: Macmillan and Co., 1928.

Gladstone, Mary (Mrs. Drew). *Her Diaries and Letters.* Edited by Lucy Masterman. London: Methuen and Co., 1930.

Godré, L. Nemours. *Parnell: Sa vie et sa fin.* Paris: P. Lethielleux, 1892.

Guedalla, Philip. *The Queen and Mr. Gladstone, 1880–1898.* London: Hodder and Stoughton, 1933.

Hamilton, Sir Edward Walter. *The Diary of Sir Edward Walter Hamilton, 1880–1885.* Vol. 1, 1880–1882. Vol. 2, 1883–1885. Edited by Dudley W. R. Bahlman. Oxford: Clarendon Press, 1972.

Hammond, J. L. *Gladstone and the Irish Nation.* Frank Cass and Co., 1964.

Harris, Frank. *My Life and Loves.* New York: Grove Press, 1979.

Harrison, Henry. *Parnell Vindicated: The Lifting of the Veil.* London: Constable and Co., 1931.

Healy, David. *James G. Blaine and Latin America.* Columbia and London: University of Missouri Press, 2001.

Healy, T. M. *Letters and Leaders of My Day.* 2 vols. London: Thornton Butterworth, 1928.

Hibbert, Christopher. *Queen Victoria in Her Letters and Journals.* London: John Murray, 1884.

———. *Queen Victoria: A Personal History.* London: HarperCollins, 2000.

Holland, Denis. *The Landlord in Donegal: Pictures from the Wilds.* Belfast: Ulsterman, [1858].

Holzman, Robert S. *Adapt or Perish: The Life of General Roger A. Pryor, C.S.A.* Hamden, CT: Archon Books, 1976.

Hopkins, Tighe. *Kilmainham Memories.* London: Ward, Lock and Co., 1896.

Jackson, Patrick. *Education Act Forster: A Political Biography of W. E. Forster (1818–1886).* London: Associated University Press, 1997.

———. *Harcourt and Son: A Political Biography of Sir William Harcourt, 1827–1904.* Madison, NJ: Fairleigh Dickinson University Press, 2004.

———, editor. *Loulou: Selected Extracts from the Journals of Lewis Harcourt (1880–1895).* Madison, NJ: Fairleigh Dickinson University Press, 2006.

Janis, Ely M. *A Greater Ireland: The Land League and Transatlantic Nationalism in Gilded Age America.* Madison: University of Wisconsin Press, 2015.

Jenkins, Roy. *Gladstone.* London: Macmillan, 1995.

Jeyes, S. H., and F. D. How. *The Life of Sir Howard Vincent.* London: George Allen and Co., 1912.

Jordan, Jane. *Kitty O'Shea: An Irish Affair.* Stroud, UK: Sutton Publishing, 2005.

Joyce, James. *Finnegans Wake.* London: Penguin Books, 1992. E-book edition.

———. *Ulysses.* London: Penguin Books, 2011. Annotated student edition.

Kee, Robert. *The Laurel and the Ivy: The Story of Charles Stewart Parnell and Irish Nationalism.* London: Hamish Hamilton, 1993.

Kehoe, Elisabeth. *Ireland's Misfortune: The Turbulent Life of Kitty O'Shea.* London: Atlantic Books, 2008.

Keneally, Thomas. *The Great Shame: A Story of the Irish in the Old World and the New.* London: Chatto and Windus, 1998.

Kenny, Kevin. *Making Sense of the Molly Maguires.* New York and Oxford: Oxford University Press, 1998.

Kettle, Andrew J. *The Material for Victory.* Dublin: C. J. Fallon, 1958.

Kinealy, Christine. *Charity and the Great Hunger in Ireland.* London and New York: 2013.

King, Carla. *Michael Davitt after the Land League, 1882–1906.* Dublin: University College Dublin Press, 2016.

Le Caron, Major Henri. *Twenty-Five Years in the Secret Service: The Recollections of a Spy.* London: William Heinemann, 1892.

Lewis, Arthur H. *Lament for the Molly Maguires.* London: Longmans, 1965.

Lloyd, Clifford. *Ireland under the Land League.* Edinburgh: Blackwood, 1892.

Longford, Elizabeth. *Victoria R.I.* London: Weidenfeld and Nicolson, 1964.

Lyons, F. S. L. *Charles Stewart Parnell.* London: Collins, 1977.

Macdonald, John. *Diary of the Parnell Commission.* London: T. Fisher Unwin, 1890.

MacGowan, Michael. *The Hard Road to Klondike.* Translated from Irish by Valentin Iremonger. Cork, Ireland: Collins Press, 2003.

Mac Suibhne, Breandán. "Agrarian Improvement and Social Unrest: Lord George Hill and the Gaoth Dobhair Sheep War." In *Donegal History and Society* (Dublin: Geography Publications, c. 1995), 547–82.

———. *The End of Outrage: Post-Famine Adjustment in Rural Ireland.* Oxford: Oxford University Press: 2017.

———. "Soggarth Aroon and Gombeen-Priest: Canon James MacFadden (1842–1917)." In *Radical Irish Priests, 1660–1970.* Edited by Gerard Moran. Dublin: Four Courts Press, 1998.

Marlow, Joyce. *Mr. and Mrs. Gladstone: An Intimate Biography.* London: Weidenfeld and Nicolson, 1977.

———. *The Uncrowned Queen of Ireland: The Life of "Kitty" O'Shea.* London: Weidenfeld and Nicolson, 1975.

Matthew, H. C. G. *Gladstone, 1809–1898.* Oxford: Clarendon Press, 1997.

Matthew, H. C. G., editor. *The Gladstone Diaries: With Cabinet Minutes and Prime-Ministerial Correspondence.* Vol. 9, January 1875–December 1880. Vol. 10, January 1881–June 1883. Vol. 11, July 1883–December 1886. Oxford: Clarendon Press, 1986, 1990.

McAdoo, William. *Guarding a Great City.* New York and London: Harper and Bros., 1906.

McCracken, Donal P. *Inspector Mallon: Buying Irish Patriotism for a Five-Pound Note.* Dublin and Portland: Irish Academic Press, 2009.

———, editor. *Ireland and South Africa in Modern Times.* South African–Irish Studies, vol. 3. [N.p.]: Ireland and Southern Africa Project, 1995.

McGee, Owen. *The IRB: The Irish Republican Brotherhood from the Land League to Sinn Féin.* Dublin: Four Courts Press, 2005.

McLaughlin, Gerry. *Cloughaneely: Myth and Fact.* [N.p.]: Johnswood Press, 2002.

Molony, Senan. *The Phoenix Park Murders: Conspiracy, Betrayal, and Retribution.* Cork, Ireland: Mercier Press, 2006.

Moody. T. W. *Davitt and Irish Revolution, 1846–82.* Oxford: Oxford University Press, 1982.

Moran, Gerard, editor. *Radical Irish Priests, 1660–1970.* Dublin: Four Courts Press, 1998.

Morley, John. *The Life of William Ewart Gladstone.* 3 vols. London: Macmillan and Co., 1903.

The Mysteries of Ireland: A Graphic and Faithful Account of Irish Secret Societies and Their Plots from the Rebellion of 1798 to the Year 1883 . . . and the History of Recent Murders in Ireland Including That of Lord Frederick Cavendish and Mr. Thomas Burke, with the Trials, Convictions, Sentences and Executions of Their Murderers . . . London: Printed for the Booksellers, 1884[?].

Ó Baoill, Dónall P. "Ar Cuireadh Iachall ar Phádraig Ó Dónaill Carey a Scaoilead?" ("Was Patrick O'Donnell Coerced into Shooting Carey?"; translation by Ailbhe Nic Golla Chomhaill). *Scáthlán* 16–32, no. 2 (1983).

O'Brien, Conor Cruise. *Parnell and His Party, 1880–90.* Oxford: Clarendon Press, 1957.

O'Brien, R. Barry. *The Life of Charles Stewart Parnell.* London: Smith, Elder and Co., 1899.

———. *The Life of Lord Russell of Killowen.* London: Smith, Elder and Co., 1902.

O'Brien, William. *Recollections.* London: Macmillan and Co., 1905.

———, editor, with Desmond Ryan. *Devoy's Post Bag, 1871–1928.* 2 vols. Dublin: Academy Press, 1979.

Ó Broin, Leon. *The Prime Informer: A Suppressed Scandal.* London: Sidgwick and Jackson, 1971.

———. *Revolutionary Underground: The Story of the Irish Republican Brotherhood, 1858–1924.* [N.p.]: Gill and Macmillan, 1976.

O'Connor, T. P. *Memoirs of an Old Parliamentarian.* London: Ernest Benn, 1929.

O'Donnell, F. Hugh. *A History of the Irish Parliamentary Party.* 2 vols. London: Longmans, Green, and Co., 1910.

Ó Dónaill, Niall. "Dálach Ghaoth Dobhair" *Donegal Annual,* 1960. Vol 4, 209–226. Donegal Historical Society.

Ó Gallchobhair, Proinnsias. *History of Landlordism in Donegal.* Ballyshannon, Ireland: Donegal Democrat, 1975.

O'Grady, Joseph Patrick. *Irish-Americans and Anglo-American Relations, 1880–1888.* New York: Arno Press, 1976.

O'Hara, M. M. *Chief and Tribune: Parnell and Davitt.* Dublin and London: Maunsel and Co., 1919.

Oliver, Cpt. S. P. *On Board a Union Steamer.* London: W. H. Allen and Co., 1881.

O'Shea, Katharine. *Charles Stewart Parnell: His Love Story and Political Life.* 2 vols. London, Toronto, and Melbourne: Cassell and Company, 1914.

Ó Siochrú, Micheál. *God's Executioner: Oliver Cromwell and the Conquest of Ireland.* London: Faber and Faber, 2008.

Parnell, John Howard. *Charles Stewart Parnell: A Memoir.* London: Constable, 1916.

Pearson, John. *Stags and Serpents: A History of the Cavendish Family and the Dukes of Devonshire.* London: Macmillan, 1983.

Ponsonby, Arthur. *Henry Ponsonby: Queen Victoria's Private Secretary; His Life from His Letters.* London: Macmillan, 1942.

Pryor, Sara Agnes. *My Day: Reminiscences of a Long Life.* New York: Macmillan, 1909.

Reid, T. Wemyss. *Life of the Right Honourable William Edward Forster.* 2 vols. London: Chapman and Hall, 1888.

Richardson, J. Hall. *From the City to Fleet Street: Some Journalistic Experiences.* London: Stanley Paul and Co., 1927.

Roberts, Andrew. *Salisbury: Victorian Titan.* London: Weidenfeld and Nicolson, 1999.

Rochefort, Henri. *Les Adventures de ma vie.* Vol. 4. Paris: Paul Dupont, 1896[?].

Rodechko, James Paul. *Patrick Ford and His Search for America.* New York: Arno Press, 1976.

Roundel, Julia, "From a Diary at Dublin Castle during the Phoenix Park Trial." *Fortnightly Review* 60, no. 356 (October 1905): 559–66.

Ryan, Dr. Mark F. *Fenian Memories.* Dublin: M. H. Gill and Son, 1945.

Shannon, William V. *The American Irish.* New York: Macmillan, 1966.

Short, K. R. M. *The Dynamite War: Irish-American Bombers in Victorian Britain.* Dublin: Gill and Macmillan, 1979.

Special Commission. *Parnellism and Crime.* London: George Edward Wright, 1888–89.

Spencer, Charles. *The Spencer Family.* London: Viking, 1999.

Spencer, John Poyntz, Earl. *The Red Earl: The Papers of the Fifth Earl Spencer.* Vol. I, 1835–1885. Vol. II, 1885–1910. Edited by Peter Gordon. Northampton, UK: Northamptonshire Record Society, 1981 and 1986.

Sullivan. A. M. *New Ireland: Political Sketches and Personal Reminiscences of Thirty Years of Irish Public Life.* 9th ed. Glasgow, Scotland: 1895.

Tóibín, Colm, and Diarmaid Ferriter. *The Irish Famine: A Documentary.* London: Profile Books, in association with *London Review of Books,* 2001.

Trollope, Anthony. *The Land-Leaguers.* London: Penguin Books, 1993.

Tuke, James H. *A Visit to Donegal and Connaught in the Spring of 1880.* London: W. Ridgway, 1880.

Tynan, Patrick J. P. *The Irish National Invincibles and Their Times.* [N.p.]: Chatham, 1894.

Vaughan, W. E. *Sin, Sheep and Scotsmen John George Adair and the Derryveagh Evictions, 1861.* Belfast: Appletree Press, 1983.

Warwick-Haller, Sally. *William O'Brien and the Irish Land War.* Dublin: Irish Academic Press, 1990.

W. B. L. *Diamonds and Gold: The Three Main Routes to the South African Ophir and How to Equip for the Journey.* London: Savoy Steam Press. 1871.

Weintraub, Stanley. *Disraeli: A Biography.* London: Hamish Hamilton, 1993.

Whelehan, Niall. *The Dynamiters: Irish Nationalism and Political Violence in the Wider World, 1867–1900.* Cambridge: Cambridge University Press, 2012.

Yanoso, Nicole Anderson. *The Irish and the American Presidency.* [N.p.]: Routledge, 2017.

Endnotes

My research has taken me to some wonderful places—whether it was the hamlet of Meen-acladdy on the savagely beautiful Donegal coast; the medieval Round Tower at Windsor Castle, where the Royal Archives are kept; or the Cape Town records office, backed by Table Mountain, which was the site of the old prison where Patrick O'Donnell was briefly held. Several libraries have been iconic destinations in themselves: the Gothic masterpiece of Oxford's Bodleian Library; the breathtaking Long Room at Trinity College, Dublin, through which its manuscript department is reached; the British Library, with its glass and bronze six-story tower housing King George's leather and vellum tomes. I experienced many goose-bump moments—most memorably in the National Archives at Kew, where among the O'Donnell trial documents I found the two actual torn scraps of paper that the jury foreman had given to the judge. But frustrations are just as memorable. Several dozen of TNA's O'Donnell papers were destroyed—probably in 1985, when the folder was declassified—and my excitement at finding his Port Elizabeth studio portraits cataloged was dashed when the folders turned out to be empty. In Dublin's National Archives of Ireland, my request slips with search codes provided by seemingly reliable bibliographies were often returned with the penciled additions "no result" or "not found." But now, as I write during Britain's latest draconian lockdown, with every archive and library closed, I realize how blessed I was to have had free access to such extraordinary material during the five years it has taken to complete this book.

In the long list of citations that follows each chapter heading in the Notes below, I credit quotations from other works and provide sources for facts in the text that I myself might have queried were I to start the book afresh. If a book or journal is mentioned only once in the Notes, I give the author's full name and publication details, but with frequently cited works, I provide only a surname and abbreviated title, reserving full information for the Bibliography. I have incorporated editorial footnotes that digress slightly from the main narrative but that strike me as interesting or illuminating. Below, I list my most important sources for each of the key characters, in alphabetical order. Call numbers for archival material are included either in the list of abbreviations or in the Notes.

JAMES CAREY

Archive

I drew mostly on a fourteen-page printed statement made to magistrate John Curran on February 21, 1883. It is held in Britain's National Archives and abbreviated in my Notes as "TNA, JC." In it, Carey describes his initiation into the Fenian organization of the 1860s and recounts the formation of the Invincibles and the gang's abortive attempts to assassinate William Forster. Details are often highly graphic—"My arm touched Mr. Forster's"—and Carey's narrative of the actual murders in Phoenix Park unfolds with the tension and urgent dialogue of a thriller.

Secondary

A leaner, less colorful account is given in the London *Times*' coverage of the Invincibles' trial (see especially the issues of February 19, 20, 23, and 24, 1883). An important find was Carey's letter to Joe Brady's mother (*Irish Times*, September 15, 1883), in which he attempts to exculpate himself by naming other informers in the gang. I could not have written my account of Carey's funeral without the recollections of the humane South African doctor Frederick Ensor in *Gleanings* (see Ensor in the abbreviations list), nor could I have discovered what became of Carey's family after his assassination without the memoir by the family's minder, the Scotland Yard detective Patrick McIntyre (*Reynolds's Newspaper*, March 31, 1895).

LUCY CAVENDISH

Archive

Of particular value among the trove of the Papers of Lady Frederick Cavendish included in the Devonshire Collections at Chatsworth are an unpublished diary (vol. 14); the typescript of a biographical essay, "Who Was Lucy Cavendish?" by Jane M. Renfrew; and a long letter from Lord Spencer minutely detailing the last two days of Frederick Cavendish's life. Further correspondence between Spencer and Lucy is among the Althorp Papers in the Archives and Manuscripts Department of the British Library. The Gladstone Papers, also held in its Western Manuscripts collection, contain several letters to and from Lucy; and there were gems to be found in the papers of Charles Masterman in the Cadbury Research Library, University of Birmingham. (I used fascinating fragments of text from an exercise book begun as preparation for a Lucy Cavendish biography by Lucy Masterman, the editor of Mary Gladstone's diaries and letters.)

Secondary

The two-volume *Diary of Lady Frederick Cavendish*, edited by John Bailey, which begins in 1865 and ends in 1884, was my prime source. Candidly self-revealing and providing an evocative picture of her world of great town and country houses, the journals are indispensable as social history and as an insider's account of Victorian politics. Their private language and nicknames can be irritatingly arch (Catherine Gladstone is "Auntie Pussy"), just as Lucy's saintliness verges at times on the cloying, but her openness, capacity for forgiveness, and devotion to the adored husband she called "My Fred" inspire nothing but admiration.

MICHAEL DAVITT

Archive

It was thrilling to discover among the Davitt Papers at Trinity College, Dublin, a diary he kept while in prison, entitled "Remarks on the capture and trial of 'the Invincibles.'" With its anecdotes unreported in the press, snatches of hearsay from fellow inmates, and Davitt's own musings and insights, it proved to be an unexpected fount of new material.

Secondary

M. M. O'Hara's *Chief and Tribune: Parnell and Davitt* is essential reading for background, while Davitt's seven-hundred-page classic, *The Fall of Feudalism in Ireland*, outlines the complex saga of the Land League and is grippingly explicit about the dirty plot by the London *Times* to discredit the league and bring down Parnell.

PATRICK EGAN

Archive

At the John J. Burns Library, Boston College, there are several long letters and numerous telegrams from Egan among the Patrick A. Collins Papers (Box 1, Folders 30 and 31). A lawyer who became a US representative and the mayor of Boston, Collins was president of the American Land League in the spring of 1881 when this correspondence began, and Egan regularly updated him about the league's land agitation. He described it as a "most judicious" combat against English "terrorism" (telegram, May 13, 1881, Folder 30) but, knowing that the moderate Collins opposed physical force, makes no mention of the assassination conspiracy he was masterminding from Paris. Nevertheless, Egan's side of the correspondence is remarkably revealing for its passionate expression of his hardline republicanism and for confirmation of his active role. On May 3, 1881, he proposed a trip to London "to *stiffen up* some of our followers and keep them on the right lines" (Folder 30), and ominously warned a fortnight later—almost exactly a year before the Phoenix Park murders—"It is now war to the knife between the entire Irish race and our brutal Saxon foes" (telegram, May 21, ibid.). A potted biography of Egan by Superintendent Mallon is held in the National Archives of Ireland (DMP [Dublin Metropolitan Police] Files, 1889 Box). Two letters written by Egan to Carey are cataloged as among NAI documents in the "CBS [Crime Branch Special] B Files, 156–268 Box" but are missing from the folders (B202 and B251).

Secondary

Henri Le Caron provides telling observations of Egan throughout *Twenty-Five Years in the Secret Service*, as well as an intriguing description of the ringleader's hasty flight to America

(228–30). Two letters from Egan to James Carey (possibly those missing from the NAI files mentioned above) are cited in evidence of the Special Commission hearing (*Parnellism and Crime*, pt. 9, 105–6; see *P and Crime* in the abbreviations list). Also in evidence to the commission, Parnell admits to Egan's unsatisfactory handling of Land League funds (*Parnellism and Crime*, pt. 20, 291–96). Superintendent Mallon provides a revealing portrait of Egan in one of his memoir extracts (*Lloyd's Weekly News*, June 20, 1909), and my information about their probable complicity is from Leon Ó Broin's *The Prime Informer: A Suppressed Scandal* (32–33).

WILLIAM FORSTER

Archive

There is a collection of letters in Britain's National Archives from Thomas Burke to Forster and his private secretary, Henry Jephson, as well as Forster's correspondence with William O'Shea (HO 144/72/A19). But the most extensive archival information is to be found among the Gladstone Papers in the British Library's Western Manuscripts collection (MS numbers supplied in the Notes).

Secondary

The Irish journals kept by Florence Arnold-Forster between June 1880 and August 5, 1882, helped me create a more rounded portrait of a much-maligned man. The immediacy and perceptiveness of Florence's observations, her authentic record of current events, and her gently humorous character drawings are compelling and important—especially her transcriptions of conversations with her father during their walks in Phoenix Park.

WILLIAM GLADSTONE

Archive

Virtually all my research took place in the Manuscript Room of the British Library, where Gladstone's original letters can be read. Also available in the Western Manuscripts collection are the papers of his private secretary, Edward Hamilton, a dedicated diarist, and the correspondence of Lord Spencer in the Althorp Papers. There are important letters in the Archive of Sir William Harcourt in the Bodleian Archives and Manuscripts in Oxford.

Secondary

Well-thumbed books were John Morley's *The Life of William Ewart Gladstone*; Roy Jenkins's *Gladstone*; and volume 10 of H. C. G Matthew's edition of *The Gladstone Diaries*. I found lively biographical color in Joyce Marlow's *Mr. and Mrs. Gladstone: An Intimate Biography*; Georgina Battiscombe's *Mrs. Gladstone: The Portrait of a Marriage*; and Mary Gladstone's *Diaries and Letters*, as well as in her memoir about her mother, written under her married name, Mary Drew. Lucy Cavendish's firsthand observations of her "Uncle W" in her published journals are unfailingly astute.

INVINCIBLES

Archive

Documents of inestimable value are held in the National Archives of Ireland. No fewer than seven bulging folders are devoted to the Phoenix Park Murders and contain numerous reports by Superintendent Mallon, including his long, handwritten account of witness statements (Police Reports 1882–1921, Box 1, 3/715/1). In another location (INL Box 9), there is a vital series of memos written between November 20, 1880, and December 10, 1881, in which Mallon gave warning of a new organization planning to assassinate "persons in high places" (November 28). His correspondence with Edward Jenkinson, Samuel Lee Anderson, the Crown solicitor, and Robert Anderson, adviser on political crime in the Home Office, is among the contents of two boxes of DMP Crime Branch Special files (CBS/B Files, 1–156 Box and CBS/B Files, 156–268 Box).

A crucial document in Britain's National Archives is entitled "Copies of Secret Official Reports made by the Dublin Metropolitan Police between December 1880 and March 1883 on the Subject of Secret Societies and the Nationalist Movement in Ireland, Together with Memoranda by Mr. E. B. Jenkinson and Others on the Same Subject." (See *Secret Official Reports* in the abbreviations list.) These forty-nine pages comprise memos by Mallon and responses by Jenkinson, and both Andersons. The report begins with Mallon's naming of executive members of the clandestine Supreme Council, suggests American involvement in the conspiracy, and outlines the formation of the Invincibles. Mallon tells of the various attempts to assassinate Forster; and transcribes the statements of his informers, "Bernard," "Andrew," "Charles," and James Mullett. In a memo, Robert Anderson confirms Frank Byrne's role in the purchase of the amputating knives; and Samuel Lee Anderson, after an interview with Carey, states that that it was indeed Mrs. Byrne who had delivered the weapons to his house in Dublin. Material about the ringleaders and their flight is scattered. I located important correspondence from Robert Anderson in the Archive of Sir William Harcourt in Oxford's Bodleian Archives and Manuscripts, where Spencer's letters to Harcourt about extradition procedures are also kept.

Secondary

There is an abundance of detail in an anonymously written little book, whose title explains its contents: *The Mysteries of Ireland: A Graphic and Faithful Account of Irish Secret Societies and Their Plots from the Rebellion of 1798 to the Year 1883 . . . and the History of Recent Murders in Ireland Including That of Lord Frederick Cavendish and Mr. Thomas Burke, with the Trials, Convictions, Sentences and Executions of Their Murderers . . .* (London: Printed for the Booksellers, 1884[?]). I found Julia Roundell's "From a Diary at Dublin Castle during the Phoenix Park Trial" to be helpful but drew most information from Superintendent Mallon's splendidly knowing "reminiscences" (serialized in *Lloyd's Weekly News*, June 27–July 25, 1909). Patrick J. P. Tynan's bombastic, self-serving tome *The Irish National Invincibles and Their Times* is required reading but has to be carefully sifted for the truth.

JOHN MALLON

Archive

For Mallon's reports see "Invincibles," above.

Secondary

Mallon's voice and personality are more vividly present in his own serialized memoir in *Lloyd's Weekly News* than in *Irish Conspiracies: The Recollections of John Mallon* by his contemporary Frederick Moir Bussy, although the book, written with engaging journalistic verve, is an essential source. Donal P. McCracken's biography *Inspector Mallon: Buying Irish Patriotism for a Five-Pound Note* is as sound and absorbing on its subject as it is on the Invincibles' plot and its Dublin setting.

PATRICK O'DONNELL

Archive

There is an important folder of O'Donnell papers and handwritten court records in the National Archives in Kew, mostly relating to the Old Bailey trial and death sentence, but on the front is a list of forty-eight documents that were destroyed without any record of their content. In Western Cape Archives, Cape Town, South Africa, I discovered fresh material in the affidavits of witnesses who did not give evidence at the Old Bailey, as well as in correspondence between the attorney general, the colonial secretary, and Port Elizabeth's resident magistrate. There was little of interest on O'Donnell in the National Archives of Ireland, although I did find proof that his Irish American supporters were paying enormous sums to defense witnesses. And if the absence of O'Donnell's name in police files on Donegal secret societies was disheartening at the time, it did allow me to write with confidence that he was unlikely to have been involved in underground activism.

Secondary

My first significant lead was an article by the late professor J. L. McCracken, "The Fate of an Infamous Informer" (available online at https://www.historyireland.com/18th-19th-century-history/the-fate-of-an-infamous-informer/). Most of my biographical information came from a long essay by Dónall P. Ó Baoill, published in *Scáthlán 2* (1983) an edition in Irish of a Gweedore journal devoted to O'Donnell and edited by Ó Baoill. I found new facts about O'Donnell's peripatetic life in a correspondence sent to the US secretary of state Frederick Frelinghuysen by a London contact named W. J. Hoppin, its purpose being to investigate the accused's right to claim American citizenship (see Hoppin in the abbreviations list). Of immense value was the in-depth interview released by the Central News Agency and published in the *Irish Times* (October 4, 1883), in which O'Donnell gives his own vibrant account of the Carey shooting. Witness depositions in contemporary South African newspapers, accessed in the superb Newsroom of the British Library (and individually cited in the Notes), were my main source for descriptive details about the *Melrose* murder. I used facts about the American Bar's criticism of the Old Bailey verdict from an anonymous pamphlet collected in *The Making of Modern Law* archive, entitled *The Life, Trial and Execution of O'Donnell, the Irish Martyr*. My final chapter, "Irresistible Impulse," was influenced by a highly convincing account "from the pen of a gentleman who received the statement from O'Donnell," published in *United Ireland* on January 4, 1884.

KATHARINE O'SHEA

Archive

I am aware of no collection of original papers between Katharine and Parnell, but her role of go-between with the prime minister is documented in correspondence in the Gladstone Papers (vol. 184, 75–313ff) in the British Library's Western Manuscripts.

Secondary

Katharine's two-volume autobiography, with its remarkably frank account of her relationship with Parnell, supported by the inclusion of his love letters, caused a sensation when it was published in 1914. The narrative time frame of *Charles Stewart Parnell: His Love Story and Political Life* is not always reliable, and it is now believed that it was "doctored in the O'Shea interest" by Katharine's son, Gerard (see R. F. Foster, "Love, Politics and Textual Corruption: Mrs. O'Shea's Parnell," in *Paddy and Mr. Punch*, 123–39). However, over a decade later came a book that attempted to set the record straight. *Parnell Vindicated: The Lifting of the Veil* was written by Henry Harrison, a twenty-four-year-old newly elected Irish MP, who had acted as Parnell's unofficial private secretary and loyal defender during the divorce scandal. After Parnell's death Harrison regularly visited Katharine in Brighton, and during October 1891 conducted a series of interviews, which provided the impetus for his book. Presenting her own side of the story, Katharine confirmed the connivance in the affair that William O'Shea had contested in court and confided astonishing examples of a passion so intense that it led to what Foster calls the "near Liebestod" of a suicide pact. There are no extant notes, but any possibility that Harrison may have exaggerated or fictionalized Katharine's account is disproved by two letters she wrote about the all-consuming liaison to Parnell's mother in words that are genuinely her own (see "Letters of Mourning from Katharine O'Shea Parnell to Delia Tudor Stewart Parnell," John D. Fair, in *Irish Historical Studies* 31, no. 122).

CHARLES STEWART PARNELL

Secondary

My main source for Parnell's upbringing and his entry into politics was the sympathetic and entertaining memoir by his brother John Howard Parnell, *Charles Stewart Parnell: A Memoir*. A comprehensive account of Parnell's life and career is *The Life of Charles Stewart Parnell*, by R. Barry O'Brien, his first biographer. Other key works are R. F. Foster's *Charles Stewart Parnell: The Man and His Family*; the magisterial biography by F. S. L. Lyons, *Charles Stewart Parnell*; and Paul Bew's enjoyable *Enigma: A New Life of Charles Stewart Parnell*. Winston Churchill's essay "Charles Stewart

Parnell" (in *Great Contemporaries*, 26–82) is a model profile—authoritative, sensitive, witty, and elegantly written.

LORD SPENCER

Archive

The bulk of material is incorporated in the Althorp Papers in the British Library's Western Manuscripts collection, but there are also many letters from Spencer among the Harcourt papers at Oxford's Bodleian Archives and Manuscripts; the Royal Archives at Windsor; and the Devonshire Collections at Chatsworth.

Secondary

There is a two-volume published collection of Spencer's papers entitled *The Red Earl* (vol. 1, 1835–1885; vol. 2, 1885–1910), edited by Peter Gordon, as well as a long article, "Lord Spencer on the Phoenix Park Murders," in *Irish Historical Studies* (vol. 18, no. 72: 583–91). Elizabeth Fingall provides a beautifully drawn account of the viceregal court in her memoir, *Seventy Years Young*.

QUEEN VICTORIA

Archive

My account of Queen Victoria's feelings, remarks, and activities was sourced from her private journals (see "QVJs" in the abbreviations list) and her letters. As so much of the correspondence is already in the public domain (see below), it was rewarding to find a number of unpublished letters scattered among Chatsworth's Devonshire Collections; the Harcourt Papers at Oxford's Bodleian Archives and Manuscripts; and the British Library's Gladstone Papers and Althorp Papers. Unsurprisingly, the most important cache is in the Royal Archives, where the horrified, scrawled response that Victoria wrote on the night of the Dublin murders is among my most prized discoveries RA VIC/ADDA12/719.

Secondary

I regularly consulted *The Letters of Queen Victoria*, vol. 3, 1879–1885 (edited by George Earle Buckle), along with Christopher Hibbert's edition, *Queen Victoria in Her Letters and Journals*. There are revealing letters about Gladstone in Arthur Ponsonby's *Henry Ponsonby: Queen Victoria's Private Secretary*; and Philip Guedalla's *The Queen and Mr. Gladstone* is excellent for its collection of letters and sharp commentary.

ABBREVIATIONS OFTEN USED IN NOTES

BL: British Library Western Manuscripts collection; items are identified by Add MS number.
B O'B: R. Barry O'Brien, *The Life of Charles Stewart Parnell*.

Bodleian, MS Harcourt: Archive of Sir William Harcourt, Bodleian Archives and Manuscripts, Oxford.

Bussy: Frederick Moir Bussy, *Irish Conspiracies: The Recollections of John Mallon.*

Chatsworth: The Papers of Lady Frederick Cavendish, the Devonshire Collections, Chatsworth.

Corfe: Tom Corfe, *The Phoenix Park Murders: Conflict, Compromise and Tragedy in Ireland, 1879–1882.*

CSP: John Howard Parnell, *Charles Stewart Parnell: A Memoir.*

DÓB: Dónall P. Ó Baoill, "Ar Cuireadh Iachall ar Phádraig Ó Dónaill Carey a Scaoilead?" ("Was Patrick O'Donnell Coerced into Shooting Carey?"; translation by Ailbhe Nic Golla Chomhaill), published in a special edition of a Donegal journal devoted to O'Donnell, *Scáthlán* 16–32, no. 2 (1983).

Ensor, *Gleanings*: Frederick Ensor, "Notes on the Case of O'Donnell," in *Gleanings*, 115–25.

Hamilton, BL: Hamilton Papers, British Library, correspondence and diaries of Sir Edward Walter Hamilton; date and MS number provided with each citation.

Hamilton, *Diary*: Sir Edward Walter Hamilton, *The Diary of Sir Edward Walter Hamilton, 1880–1885* (vol. 1, 1880–82; vol. 2, 1883–85). Edited by Dudley W. R. Bahlman.

Hoppin: Correspondence from W. J. Hoppin to Frederick Frelinghuysen, October 18–December 15, 1883 (nos. 253–69). Papers Relating to the Foreign Relations of the United States, 1880–1888.

Le Caron: Henri Le Caron, *Twenty-Five Years in the Secret Service: The Recollections of a Spy.*

Love Story, vol. 1 or 2: Katharine O'Shea, *Charles Stewart Parnell: His Love Story and Political Life.*

Lucy, vol. 1 or 2: Lady Frederick (Lucy) Cavendish, *The Diary of Lady Frederick Cavendish.* Edited by John Bailey.

Lyons: F. S. L. Lyons, *Charles Stewart Parnell.*

Mary, *Diaries*: Mary Gladstone (Mrs. Drew), *Her Diaries and Letters.* Edited by Lucy Masterman.

McIntyre: Patrick McIntyre memoir. *Reynolds's Newspaper*, March 24 and 31, 1895.

MD Invincibles Diary: Michael Davitt, "Remarks on the capture and trial of 'the Invincibles,'" Davitt Papers, Trinity College, Dublin, MS 9537/33.

NAI: National Archives of Ireland.

Old Bailey: Trial of Patrick O'Donnell, November 19, 1883, Proceedings of the Old Bailey, London's Central Criminal Court, ref. no. t18831119-75. Available at www.oldbaileyonline.org.

P O'D file: Patrick O'Donnell file, the National Archives, Kew, CRIM 1/19/4; previously cataloged as HO 144/122/A30424.

P and Crime: *Parnellism and Crime*, the Special Commission (London: George Edward Wright, 1888–89). Reprinted from the *Times* (London).

QVJs: Queen Victoria's Journals. Available at www.queenvictoriasjournals.org.

RA: Royal Archives, Windsor Castle.

Secret Official Reports: *Copies of Secret Official Reports made by the Dublin Metropolitan Police between December 1880 and March 1883 on the Subject of Secret Societies and the Nationalist Movement in Ireland, Together with Memoranda by Mr. E. B. Jenkinson and Others on the Same Subject.* Printed for use of the Cabinet, April 1889 the National Archives, Kew Balfour Papers, CAB 37/24.

TCD: Trinity College, Dublin.

TNA: The National Archives, Kew.

TNA, JC: James Carey's statement made to magistrate John Curran on February 21, 1883, TNA, HO 144/98/A16380C.

Tynan: Patrick J. P. Tynan, *The Irish National Invincibles and Their Times.*

WCA: Western Cape Archives.

A Brief History

ix **Anglo-Normans:** They had been sent by Henry II, the Plantagenet king, who had "long cast hungry eyes towards Ireland" (W. L. Warren, *Henry II* London: Eyre Methuen, 1973, 194), and had the pope's permission to invade. Henry had been asked for military aid by one of Ireland's warring chieftans, Dermuid Mac-Murrough, a giant of a man with a fiery red beard who had been ousted from his kingdom after running off with the wife of the omnipotent chieftan the High King. The challenge was taken up by the Earl of Pembroke, known as "Strongbow," who raised an army in return for the hand of MacMurrough's beautiful daughter and succession to his kingdom. As a result, the Norman allies were rewarded with land on which they built castles and garrisons; Irish land became fiefs held by the Crown; and Henry II was declared supreme lord of Ireland.

ix **"Us and Them . . . their religion . . . our religion":** Anna Burns, *Milkman* (London: Faber and Faber, 2018), 22.

x **Edmund Spenser:** Spenser's seized lands included Cork's Kilcolman Castle, an estate that had belonged to the "Rebel Earl" Gerald Fitzgerald, a descendant of the first Norman conqueror (and, incidentally, the namesake centuries later of John Fitzgerald Kennedy).

x **until "half dead":** Thomas Addis Emmet, *Ireland under English Rule*, 2 vols. (New York and London: G. P. Putnam's Sons, 1903), 96. See also Dennis Taaffe, *An Impartial History of Ireland* (Dublin: Christie, 1810), vol. 3, 338–39: Under the penal laws, every Catholic priest was deemed guilty of rebellion and sentenced to be hanged "until he was half dead."

x **"So the name of an Inglysh man . . .":** Canny, *The Elizabethan Conquest of Ireland*, 121.

x **"anatomies of death":** Edmund Spenser, *A View of the Present State of Ireland*, vol. 7, 430. See also Emmet, *Ireland under English Rule*, vol. 1, 66; Raymond Jenkins, "Spenser and Ireland," *ELH* 19, no. 2, 131–42; and Willy Maley, " 'To Weet to Work Irenaes Franchisement': Ireland in 'The Faerie Queene,' " *Irish University Review* 26, no. 2, 303–19.

x **"raw-bone cheeks":** Spenser, *The Faerie Queene* (1.9.35–36), ed. Thomas P. Roche Jr. (London: Penguin Books, 1978), 154–55.

xi **1641 uprising:** Available online at "1641 Depositions," Trinity College Library, Dublin, http://1641.tcd.ie/.

xi **" 'Tis madness to resist . . .":** Andrew Marvell, "An Horation Ode upon Cromwell's Return from Ireland." Available online at the Poetry Foundation, https://www .poetryfoundation.org/poems/44683/an-horatian-ode-upon-cromwells-return

-from-ireland. I am indebted to Peter Conrad for urging me to read Marvell's Cromwell poem.

xii *I See a Dark Stranger:* I watched this highly entertaining film—once again, thanks to Peter Conrad—on YouTube; it is also available on DVD.

xii **"that murdering bastard . . . portrait of Eichmann":** Remarks by the comedian, writer, and polymath Stephen Fry, in the introduction to Micheál Ó Siochrú, *God's Executioner: Oliver Cromwell and the Conquest of Ireland,* I. At the Dublin launch of Dr. Ó Siochrú's book, Ahern denied walking out of Robin Cook's office but admitted having startled the foreign secretary with his "forthright" denunciation of Cromwell. *Irish Times,* October 10, 2008.

xii **"taunting, long-memory . . . bygones":** Burns, *Milkman,* 24–25.

xiii **"That one million people . . .":** Tony Blair, quoted in the *Guardian,* February 21, 2012.

xiii **"The Almighty, indeed . . .":** John Mitchel, *The Last Conquest of Ireland (Perhaps),* ed. Patrick Maume (Dublin: University College Dublin Press, 2005), 219.

xiii **"God had sent the calamity":** Jennifer Hart, quoted in Robin Haines, *Charles Trevelyan and the Great Irish Famine* (Dublin: Four Courts Press, 2004), 14.

xiv **"as a means of keeping people down":** Ibid., 15.

xiv **"Feed your family first . . .":** The quotation and information about mass evictions during the famine is from Peter Gray's comprehensive account, *The Irish Famine* (New York: Harry N. Abrams, 1995). Available at http://freepages.rootsweb .com/~emeraldidyll/genealogy/Ireland/Irish_Famine_Mass_Evictions.htm.

xv **"a holocaust" of themselves:** Davitt, *Fall of Feudalism,* 259.

Before

2 **"curious social experiment":** Mac Suibhne, "Agrarian Improvement and Social Unrest: Lord George Hill and the Gaoth Dobhair Sheep War," 556. This enlightening essay was my handbook on Gweedore and its landlord issues.

4 **Landlord-tenant conflict:** In response to its escalation ten priests met at Dunfanaghy on January 14, 1858, to establish a relief committee and issue a public appeal for assistance. Between June 8 and July 2, 1858, the House of Commons Select Committee heard evidence on the topic of destitution in Gweedore and Cloughaneely, where eight hundred families were living in dire poverty. The committee ruled in the landlords' favor and declared that there was no evidence of destitution. *Report from the Select Committee on Destitution in Gweedore and Cloughaneely* (hereafter, *Destitution Report*), British House of Commons Sessional Papers, 1857–58. Additional information about Holland's tour of Gweedore with Father Doherty comes from his interview with the Select Committee. See *Destitution Report,* vol. 13, 93–95.

4 **"a means of generating pauperism":** *Destitution Report,* 437, 457.

5 **"We got it out of rundale . . ." and remarks by John Obin Woodhouse:** June 22, 1858. Ibid., 257–72. Woodhouse had 1,119 acres of land in Meenacladdy and owned Tory Island and two others, Innishdowey and Innishbeg. He told the inquiry

that Michael Art O'Donnell held a farm at £1.5s, and when O'Donnell decided to emigrate to America, Woodhouse's manager bought his tenant right in the farm for £20. On his return to Meenacladdy, O'Donnell was charged a rent of £4 by Woodhouse, who gave as his reason for the increase the £74 he had spent on improvements in the interim. "And yet I have been held up as an oppressor and a tyrant because I do so." Woodhouse swore that he had never ejected a tenant or taken mountain grazing from them, and yet he was found to have taken six to seven hundred acres away from the tenants of Meenacladdy, who had no grazing rights to the land.

5   "We got it out of rundale . . .": Woodhouse, quoted in *Destitution Report*, 256.

5   settling . . . in Janesville, Pennsylvania: Hoppin, October 23, 1882, no. 256.

5   "Sure if it wasn't for burning . . .": All quotations during the encounter between Michael O'Donnell, Denis Holland, and Father Doherty are from Holland, *The Landlord in Donegal*, 52.

6   "a bigoted, a persecuting . . .": Jay P. Dolan, *The American Catholic Experience* (New York: Doubleday and Company, 1985), 266.

6   "Better for many of our people . . .": Arnold Schrier, *Ireland and the American Emigration, 1850–1900* (New York: Russell and Russell, 1958), 36–37.

7   "the New Ireland . . .": Ibid.

7   Late nineteenth-century emigration from Donegal: Mící Mac Gabhann, *Rotha Mór an tSaoil*, trans. Ailbhe Nic Giolla Chomhaill. Indreabhán Conomara: Cló Iar-Chonnachta, 1959, 1996, 83–85.

ONE: THE LEADER

9   IRELAND FOR THE IRISH! and subsequent quotations relating to Westport tenants' rights meeting: *Connaught Telegraph*, June 14, 1879.

11   "The unfeeling society . . . Constantly thinking . . .": William Parnell, introduction, *Maurice and Berghetta; or, The Priest of Rahery, a Tale* (Boston: Wells and Lilly, 1820), x.

12   "the one impetuous act . . .": Foster, *Parnell: The Man and His Family*, 42.

12   "a flaring exotic": Lyons, 8.

13   "who would mother [Charles] . . .": B O'B, 36.

13   "spring up panic-stricken . . .": *Love Story*, vol. 2, 46.

14   "the Fenian stronghold": *CSP*, 70.

14   turning up at the door for handouts: The men are believed to have been demobilized Irish American soldiers looking for help after the US Civil War from a prominent fellow countrywoman. "They probably had Fenian sympathies," says historian and author Roy Foster. "But I think that retrospectively this aspect was played up." (Email to author, May 21 2020.) Delia Parnell did, however, support an amnesty organization on behalf of Fenian prisoners.

14   "He distinctly resented . . .": Ibid., 71.

14   "sons of monied parvenus . . .": Foster, *Paddy and Mr. Punch*, 109.

14   "keen about nothing": Ibid., 108. Foster quotes Samuel Sproston, "Magdalene in the Sixties," *Magdalene College Magazine* I (March 1910): 65–66.

15 He is said to have taken pride . . .: Bew, *Enigma*, 23. See also O'Connor, *Memoirs of an Old Parliamentarian*, vol. I, 99.

15 "Driven wild": Bew, *Enigma*, 11.

16 "These English despise us": B O'B, 39.

16 Parnell's courtship of Abby Woods: Quotations are from "Jilted—Parnell and the American Heiress," *History Ireland* 23, no. 1.

17 "How could you expect . . .": William O'Brien, *The Parnell of Real Life*, 41.

18 "things were as . . .": *CSP*, 78.

18 "he was only an Irish gentleman": Ibid.

18 "I want you to . . . poured forth the pitiful tale": Ibid.

19 "it was a jilting": O'Connor, *Memoirs of an Old Parliamentarian*, vol. I, 234. John Parnell was convinced that the rejection had impelled his brother to take to the political stage, because "he was deeply hurt at the idea of being considered a country gentleman without any special abilities." (*CSP*, 130.) This was also the view of their sister Emily, who maintained that Charles's parliamentary career "had its origin in a woman." Dickinson, *A Patriot's Mistake*, 111.

20 "Now . . . something can be done": B O'B, 50.

20 "Charley and myself . . .": *CSP*, 142.

20 "He broke down utterly . . . He faltered": B O'B, 64.

21 "a revelation": Lyons, 44.

21 "a beautiful fighter": B O'B, 90.

21 "could not bear to see": O'Hara, *Chief and Tribune*, 59.

22 "Everything was ready": Ibid., 65.

22 "the wrongs committed . . . so fired": Ibid., 21.

23 "New Departure of 1878": Davitt, *Fall of Feudalism*, 116.

24 "This was superb": Ibid., 153.

24 "The speech was so full": Elbert Hubbard, "Parnell and Kitty O'Shea," in *Little Journeys to the Homes of the Great*, vol. 13, *Little Journeys to the Homes of Great Lovers* (New York: [n.p.], 1916). Available at http://www.gutenberg.org/files/23458/23458-h/23458-h.htm#PARNELL_ AND_KITTY_OSHEA.

25 "When I saw this sleek": Lyons, *John Dillon: A Biography*, 35.

25 "I feel confident that": Ibid.

25 "Man is a land-animal": Hubbard, "Parnell and Kitty O'Shea."

25 "The cause of the poor": *Irish World*, January 8, 1880.

26 COLUMBIA'S WELCOME: Ibid., January 10, 1880.

26 "Million Fund" . . . "to help": Ibid., January 3, 1880.

26 "Parliament dissolved": March 8, 1880, T. M. Healy, *Letters and Leaders*, vol. I, 83.

TWO: THAT HALF-MAD FIREBRAND

27 "terrible telegram": Queen Victoria to Henry Ponsonby, April 3, 1881. Buckle (ed.), *Letters of QV*, vol. 3, 73.

27 "dear little": March 27, 1880. QVJs.

28 "A whip with . . .": April 5, 1880. Ibid.

28 "I grieve at the thought . . .": Ibid.

28 "poetry, romance and chivalry": Hibbert, *QV: A Personal History*, 317.

28 "It is just settled . . .": Ibid., 361.

28 "If *we* are to *maintain* . . .": Letter of July 28, 1879. Buckle (ed.), *Letters of QV*, vol. 3, 87.

29 "Everybody knew the great . . .": Morley, *Life of Gladstone*, vol. 2, 589.

29 "unpatriotic ravings": Queen Victoria to the crown princess of Prussia, April 5, 1880. Hibbert, *QV in Her Letters and Journals*, 260.

29 "*That half mad firebrand* . . .": Ponsonby, *Henry Ponsonby*, 184.

30 "forget all rest . . .": Battiscombe, *Mrs. Gladstone*, 157.

30 "We are told the Queen . . .": December 1, 1879. Mary, *Diaries*, 183.

31 "on the great hand . . .": Matthew (ed.), *Gladstone Diaries*, vol. 9, 478.

31 "For the first time . . .": December 1–7, 1879, Lucy, vol. 2, 241.

32 "I must keep my promise . . .": April [day omitted] 1859. As cited in Battiscombe, *Mrs. Gladstone*, 117.

32 "How marvelously, miraculously . . .": Drew, *Mrs. Gladstone*, 79.

32 "an unchangeable certainty": Introduction to Books 1 and 2, Lucy, vol. 1, 13.

33 "He's such a compound of gallantry . . .": August 8, 1873. Lucy, vol. 2, 162.

33 "having his blinkers on": Lucy Masterman notebook, Masterman Papers, University of Birmingham, Cadbury Research Library, Special Collections, CFGM/24/1/2.

33 "a very general, a nearly unanimous . . .": Morley, *Life of Gladstone*, vol. 2, 598.

33 "if you were staunch . . .": Jackson, *Harcourt and Son*, 75.

33 "Can Father, having brought up . . .": Battiscombe, *Mrs. Gladstone*, 177.

34 "Every person I meet . . .": Undated. Ibid., 178–79.

34 "would far prefer . . .": April 19–25, 1880. Lucy, vol. 2, 250.

35 "He is, as you know . . .": The Duke of Connaught to Queen Victoria, April 18, 1880. Buckle (ed.), *Letters of QV*, vol. 3, 79–80.

35 "Almost all the newspapers . . .": April 9, 1880. Ibid., 77.

35 "I can't understand . . .": The Duke of Connaught to Queen Victoria, April 11, 1880. Ibid., 78–79.

36 "Such a *good* man": Hibbert, *QV: A Personal History*, 319.

36 "She seems now . . . violent, passionate . . .": Guedalla, *The Queen and Mr. Gladstone*, 13.

36 "She can't bear to see . . .": September 27, 1883. Hamilton, *Diary*, vol. 2, 486.

36 "the subordinate of one . . .": Morley, *Life of Gladstone*, vol. 2, 620.

37 "She seemed to me . . .": Ibid., 628.

37 "conciliatory": April 23, 1880. QVJs.

37 "I ended by kissing . . .": Morley, *Life of Gladstone*, vol. 2, 628.

37 "A look of detached disgust . . .": Longford, *Victoria R.I.*, 433.

38 "spicy and high bred . . . arranged in hideous . . .": May 20, 1880. Mary, *Diaries*, 198.

38 "the dark thunderclouds": Churchill, *Great Contemporaries*, 269.

38 "that was already swelling . . .": Gladstone's Edinburgh speech of September 1, 1884. As quoted in Morley, *Life of Gladstone*, vol. 3, 48.

THREE: The "Irish Soup" Thickens

39 "admirable zeal . . .": "James H. Tuke's Report," in *Transactions of the Central Relief Committee of the Society of Friends during the Famine in Ireland in 1846 and 1847* (Dublin: Hodges and Smith, 1852), 149.

40 "I feel, after a lapse . . .": Tuke, *A Visit to Donegal*, 25.

41 "We are beaten . . .": Ibid., 11.

41 "I would be a long time . . .": *Times* (London), January 29, 1883.

41 "the most minute subdivision": From Tuke's letter to the *Times* (London), April 18, 1881, regarding the Canadian government's offer of free grants and land.

41 "He had a lot of people . . .": In conversation with the author, Dublin, October 18, 2016.

42 "thought no more of . . .": MacGowan, *The Hard Road to Klondike*, 58–59. This is a wonderfully evocative book. Micky MacGowan's oral account of his tough upbringing in Gweedore's neighboring parish of Cloughaneely and his observations as a young emigrant traveling from Donegal to America, where he first worked in the Montana mines, allowed me to imagine the parallel experience of the young Patrick O'Donnell. The story of the abducted O'Donnell wife is recounted on pp. 63–64.

42 "Everything was good enough . . .": This quotation and the description of O'Donnell in a cowboy suit comes from an account by Jack Curran (DOB). The Curran family lived three miles from Allentown, and O'Donnell had a relative there. Patrick O'Donnell file, WCA, 1/PEZ 1/1/1/7.

42 "such a restless rover" and descriptions of Margaret O'Donnell: *Times* (Philadelphia), November 1–2, 1883.

42 O'Donnell's various occupations: See Hoppin, October 18–December 15, 1883. For his employment and illness in Edinburgh, see the *Times* (London), September 20, 1883. For Dan O'Donnell's loan of money, see the *Star* (London), September 22, 1883.

43 "an absolute reign of terror": *Derry Journal*, October 28, 1881.

43 "Long Forster" . . . "almost too full . . . those queer dressed . . .": Jackson, *Education Act Forster*, 16.

44 "more like famished dogs . . .": "William Edward Forster's Report," in *Transactions of the Central Relief Committee of the Society of Friends during the Famine in Ireland in 1846 and 1847*, 156.

45 "The state of our fellow country-men . . .": Gordon, quoted in B O'B, 193.

45 "That wretched Bill . . .": July 10, 1880. Hamilton, BL, Add MS 48630.

45 "retain in the country . . .": July 16, 1880. Ibid. Hamilton is quoting Lord Fitzwilliam making an appeal to Gladstone about proceeding with the bill.

45 "Do *you* EVER remember . . . wild excess of landlordism . . .": Quoted in Corfe, 81.

46 "more interested in partridges . . .": Lyons, 128.

46 "Now I think I heard . . .": *Freeman's Journal*, September 20, 1880.

46 Dillon and Davitt advocating social ostracism: See Corfe, 90–91.

46 Boycotting: See Forster's account in the House of Commons on January 24, 1881, "Motion for Leave, 'Protection of Person and Property (Ireland) Bill,' Hansard's Parliamentary Debates," 1210–36.

49 "The Irish 'soup' . . .": December 7, 1880. Hamilton, BL, MS 48630.

49 "I was talking to Homer . . .": Gladstone, *After Thirty Years*, 186.

49 "Had there been no Land League . . .": Davitt, *Fall of Feudalism*, 259.

50 "broken in mind and body": Lewis "Loulou" Harcourt to his father, William, December 13, 1880. Quoted in Jackson, *Harcourt and Son*, 99.

50 "more like an inebriated . . .": December 7, 1880. Hamilton, BL, Add MS 48630.

50 "getting [in] a twist": November 30, 1880. Ibid.

50 "It is impossible for anyone . . .": Letter to Gladstone, November 8, 1880. Reid, *Life of Forster*, vol. 2, 264.

51 "very much more pleasure . . .": January 17, 1864. Lucy, vol. 1, 200.

51 "shrieked and kicked . . .": Lucy, vol. 1, Introduction, xv.

51 "capital little dance": December 9, 1863. Ibid., 193.

51 "grave and simple . . .": April 26, 1864. Ibid., 212.

52 "She came towards me . . .": May 13, 1864. Ibid.

52 "The dear Queen . . .": April 15, 1869. Lucy, vol. 2, 68.

52 "Sweet peace . . . And no wonder . . .": December 12, 1880. Ibid., 275.

52 "People only go . . .": Gladstone, *After Thirty Years*, 265.

53 "There is to be a Cabinet . . .": December 25, 1880. Buckle (ed.), *Letters of QV*, vol. 3, 165–66.

54 "By this time next week . . .": December 25, 1880. Arnold-Forster, *Irish Journal*, 44.

54 "I, with many a fear . . .": William Wordsworth, "Composed by the Sea-side near Calais," August 1802.

54 "Poor Uncle W": December 31, 1880. Lucy, vol. 2, 276.

54 "After dinner he took me . . .": Quoted in Jenkins, *Gladstone*, 475.

55 "I finally acquiesced . . .": Morley, *Life of Gladstone*, vol. 3, 50.

55 "rests on coercion . . ." and subsequent quotations: Forster's account in the House of Commons on January 24, 1881, "Motion for Leave, 'Protection of Person and Property (Ireland) Bill,' Hansard's Parliamentary Debates," 1210–36.

56 "His earnestness was . . .": Quoted in Jackson, *Education Act Forster*, 273.

56 "a ring of intense fervor . . .": January 28, 1881. Mary, *Diaries*, 217.

57 "The dinner hour came . . .": Tynan, 197.

57 The Ladies' Gallery: The grille, dubbed "The Ladies' Cage" by Anna Parnell (*Celtic Monthly*, May–July 1880), was intended to shield male politicians from the distraction of women in the House of Commons. It remained in place until 1917, almost a decade after suffragettes had chained themselves to the metal in protest. Until then, Victorian women were resigned to hearing rather than fully seeing parliamentary debates.

58 "The lonely man . . .": Churchill, *Great Contemporaries*, 273.

FOUR: FIRE BENEATH THE ICE

59 "He looked straight at me . . .": *Love Story*, vol. I, 155.

60 "miserable": T. P. O'Connor quoted in Jordan, *Kitty O'Shea*, 30.

60 "cold and suspicious": *CSP*, 110.

60 "notwithstanding the powerful . . .": *Love Story*, vol. I, 136.

60 "He would urge me . . .": Harrison, *Parnell Vindicated*, 123.

61 "with someone else's money": Dungan, *The Captain and the King*, 37.

61 two French mistresses: In her affidavit in the UK Civil Divorce Records, 1858–1911, quoted in the *Irish Independent*, March 3, 2013, Katharine claimed that the affairs with two Frenchwomen took place in the spring of 1874. Her husband, she said, "habitually committed adultery with divers prostitutes," and she gives the date of his infidelity with their parlor maid Sarah in 1875. She knew of affairs with a Maria Domingues in Spain in 1877, a Mrs. Deerehurst in Haymarket in 1881, and an Elise Guerin in Paris in 1882. She swore that O'Shea had seduced her sister, Anna and that he was guilty of "inducing, directing and requiring" her to form a liaison with Parnell in order to gain favors in his own interest.

62 "Sex love between us . . .": Harrison, *Parnell Vindicated*, 122.

62 she was "My Dick," and he "Your Boysie": See "Captain O'Shea's Letters," *Love Story*, vol. 2, 194–211.

62 "I did what I could . . . ": Harrison, *Parnell Vindicated*, 123.

62 "the prototype of 'the wild Irish girl'": Lyons, 13.

62 "arch-rebel": *CSP*, 70.

63 "with golden hair, small features and blue eyes": *Love Story*, vol. I, 138.

63 "great brother Charles . . . How famous . . .": *CSP*, 80.

63 "I could not do all that . . . ": *Love Story*, vol. I, 139.

63 "his desertion": Ibid.

63 "as though I had always known . . .": *Love Story*, vol. I, 138.

64 "He promised he would do his best . . . ": *Love Story*, vol. I, 140.

64 "There must be a lady in the case . . .": Jordan, *Kitty O'Shea*, 24.

64 "I was under the impression . . .": *Love Story*, vol. I, 141.

64 "dangerous" long silences: Ibid.

65 "I slipped my hand into his . . .": *Love Story*, vol. I, 93.

65 "My own love": *Love Story*, vol. I, 153.

66 Yeats's delight in the incident: See Foster, *Paddy and Mr. Punch*, 138.

66 "A husband that had sold . . .": The anecdote was told to Henry Harrison. See his *Parnell Vindicated*, 125–26.

66 "It was a mixture of secrecy . . .": Churchill, *Great Contemporaries*, 273.

66 "Of course he knew . . .": Harrison, *Parnell Vindicated*, 123.

66 "the dour, silent, handsome . . .": Harris, *My Life and Loves*, 453–54.

66 "the fellow's name": *Love Story*, vol. I, 174.

67 "He was always a man apart . . . the loyalty . . .": *CSP*, 132.

67 "the exquisite beauty . . .": Fair, "Letters of Mourning."

67 "He was so absolutely self-controlled . . .": *Love Story*, vol. 2, 248–49.

67 **Parnell's life in danger:** Michael Davitt was convinced that his own life was at risk. In a semi-coded letter to the Clan na Gael leader, John Devoy, on December 16, 1880, he had written:

> I have seen no-one of the firm, Osborne & Co [the Supreme Council, IRB] since my return and cannot therefore give you any news in ref to *that* branch of business. Fitz [P. N. Fitzgerald, the principal agent of an IRB arms importation scheme, who fiercely opposed the Land League] . . . is still distinguishing himself by inciting opposition to the Rival House [the Land League]. He it was, I am assured, who got the boys in Clomel and Athlone to plan the "downfall" of the platforms in these places. . . . He was in Sligo the day before the meeting there, when four bottles of powder were discovered under the platform from which Kyle [Davitt] was to speak. Of course, all this is suspicion and not evidence, but suspicion points so strong to him in these enterprises that there is little room left for doubt. I am also assured that both Jacob's [Jeremiah O'Donovan Rossa's] man, Jack S, and Osborne's man M (that is Leinster Man) have each resolved to put Kyle [Davitt] out of the way. *Devoy's Post Bag*, vol. 2, 22.

67 "of the lights and shades . . .": Kettle, *The Material for Victory*, 48.

69 "almost too disgusting . . .": O'Hara, *Chief and Tribune*, 28.

70 "The sudden and involuntary . . .": Davitt Papers, TCD, MS 9320/3.

70 "Do you see that scoundrel . . .": Moody, *Davitt and Irish Revolution*, 463.

70 "a gagging": Tynan, 202.

70 "the Right Honourable gentleman . . .": Ibid.

70 "monstrous": Queen Victoria to Parnell, July 1, 1882. RA VIC/MAIN/D /34/9.

71 "Some attribute it . . .": February 14, 1881. Hamilton, BL, Add MS 48630.

72 "Don't you know me?": *Love Story*, vol. 1, 181.

72 "where the blazes": Kettle, *The Material for Victory*, 44.

72 "in the national interest": T. M. Healy, *Letters and Leaders*, vol. 1, 108.

72 **Barmaid said to have given birth to Parnell's child:** Parnell is alleged to have met "Lizzie" at the Wellington Hotel in Manchester, an Irish center, in 1878, and briefly lived with her in London; an emissary sent to her address found a woman with a baby in sparsely furnished lodgings in Holloway. An account by the MP Henry Labouchère claimed that "Parnell, having taken up with Mrs. O'Shea would do nothing for her," but Healy insists that as she never again sought further help, "Parnell must have made amends for his temporary neglect." See Callanan, *T. M. Healy*, 53–54.

73 "Well, what have you . . . Gentlemen, if we get . . .": Kettle, *The Material for Victory*, 44–45.

73 *l'Agitation Irlandaise*: *Le Figaro*, February 14, 1881.

74 "It's the slow rolling gaze . . .": Ibid., February 19, 1881.

74 **Henri Rochefort:** After living in exile in London and Geneva, Rochefort had only recently returned to Paris under the 1880 amnesty and founded the left-wing newspaper *L'Intransigeant*. It was his support of the Paris Commune that had led to his deportation to the penal colony of New Caledonia, but Rochefort had managed to escape, and O'Kelly got the scoop interview for the *Herald*. The journalist had a revolutionary past himself, having been an arms agent for the Irish Republican Brotherhood, and narrowly escaped a death sentence imposed by the Spanish army for crossing into rebel-held territory in an attempt to help free Cuba. O'Kelly's bravery and high ideals had won him the esteem and affection of Rochefort, who had no hesitation about agreeing to see Parnell.

74 **"the idol of the Irish people":** Tynan, 212.

74 **"It will be pure despotism . . .":** *L'Intransigeant*, February 18, 1881.

74 **"Strictly a social question . . .":** Ibid.

75 **"entailed the betrayal . . .":** Godré, *Parnell: Sa vie et sa fin*, 65–66.

75 **"anarchists and communists":** Callanan, *T. M. Healy*, 52.

75 **"the cape-work . . .":** Quoted in ibid., 51.

75 **"I feel he is eminently deserving . . .":** Devoy, *Devoy's Post Bag*, vol. 2, 40.

76 **"some plot on foot . . .":** Parnell letter, February 27, 1881. *Love Story*, vol. 1, 179.

76 **Plot against the Land League:** Telling Katharine that this conspiracy had been planned in Cork—"and you will guess the original source" [Ibid]—Parnell, like Michael Davitt, suspected that the Cork-based, leading IRB man P. N. Fitzgerald was behind it. Fitzgerald was believed to be out to destroy the Land League "on grounds," writes historian Owen McGee, "that it appealed only to material self-interest and was too much under the control of the Irish Parliamentary Party." *Dictionary of Irish Biography* (online membership access required).

76 **"laughing in the face":** *Le Figaro*, February 19, 1881.

76 **"*adieu* . . . I dare not say . . .":** Tynan, 213.

76 **"There it remained . . .":** *Love Story*, vol. 1, 167.

FIVE: CAPTAIN MOONLIGHT

77 AMERICA'S ANSWER TO COERCION: February 12, 1882.

77 **"I never saw in my life . . .":** Cross-examination of Somerset Ward in *Report of the Royal Commission on the Land Law Ireland Act (1881), and the Purchase of Land (Ireland) Act (1885)*, vol. 2, 245–51. (Hereafter, *Royal Commission*.)

77 **"This was the great heroic man . . .":** Translated by Breandán Mac Suibhne and quoted in "Soggarth Aroon and Gombeen-Priest."

78 **"You consider me the enemy . . .":** Somerset Ward cross-examination, *Royal Commission*.

78 **MacFadden advocated:** MacFadden ruled Gweedore in other ways too. A rigid disciplinarian, he insisted on regular attendance at Sunday Mass, severely punished nonconformists (allegedly to the point of whipping a single mother), railed against illicit distillation of poteen, and established a branch of the Temperance

League. Dan O'Donnell's public house had a loft where young people gathered to drink ale and dance to the fiddle on public fair days. "If MacFadden learned about this he would come with his blackthorn stick and people would run helter skelter. . . . [They] would then move down to Carrick Beach to have the dancing there. MacFadden certainly wasn't a man for amusement." Quotations from "Father McFadden [sic] of Gweedore," *Documentary on One*, RTÉ Radio 1, Ireland, presented and produced by Proinsias Ó Conluain, broadcast July 27, 1975.

To him dancing and music were sinful, pagan practices that risked corroding his parishioners' faith and morals. Ireland's "Great Piper," Torlogh MacSweeney, was a Gweedore man whose family had been evicted by Black Jack Adair and who a decade later won the piping championship at the Chicago World's Fair. Naturally, he was in great demand, but MacFadden did his best to prevent the piper from appearing at any celebration, noting the name of everyone he discovered listening to him and announcing from the altar the following Sunday that they must come barefoot to Mass for the next fortnight. At every opportunity, he berated MacSweeney, and once he quizzed him about his whereabouts the night before:

"I was over in Bun a'Leaca in Maire Og's house."
"You weren't over in Bun a'Leaca! You weren't. You were on the flagstones of Hell!"
"Well, if that's where I was, I wouldn't ever ask to leave it!"

This oral communication was quoted and translated by Breandán Mac Suibhne in "Soggarth Aroon and Gombeen-Priest."

78 "Optimistic and impatient . . .": Ibid., 163.
79 "Mr. Keown gave the hungry . . .": *Londonderry Sentinel*, May 26, 1881.
79 "Go on with your ordinary work . . .": *Derry Journal*, May 25, 1881.
80 "They are absolutely under . . ." and subsequent quotations: *Royal Commission*.
81 "the appellant had expressed . . .": *Derry Journal*, October 28, 1881.
81 "I didn't go to it . . .": *Irish Times*, October 4, 1883.
81 "It's said that Patrick . . .": DÓB.
81 "If [the people] drive us . . .": Reid, *Life of Forster*, vol. 2, 323.
81 "The Irish have always said . . .": Lewis Harcourt diaries, November 4, 1881. Bodleian, MS Harcourt 349.
82 "I have had to put the Act . . .": Quoted in Reid, *Life of Forster*, vol. 2, 330.
82 "Oh, my friends, beware . . .": Lloyd, *Ireland under the Land League*, 191.
82 "We tell the people of Ireland . . .": *Irish World*, August 6, 1881.
83 "the hollowness of the Act": C. C. O'Brien, *Parnell and His Party*, 71.
83 "For what he had to do . . ." and subsequent quotations: October 8, 1881. Lucy, vol. 2, 292–93.
84 "the anxious effort . . .": October 7, 1881. Matthew (ed.), *Gladstone Diaries*, vol. 10, 139.

84 "You will see that . . .": October 8, 1881. Ibid., 142.

84 "the last landlord": *Freeman's Journal*, October 10, 1881.

84 "the greatest coercionist . . . perfidious and cruel . . . unscrupulous and dishonest": Ibid.

84 "We have pushed this movement . . .": T. M. Healy, *Letters and Leaders*, vol. I, 136.

85 "If I am arrested . . .": B O'B, 240.

85 "Even such a benevolent . . .": October 10, 1881. Arnold-Forster, *Irish Journal*, 267.

86 "Proceed": October 12, 1881. Ibid., 269.

86 "the Irish Sherlock Holmes": Paul Craven, "Ireland's Sherlock Holmes Died 100 Years Ago," *Ireland's Own*, September 29, 2015. https://www.irelandsown.ie/irelands-sherlock-holmes-died-100-years-ago/.

87 "final excited colloquy": W. O'Brien, *Recollections*, 347–48.

87 "When I heard that . . .": *Love Story*, vol. I, 212.

88 "My own Queenie . . .": Ibid., 207.

88 "However, I had a cab . . ." and subsequent quotations: *Lloyd's Weekly News*, June 27, 1909.

89 "Even within these few moments . . .": October 14, 1881. Matthew (ed.), *Gladstone Diaries*, vol. 10, 144.

90 "well-contrived effect": Hopkins, *Kilmainham Memories*, 21.

90 "As the news of Mr. Parnell's . . .": October 12, 1881. Buckle (ed.), *Letters of QV*, vol. 3, 244.

90 "The most dreadful . . .": October 14, 1881. QVJs.

91 "Willie was so fiercely . . .": *Love Story*, vol. I, 206.

91 her husband had long been aware: The date of O'Shea's letter issuing the duel challenge was July 13, 1881, but a note to Katharine from Parnell suggests that her husband had discovered the portmanteau six months earlier. On January 7, 1881, Parnell wrote, "Kindly ask Captain O'Shea where he left my luggage." Dungan, *The Captain and the King*, 80.

92 "Let them manacle . . .": Quoted in Callanan, *T. M. Healy*, 63.

92 "A remark I made . . .": Diary, October 14, 1881. Quoted in Gladstone, *After Thirty Years*, 270.

92 "Mr. Parnell was safe in Kilmainham": October 13, 1881. QVJs.

93 "Your suggestion is approved . . .": B O'B, 247.

93 At Parnell's request: The decision to go ahead with a rent strike was far from unanimous: John Dillon and James O'Kelly both condemned this extreme measure; Davitt, in Portland Prison, had his name attached without his permission; and Parnell (according to Katharine) adamantly opposed it, although other accounts differ.

93 "A thousand cheers . . .": Sent on October 19, 1881. Quoted in *Irish World*, October 29, 1881.

93 "Captain Moonlight and his murder clubs . . .": W. O'Brien, *Recollections*, 376.

93 "Well John, what is to be the outcome . . ." and subsequent conversation: Quoted in O'Hara, *Chief and Tribune*, 188.

SIX: The Invincibles

94   "His business most important . . .": Memo to Forster, October 8, 1881. NAI, INL/Box 9.

94   "a set of assassins . . .": Mallon memo, December 2, 1880. Ibid.

94   "persons in high places": November 28, 1881. Ibid.

95   "they could not control the fanatics . . .": Ibid.

95   "I have received further confirmation . . .": Postscript to ibid.

95   "This was the first occasion . . .": Mallon memo, November 6, 1882. *Secret Official Reports*, 26.

95   Supreme Council: On p. 25 of ibid., Mallon lists members of the Supreme Council in February 1882: President: Charles Kickham; secretary: Patrick Egan; Joseph Biggar MP; James Mullett, Dublin; John Walsh, Middlesbrough. Thomas Brennan, secretary of the Land League, was also general secretary of the Supreme Council. The local directory for Dublin included James Mullett, James Carey, and Daniel Curley. See also McGee, *The IRB*; Ó Broin, *Revolutionary Underground*; and Ó Broin and T. W. Moody, "The I.R.B. Supreme Council, 1868–78," *Irish Historical Studies* 19 (1974–75).

96   "the ablest strategist . . .": A. M. Sullivan, quoted in B O'B, 189.

96   "I am a Land Leaguer . . .": Quoted in Le Caron, 168.

96   It was John Walsh: Walsh (alias "Hanrahan") had been entrusted by Egan in 1876 to participate in the rescue in Australia of six Fenian convicts who were successfully transported to America on the whaleboat *Catalpa*—a legendary feat in IRB history. For years he had held a responsible position in England's Middlesbrough shipyard but gave it up to devote himself exclusively to Irish nationalism, troubling his respectable family with his advanced ideas. *Freeman's Journal*, March 3, 1883.

96   "Mr. Walsh said . . .": Statement of James Mullett, Kilmainham Gaol, March 9, 1883. *Secret Official Reports*, 43–45.

97   "Mr. Kickham's old-fashioned notions": Ibid., 44.

97   "a clergyman from the country": Ibid.

98   "My object was to assist . . .": *Times* (London), February 20, 1883.

98   "The young fellow's religion . . .": *Lloyd's Weekly News*, July 11, 1909.

99   "Facts came to my knowledge . . .": Ibid.

99   he had been "personally responsible": The police also suspected that Carey was the murderer of George Clark, an informer, on February 9, 1866, at Pin Mill, on the bank of the Royal Canal; and of Andrew Mullen, a gas fitter, shot dead on February 20, 1870, while walking down Usher's Quay. Carey claimed to have overseen the attack, during the Fenian Rising of 1867, on two policemen, one of whom was shot dead; to have been present at the dynamite attack on the Prince Consort memorial; and to have led the party that attempted to blow up Lord Carlisle's monument in Phoenix Park. He boasted that he had pointed out Head Constable Thomas Talbot to the man who murdered him in Hardwicke Street in 1871. Carey

said he had kept the assassin, Robert Kelly, on a retainer, paying him a pound a week for several months. *Dundee Courier and Argus*, September 28, 1883.

99 "It could not come by . . .": Quoted in *P and Crime*, pt. 9, 124.

99 "Pat Egan urged him on . . .": Ibid., 104.

99 "My dear James . . .": Ibid., 105.

100 "make history" and subsequent Carey quotations: TNA, JC.

100 "might have aroused": *Lloyd's Weekly News*, July 4, 1909.

101 "Egan is now Dictator . . .": NAI, Mallon Reports, INL/Box 9.

101 "A very remarkable man": *Lloyds Weekly Review*, June 29, 1909.

101 "storm signals . . . Suddenly . . . he flamed . . .": W. O'Brien, *Recollections*, 136.

102 "querulous bully": *Lloyd's Weekly News*, June 20, 1909.

102 "the prince of spies": John Devoy's name for Le Caron. *Devoy's Post Bag*, vol. 2, 46.

102 "He was the last person . . .": Le Caron, 161.

102 "the poor dupes . . .": Ibid., 167.

102 "You remember the committee . . .": Egan, quoted in *P and Crime*, pt. 12, 43. The claim about the dispersal of £70,000–£100,000 of Land League funds is made during the Special Commission's interrogation of Parnell. *P and Crime*, pt. 20, 298–99.

103 "the exact nature . . . I cannot tell you exactly . . .": *New York Herald*, October 21, 1881.

103 "TO THE PEOPLE OF IRELAND . . .": Flyer, NAI, INL/Box 9.

103 Patrick Ford's *Irish World*: Although no single publication was more vocal or philanthropic in driving the Irish cause, the Coercion Act followed by Parnell's imprisonment triggered nationwide fury in Irish America. Catholic journals, including the New York *Tablet* and the Boston *Pilot*, urged their readers to reach deep into their purses, and in a memo dated February 3, 1882, Consul General Edward Archibald reported to Lionel Sackville West at the British legation in Washington that "$232,983 have been collected and nearly all remitted to the Treasurer Egan at Paris. Of this amount the sum of $69,000 was received by the Editor of the *Irish World*." TNA, FO 5/1816.

Through the *Irish World*, Ford established twenty-five hundred branches of the Land League and contributed a total of $342,072, but his activism had angered the president of the American Land League, Patrick A. Collins, who believed (rightly) that Ford intended to usurp the organization's supremacy. Tensions between the two men erupted, and Patrick Egan, anxious not to jeopardize funds raised by Collins, acted as peacemaker. Urging the two men to meet halfway, and even enlisting Parnell as a go-between, he wrote Collins a twelve-page placatory letter.

Hotel Brighton
March 7, 1881

I could not see why all friends would not at the present momentous crisis work in harmony for the cause of Ireland. . . . The *Irish World* has

been an exceedingly powerful ally and a very good friend of our movement from the very beginning and we could not nor would not do anything like throwing them over, but I see the full force of your statement
that the movement should not be—as you say in America—bossed [?] by
any one paper to the exclusion of the various other influential journals
throughout the States who are willing to lend their aid, and I am writing
to Mr. Ford fully and candidly upon the whole matter . . . and urging
upon him in the interest of the cause to co-operate cordially with your
organisation. . . .

The spirit of the people in Ireland is simply magnificent. We are
now face to face with coercion and so far there is no flinching, no yielding. . . . The Whigs [Gladstone's Liberal Party] think that they will
under cover of coercion be able to raise their heads again, that they can
patch up the Land Act of 1870 and that the country will accept this
bill and settle down. . . . They think they are dealing with the usual type
of agitation. They cannot see that during the past two years we have
created not only a *young* Ireland but a *new* Ireland and that nothing can
now satisfy the country short of rooting the English Landlord garrisons
out of the land. *One of the greatest sources of our power is that we have money.*
Having that in view, we are keeping our outlay as close as possible and
our friends in America may rest assured that every cent of their money
will be put to the best possible account for the furtherance of the cause
of Ireland. (Patrick A. Collins Papers, Box 1, Folder 30, John Burns
Library, Boston College.)

But the antipathy continued. The *Irish World*'s thunderous promotion of the No
Rent policy had divided Irish Americans, the more conservative (such as Collins)
viewing its editor as a dangerous friend of the cause. Ford neither publicized nor
attended a Land League convention arranged by Collins in Washington, DC, in
April 1882. By then, he and Egan were in control.

My information is drawn from the Patrick A. Collins Papers and from two
essays, Lawrence W. Kennedy, "Young Patrick A. Collins and Boston Politics
after the Civil War," *Historical Journal of Massachusetts* 38 (Spring 2010), 39–59; and
James J. Green, "American Catholics and the Irish Land League, 1879–1882,"
Catholic Historical Review 35, no. 1 (April 1949), 19–42, https://www.jstor.org/
stable/25014992.

104 "loud-tongued apostle": Le Caron, 134.

104 "Brothers, English despotism . . .": *New York Times*, October 22, 1881.

105 Sullivan and Egan in Paris: See Campbell, *Fenian Fire*, 126.

105 "like an Irish farmer . . .": Devoy, quoted in ibid.

105 "to be used at some future time . . .": Le Caron to Robert Anderson, December 12,
1881. TNA, Robert Anderson Papers, HO 144/1538/6.

105   "We can't continue to be the tail . . .": Undated. National Library of Ireland, Manuscripts, John Devoy Papers, MS 18,012/(16).

105   "The game is being played . . .": Mallon to Talbot, December 10, 1881. NAI, INL/ Box 9.

105   "The Miller has stated . . .": November 26, 1881. Ibid.

106   "It is also understood": December 10, 1881. Ibid.

106   "[The Queen] has today . . .": December 31, 1881. Buckle (ed.), Letters of QV, vol. 3, 249.

107   "horrors and sorrows . . . Irish Atrocities": December 31, 1881. QVJs.

107   "overwhelming": Weintraub, Disraeli, 659.

107   "an unguarded exchange . . .": Ibid., 649.

107   "It is better not . . .": Ibid., 655.

107   "the extraordinary powers . . .": April 21, 1881. QVJs.

107   "Oh William dear . . .": Jenkins, Gladstone, 55.

107   "Do pet the Queen": Hibbert, QV: A Personal History, 320.

107   "The repellent power . . .": Battiscombe, Mrs. Gladstone, 150.

108   "I am always outside . . .": November 30, 1881. Jenkins, Gladstone, 468.

108   "accidental, conditional . . .": To Mary Gladstone, November 15, 1881. Mary, Diaries, 234.

108   "intolerable . . . Nor can the moment . . .": November 4, 1881. Lucy, vol. 2, 295–96.

108   "It may seem unfriendly . . .": November 25, 1881. Fitzmaurice, The Life of Granville, 302.

109   "Seriously, I think . . .": November 4, 1881. Arnold-Forster, Irish Journal, 304.

109   "the Pendulum": December 27, 1881. Hamilton, Diary, vol. 1, 206.

109   "by someone not tarred . . .": November 1, 1881. Reid, Life of Forster, vol. 2, 358.

109   "his hand-writing showed this": Cowper, Earl Cowper, 542.

109   "He looks ill . . .": January 8, 1882. QVJs.

110   "a giant in stature . . .": Mallon's description. Lloyd's Weekly News, July 4, 1909.

111   "Mr. Forster was referred to . . .": James Carey statement. TNA, JC.

111   "scowling visage": Poster, "Wanted Fenian John McCafferty, 1867," accessed at Rare Irish Stuff: https://www.rareirishstuff.com/irish-historical-memorabilia-/fenian -wanted-poster-john-mccafferty-1867.7853.html.

111   "The gun is mightier . . .": Ibid.

112   "The doctor has been buying . . . I was somewhat surprised . . .": Evidence given by James Leavy, P and Crime, 103–5.

112   Mary Ann Byrne: See account in Tynan, Appendix E, 554; and police reports in the Crime Branch Special files, NAI, CBS/B Files, 156–268 Box.

113   "do the remainder": Evidence given by Robert Farrell. Times (London), January 22, 1883.

113   "You see, he likes them": March 8, 1882. Arnold-Forster, Irish Journal, 396.

113   "the worst part of Galway": March 2, 1882. Ibid., 390.

113   "Let out the suspects!": Reid, *Life of Forster*, vol. 2, 403.

114   "Why did he not do this . . .": March 12, 1882. Hamilton, *Diary*, vol. 1, 237.

114   "leaning forward . . .": Horace West, assistant private secretary, April 5, 1882. Arnold-Forster, *Irish Journal*, 436.

115   "staggered and astonished . . . in the very chamber . . .": Tynan, 448.

115   "If he left a note . . .": TNA, JC.

115   "a few more good men . . .": Statement by Carey's brother, Peter. TNA, JC.

115   "How easily this tyrant . . .": Tynan, 454.

116   "Carey suffered in their estimation": Ibid., 459.

117   "should have been made . . .": Ibid., 460.

117   "What are those confounded fellows": April 5, 1882. Arnold-Forster, *Irish Journal*, 436.

117   "She would think it so dreadful": March 23, 1882. Ibid., 416.

117   "I go into the Castle . . .": Cowper to Gladstone, December 28, 1881. Cowper, *Earl Cowper*, 545.

118   "a sudden Council of War": Ibid., 566.

118   "Have just heard of the death . . .": April 9, 1882 (Easter Sunday). Arnold-Forster, *Irish Journal*, 441.

SEVEN: COERCION-IN-COTTONWOOL

119   "Do not crowd what you write . . .": March 30, 1882. *Love Story*, vol. 1, 242.

120   "Has he left yet? . . .": November 21, 1881. Ibid., 220.

120   "I do trust you have . . .": January 11, 1882. Ibid., 231.

120   "really the only reason . . .": January 17, 1881. Ibid., 232.

120   "inexpressibly consoling": O'Connor, *Memoirs of an Old Parliamentarian*, 127.

120   "Coercion-in-cottonwool": O'Donnell, *A History of the Irish Parliamentary Party*, vol. 2, 44.

120   "He makes me a soda . . .": Parnell letter to Katharine, November 5, 1881. *Love Story*, vol. 1, 217–18.

121   "He himself told me . . .": O'Connor, *Memoirs of an Old Parliamentarian*, 127.

121   "surely killing": Parnell letter to Katharine, December 14, 1881, quoting her remark to him, *Love Story*, vol. 1, 225.

121   "I could not very well . . .": December 16, 1881. Ibid., 226.

121   "*Tell one of them* . . .": December 30, 1881. Ibid., 228.

121   "You must tell the doctor . . .": January 7, 1882. Ibid., 229.

121   "I shall love her . . .": March 16, 1882. Ibid., 238.

121   "it might make suspicions": March 30, 1882. Ibid., 242.

122   "very much like a father": March 16, 1882. Ibid., 238.

122   "my pain was the greater . . .": Ibid., 244.

122   Invincibles leader Frank Byrne: It had been Byrne who, on Parnell's arrest, had organized a mass protest in London's Hyde Park, distributing a circular denouncing the imprisonment without trial of the political suspects and the attempt to suppress

by force freedom of speech and the right to protest against grievances in Ireland. *Daily News* (London), October 24, 1881.

123   "practically withdrawn": Parnell's evidence, *P and Crime*, pt. 20, 60.

123   "the unspeakable comfort": *Love Story*, vol. I, 245.

123   "to conciliate Willie . . .": Ibid., 247.

123   "brought Mr. Parnell within . . .": BL, Gladstone Papers, Add MS 44269.

123   "the unfortunate tenants . . .": Chamberlain to Gladstone, December 14, 1881. Garvin, *Life of Chamberlain*, vol. I, 346.

123   "What the French call . . .": April 18, 1881. Chamberlain, *A Political Memoir*, 35.

123   "was sick of prison . . .": Ibid., 26–27.

123   "I had hitherto refrained . . .": April 18, 1881. Ibid., 36.

124   "astonishing proposal . . . Instead of feeling inclined . . .": Letter to the Hon. H. Cowper, April 22, 1882. Cowper, *Earl Cowper*, 571.

124   "purely and exclusively his own": Ibid.

124   "Old 'Buckshot' actually suggested . . .": April 5, 1882. Hamilton, *Diary*, vol. I, 247.

124   actually brushed Forster's arm: From Carey's statement to John Curran on February 21, 1883: "On Tuesday I met him myself in Dame street where he was coming down with a gentleman, a tall young gentleman. My arm touched Mr Forster's. They stopped at the post office at College Green, and went in there." TNA JC.

125   "He said that from what . . .": Tynan, 465.

125   "He was to be shot . . .": Carey evidence, February 17, 1882. *Times* (London), February 19, 1883.

125   "We left by the quarter to six . . .": Jephson, quoted in Reid, *Life of Forster*, vol. 2, 429.

125   "I think I caught it . . .": *Love Story*, vol. I, 246.

126   "Willie wanted me to join them . . .": Ibid., 247.

126   "wretched state . . .": Katharine to Parnell, April 24, 1882. Quoted in Jordan, *Kitty O'Shea*, 68.

126   "to be disavowed if he failed": Quotation from Charles Dilke's diary. BL, Add MS 43936.

126   "pimped [Katharine] to the Irish party leader": Dungan, *The Captain and the King*, 83.

126   "What do you think . . .": April 25, 1882. *Love Story*, vol. I, 253.

127   "Parnell and Co must publish . . .": Garvin, *Life of Chamberlain*, vol. I, 354.

127   "so shifty": *Love Story*, vol. I, 256.

127   exchange of correspondence: Giving instructions to his private secretary, Henry Jephson, Forster wrote: "My object [is] that private unopened letters should pass between O'Shea & Parnell & that their having passed should not be mentioned." In a note to William O'Shea, Forster added: "I will take care your letters to Mr Parnell and his to you are not interfered with. Do not however let this be known, and put your name in the corner of your letter. Yrs W.E.F. Upon second thoughts I think the best plan would be for you to send your letters to the Irish Office, sealed of

course, and for me to send it under cover to the Governor [of Kilmainham Gaol] to give to Mr Parnell without delay & of course unopened, and to ask him to give the Govenor his reply which the Govenor shall post of course unopened direct to you." TNA, HO 144/72/A19.

127 "two private letters each way": Ibid.

127 "If you come to Ireland . . .": O'Shea evidence, Special Commission. *Times* (London), November 1, 1880.

127 "knew everybody . . . the first run at them": Ibid.

128 "The accomplishment of the program . . .": B O'B, 264.

128 "He came over to see me . . .": *Love Story*, vol. I, 255.

128 "Is that all, do you think . . . What more . . . That the conspiracy . . .": B O'B, 264–65.

129 "a very dangerous troublesome fellow": Thomas Burke letter to Forster, March 21, 1881. TNA, HO 144/72/A19.

129 "which might be interpreted . . .": B O'B, 265.

129 "But is Mr. Gladstone impressed . . .": Arnold-Forster, *Irish Journal*, 469.

129 "an *hors d'oeuvre* . . .": Matthew (ed.), *Gladstone Diaries*, vol. 10, 247.

129 "the most extraordinary . . .": B O'B, 266.

129 "It would hardly be possible . . .": BL, Gladstone Papers, MS 44545.

130 "It seems that Mr. Gladstone . . .": May 3, 1882. Arnold-Forster, *Irish Journal*, 472.

130 "He need hardly assure . . .": May 1, 1882. Buckle (ed.), *Letters of QV*, vol. 3, 274–75.

130 "*let out* to attend . . . Surely this ought not . . .": Undated letter to Forster. RA VIC/MAIN/D/32/13a.

130 "I *very reluctantly* . . . ": May 2, 1882. QVJs.

131 "He has resigned": Arnold-Forster, *Irish Journal*, 470.

131 "growled out . . .": May 2, 1882. Mary, *Diaries*, 247.

131 "Well, I think you might . . .": Arnold-Forster, *Irish Journal*, 471.

131 "who must know . . .": Letter to Gladstone, May 3, 1882. RA VIC/MAIN/D/32/50.

132 "She cannot conceal from him . . .": Ibid.

132 "a better man": Letter to the Hon. H. Cowper, April 22, 1882. Cowper, *Earl Cowper*, 571.

132 "for a gross violation . . .": B O'B, 267.

132 "Oh Master Charley . . . I thought he was . . .": Ibid., 268.

133 "Not the slightest . . .": *Irish World*, May 5, 1882.

133 "dragged into . . . I cannot describe . . .": *Love Story*, vol. I, 235.

133 "I was very anxious . . .": Ibid., 257.

134 "For myself, I believe that . . .": See Patrick Maume's groundbreaking discovery in his essay, "Parnell and the IRB Oath," *Irish Historical Studies* 29 (May 1995): 363–70.

134 "Mr. Speaker I have received . . .": Arnold-Forster, *Irish Journal*, 475.

134 "the hon. Member for the City of Cork": B O'B, 270.

134 "Nothing can be more clear . . .": Memo to Lord Spencer. Quoted in Richard Hawkins, "Gladstone, Forster, and the Release of Parnell, 1882–8," *Irish Historical Studies*, vol. 16, no. 64, 417–45.

134 "I locked him up in '81 . . .": May 16, 1887. Lucy Cavendish, unpublished diary, vol. 14, Chatsworth, DF19/1/12.

135 "the evil genius of Ireland": Ibid.

135 "His words are so important . . .": May 4–5, 1882. Buckle (ed.), *Letters of QV*, vol. 3, 280.

135 "There has been *no* negotiation . . .": May 1, 1882. Matthew (ed.), *Gladstone Diaries*, vol. 10, 247.

EIGHT: MAYDAY

136 "He was much disturbed . . .": May 2, 1882. Lucy, vol. 2, 304–5.

136 "almost inevitably one of odium": Ibid., 305.

136 "I told him I had no tact . . .": Ibid.

136 "almost unmixed mischief": Gladstone letter to John Morley, August 11, 1888. Quoted in Chamberlain, *A Political Memoir*, 58.

137 "I told him I considered him . . .": May 11, 1882. Lucy, vol. 2, 326.

137 "very rash course of action": Pearson, *Stags and Serpents*, 219.

137 "F. seems to have nearly . . .": May 3, 1882. Ibid.

138 the Devonshire properties: William Cavendish, when becoming Duke of Devonshire at age fifty, had inherited Chatsworth House, only to find himself encumbered with the formidable debts of his predecessor, the profligate "Bachelor Duke." Turning to modern business as a way of securing his legacy, he became a prominent tycoon, expanding the Lancashire docklands, transforming the small fishing port of Eastbourne in Sussex into a select seaside resort, and supervising the conversion of the local village of Barrow into an iron-rich industrial mecca.

138 "F. is much disturbed . . .": May 4, 1882. Lucy, vol. 2, 308.

138 "O, she is as brave as possible . . .": May 3, 1882. Ibid., 306.

138 "sprinkling itself with grey": Ibid., 266.

138 "If only he could learn . . .": Ibid., 91.

138 "his defective 'r' and 'th' . . .": Ibid., 315.

139 "I felt half afraid . . .": Ibid., 310.

139 "By the God of Heaven . . .": Corfe, 176.

139 "I suppose it is all . . .": Lewis "Loulou" Harcourt, quoted in Jackson, *Harcourt and Son*, 105.

139 "Never was so small . . .": Curran, *Reminiscences*, 132.

139 "the greatest horror of it": Corfe, 174.

139 "Had I known . . .": Letter to Morley, August 11, 1888. Chamberlain, *A Political Memoir*, 58.

139 "disgraceful surrender . . .": Tynan, 470.

140 "the old tyrant escaping": Ibid., 468.

140 **A conscientious civil servant:** Undersecretary Burke's usefulness to Forster is borne out by a collection of letters held in the National Archives that contains long reports on Irish land issues and local intelligence. (TNA HO 144/72/A19.) Herbert Gladstone, who got to know Burke when they worked together at Dublin Castle, described him as a strong, high-minded man, "who was thought to have the reigns of coercion in his hands." When he asked Burke whether he carried a handgun, the undersecretary replied with indifference: "No, if they want to get me they can." (*After Thirty Years,* 277.)

140 **"Over and over again . . .":** *Hansard's Parliamentary Debates,* vol. 269 (1882), 324.

140 **Phoenix Park:** The name of the park has nothing to do with the mythical, transcendent bird but is a corruption of the Irish words *Fionn-uisge,* meaning "clear water," and refers to the mineral spring near the Viceregal Lodge.

141 **"told us Mr. Burke had gone . . .":** *Times* (London), February 23, 1883.

141 **the new invaders:** Tynan, 468.

141 **"a massacre":** Corfe, 178.

141 **"We must see that this hideous deed . . .":** Ibid.

142 **"We talked a while . . .":** Letter to Lucy Cavendish, May 6, 1883. Chatsworth, DF19/2/6.

142 **"It was a magical country . . .":** Fingall [née Plunkett], *Seventy Years Young,* 48.

142 **Isle of Portland . . . prison yard:** Portland was where the exiled revolutionary Jeremiah O'Donovan Rossa had been incarcerated in the 1860s, his demeaning treatment the trigger for his "Skirmishing" dynamite campaign against Britain. He never cleaned out Portland's lavatories, he declared, "without wishing that the Prime Minister of England and the Secretary of State were within the reach of my shovel." *Prison Life: Six Years in English Prisons.* New York: P. J. Kennedy, 1874, 137. O'Donovan Rossa dedicated his book to Irish convicted felons.

143 **"after their singular mode . . .":** *Recollections of Portland Prison, 1881,* 337–47. Davitt Papers, TCD, 9641.

143 **"In spite of my prowling enemies . . .":** Ibid.

143 **"My dear Sir . . . We were ourselves . . .":** Davitt, *Fall of Feudalism,* 355.

144 **The splendor of castle seasons:** "Only at Buckingham Palace and the Viceregal Lodge have I eaten off gold plate. Nasty and scratchy," wrote Elizabeth Fingall, née Plunkett, in her memoir, *Seventy Years Young,* 76.

144 **"The atmosphere seems tainted . . .":** C. Spencer, *The Spencer Family,* 267.

145 **"Jenkinson would not reply . . .":** Letter to Lucy Cavendish, May 6, 1883. Chatsworth, DF19/2/6.

145 **"Certainly the best reception . . .":** Spencer, *The Red Earl,* vol. I, 189.

145 **"an occasional faint hiss":** Molony, *Phoenix Park Murders,* 14.

145 **"a respectable . . . My fine fellow . . .":** Anonymous letter from "An Englishman Occasionally Resident in Ireland," *St. James's Gazette,* May 11, 1882.

146 **"No-one is of the slightest use . . .":** Cowper, *Earl Cowper,* 450.

146 **"I thought that, although . . .":** Cooke and Vincent, "Lord Spencer on the Phoenix Park Murders."

147 "There are some of the 'boys' . . .": Bussy, 62.

147 "How bright the future looked . . . ": MD Invincibles Diary, headed "May 5th & 6th [1883] Anniversary of my release from Portland and of the Park murder."

148 "I see no reason why . . .": Davitt, *Fall of Feudalism*, 356.

148 "Ireland a Nation . . ." and other quotations: *Derry Journal*, May 8 and 10, 1882.

148 "half condoling, half congratulating": May 3, 1882. Arnold-Forster, *Irish Journal*, 474.

148 "It is selfish to find . . .": May 4, 1882. Chatsworth, DF19/2/3.

149 "the shower of contemptuous . . .": Letter (undated) to Lady Louisa Egerton. Quoted in Lucy, vol. 2, 268.

149 "I cannot congratulate you" . . . "the cold-shouldering . . .": May 4, 1882. Ibid., 311.

149 "Thou shalt keep him" . . . "I thought 'O, these are . . .'": May 6, 1882. Ibid., 316.

150 Samuel Ferguson: Ferguson followed "At the Polo Ground" with a companion piece, "In Carey's Footsteps," dated February 18, 1886. Described as "a Dublin eclogue," it is a long meditation entering the mind of a Catholic priest who walks through Phoenix Park, commenting on the two statues that symbolized British imperialism in Ireland.

Reminding one at every step he takes
In his own grounds, at home, that some one else
Confers his culture on him from outside.

Passing the zoological garden, he reaches the polo ground and realizes that he is standing on the very spot where Carey waited to signal the Invincibles to act. The narrator struggles to banish "foul images" from his mind, wondering whether his own nationalist sympathies might have set "wits imagining" among his congregation and prompted an avenger to carry out his private war. The poem seems to consider whether a patriotic sense of duty can be reconciled with the better nature of human beings and ends by imagining Carey making the choice to leave the scene.

In his pausing footsteps, here stand I,
Still free to turn whichever way I will.

Ferguson, *Sir Samuel Ferguson*, vol. 1, 263–66.

150 "Here I am . . ." and further quotations: Ferguson, *Sir Samuel Ferguson*, vol. 1, 258–62.

151 memorial of the war hero Lord Gough: The 1878 unveiling of John Henry Foley's statue of the British commander was witnessed by the four-year-old Winston Churchill, whose earliest memory was that of his formidable lord lieutenant grandfather proudly bellowing to the crowd, "And with a withering volley he shattered the enemy's line!" (The Rt. Hon. Winston S. Churchill C.H. M.P., *My Early Life: A Roving Commission* London: Thornton Butterworth Ltd, 1930, 15.)

Beheaded on Christmas Eve 1944, and bombed in 1957, the Gough statue inspired a bawdy ballad, the most-quoted lines being:

Neath the horse's prick, a dynamite stick
Some gallant "hayro" did place
For the cause of our land, with a match in his hand
Bravely the foe he did face.

Wrongly attributed to Brendan Behan, the ballad is now known to have been written by Vincent Caprani, a young printer and writer, whose "Rowdy Rhymes and Rec-imitations" appeared in an anonymous broadsheet in 1982. Caprani's doggerel has been collected in a volume of the same name (Dublin: Gill and Macmillan, 2011).

151 "so deeply and tranquilly": A remark in Lucy Cavendish's undated letter to her brother, Alfred, quoted in Introduction to Book 14, Lucy, vol. 2, 266.

152 "Fine evening": Spencer letter to Lucy Cavendish, May 6, 1883. Chatsworth, DF19/2/6.

152 "the Castle Rat": Corfe, 26.

152 "I will not carry arms . . .": Bussy, 169.

153 "Those are Castle swells . . . Forster's policy": Roundell, "From a Diary at Dublin Castle."

153 "Two men . . . Two by two": Joyce, "Aeolus," Ulysses, 175.

153 "What are you doing here?" and subsequent quotations: Times (London), February 23, 1883.

154 "Ah, you villain!": The Mysteries of Ireland, 287.

154 "at Mr. Burke": Times (London), February 19, 1883.

155 "I was so startled . . .": Lloyd's Weekly News, May 14, 1882.

155 "This looks like murder": Ibid.

155 "No-one that I told . . .": Corfe, 188.

155 "Halloa, There has been a murder . . .": Standard (London), May 8, 1882.

155 "He did not get excited . . .": Ibid.

155 "a shriek which I shall never forget . . .": B O'B, 273.

155 "Murder, murder!": Cooke and Vincent, "Lord Spencer on the Phoenix Park Murders."

156 "Good God, it's Lord Frederick!": Corfe, 197.

156 "I noticed that Lord Frederick's socks . . .": This quotation and account is from the typescript of a notebook written by Conor Maguire, MD, of Claremorris District of County Mayo, "The Murder of Lord Frederick Cavendish and Mr. Burke, Under-Secretary, in the Phoenix Park on the 6th May, 1882." Irish National Folklore Collection, MS 1304, 146–48.

156 "inflicted by a man of Herculean strength": Irish Times, April 12, 1882.

156 "The clean edges . . . The weapon . . .": Lloyd's Weekly News, May 14, 1882.

157 "Is it true what I hear . . . It is so . . .": Times (London), February 19, 1883.

157 "Executed by order . . .": Ibid.

157 "The whole thing . . .": Cooke and Vincent, "Lord Spencer on the Phoenix Park Murders."

158 "quite conscious . . . He well knew that . . .": May 6, 1882. Devonshire Collections, Chatsworth, Correspondence of the Eighth Duke of Devonshire, CS8/340/1147.

158 "We are in God's hands . . .": Battiscombe, *The Spencers of Althorp*, 229.

158 "I must go in search of Hartington": May 8, 1882. Hamilton, BL, Add MS 48632.

159 "Put your things on . . . I shall go . . . I feel it most . . .": May 6, 1882. Arnold-Forster, *Irish Journal*, 481.

159 "someone stammer 'bad news'": Mary, *Diaries*, 249.

159 "Mr. and Mrs. Gladstone have not yet returned . . .": RAVIC/MAIN/D/32/76.

159 "nothing about Mr. Gladstone": Rhys Jenkins, *Sir Charles Dilke: A Victorian Tragedy* (London: Collins, 1959), 153.

160 "I briefly told her . . .": May 8, 1882. Hamilton, BL, Add MS 48632.

160 "Was ever such a May-day . . .": *Morning Post* (London), May 8, 1882.

160 "Nothing but loyal expressions . . .": May 6, 1882. QVJs.

160 "This is awful—terrible!": RAVIC/ADDA12/719.

161 "the *direct result* . . .": Corfe, 201.

161 "All is over with Lord Frederick": QVJs.

161 "[I] could think of nothing else": Ibid.

161 "Oh, come . . . This is a patent . . .": Davitt, *Fall of Feudalism*, 357.

NINE: Falling Soft

162 "Please to ask Freddy . . .": BL, Gladstone Papers, Add MS 44124.

162 "No thought of fear . . .": Lucy, vol. 2, 318. This, and Lucy's subsequent entries about trauma of her husband's murder, and of the Invincibles Trials, were written in the religious Retreat at St. Mary's Stone on November 14 and 15, 1882.

163 "Oh I know . . . Tell me everything . . .": Meriel Talbot appendix, Lucy, vol. 2, 330–32.

163 "[He] was all I had . . .": Lord Granville to Queen Victoria, May 7, 1882: "Lady Louisa had gradually broken it to Lady Frederick: '[He] was all I had, I have no-one else' was her first exclamation but she showed courage and some self-possession." RAVIC/MAIN/D/32/74.

163 "It is cruel . . . Don't let them hate . . .": Quoted in an appendix by Lucy's younger sister, Lavinia Talbot, Lucy, vol. 2, 330–32.

163 "I saw his face . . ." and subsequent quotations: Lucy, vol. 2, 318.

164 "like an oak . . .": Talbot appendix, ibid., 331.

164 "She never seemed bewildered . . ." and subsequent quotations: Ibid.

164 "a marvelous manifestation . . .": Ibid., 332.

164 "All through the long awful night . . .": Lucy, vol. 2, 320.

165 "King, what is it? . . . No, you are not a coward": Quoted in Jordan, *Kitty O'Shea*, 75.

165 "stabbed in the back": Ibid., 76.

165 "of a few hare-brained fanatics": Tim Healy, quoting Parnell. *Boston Republic*, June 17, 1882.

165   "I regarded them as . . .": Parnell's evidence to the Special Commission. Quoted in Harrison, *Parnell Vindicated*, 326.

165   "One of the worst things . . .": Davitt, *Fall of Feudalism*, 357.

165   "One act of hellish vengeance . . .": May 7, 1882. Diary, Davitt Papers, TCD, MS 9535.

166   "He was wild . . . Talk of the calm . . .": B O'B, 274.

166   "The murder has ruined us . . .": May 12, 1882. T. M. Healy, *Letters and Leaders*, vol. I, 161.

166   "We feel that no act . . .": Bew, *Enigma*, 98–99.

166   "this dark Sunday": Written beside the date of May 7, 1882, on a letter to Lord Granville. BL, Gladstone Papers, Add MS 44545.

167   "He wrote evidently under . . .": Quoted in Jordan, *Kitty O'Shea*, 76.

167   "The conviction was borne in upon . . .": Churchill, *Great Contemporaries*, 270.

167   "Dear Mr. O'Shea . . .": May 7, 1882. BL, Gladstone Papers, Add MS 44545.

167   "flaming for reprisals": Garvin, *Life of Chamberlain*, vol. I, 369.

167   "the *people* of Ireland": Letter to Roundell Palmer, the lord chancellor, May 9, 1882. BL, Gladstone Papers, Add MS 44545.

167   "Even in this black crime . . .": Ibid.

168   "They will strike at me next": Chamberlain, *A Political Memoir*, 62–63.

168   "He must show that . . ." and subsequent quotations: *Love Story*, vol. I, 264.

168   "sacred band": Tynan, 746.

168   "the glorious 6th of May": Ibid., 274.

169   "a thousand times greater . . .": Ibid., 480.

169   "Only for himself . . . [When] the strange gentleman . . .": Corfe, 200.

169   "impressing upon them the necessity . . .": Tynan, 483.

169   "When [Egan] opened and looked . . . For perhaps five minutes . . .": Article by the Paris correspondent of the *Daily News* (London). Quoted in Macdonald, *Diary of the Parnell Commission*, 314.

170   "They knew nothing . . .": Tynan, 482.

170   "an old Castle official": *Daily News* (London), May 9, 1882.

170   "Lord Frederick Cavendish had only been . . . He had been so long . . .": Ibid.

170   "stupid as well as atrocious": Ibid.

170   "None but the most stupid ass . . . ": Dr. William B. Wallace, quoted in the *New York Times*, June 4, 1894.

170   "The most anti-English of us . . .": Katharine Tynan, quoted in Teresa O'Donnell's essay "Skin the Goat's Curse on James Carey: Narrating the Phoenix Park Murders through Contemporary Broadside Ballads," in *Crime, Violence and the Irish in the 19th Century*, ed. Kyle Hughes and Donald MacRaild, (Liverpool University Press, 2018), 28.

170   "abhorrent to every true friend . . .": *Daily News* (London), May 9, 1882.

170   "What harm if it was only Burke . . .": B O'B, 273.

171   "first disgusted me": This remark is from a memo of January 3, 1883, sent to Britain's US ambassador Lionel Sackville West. It recounts an interview with an

informer named Lionel Crowley, questioned about a plot by Jeremiah O'Donovan Rossa to assassinate, "by means of an infernal machine," the Prince of Wales, the Earl of Derby, and Herbert Gladstone. Formerly schoolmates, Crowley and O'Donovan Rossa had met again after seventeen years in June 1882. "It was the Phoenix Park Murders which first disgusted me with what was going on. I left Ireland shortly after them. Lord Frederick Cavendish was a tip-top man. Had I known beforehand that the murders were going to take place I had influence enough to have stopped them." Crowley said that he heard that the Dublin murders had been planned in New York, and that the murderers had gone from New York to commit the crime. I said, 'Do you suppose any of them came back here?' He replied, 'One must have anyhow.' I asked him why he thought so. He then told me that shortly after his arrival in New York, he had been shown a blade of grass plucked from the spot on which Lord Frederick Cavendish fell, and which had been brought to the possessor by one of the assassins. 'Rossa has it,' he said. 'It was given to him. He knows the name of the man who brought it over.'" Crowley claimed that a long time would have to elapse, perhaps two years, before there would be any relaxation in "the dead secrecy maintained in connection with this crime." TNA, FO 5/1860.

171 "allegiance to the enemy . . . Was this hypocrisy . . .": Tynan, 484.

171 "You surely do not think . . .": *Daily News* (London), May 9, 1882.

171 "I yield to no man . . .": June 8, 1882. Davitt Papers, TCD MS 9368.

172 "after the signal failure . . ." and "Mr. Forster is proved . . .": Quoted by the Paris correspondent of the *Standard* (London), May 8, 1882.

172 "Even Mr. Gladstone's bitterest enemies . . .": Hamilton, BL, Add MS 48632.

172 "dry man of figures": Lucy, vol. 2, 325.

173 "give way and make a scene": Letter to Lord Hartington, Devonshire Collections, Chatsworth, Correspondence of the Eighth Duke of Devonshire, CS8/340/1149.

173 "The hand of the assassin . . .": Morley, *Life of Gladstone*, vol. 3.

173 "I am so thankful it's over": Arnold-Forster, *Irish Journal*, 488.

173 "the Prime Minister's face and hands": *St. James's Gazette*, May 11, 1882.

173 "assassin guerrillas . . . I lay the guilt . . .": Corfe, 158.

174 "What had this man to say?": John E. Redmond, MP, *Historical and Political Addresses: 1883–1897* (Dublin and London: Sealy, Bryers and Walker, 1898), 13–14.

174 **most hated, distrusted, and feared man in England:** Until the time of his imprisonment, Parnell had voiced decidedly revolutionary ideas, but had he known anything of the assassination conspiracy? John Walsh told James Mullett, the original Dublin leader, that "the new business" had been planned in Kilmainham Gaol. Statement of James Mullet, Kilmainham Gaol, March 9, 1983 (NAI CBS B BOX 198).

This is something that Joe Brady's father attested at a future date to the Irish MP Frank O'Donnell: "Do ye think there could be 500 Land Leaguers in Kilmainham, with everybody free to see his friends, and not one of them tell Parnell that brave men had their knives waiting to kill Forster and coercion?" O'Donnell said, "Money could be used without Mr. Parnell knowing it." Brady Sr. replied, "Of course. That was the plan. There were no bridges leading to Parnell. They were kept cut. But he could make the connexions, if he liked." (O'Donnell, *Irish Parliamentary Party*, vol. 2, 131.)

The spy Henri Le Caron felt sure that Parnell had not been aware of the crime, but Le Caron claimed to have "positive and unquestionable means of knowing that his most intimate advisers were both cognizant of and parties to these murders." *Devoy's Post Bag*, vol. 2, 50.

174   "He was satisfied with the respect . . .": *Hansard's Parliamentary Debates*, vol. 269 (1882), 324.

175   "a more utterly crushed being": Remark by Winifred Howard in a letter to her mother, May 8, 1882. Chatsworth, DF19/2/12.

175   "Do not let him lose . . .": Telegram from Cannes, May 8, 1882.

175   "I apprehend a violent burst . . .": May 9, 1882, Acton, *Letters of Lord Acton*, 154–55.

175   "It is impossible to describe . . .": May 9, 1882. RA IC/MAIN/D/32/112.

175   the old duke fell to his knees: This was yet another tragedy in a life that had physically bowed William Cavendish with grief: When he was a child, his father had been killed in a driving accident in the park of Holker Hall; William and his beloved young wife, Blanche, had lost their firstborn son at the age of three; and then Blanche herself had died. The last had happened on his birthday—an annual day of mourning, as he never remarried or allowed his memory of her to fade. A decade earlier, he had come close to losing Frederick in a fire that destroyed the entire west wing of Holker, along with its priceless paintings. His son had been asleep when the flames had begun raging in the adjoining dressing room and had woken in time to escape in his nightclothes. Now, the duke's only solace was hearing that his "dearest boy is not supposed to have suffered much pain." Pearson, *Stags and Serpents*, 220.

175   "My Freddy": May 11, 1882. Arnold-Forster, *Irish Journal*, 492.

175   "papa-in-law . . . horribly shy . . .": April 13, 1868. Lucy, vol. 2, 48.

176   "He was the best son . . .": Ibid., 323.

176   "this dear dear face": Pearson, *Stags and Serpents*, 220.

176   "sacrifice for Christ's sake": Lucy, vol. 2, 318.

176   "His face beautiful and serene . . .": Ibid., 323.

176   "I have never seen her . . .": May 9, 1882. BL, Althorp Papers, Add MS 76820.

176   "the pride and center . . .": May 7, 1882. Arnold-Forster, *Irish Journal*, 483.

177   she threw herself on his body: May 11, 1882. Ibid., 492.

177   "as if I was indeed falling . . .": Lucy, vol. 2, 321.

177   "If by God's Almighty power . . .": May 9, 1882, letter to Queen Victoria, RA VIC/MAIN/D/32/113.

177   "most painfully interested": Letter to Lord Spencer, May 8, 1882. RA VIC/MAIN/D/32/106.

177   Lieutenant Ross of Bladensburgh: A member of the Coldstream Guards who had recently been attached to Forster as a type of military secretary, Ross saw Queen Victoria at eleven p.m. on May 7. After filling her in about various secret societies,

he remarked, "The semi savage condition of many of the people in Ireland reckless of life make these societies possible." He told her that the Fenians were said to be furious at the so-called agreement between the Parnellites and the government, adding, "The release of the suspects and above all of Michael Davitt is simply looked upon as lamentable weakness leading to contempt for the Government and an agitation for further concession. Mr Forster knew this well and had he been supported in the early days of the agitation would have endeavoured to have crushed it in the bud—but he was not supported." RA VIC/MAIN/D32/86.

177 "fatal policy"; "dreadful details . . .": May 7, 1882. QVJs.

178 "Every detail is of interest . . .": BL, Althorp Papers, Spencer-Ponsonby correspondence, January 1882–December 1883, Add MS 76834.

178 "Why they gave no arms . . .": Ibid.

178 "think of nothing, nothing else . . .": Letter to her daughter, the crown princess of Prussia. Hibbert, *QV in Her Letters and Journals*, 273–74. Victoria makes the same remark in a letter to Lord Spencer, May 8, 1882, noting, "The Queen . . . can think of nothing else" (RA VIC/MAIN/D/32/106), and notes in her journal, May 6, 1882, "[I] could think of nothing else" (QVJs).

178 "poor dear Lucy": May 8, 1882. RA VIC/MAIN/D/32/107.

178 "poor Miss Burke": Letter to Gladstone, May 11, 1882. RA VIC/MAIN/D/32/134.

178 "She ought never to have been asked . . .": May 6, 1882. RA VIC/ADDA12/719.

178 "The barbarity & daring . . .": May 8, 1882. RA VIC/MAIN/D/32/106.

179 "One person is solely responsible . . .": RA VIC/MAIN/D/32/79.

179 "a very strange" letter: May 7, 1882. QVJs.

179 "which best compresses . . .": May 7, 1882. RA VIC/MAIN/D/32/84.

179 "he was still stunned . . . to those whose actions . . .": Draft of letter to Gladstone. RA VIC/MAIN/D/32/116.

179 "She will never be happy . . .": May 9, 1882. Hamilton, *Diary*, vol. 1, 269.

179 "an indescribable thrill of horror": May 8, 1882. RA VIC/MAIN/ D/32/107.

179 "very intelligent": Letter to Spencer, May 8, 1882. Ibid., 106.

179 "A minister of the Crown . . .": May 10, 1882. Ibid., 126.

179 "if the Government have judged . . .": May 10, 1882. Ibid., 133.

180 "Better not to draw . . .": Letter to QV, May 11, 1882. Ibid., 140.

180 "I never saw anything so like . . . She was looking up": Arnold-Forster, *Irish Journal*, 492.

181 "Her faith never failed her . . . It was *there* . . .": Talbot appendix, Lucy, vol. 2, 332.

TEN: MALLON'S MANHUNT

182 "It is a great occasion . . .": May 11, 1882. Matthew (ed.), *Gladstone Diaries*, vol. 10, 260.

182 epitaph: "While I—reversed our nature's kindlier doom / Pour forth a father's sorrows on thy tomb." The poem, "Lines on the Death of the Hon. G. C. Canning,"

was written in 1820. Thomas Rede Leman, *Memoir of the Right Hon. George Canning* (London: Virtue, 1827), 97.

182   "forced their way": May 12, 1882. Ibid.

182   "dearly loved son": Letter to Lord Ripon, June 1, 1882. Morley, *Life of Gladstone*, vol. 3, 69.

182   "dreadful murder": May 12, 1882. QVJs.

182   "He defended himself . . .": Letter to crown princess of Prussia, May 13, 1882. Hibbert, *QV in Her Letters and Journals*, 274.

183   "The whole country cries out . . .": May 11, 1882. RAVIC/MAIN/D/32/134.

183   "little, if any, short of martial law": May 11, 1882. RAVIC/MAIN/D/32/143.

183   "We have committed ourselves . . .": May 24, 1882. Garvin, *Life of Chamberlain*, 370.

183   "You will be simply playing . . . We have posted placards . . .": *Hansard's Parliamentary Debates*, vol. 269 (1882), 491.

184   "handing over the Irish Party . . .": "May 5th and 6th [1883]: Anniversary of my release from Portland and of the Park murder. MD Invincibles Diary.

184   "The whole public burden . . .": Callanan, *T. M. Healy*, 73.

184   "the Capitulation of the Land League": May 18, 1882. Diary, Davitt Papers, TCD, MS, 9535.

184   Parnell . . . selling out: On May 19, Davitt wrote: "Smothered feeling of discontent at CSP's compact with Whigs [the Liberal government]. How long has he been negotiating with Gladstone? . . . P not called upon me for a week . . . yet I firmly believe that he has been activated by honest motives but finding himself landed in a false position he lacks the moral courage to escape from it." Ibid.

184   "directly or indirectly": Callanan, *T. M. Healy*, 73.

184   "to take some step or other": Quoted in Curran, *Reminiscences*, 140.

184   "But *we all lost our heads*": Callanan, *T. M. Healy*, 74–75.

184   "Davitt will do anything . . .": Gardiner, *Life of William Harcourt*, vol. 1, 435.

184   "Have you seen how Davitt . . .": Bodleian, MS Harcourt 2.

185   "If he does mischief . . .": Ibid.

185   "It was from being so entirely . . .": Lucy Cavendish. Unpublished diary, vol. 14, 1889, Chatsworth, DF19/1/12.

185   "Everything looked so fair . . .": May 12, 1882. RAVIC/MAIN/D/32/156.

186   "I do not in the least care . . .": Battiscombe, *The Spencers of Althorp*, 232.

186   "He purposefully rides very fast . . .": Julia Roundell, "From a Diary at Dublin Castle during the Phoenix Park Trial," *Fortnightly Review* 60, no. 356: 559–66.

186   "a capital fellow": Remark by Lord Northbrook in a letter to Lord Spencer, May 8, 1882. Spencer, *The Red Earl*, vol. 1, 193.

186   "by justice & *sympathy*": Lucy Cavendish. Unpublished diary, vol. 14, Chatsworth, DF19/1/12.

186   The ordeal he would face: By two years later, Trevelyan had resigned, the intense stress having turned his hair white. Meeting him around that time, Lucy Cavendish had been shocked and saddened by how embittered he was about Ireland taking up too much of England's time and by his total loss of hope. "The effect of ceaseless

strain, everyday peril of his life etc. had been to break his nerves to pieces. He ended by never sleeping & if he had gone on much longer he would probably have had a complete mental collapse." (Ibid.)

186 **bloodstained coat of Frederick Cavendish:** Sir Algernon West, *Recollections, 1832–1886*, vol. 2, (London: Smith, Elder and Co., 1899), 152.

187 **"in a position to know" and other Le Caron quotations:** Le Caron report, June 1, 1882. TNA, Robert Anderson Papers, HO 144/1538/6.

187 **Le Caron was certain:** He explained:

> [Frank Agnew] claimed to have had knowledge that something of the kind could be expected and he included especially Forster as one of the expected victims. His and others' opinion is that individuals in the org at home have for a twofold purpose done it. Some of them upon your side have still a very bitter feeling against the leaders of the Land League and if an act of this kind would tend to injure them they would not hesitate to kill an individual to revenge supposed wrongs. . . . The development since the release of Parnell in and outside Parliament has injured the cause very much. It looks very much as if there would be an open rupture between the Land League and nationalists. There is a bitter feeling against Davitt for his supposed abandonment of his national ideas. (Ibid.)

187 **"this foul deed":** Gardiner, *Life of William Harcourt*, vol. 1, 436–37.

187 **umbrellas with sword-stick handles:** NAI, CBS/B Files, 1–156 Box, B14.

187 **"utter incompetence":** *St. James's Gazette*, May 13, 1882.

187 **wheel tracks of the assassins' cab:** "A pursuit on horseback . . . would assuredly have led to some information respecting this important vehicle." Ibid.

187 **"two rough-looking Irishmen . . .":** Ibid., May 10, 1882.

187 **a poor psychotic in London's Whitechapel:** Ibid., May 11, 1882.

187 **man seen wearing bloodstained trousers:** Spencer, *The Red Earl*, vol. 1, 190.

188 **"No force could have behaved better . . .":** May 10, 1882. RA VIC/MAIN/D/32/133.

188 **"Carey, a bricklayer . . .":** December 2, 1880. NAI, Mallon Reports, INL/Box 9.

188 **"failing assistance from the persons . . ." and subsequent quotations:** These quotations, the conflicting descriptions of the vehicle and its driver, and the claim that all the cab drivers had alibis "except Kavanagh, who said he was drinking," are from Mallon's handwritten memo. NAI, Police Reports, 1882–1921, Box 1, 3/715/1.

189 **"They are sufficiently wicked . . .":** Mallon Report, May 15, 1882. NAI, CBS/B Files, 1–156 Box.

190 **"the low desperadoes . . . All this makes me incline":** Mallon Report, May 20, 1882. Ibid.

190 **"the most noiseless weapons . . . The writer . . .":** NAI, CBS/B Files, 156–268 Box, B245.

190 "This is a remarkable letter . . . Of course I was said to be demented . . .": A postscript added by Mallon to the anonymous letter on April 2, 1883.

191 political mentor: Egan had briefed Parnell on how to secure election to Parliament
and may even have manipulated him, confiding to Henri Le Caron that their leader
had not been allowed to join the IRB, as it might have "interfered with the usefulness of Mr Parnell." *P and Crime*, pt. 12, 40.

191 "There seems to be proof . . .": Bodleian, MS Harcourt 39.

191 "made inquiries of Mr. Egan": *P and Crime*, pt. 20, 291.

191 "at daggers drawn with Egan": Callanan, *T. M. Healy*, 76.

191 "Anything but welcome visitor . . .": Diary, Davitt Papers, TCD, MS 9535.

191 "atrocious accusation": May 18, 1882. Dillon Papers, TCD, MS 9368.

191 Egan's cashbooks: An 1890 pamphlet printed a letter dated October 14, 1882,
from Egan to Parnell that gave a cursory account of Land League expenditure (figures were described as "about" or "over" and given in round sums). General Land
League and Ladies' Land League expenses for support of evicted tenants—from
the provision of wooden houses to their legal costs—came to a total of £148,000.
About £40,000 was accounted for in evidence to the commission, but no details
were given about the money provided to the Ladies' Land League or the remaining
£108,000. (John Sampson York, *Plums from the Report of the Parnell Commission* London:
Simpkin, Marshall, 1890, 15–16). See also *P and Crime*, pt. 20, 298, for the claim
that "between £70,000 and £100,000 had been disbursed by the Land League in
various ways by the end of 1881."

192 "negotiated in secret . . .": Attack by the powerful Conservative MP Arthur Balfour,
on May 16, 1882. Quoted in Jenkins, *Gladstone*, 471.

192 "the letter in question": *Hansard's Parliamentary Debates*, vol. 269 (1882), 672.

192 "his furrowed brow": T. M. Healy, *Letters and Leaders*, vol. I, 161.

192 "Might I be allowed" . . . "Hon. Friend the Member . . .": *Hansard's Parliamentary
Debates*, vol. 269 (1882), 673.

192 "I think the best plan . . .": Ibid., 674.

192 "As long as the matter . . .": May 3, 1882. Arnold-Forster, *Irish Journal*, 472.

192 "Read the last paragraph . . .": *Hansard's Parliamentary Debates*, vol. 269 (1882), 674.

193 "We felt that the Chief . . .": T. M. Healy, *Letters and Leaders*, vol. I, 162.

193 "blow below the belt": Remark to John Morley, August 16, 1882. Chamberlain, *A
Political Memoir*, 59.

193 "That the conspiracy which has been . . .": T. M. Healy, *Letters and Leaders*, vol. I, 161.

193 "coming backwards and forwards . . .": *Hansard's Parliamentary Debates*, vol. 269
(1882), 788.

193 "This damned fellow . . .": T. M. Healy, *Letters and Leaders*, vol. I, 162.

193 "I am writing in perfect confidence . . .": May 23, 1882. BL, Gladstone Papers, Add
MS 44269.

194 "She is said to be . . .": May 24, 1882. BL, Gladstone Papers, Add MS 44174.

194 "inexpressibly sorry": May 26, 1882. BL, Gladstone Papers, Add MS 44269.

194 "actually inveigled Mr. G. . . .": June 20, 1882. Hamilton, *Diary*, vol. I, 290.

194   the prime minister's new acquaintance: Gladstone first met Lillie Langtry at the
      Pre-Raphaelite painter John Everett Millais's studio in January 1882 and soon
      afterward had his attention drawn by Lucy Cavendish to a note sent by the drama
      critic of the *Times*: "Recommends you, if you have time, to call on Mrs. Langtry,
      who is a great admirer of yours. (You are aware that she has gone upon the stage)."
      (Ernest Dudley, *The Gilded Lily: The Life and Loves of the Fabulous Lillie Lantry* London:
      Odhams Press, 1958, 221.) Gladstone is said to have helped the actress with the
      interpretation of her roles and read aloud to her from Shakespeare and the Bible.

194   "intimacy on paper": April 20, 1882. Hamilton, *Diary*, vol. I, 257.

194   "I took the occasion . . .": April 1, 1882. Hamilton, *Diary*, vol. I, 245.

194   engaging prostitutes in conversation: Walking back to Downing Street on the
      night of the Phoenix Park murders, Gladstone was seen talking to a woman near
      the Duke of York Column. "[He] was perfectly frank . . . [and] promptly related
      everything he remembered of the incident, which was merely that this woman had
      followed him and begged to be allowed to talk to him," writes Hamilton. "On find-
      ing that her tale was an idle one, he passed on. Of course the story had been dressed
      up; 'they were walking arm-in-arm etc.' . . . I know for certain that it is only from
      high, unselfish and kind motives and from no others that he addresses himself to
      women in the street in the hope (which he says has often been realized) of reclaim-
      ing the poor creatures from their fallen position." May 9, 1882, Hamilton, *Diary*,
      vol. I, 269–70.

194   "It is a terribly unfortunate . . .": February 8, 1882. Ibid., 221.

194   "for Mr. G. to decline . . .": June 20, 1882. Ibid., 290.

195   "what I desired . . .": *Love Story*, vol. I, 270.

195   "It might be advantageous . . .": Ibid., 271–72.

195   "on F.C.'s noble end": May 17, 1882. Matthew (ed.), *Gladstone Diaries*, vol. 10, 263.

195   "noble monument": Article by Gladstone on Arthur Hallam, his intimate friend at
      Eton College. *Daily Telegraph*, January 5, 1898.

195   "On Reconcilement's altar laid . . .": Pages of rough notes, one headed "May 6
      1882." BL, Gladstone Papers, Add MS 44766, vol. 681, 93–95.

195   "the blackest [day] . . .": May 7, 1882. Diary, Davitt Papers, TCD, MS 9535.

196   "which still abides with me . . .": Retrospective account of May 6, 1882. Lucy,
      vol. 2, 320.

196   "All my darkened life . . .": June 7, 1882. BL, Gladstone Papers, Add MS 44766.

196   "so that it may have some good . . .": May 9, 1882. BL, Althorp Papers, Add MS
      76820.

196   "Money—plenty of money . . . Should I be able to show . . .": Brackenbury to
      Spencer, May 31, 1882. BL, Althorp Papers, Add MS 77088.

197   "I venture to think . . .": Ibid.

197   "The sum asked for . . .": Copy of Spencer letter (no addressee), June 7, 1882. Ibid.

197   "I very urgently pressed . . .": June 18, 1882. Bodleian, MS Harcourt 39.

198   General J. D. McAdaras: The advanced political stance that had caused alarm was
      later exposed by John Devoy to be a sham: "McAdaras for several years posed as

the representative of the Irish Revolutionists, which he was not. He was the most successful of all the fakers who traded on the Irish Movement, but he never got into it." Living lavishly as a result of his marriage to a widowed heiress from St. Louis, McAdaras is portrayed by Devoy as a seasoned con man who had tricked the French minister of war into appointing him a general. He was lame from wounds received in India, where he had been a general in the British army, he told the French. "General be damned. . . . He's the damnedest scoundrel from here to hell!" exclaimed an officer in whose troop McAdaras had served as sergeant-major. Devoy, *Recollections of an Irish Rebel*, 338.

198 "a most dynamitic speech . . . If he is taking a house . . .": Undated letter from Chalmers (the banker) to a Mr. Hershell. NAI, CBS/B Files, 1–156 Box.

198 "a great deal of swagger . . .": Report to Samuel Lee Anderson, which has the notation "seen by Lord Spencer," August 8, 1882. NAI, CBS/B Files, 156–268 Box.

198 Irish secret societies: Brackenbury's first memorandum reports that the most active center of Land League operations is Paris, "whence money is being sent to aid the Fenians"; the Fenian societies have their headquarters in America; and the leaders of the conspiracy depend on American subscriptions, which supply the bulk of the money. "To induce men to subscribe, action must be constant; there must be proof to show that they are not idle. . . . Everything points to the existence of small secret assassinations gangs." To Spencer, May 31, 1882. BL, Althorp Papers, Add MS 77088.

198 "for a five-pound note": *Buying Irish Patriotism for a Five-Pound Note* is the subtitle of Donal McCracken's biography, *Inspector Mallon*.

199 "The informant says he has . . .": NAI, CBS/B Files, 156–268 Box.

199 remained unaccounted for: "Mr. Egan's books would be entirely separate from the cash-books of the League," Parnell later remarked. "These were Mr. Egan's private books. . . . They would not show the details of the expenditure of Land League money, but simply such items as 'remittance of £5,000 to the Ladies' Land League.'" (*P and Crime*, pt. 20, 295.)

199 "I was anxious . . .": *P and Crime*, pt. 20, 69.

199 "Parnell wants Mr. Gladstone to know": Letter to Chamberlain, June 9, 1882. Algar Labouchere Thorold, *The Life of Henry Labouchère* (London: Constable and Company, 1913), 165.

200 "Parnell has put his finger . . .": Spencer was quoting William Shaw, the previous Irish leader, in a letter to Lord Granville. TNA, A and B Granville Papers, PRO 30/29/29.

200 "I beg you will not 'boycott' me . . .": Gladstone Papers, BL, Add MS 44269.

200 "The news of another double . . .": June 29, 1882. Ibid., Add MS 44545.

200 "the person subsidized by Egan . . ." and subsequent quotations: NAI, Mallon Reports, CBS/B Files, 156–268 Box.

201 "that man he called No 1 . . .": From James Mullett's statement, Kilmainham Gaol, March 9, 1882. Ibid., B198.

201 "directions as to the working . . . But the fact of his . . .": *Dublin Evening Mail*, June 6, 1883.

202 "I feel morally satisfied . . .": NAI, CBS/B Files, 1–156 Box.

ELEVEN: CONCOCTING AND "PEACHING"

203 Pinkerton National Detective Agency: The detectives, known as "the Pinks," had been employed to protect Abraham Lincoln during his inauguration and successfully thwarted an assassination attempt; Pinkerton always maintained that if he had continued to provide security for Lincoln, the 1865 fatal shooting would not have occurred.

204 "My plan would be as follows . . .": July 8, 1882. TNA, HO 144/1538/4.

204 "with great interest . . .": Letter to Spencer, July 21, 1882. As quoted in Spencer, *The Red Earl*, vol. 1, 217.

204 "what advice or suggestions . . .": Ibid.

205 "all sorts of prospective arrangements . . .": Harcourt letter to Spencer, July 8, 1882. Bodleian, MS Harcourt 39.

205 "Should it be endangered . . .": August 1, 1882. Buckle (ed.), *Letters of QV*, vol. 3, 318.

205 "The news from Alexandria . . .": Hamilton, BL, Add MS 48632.

205 "above all things a soldier . . . I could hand over . . .": July 14, 1882. BL, Althorp Papers, MS 77088.

205 "shocked at Brackenbury's behavior": July 20, 1882. Hamilton, BL, Add MS 48632.

205 "He has behaved quite infamously . . .": July 8, 1882. Bodleian, MS Harcourt 39.

206 "very angry" Queen Victoria: Ponsonby to Courtenay Boyle, July 22, 1882. BL, Althorp Papers, Spencer-Ponsonby correspondence, January 1882–December 1883, Add MS 76834.

206 thwart Brackenbury's military ambitions: Brackenbury followed Wolseley's advice and withdrew his resignation but was categorically refused. In hindsight, he admitted that the offense he caused by abandoning the Irish mission had been the most unfortunate episode of his career.

206 "If his appointment to any post . . .": Ponsonby to Spencer, July 22, 1882. BL, Althorp Papers, Spencer-Ponsonby correspondence, January 1882–December, Add MS 76834.

206 "I wish he had been . . .": August 1, 1882. As quoted in Spencer, *The Red Earl*, vol. 1, 217.

206 "I confess I was more than anxious . . .": *Lloyds Weekly News*, July 18, 1909.

207 "broken up into little bits . . .": TNA, JC.

207 preserve the weapons as patriotic relics: "As a national relic, or any way you like to put it." Carey, as quoted in Corrigan (ed.), *A History of the Phoenix Park Patriots*, 31.

207 cache . . . found by one of his tenants: This was John Fitzsimons, who rented Carey's property in South Cumberland Street and had first been made suspicious by his landlord's violent reaction to his investigation of the leak. "Were you on the roof of my house?" Carey had roared. "If I thought you were, by God I'd turn

you out in the street!" A few weeks later, after another heavy rainfall, and as Carey was in prison at the time, Fitzsimons ventured through a trapdoor onto the roof. He noticed that two large slates had recently been removed and, searching under scrunched-up paper and wood shavings, came across the weapons. Mallon report, August 9, 1882. NAI, CBS/B Files, I–156 Box.

207   Egan . . . subscribed £500: *Dublin Daily Express*, August 16, 1882.

207   "to assail this tyrant . . .": Tynan, 500.

208   "must come off at once . . .": Ibid., 513.

208   "would sooner go in for Spencer" and subsequent quotations: Evidence of Patrick Delaney. *P and Crime*, pt. 9, 96–99.

208   Ladies' Land League expenditure: The total submitted in June 1882 by Anna Parnell to Michael Davitt for catering to the prisoners amounted to £21,637.16.40. See Jane McL. Côté, *Fanny and Anna Parnell: Ireland's Patriot Sisters* (London: Macmillan, 1991), 218.

208   "No. Not a shilling . . . They will get no more . . .": Devoy, *Devoy's Post Bag*, vol. 2, 127.

208   family connection seemed to count for nothing: Anna Parnell had been one of the severest critics of her brother's treaty with the government—"The Treachery of Kilmainham," she called it (Patricia Groves, *Petticoat Rebellion: The Anna Parnell Story*. Cork: Mercier Press, 2004, 224), and she found this ruthless dismissal of their thankless work aiding land agitation to be unforgivable. She never spoke to him again.

209   "Parnell never made a greater mistake . . .": August 24, 1882. Davitt Papers, TCD, MS 9403.

209   "The two Ds have quarreled . . .": August 20, 1882, *Love Story*, vol. 2, 51.

209   "Once, to my horror . . .": *Love Story*, vol. 2, 57.

209   "If I turn to the Government . . .": Ibid., 56.

210   "I can hardly think of . . .": As quoted in Marlow, *The Uncrowned Queen*, 109.

210   "Mr G. thinks the Government . . .": August 29, 1882. Hamilton, BL, Add MS 448632.

210   "that bothersome woman": As quoted in Marlow, *The Uncrowned Queen*, 109, footnote.

210   "I can't say how greatly . . .": September 24, 1882. As quoted in Spencer, *The Red Earl*, vol. 1, 223.

210   "unpleasantly struck": Ibid., 222.

210   "How I wish she would not . . .": Ibid., 223.

211   "Some time ago I signified . . .": September 26, 1882. Ibid., 226.

211   "A letter came to me . . .": TNA, JC.

211   "Carey promised obedience . . .": Tynan, 494.

211   "to get out of the affair . . .": Spencer to Harcourt, February 12, 1882. Bodleian, MS Harcourt 39.

211   "James Carey: Builder . . .": *Flag of Ireland*, October 7, 1882.

211   "from Welsh stone to . . .": *Freeman's Journal*, November 23, 1882.

212   "with a keen sense . . . A quietus . . . 'best men . . .'": *Irish World*, October 14, 1882.

212   "the complete eclipse . . .": King, *Michael Davitt after the Land League*, 52.

212 "shake himself free . . .": BL, Gladstone Papers, Add MS 44269.

212 "He is anxious to be . . .": *Love Story*, vol. 2, 9 (from Parnell's notes written in preparation for Katharine's memo to Gladstone).

213 "mysterious cheque . . . Mallon could not for the life . . .": Bussy, 222.

213 "They are, I am sure . . .": To Spencer, October 10, 1882. BL, Althorp Papers, Add MS 77031.

213 "so stupid and blundering": Tynan, 504.

213 "feigned the attack . . .": Remark by Lucy Cavendish, October 23, 1884. Unpublished diary, vol. 14, Chatsworth, DF19/1/12.

214 "Ah, you villain!": Curran, *Reminiscences*, 156.

214 "We depend in Dublin . . .": As quoted in McCracken, *Inspector Mallon*, 95.

214 "ashamed and vexed": Bussy, 81.

214 three informers in his confidence: "Minutes of Evidence of the Dublin Metropolitan Police Committee of Enquiry." TNA, T1/14746.

215 "I disremember": Bussy, 87.

215 "He could have beaten them . . .": T. M. Healy, *Letters and Leaders*, vol. 1, 192.

215 word reached them of serious intention: Frederick Bussy tells of a letter Mallon received on January 8 from the wife of an unnamed nationalist MP, warning that he and Curran were in imminent danger. "If certain men she mentioned—Brady was one of them and Curley another—were not at once arrested, neither he nor Curran would be alive to continue their inquiry on the following Monday morning." Mallon knew the source of her information and took it seriously enough to act. Bussy, 200–201.

215 "a better Catholic . . .": Bussy, 87.

216 "I had the whole of our men . . .": *Lloyd's Weekly News*, July 11, 1909.

216 "We took a very decided step . . .": BL, Althorp Papers, Add MS 76930.

216 "The witness bore himself . . .": Ibid., Add MS 76832.

217 "Farrell cannot be seen . . .": January 20, 1883. NAI, DMP Files, 1883.

218 Mallon produced a letter from a man: Curran, *Reminiscences*, 179–80.

TWELVE: *Who Is Number One?*

219 "totally unfitted for the Premiership": Mary, *Diaries*, 277.

219 "We have had great difficulty . . .": Gardiner, *Life of William Harcourt*, vol. 1, 469.

219 "much to answer for": January 17, 1883. TNA, A and B Granville Papers, PRO 30/29/29.

219 "somewhat sudden breakdown": QV to Granville, January 20, 1883. Buckle (ed.), *Letters of QV*, vol. 3, 399.

219 "He must be really quiet . . .": January 10, 1883. Ibid., 279.

219 "He ought to be persuaded": QV to Granville, January 20, 1883. Ibid., 399.

220 "I am stunned . . .": Morley, *Life of Gladstone*, vol. 3, 103.

220 "P.M. A changed man": Mary, *Diaries*, 277.

220 "an ecclesiastical statesman": Herbert Paul, "Introductory Memoir," in Acton, *Letters of Lord Acton*, xiii.

220 **Lord Acton was Gladstone's main reason:** Gladstone's regard dated back to 1859, when he read an article by Acton, then a student half his age, and sent him a complimentary letter. "Its principles and politics I embrace; its research and wealth of knowledge I admire; and its whole atmosphere is that which I desire to breathe," he wrote. (Drew, *Acton, Gladstone*, 6). Descending on one side from a prime minister of Naples (his grandfather) and from the great German house of Dalberg on the other, Acton was the husband of an aristocratic Bavarian wife who had borne him six children. Acton's familiarity with the highest level of British and European political society had given him a cosmopolitan outlook much appreciated by Gladstone. For a short time, he had served as an MP, but he had not shone; his great success was his power over the prime minister, whose indefatigable optimism sometimes led him astray, and who invited Acton's criticism as proof of their friendship. "No man admired Mr. Gladstone more," wrote one observer. "No man flattered him less." (Herbert Paul, "Introductory Memoir," in Acton, *Letters of Lord Acton*, (xiii).

220 **"In three things they believed . . .":** Drew, *Acton, Gladstone*, 4.

220 **"power tends to corrupt":** Letter to Bishop Creighton, April 5, 1887. "Lord Acton writes to Bishop Creighton . . . ," Online Library of Liberty, oll.libertyfund.org /quotes/214.

220 **"Gladstone influences all around . . . In truth, they acted . . .":** Drew, *Acton, Gladstone*, 2.

221 **"We have no thread . . .":** Ibid., 5.

221 **Mary Gladstone's friendship with Acton.:** M Gladstone was far more questioning than her father was about their mentor's transcendent idealism. She was staying for a few days with Acton at his villa, La Madeleine, and noted in his study the innumerable reference books tagged with marking slips, the black leather files and boxes of index cards—"all the signs of a tome or tomes in gestation." (Owen Chadwick, *Acton and History*. Cambridge: Cambridge University Press, 1998, 152.) Acton's life's ambition was to write a "History of Liberty," but it was to be the greatest book never written, as Mary pointed out, unsparingly drawing Acton's attention to a recent Henry James story, *The Madonna of the Future*, in which an artist is "for ever preparing for a work for ever deferred." (Henry James, *The Madonna of the Future and Other Tales*. London: Macmillan and Co., 1879, 31.) Acton too, Mary infers, chose not to manifest himself by imperfection and "the vulgar effort and hazard of production." (Ibid., 11.) Gladstone, however, appears to have had no reservations about their friend's vocation.

221 **"We fell in with the foreign hours . . .":** Morley, *Life of Gladstone*, vol. 3, 103.

221 **"Dr. Clark thinks it possible . . .":** January 26, 1883. Buckle (ed.), *Letters of QV*, vol. 3, 403.

222 **"Am coming to Cannes . . . Mr. Tisdale":** Bussy, 112.

222 **hard-drinking, voluble extremist:** Michael Davitt had little regard for Joseph Casey: "Bombs, dynamite, daggers, poison were his revolutionary media whenever those who wanted this sort of talk 'stood' the necessary absinthe or cognac, for which it could be produced *ad libitum*." (Davitt, *Fall of Feudalism*, 435.) In an article in the *Irish Times*

(March 22, 1947), Kathleen Fitzpatrick says that James Joyce often met Joseph in a Paris café in 1903 and used him as the model for the old Fenian Kevin Egan in *Ulysses*: "In gay Paree he hides, Egan of Paris, unsought by any save by me . . . loveless, landless, wifeless. . . . They have forgotten Kevin Egan, not he them."

222　"the most decent place . . .": Bussy, 112.

223　"Skin giving Mallon information . . .": MD Invincibles Diary.

223　"Sure, Mr. Mallon . . .": *Lloyd's Weekly News*, July 11, 1909.

223　"This quickened his memory . . .": Ibid., July 18, 1909.

223　"Bring up Michael Kavanagh": *Times* (London), February 12, 1883.

223　"The prisoners looked wonderfully . . .": February 10, 1882. RA VIC/ MAIN/D/35/13.

223　"One of them is there": *Times* (London), February 12, 1883.

224　"You scorpion! . . ." and "You are a liar!": Ibid.

224　"A small table, a chair . . ." and subsequent quotations: Bussy, 99–106.

225　"It is not so much the loss . . .": Tynan, 289.

225　"He commenced to tell me . . . So I said to him sharply . . .": *Lloyd's Weekly News*, July 18, 1909.

225　"about as bad a lot . . .": Ibid., July 11, 1909.

225　profaning the Holy Sacrament: Carey subsequently swore in court that he did not receive Holy Communion on any occasion during May 1882; indeed, it has been contested that had he confessed the severity of his crime to any priest, "he would have been refused absolution and on no account permitted to approach the altar." (Dillon Cosgrave, "The True History of the Phoenix Park Murders," *New Ireland Review* 25 [1906]: 225–35.)

225　"who could in any degree . . .": Mallon report, June 20, 1882. NAI, CBS/B Files, 156–268 Box.

226　"the only well dressed . . .": Elizabeth Dillon diary, December 1882–July 1883. Dillon Papers, TCD, MS 6677.

226　"extraordinary triumph . . .": Corfe, 238.

226　"a very useful kind of . . .": *Lloyd's Weekly News*, July 11, 1909.

226　"See here, Carey . . .": Ibid., July 18, 1909.

226　"James Carey the Town Councilor . . .": February 12, 1883. BL, Althorp Papers.

227　"he & his family will be damned . . .": February 12, 1883. BL, Althorp Papers, Add MS 76931.

227　"The great importance of getting . . .": Gardiner, *Life of William Harcourt*, vol. I, 474.

228　"I am ready now": *Lloyd's Weekly News*, July 11, 1909.

228　"I was before ye's . . .": *Times* (London), February 23, 1883.

228　"His evidence was given . . .": February 18, 1883. RA VIC/MAIN/D/35/23.

229　"Evidence tomorrow will make . . .": To Harcourt, February 16, 1883. BL, Althorp Papers, Add MS 76931.

229　"the more important scoundrels": To Lady Louisa Egerton, February 18, 1883. Devonshire Collections, Chatsworth, Correspondence of the Eighth Duke of Devonshire, CS8/340/1329.

229 "Will you do all you can . . .": February 17, 1883. BL, Althorp Papers, Add MS 76931.

229 "but the stupidity of the police . . .": To Hartington, February 21, 1883. Devonshire Collections, Chatsworth, Correspondence of the Eighth Duke of Devonshire, CS8/340/1331.

229 "There is no doubt he is in Paris . . .": January 31, 1883. NAI, CBS/B Files, 156–268 Box.

229 "to enable the wanted parties . . .": Robert Anderson to Jenkinson, February 24, 1883. NAI, Police Reports, 1882–1921, Box 1, 3/715/1.

230 "Whether she had left before . . .": Ibid.

230 "I will tell you a very . . .": Gardiner, *Life of William Harcourt*, vol. 1, 476.

230 "Please step forward . . .": Richardson, *From the City to Fleet Street*, 186.

230 "He came in sideways . . .": *North London News*, February 24, 1883.

230 "You must remember . . .": Curran, *Reminiscences*, 195.

231 "most painfully interested . . . They are quite thrilling . . .": February 15, 1882. RA VIC/MAIN/D/35/19.

231 "Is there any further news?": Bodleian, MS Harcourt 2.

231 "She was anxious . . .": Gardiner, *Life of William Harcourt*, vol. 1, 474.

231 "shut the mouths": February 18, 1883. QVJs.

231 "The public will at last know . . .": February 17, 1883. Buckle (ed.), *Letters of QV*, vol. 3, 409.

231 *"appalling"*: February 18, 1883. Ibid., 411.

231 "Will not Mr. Gladstone be dreadfully . . .": Gardiner, *Life of William Harcourt*, vol. 1, 474.

232 "Sir William believes Ireland . . .": February 21, 1883. QVJs.

232 "It is my nature . . .": Retrospective account of May 6, 1882. Lucy, vol. 2, 320–21.

232 obsessing over tiny details: "His liability to rheumatism always made him careful not to get caught even in a shower without an umbrella, & he never walked without one or other. . . . I remember hearing at the time, or reading perhaps in some paper, that his umbrella was lying near him broken; & I thought its being broken was the reason I did not get it back. Whatever gave me any reason to fear that he had had some minutes' struggle I could not forget; & so I have always remembered this about the umbrella being broken." (To Spencer, February 19, 1883. BL, Althorp Papers, Add MS 76820.)

Lucy's umbrella fixation anticipated James Joyce's reference to Cavendish's murder in *Finnegans Wake*—one of the book's most lyrical lines: "Here all the leaves alift aloft, full o'liefing, fell alaughing over Ombrellone . . ." (Joyce, *Finnegans Wake*, 831).

232 "terrible week . . . I went down earlyish . . .": February 12, 1883. Devonshire Collections, Chatsworth, Correspondence of the Eighth Duke of Devonshire, CS8/340/1328.

233 "My dear Lady Frederick . . .": February 22, 1882. Chatsworth, DF19/2/12.

233 "How content I was . . .": July 30, 1883. BL, Althorp Papers, Add MS 76820.

233 "It makes his death noble . . . There can be no reopening . . .": February 19, 1883. Devonshire Collections, Chatsworth, Correspondence of the Eighth Duke of Devonshire, CS8/340/1330.

234 "I can't help hoping . . .": Ibid.

234 "Oh, I have yearned . . .": Battiscombe, *Mrs. Gladstone*, 188.

234 "I hope Mr. Gladstone will come back": February 19, 1883. BL, Althorp Papers, Add MS 76820.

234 "Mr G's plans are still undecided . . . But there seems . . .": February 29, 1883. Hamilton, BL, Add MS 48633.

234 "bored to death . . . The P.M. is only too . . . Everybody's minds . . .": Mary, *Diaries*, 277.

234 "the long and harrowing . . .": February 20, 1883. Matthew (ed.), *Gladstone Diaries*, vol. 10, 408.

234 "There could not be any doubt . . .": February 27, 1883. Ibid., 410.

235 "About Carey, the spectacle . . .": February 19, 1883. BL, Add MS 44546.

235 "In a pouring Scotch rain": TNA, A and B Granville Papers, PRO 30/29/29 (box Misc. C).

235 "We have disestablished . . .": Undated clipping from the *Daily News* (London). Ibid.

235 "without detriment . . .": TNA, A and B Granville Papers, PRO 30/29/29 (box Misc. C).

235 "Part of it was much more precipitous . . .": Ibid.

235 "It has got better . . .": February 21, 1883. Morley, *Life of Gladstone*, vol. 3, 104.

235 "sitting tight for a messenger . . .": February 17, 1883. Mary, *Diaries*, 277.

236 "There is a noise . . .": February 15, 1882. Matthew (ed.), *Gladstone Diaries*, vol. 10, 407.

236 "It is not that he . . . It is a lie . . . Those miserable wretches . . .": As quoted in Lyons, 245–46.

236 "a fierce joy": *Love Story*, vol. 2, 60.

236 "we had to force him": B O'B, 295.

236 "He has not even the pretext . . .": February 23, 1883. *The Field Day Anthology of Irish Writing* (Derry: Field Day Publications, 1991), vol. 2, 306–7.

237 "Call him back to his post! . . .": Ibid.

237 "It struck a note . . .": Davitt, *Fall of Feudalism*, 461.

237 "I have been for some time . . .": *Freeman's Journal*, February 23, 1883.

238 a Mr. "Lisdale": *Times* (London), March 1, 1883.

238 "There she is . . ." and other quotations: *Daily News* (London), February 26, 1883.

239 "*Who* is N° 1?": February 20, 1883. Bodleian, MS Harcourt 2.

239 "supposed with good reason . . .": RA VIC/MAIN/D/35/32.

239 "During the last year . . .": *Times* (London), February 19, 1883.

240 "used very serious threats": Mallon report (undated). NAI, CBS/B Files, 156–268 Box.

240 "one of the head men": Mallon report, February 23, 1883. Ibid.

240   "The photograph is the likeness . . .": TNA, HO 144/98/A16380C.

241   "a needy and seedy . . . He was regarded . . .": *Lloyd's Weekly News*, July 4, 1909.

241   "Mr. Egan's flight to America . . . There was not enough . . .": March 14, 1883. RA VIC/MAIN/B/34/117a.

241   "Some of them appertaining . . . and thus got out . . .": Le Caron, 229.

242   "He volunteered no definite information . . .": *Lloyd's Weekly News*, July 18, 1909.

242   alleged by a colleague: Ó Broin, *The Prime Informer*, 159.

242   "He certainly gave Egan the nod: Interview with the author, October 16, 2016.

242   "all up with [Mallon]": Bussy, 223–24.

242   "I believe I would have been assassinated . . .": Mallon made a formal report of this on March 23, 1883: "On the 17th and 18th August [1882] 'Skin the Goat' drove Joseph Brady, Tim Kelly, Peter Carey and Mrs Peter Carey in his cab to the gate on the North Circular Rd leading to the RIC [Royal Irish Constabulary] Depot and on that occasion they intended to assassinate me. I believe I would have been assassinated only for No 1." Mallon report, March 23, 1883. NAI, CBS/B Files, 156–268 Box.

243   "Now, it was perfectly well known . . .": July 20–August 9, 1883. *Hansard's Parliamentary Debates*, vol. 282, 1062. Parnell's speech was in response to a claim by the chief secretary that the Constabulary and Police Administration (Ireland) Bill was justified by "the success of Mr. Jenkinson in discovering the existence of the Invincibles in Dublin."

243   "[Jenkinson] got all the credit . . .": BL, Althorp Papers, Add MS 76832. Spencer to Harcourt, February 10: "I hear that nothing could have been better than today's evidence. The car driver turned on Thursday, it was cleverly managed by Jenkinson. He allowed him to see another witness who has turned & he told him that they turned not to be hung for the others & he [illeg] to split. Kavanagh then said he would do the same & immediately gave evidence of the most circumstantial kind with the Field case & in the Phoenix Park" (Bodleian, MS Harcourt 41); Harcourt to Spencer, February 14: "I hope you will tell Jenkinson how much I admire the style in which he has handled this most difficult business" (ibid.); Edward Hamilton, February 23: "He could only be got to turn informer after Jenkinson (to whom too much credit in all this business cannot be given) had for three hours depicted to Carey the certain prospect of the horrors of the gallows" (BL, Add MS 48633, vol. 4); Gladstone to Spencer, February 27: "Jenkinson seems to have rendered splendid service" (Matthew [ed.], *Gladstone Diaries*, vol. 10, 410).

243   "I contemplate with alarm . . .": February 20, 1883. TNA, A and B, Granville Papers, PRO 30/29/29.

243   "But how can he govern England . . .": Granville to QV, February 23, 1882. Buckle (ed.), *Letters of QV*, vol. 3, 413.

243   "immediate summons": February 20, 1883. TNA, A and B Granville Papers, PRO 30/29/29.

244   "like a boy going back to school": March 1, 1883. Hamilton, BL, Add MS 48633.

244 "This foreigner . . .": *Times* (London), March 1, 1883.
244 The Byrnes' passage paid by Thomas Quinn: Mallon report, December 10, 1887. NAI, DMP Files, 1889.
244 "Man believed to be Walsh . . .": February 26, 1883. NAI, CBS/B Files, 156–268 Box.
244 "Your Majesty will remember . . . He is the recognized . . .": March 2, 1883. RA VIC/MAIN/D/35/56.
245 the name Stephen Hyland: *Leeds Mercury*, March 3, 1883.
245 "Will the French admit . . .": March 5, 1883. Bodleian, MS Harcourt 41.
245 "So they let Walsh go . . .": Bussy, 163.
245 "The Invincible Directory threw . . .": Tynan, 525.
245 "The case against No 1 . . .": March 5, 1883. Bodleian, MS Harcourt 41.
245 "Request French Government to arrest No 1": February 26, 1883, cable to Anderson. NAI, CBS/B Files, 156–268 Box.
245 "Is there any use . . .": March 5, 1883. Ibid.
245 "See no prospect . . .": March 10, 1883. Ibid.
246 "If [he] had been silent . . .": February 17, 1883. RA VIC/MAIN/D/35/22.
246 "I have no doubt whatever . . .": June 4, 1883. NAI, CBS/B Files, 156–268 Box.

THIRTEEN: MARWOODED

247 "Have heard that car man . . ." and subsequent quotations: MD Invincibles Diary.
248 as if their guilt were already established: Davitt had experienced this injustice himself when, on his arrest in 1870, he had been questioned and searched in London's Paddington police station as if he were already a convicted prisoner. He particularly objected to the callous treatment in Kilmainham of Harry Rowles, the Invincible who failed to see the white handkerchief signaling Forster's arrival, who died in the jail a week before the trials began. "Though he was seriously ill on Thursday and was beyond recovered on Saturday, it was only on Sunday after his death or when he was past all consciousness that his wife & son were permitted to come to his bedside." As if in explanation, a later penciled addition to the entry notes, "This man was an informer." Rowles was Mallon's "Bernard." Ibid.
248 "The identical car now also on view": *Times* (London), April 10, 1883.
249 "about those dreadful . . . Mr. Gladstone is . . . But still does not realize": April 8, 1883. QVJs.
249 "my dearest best friend . . . There is no rebound . . . Now all, all . . .": To the crown princess of Prussia, April 8, 1883. Hibbert, *QV in Her Letters and Journals*, 281.
249 "very curious": April 8, 1883. QVJs.
250 "The failure in Kelly's case . . .": April 30, 1883. RA, VIC-MAIN, D2018.
250 "among the lower classes . . . They no doubt . . .": April 13, 1883. Add MS 76832.
250 "Conspiracy to murder . . . Their keeping out of the way . . .": February 17, 1883. BL, Althorp Papers, Add MS 76931.

250 a kind of headquarters: John J. Breslin to Devoy, April 14 1883. "P.J.S. [Sheridan] took both of them to the *I.W.* and I hear that both of them are staunch Ford men." Devoy, *Devoy's Post Bag*, vol. 2, 189.

250 staying on his arrival with Hamilton Williams: Tynan, Appendix F, 558.

251 "I don't know 'Number One' . . .": *Irish Times*, November 13, 1883.

251 "more than satisfied": Le Caron, 211.

251 "active work": Ibid.

251 "He has evidently used P the Little . . .": April 23, 1883. Diary, Davitt Papers, TCD MS 9537/38.

251 "Messrs. Sullivan and Egan's big machine": Devoy, *Devoy's Post Bag*, vol. 2, 222.

251 "a conference (informal) . . .": To Devoy, April 18, 1883. Ibid., 190.

251 "I have been reading up . . .": Le Caron, 231.

252 "nitro-glycerine methods . . .": Ibid., 215.

252 "I would advise that . . .": Lyons, 250–51.

253 Unacceptable coercive measures: *P and Crime*, pt. 20, 86.

253 "sometimes, but not often": Jordan, *Kitty O'Shea*, 101.

253 Katharine's hair "all flying": Ibid., 102.

253 "There must be a powerful sentiment . . .": *Times* (London), December 11, 1883.

254 letter of forgiveness: Jane M. Renfrew, "Who Was Lucy Cavendish?" Devonshire Collections, Chatsworth, Secondary Source file for Lucy Cavendish.

254 "obeying orders . . . for Ireland . . . They did not seem . . .": Lucy, vol. 2, 327.

254 "this relation of poor Mr. Burkes . . . She had the greatest difficulty": July 12, 1883. QVJs.

254 Spencer replied at length: RA VIC/MAIN/D/36/23.

255 government would be blamed: In the event, Spencer decided against calling on Delaney as a witness, but because he had "constantly offered important evidence," (ibid.) Spencer told the queen that he had felt obliged to lift the death penalty. To Harcourt, she exploded, "Those who are imprisoned for Penal Servitude for life ought *never* to get tickets of leave!" (May 7, 1883. Bodleian, MS Harcourt 2.) (Michael Davitt, who spoke from experience, considered "P.S. for life" [MD Invincibles Diary], a worse sentence than execution.) As it happened, both Delaney and McCaffrey were given relatively lenient sentences of ten years.

255 "It was even said that the Crown . . .": MD Invincibles Diary.

255 "a man of sound business . . .": *United Ireland*, March 24, 1883.

255 "How many have been *refused* . . . It is nevertheless . . .": MD Invincibles Diary.

255 "Skin, honorably excepted": Skin-the-Goat (James Fitzharris) was acquitted for being an accessory to murder after the fact, on the grounds that it was open to doubt that he knew he was driving men engaged in murder. But he too was sentenced to ten years for his involvement on May 6. Fitzharris became a nationalist folk hero, inspiring a number of broadside ballads, several of which he is said to have written himself. This vengeful verse about James Carey may well be one.

When the equator is crossed, may the rudder be lost,
And his vessel be wafted ashore,
To some cannibal isle near the banks of the Nile,
Where savages jump and roar;
With a big sharp knife may they take his life,
While his vessel is still afloat,
And pick his bones as clean as stones,
Is the prayer of poor Skin the Goat.

(Georges-Denis Zimmermann, *Songs of Irish Rebellion: Political Street Ballads and Rebel Songs 1780–1900*. Dublin: Figgis, 1967, 284.)

255 **"told all before I said . . .":** *Morning Post* (London), December 10, 1883.

256 **provide names:** "They are—Martin Poules (died in gaol), Farrell, P. Delaney, Peter Carey, Kavanagh, James Mullett, Dan Curley, after me E. McCaffrey, Dan Delaney, G. Smith, J. Smith, Joe Hanlon, old O'Brien, and Dwyer, I forgot, told all before me. A nice lot of martyrs! A woman done all the harm. Mrs. —— [probably Peter Carey's wife, Susan, a government informer] got money from Buckshot. . . . Skin-the-Goat, Joseph Mullett, and Larry Hanlon every one told all on poor Joe and on James Carey." The letter is undated and said to have been "smuggled out of Kilmainham two days before [Carey] sailed." Ibid.

256 **"a clean breast of it . . .":** Bussy, 138.

256 **"I have my lord . . .":** Ibid.

256 **"an ardent nationalist . . .":** Cooke and Vincent, "Lord Spencer on the Phoenix Park Murders."

256 **"Putting aside the alibi . . .":** Molony, *Phoenix Park Murders*, 223.

257 **"Dear Mr. Kelly . . .":** National Library of Ireland, Manuscript Department, Letters to Kilmainham Inmates, MS10700, Acc. 2123.

257 **"lad of nineteen . . .":** *The Mysteries of Ireland*, 287–90.

257 **"I'll bet you a bob . . .":** Bussy, 137.

258 **more humane method:** The gruesomely botched execution of one of the three Manchester Martyrs in November 1867 had become an infamous example of the threat posed by an incompetent hangman. When the drop failed to kill the prisoner Michael Larkin, the hangman had to jump into the pit to finish off the job—by strangling Larkin, in one account, or by climbing onto his shoulders, in another.

258 **"Marwood will have a terrible job . . .":** From Carey's letter to Mr. and Mrs. Brady. *Morning Post* (London), December 10, 1883.

258 **It was Brady's head:** Bussy, 156.

258 **Brady's head:** This was delivered by Mallon to Dr. William Carté, who gave him a section of the spinal cord they removed as a memento. "For years Mallon carried [it] in his waistcoat pocket," writes Donal McCracken in his biography, *Inspector Mallon*, 223–24.

258 **"a brave self-sacrificing misguided man":** *Irishman*, May 19, 1883.

258   "The Catholic Church is the only one . . .": W. O'Brien, *Recollections*, 403.

258   "work of ruling Ireland . . . The hangman . . .": *P and Crime*, pt. 20, 270.

259   "marwooded": May 28, 1883. MD Invincibles Diary.

259   "The third life . . .": Ibid.

FOURTEEN: AN ABYSS OF INFAMY

260   beginning of June 1883: *Times* (London), September 19, 1883; *Star*, September 22, 1883.

261   "the sufferings of this . . .": Letter dated January 19, 1884. Davitt Papers, TCD, MS 9602/13.

261   "The burning memory . . .": *Freeman's Journal*, November 13, 1882.

261   "The horror of hunger . . .": *United Ireland*, July 7, 1883.

261   America was "played out": *Times* (London), September 19, 1883.

261   diggings near St. Louis: Hoppin, November 2, 1883, no. 261.

261   "He often said he would go . . ." and subsequent quotations and information: *Times* (Philadelphia), October 31 and November 1, 1883.

262   Londonderry on May 27 and subsequent information: Letterkenny correspondent, *Irish Times*, September 18 and 19, 1883.

262   long conversations with Neil McDevitt: Confidential police report, City of Londonderry, October 8, 1883: "While here, he was in company with Neil McDevitt, Thomas O'Hanlon and a shot boy of O'Hanlon's named Black, all nationalists of this city. He had a long conversation with McDevitt in O'Hanlon's public house on the day he arrived. While O'Donnell was in Derry he stopped in McDevitt's house. [Also] made some enquires as to O'Donnell's dealings in the Belfast Bank in Londonderry. Gave his name as Mr. Collins, clerk to a London solicitor. NAI, Police Reports, 1882–1921, Box 1, 3/715/1.

262   "I would not shoot him . . .": *Irish Times*, September 18, 1883.

263   "A Corydon, a Nagle, or a Carey . . .": McAdoo, *Guarding a Great City*, 264.

263   "traitor, decoyer of the innocent . . .": *The Mysteries of Ireland*, 279.

263   "It impossible for human power . . . He sinks into an abyss . . .": *Freeman's Journal*.

263   "We hereby call upon . . .": *Times* (London), February 24, 1883.

263   "the hereafter opening slowly . . .": *Lloyd's Weekly News*, July 25, 1909.

263   forgive his betrayer: Proof of this is in their dialogue written on the flyleaf of a prison prayer book, *Catholic Piety, with Epistles and Gospels*: "Joseph Brady, condemned to death by the perjured traitor, Carey," Brady has scrawled, and underneath, in Carey's hand, is: "James Carey was no traitor. He gave evidence only when he had been betrayed himself. He saved the lives of innocent men, and one woman." Another entry reads, "Cell No 26. James Carey, TC, conspired to murder, arrested 12 Jan 1883. 20th Feb is on remand yet." Brady: "[Carey is] an informer of the darkest dye." Carey: "After everyone betraying him he saved himself and many others." This volume was smuggled out of Kilmainham by Carey and delivered to Brady's parents along with his letter attempting to justify himself:

No one regrets poor Joe more than I do. His sad and untimely fate would have been carried out without me. The week before I said one word . . . everyone here except Joseph Brady told all they knew. . . . I send you the prayer-book he held in his hand on the fatal day. . . . I had the book; Joe got it, and wrote in it.

Morning Post (London), December 10, 1883.

263   "rather have died with Brady . . .": Ensor, *Gleanings*.

264   "never more be parted . . .": Unmarked clipping. RA VIC/MAIN/D/36/68.

264   "most earnestly": *Times* (London), February 23, 1882.

264   "cursed informer": Ibid.

264   "unavoidable absence": Molony, *Phoenix Park Murders*, 236.

264   "I might draw your attention . . .": Ibid., 240.

264   "We are glad to hear . . . He must be a nuisance . . .": To Courtenay Boyle, June 11, 1883. BL, Althorp Papers, Add MS 76834.

265   "Not improbable. He of course . . .": May 20, 1883. MD Invincibles Diary.

265   "to find and kill Carey": *Leeds Mercury*, February 3, 1883.

265   "a blunder to Irish brotherhood . . . he would soon . . .": Ibid.

266   "He showed me where the acid . . .": *Argus* (Melbourne), February 24, 1885.

266   "He came over here . . . dreadfully upset": Campbell, *Fenian Fire*, 159.

266   nearly resulted in his murder: "A Dynamiter's Story," in which Phelan told of his attempt to save the *The Queen* from destruction, appeared in the *Kansas City Journal* on December 21, 1885. Three weeks later, Phelan was decoyed by Kearney to O'Donovan Rossa's office in New York, where he was seized by a man named Richard Short and repeatedly stabbed in the face and neck. The assassin was arrested before he could escape, and Captain Phelan narrowly survived the attack.

266   "out of his time": T. M. Healy, *Letters and Leaders*, vol. I, 193.

266   "the sods being . . . From that moment . . .": Cooke and Vincent, "Lord Spencer on the Phoenix Park Murders."

266   sweetly singing hymns: Bussy, 139.

267   "Won't you let me kiss . . .": *The Mysteries of Ireland*, 301.

267   "The Trials are over . . .": TNA, Robert Anderson Papers, HO 144/1538/4.

268   "loathed and shunned": Bussy, 150.

268   "laughing at Carey": Molony, *Phoenix Park Murders*, 237.

269   fresh start for them both: The scenario is almost that of James Joyce's short story "Eveline," in his collection *Dubliners* (London: Jonathan Cape, 1971, 37–43). A nineteen-year-old met a well-traveled, middle-aged man who had returned to Ireland for a holiday. Frank beguiled Eveline with tales of distant countries and wanted her to come away with him to South America, promising that he would marry her. A shop girl leading a blank life, she had relished the chance to escape. "Frank would save her. He would give her life, perhaps love, too." When Eveline, standing on the North Wall quay, hears the steamer's departure whistle, she panics, and decides to stay behind. Clearly Susan Gallagher was more intrepid.

269   "on the grounds that . . .": *New York Times*, January 30, 1885.

269   "Mr. and Mrs. O'Donnell": Shipping Intelligence. *Eastern Province Herald*, August 1, 1883.

269   "kidnapped": *Derry Journal*, August 1, 1883.

270   "Very well, James . . .": Bussy, 149.

270   "most loquacious": *Londonderry Sentinel*, August 2, 1883.

270   "I know how long . . .": To Horace Seymour, August 3, 1883. Spencer, *The Red Earl*, 250.

270   "The Rats Adrift or the Carey Family at Sea": *United Ireland*, June 23, 1883. In the foreground are Carey Junior, James Carey, two children, and a baby in Maggie Carey's arms. "Lord Spencer" is quoted saying, "I'm done with you now. If you ever reach the Australian bush I hope you will not be found out there."

FIFTEEN: THE ASSASSIN'S ASSASSIN

271   "There is something suspicious . . .": *Cape Times*, August 1, 1883.

272   "very companionable fellows . . . [I] don't seek . . . less than kith": *Freeman's Journal*, September 18, 1883.

272   "the miscreant Carey": *Derry Journal*, August 1, 1883.

272   "We used to be alone . . ." and subsequent O'Donnell quotations: *Irish Times*, October 4, 1883.

273   "I tell you I have been accustomed . . .": *Cape Argus*, July 31, 1883.

273   "Where I come from . . .": *Irish Times*, October 4, 1883.

274   "O'Donnell has taken a fancy to me . . .": Robert Hardy deposition, August 16, 1883. WCA, 1/PEZ 1/1/1/7.

275   "'Twas pitch dark . . .": *Irish Times*, October 4, 1883.

276   "Did you see this . . . awfully excited . . . If I had known . . .": *Times* (London), August 22, 1883.

276   "I would have swung for him!": The steward thought the expression meant to swing a punch, but Senan Molony, author of *The Phoenix Park Murders*, points out a more likely interpretation—"that Carey's fellow Irishman could have been content to swing on the gallows for the man's murder." (252.)

276   "I recognized that likeness . . . Have you seen . . .": Robert Thomas Cubitt evidence, November 19, 1883, Old Bailey.

276   "I will shoot that man": Letter from John James Graham, the clerk of the peace for Cape Town, to the colonial secretary, August 27, 1883: "Robert Cubitt has returned to England. His brother Frank who came out with him is still at the White House [Hotel]. The two were down at the docks when the *Melrose* left. Frank Cubitt states that on this occasion O'Donnell showed him a woodcut of Carey & said, 'I will shoot that man.' Cubitt paid very little attention to the remark however, as he thought O'Donnell was merely chaffing." WCA, 1/PEZ 1/1/1/7.

277   "I will go to the other end . . .": Charles Russell, queen's counsel, quoting a remark during the O'Donnell trial that Tom Carey had made about his father's nervousness. *The Life, Trial and Execution of O'Donnell*.

277 "the greatest monster . . ." and subsequent O'Donnell quotations: *Irish Times*, October 4, 1883.

278 "The man who drew the short straw . . ." and rest of Jack Curran account: DÓB.

278 "I'd rather have been under . . .": *Irish Times*, October 4, 1883.

278 "the worst of the crowd . . . He won't escape . . .": Charles Schofield deposition, Port Elizabeth Preliminary Trial. WCA, 1/PEZ 1/1/1/7.

279 "I don't know . . . Will you take a bottle of ale?": Maggie Carey evidence. *Natal Witness*, August 2, 1883.

279 "Oh Maggie, Maggie . . .": Tom Carey evidence. *Natal Witness*, August 2, 1883.

279 "He said that we need not . . .": *Eastern Province Herald*, August 1, 1883.

279 "in a grieving, frantic way": Nathan Marks evidence. Old Bailey.

280 "Shake hands, Mrs. Carey, I had to do it": Charles Russell to Harcourt, December 10, 1883. "[O'Donnell's] remark, 'Shake hands, Mrs. Carey, I couldn't help it' or 'I had to do it' affords a strong moral argument that he had not in cold blood murdered the husband of the woman whom he thus addressed." TNA, HO 144/122/A30424.

280 "No matter, O'Donnell, you are no informer": Evidence of Thomas Jones, Old Bailey. Tom Carey and Maggie Carey's evidence cited in *Cape Times*, August 1, 1883.

280 "He tried to get to his wife": *Eastern Province Herald*, August 1, 1883.

280 "some sort of electric machine": *Cape Argus*, July 31, 1883.

280 "It was unlike anything . . .": *Eastern Province Herald*, August 1, 1883.

281 "some roughs": *Cape Times*, July 31, 1883.

281 "We do not remember seeing . . .": *Eastern Province Herald* (Port Elizabeth), August 1, 1883.

281 "Well deserved, but shocking!": July 30, 1883. QVJs.

281 "That shooting of Carey . . .": August 2, 1883. Ibid.

281 "There can be no doubt . . .": August 1, 1883. Buckle (ed.), *Letters of QV*, vol. 3, 437.

282 "Last evening and through . . .": July 31, 1883. NAI, Police Reports, 1882–1921, Box 1, 3/715/1.

282 "Give me a penny . . .": *Londonderry Standard*, July 31, 1883.

282 "No man can betray . . .": As quoted in Campbell, *Fenian Fire*, 83.

282 "The popular conscience . . .": Davitt, *Fall of Feudalism*, 454.

282 abhorrence for Carey: James Joyce loathed Carey and in *Ulysses* repeatedly expresses his contempt for the informer "that blew the gaff on the invincibles." In "Lotus-Eaters" Leopold Bloom goes into the church of All Hallows, where the sight of the priest stowing away the Communion cup prompts him to muse: "That fellow that turned queen's evidence on the invincibles he used to receive the, Carey was his name, the communion every morning. This very church. . . . And just imagine that. Wife and six children at home. And plotting that murder all the time." (*Ulysses*, 100.) Later, in "Lestrygonians," Joyce accuses Carey of "Egging raw youths on to get in the know all the time drawing secret service pay from the castle. [Untrue.] Drop him like a hot potato." (*Ulysses*, 206–207.) Among today's older generation of

Irish, "a carey is still a synonym for a traitor." (Remark by Brian Friel to the author in June 2015.)

282   "It was his efforts . . .": *Times* (Philadelphia), August 6, 1883.

282   "The incident certainly reflects . . .": July 31, 1883. Hamilton, BL, Add MS 48634.

282   "O'Donnell then seems . . .": August 1, 1883. Buckle (ed.), *Letters of QV*, vol. 3, 437.

282   duty to protect him: The dispatching of the other Invincibles informers had also been mismanaged. Spencer had assured the colonial secretary that the five being sent to Australia and New Zealand were not dangerous—"They were dupes and not leaders of the Conspiracy."(June 13, 1883. TNA, HO 144/98/A16380C.) And yet they had been shipped off before the New South Wales government had agreed to have them. Not only that, Michael Kavanagh, Joseph Hanlon, and Joe Smith, who should have been put on separate vessels, had been spotted aboard the SS *Pathan* before it had even departed. A Dublin publican, who had served on the Invincibles jury, was seeing off emigrating relatives at Gravesend and recognized them at once. "The secret was no longer a secret." (Unmarked Melbourne newspaper clipping. Ibid.)

Prohibited from disembarking in Adelaide or Melbourne at the beginning of August, the three men were taken off the *Pathan* by uniformed officers in Sydney and kept on another steamer in the harbor until they could be conveyed elsewhere (this turned out to be Cyprus). Robert Farrell had been bound for Wellington, and Peter and Susan Carey for Auckland, but Spencer was told that there was little chance of their being allowed to stay. He was said to be furious, and Harcourt to be "in as great a state of anxiety as he ever was," as the tracking of Carey and the other informers showed that Irish conspiracy was far from crushed. August 8, 1883. Hamilton, BL, Add MS 48634.

283   "as if he had been under discipline . . ." and other quotations: Ensor, *Gleanings*.

283   "her mistress mistreated her": In another account of the conversation she is "Susan O'Donnell," and her "mother" ill-treated her. *Cape Times*, August 1, 1883.

284   "What I did was in self-defense . . .": Bow Street court depositions. TNA, CRIM 1/19/4.

284   "rolled up tightly . . . showing that": *Eastern Province Herald*, August 6, 1883.

284   "I did not hear O'Donnell make . . .": *Cape Times*, August 1, 1883.

284   "no quarrel . . . standing a couple of yards off": Ibid.

285   the name "Carey": WCA, 1/PEZ 1/1/1/7.

285   "If there had been angry words . . .": *Natal Witness*, August 2, 1883.

285   "I thought he might want it . . . who put out his hand . . .": *Cape Times*, August 1, 1883.

285   "He said, 'Mrs. Carey . . .'": Old Bailey.

285   "known to him only as . . .": *Derry Journal*, August 2, 1883.

285   "It was first suspected . . .": *Leeds Mercury*, February 3, 1885.

286   "He said nothing . . . eked out . . . a sort of agent . . .": J. L. McCracken, "The Death of the Informer James Carey: A Fenian Revenge Killing?," in Donal P. McCracken, *Ireland and South Africa in Modern Times*, 195.

286   "There was nothing but Fenians . . .": DÓB.

286 **"many simple souls"**: Le Caron, 27.

286 **notorious massacre**: Margaret O'Donnell lived in a large house with her two sons, Charles and James "Friday" O'Donnell; her daughter Ellen; and her son-in-law Charles McAllister. In the early hours of December 10, 1875, a gang of masked vigilantes forced their way in and shot Charles O'Donnell and the heavily pregnant Ellen in cold blood. Their mother was pistol-whipped but survived; James and Charles McAllister were able to flee. The attack was said to be in retaliation for the O'Donnells' involvement in the murder of two English mine officials, and the perpetrators were never found.

287 **"The mob gathering . . . I knew when . . ."**: As quoted in Lewis, *Lament for the Molly Maguires*, 187.

287 **"peculiarly misleading mixture . . . "**: The view of Arthur H. Lewis's book *Lament for the Molly Maguires* by Kevin Kenny, author of the much-admired *Making Sense of the Molly Maguires*. The quotation is from Kenny's article "The Molly Maguires in Popular Culture," *Journal of American Ethnic History* 14, no. 4 (Summer 1995), 40.

287 **"It was reported that . . ."**: Hagley Museum and Library, Wilmington, Delaware, acc. 1520, Reading Railroad McParlan Reports, Box 1001.

288 **earned him the $700**: *Times* (Philadelphia), October 31, 1883.

288 **"I don't mix much . . ."**: *Irish Times*, October 4, 1883.

288 **"They say he was a quiet . . . There is genuine sympathy . . ."**: *Irish Times*, September 18, 1883.

288 **"misfortune and a curse . . ."**: McAdoo, *Guarding a Great City*, 266.

288 **"It seemed so shocking . . ." and subsequent quotations**: Ensor, *Gleanings*.

289 **"for the benefit of his niece"**: Telegram from Alfred Carrington Wylde, resident magistrate to Cape Town's attorney general. WCA 1/PEZ 1/1/1/7. Three studio photos of O'Donnell taken in Port Elizabeth on August 28, 1883, by the photographer C. W. Smart are cataloged in the National Archives at Kew (COPY 1/365/184, 185, and 186). Described as "Photograph of P O'Donnell assassinator of James Grey [*sic*]." However, although the typed captions exist, the three envelopes no longer contain the photographs.

289 **"pacing his cell . . ."**: Ensor, *Gleanings*.

289 **"Can I see the little girl?"**: John Cherry, Port Elizabeth inspector of police. Old Bailey.

289 **"partook of a hearty breakfast"**: *Eastern Province Herald*, August 6, 1883.

290 **"wrenched the weapon . . ."**: *Irish Times*, September 18, 1883.

290 **"I therefore am compelled . . ."**: *Eastern Province Herald*, August 6, 1883.

290 **"ascertain the wishes . . ."**: Telegram to attorney general, Cape Town. WCA, 1/PEZ 1/1/1/7.

290 **"*must* be tried . . . Sir Henry James . . ."**: August 10, 1883. BL, Althorp Papers, Add MS 77032.

291 **"England wanted to make . . ."**: *The Life, Trial and Execution of O'Donnell*, 60.

291 **"if he is likely to be tried . . ."**: August 11, 1883. Spencer letter to Jenkinson, BL, Althorp Papers, Add MS 77032.

291 "Afrikaner from Cork": J. L. McCracken, "The Death of the Informer James Carey," 193.

291 "The prisoner will leave . . .": August 27, 1883. WCA 1/PEZ 1/1/1/7.

292 "I suppose they are afraid . . .": *Irish Times*, September 18, 1883.

292 "O'Donnell does not so much . . . He states . . .": Ibid.

293 "Have you got Number One . . . Number One is a tall . . .": *Irish Times*, September 22, 1883.

293 Michael O'Donnell, puddler . . . thought it right . . .": *Morning Post*, September 19, 1883.

294 "That didn't take long": *Irish Times*, September 18, 1883.

294 "a tall, quiet, comely woman . . ." and subsequent quotations: *Herald* interview, as cited in *St. Louis Post-Dispatch*, September 25, 1883.

294 uniform of a female warder: McIntyre.

294 "No one guessed . . .": Ibid.

295 "[Pat] also told me . . .": Corrigan (ed.), *A History of the Phoenix Park Patriots*, 110.

295 "The governor pressed me . . .": *New York Times*, September 30, 1883.

295 "In all parts of the world . . .": *Irishman*, September 22, 1883.

295 "Talbot was shot in Dublin.": A reference to Robert Kelly's 1871 shooting of Head Constable Thomas Talbot, the archetype of informers and model for Harvey Duff in Dion Boucicault's play *The Shaughraun*. The controversy of Kelly's trial—whether Talbot died as a result of the bullet wound in the neck or of an infection and hemorrhaging following an operation performed by the eminent Sir Wiliam Stokes—was the subject of Roger McHugh's 1945 play *Trial at Green Street Courthouse*.

296 "the well-known dynamite advocate . . .": Le Caron, 206.

296 "never was there a nobler . . . Did it ever occur . . .": September 29, 1883. Davitt Papers, TCD, MS 9602/32.

296 $55,000: Audit of Account, *Irish World*, February 16, 1884.

296 "a firm and devoted friend . . .": Tynan, 337.

297 "revolutionary sentiments . . .": Le Caron, 177.

297 "an act designed to roil . . .": Sullivan, *New Ireland*, 462.

297 "There is probably no part of Ireland": Ibid., 228.

297 "I am not ashamed to say . . .": Ibid.

298 "the biggest advocate . . .": Remark by Lord Coleridge, as quoted in B O'B, 103.

298 "Did you not hear him . . ." and subsequent quotations: *Irish Times*, October 4, 1883.

300 "to connect the Prisoner . . .": Office of the Resident Magistrate, August 7, 1883. WCA 1/PEZ 1/1/1/7.

300 "I can't read . . .": *Irish Times*, October 4, 1883.

300 "We all hoped and prayed . . .": Katharine Tynan, *Twenty-Five Years: Reminiscences* (London: Smith, Elder and Co., 1913), 95.

300 "under great emotion . . . The man who . . .": *Derry Journal*, August 2, 1883.

SIXTEEN: IRRESISTIBLE IMPULSE

301 **distribute a "Martyr's Fund":** Mallon reports, October 20 and 22, 1883. NAI, Chief Secretary's Office Registered Papers (CSORP)/Police Crime, Carton 2.

301 **"in sympathy with . . . they will likely . . .":** Ibid.

302 **From police reports . . . and subsequent Hoppin quotations and facts about O'Donnell:** Hoppin, October 18–December 15, 1883, nos. 253–69.

302 **discharged from the US Army:** Inspector Littlechild, the officer who had met O'Donnell on arrival in England, had been given further information: "2 or 3 times he took bounty and deserted, never belonging to any regiment" (Hoppin). However, an officer of Company H of the 124th Ohio Regiment at Cleveland declared that O'Donnell had enlisted as a substitute: "While with us he was never in any engagement with the enemy but boasted a great deal about the deeds of valor he performed as a member of Gen. Mulligan's corps. I don't believe any effort was made to capture O'Donnell after his final desertion" (*Chicago Daily Tribune*, December 21, 1883). An account by Jack Curran confirms that O'Donnell had served as a substitute: "They would pay him a few hundred pounds, and as soon as he got this money he would head off and the first town he arrived in he would jump on the train and he would go walking through the big city. And then he would get another few hundred pounds from another man and off he would go again. He worked away like this until the war was almost over and he had never gone out to fight at all" (DÓB).

302 **"wrong in this and other matters":** Hoppin, October 31, 1883, no. 256. Another area of doubt is when the family had returned to Ireland. O'Donnell said that he had been twelve years old, but this is unlikely, given that this would have been at the time of the Great Famine. It was almost certainly 1852 or '53, when Michael Art bought back his land from Lord Woodhouse.

303 **"a shebeen house in Toronto . . .":** Ibid.

303 **"in the absence of proof to the contrary," "he was to be regarded as an American citizen" and "a courteous relaxation":** Hoppin, November 19, 1883, no. 256.

304 **"cheerfully withdraw . . . already not too strong":** *New York Times*, December 22, 1883.

304 **"They would have retired . . .":** Ibid., December 17, 1883.

304 **"a matter of sheer impossibility . . . Therefore the Clan-na-Gael . . .":** McIntyre.

305 **"The people fear . . .":** Undated, unsigned memo. NAI, Police Reports, 1882–1921, Box I, 3/715/I.

305 **"a shot boy . . . all nationalists . . .":** October 1883. Ibid.

305 **"keeping his word true . . .":** *New York Times*, November 30, 1883.

305 **"greatly disturbed . . . it was with plans . . .":** *Times* (Philadelphia), October 31, 1883.

305 **"Then at the last moment . . .":** *Nation*, January 5, 1884.

306 **possibly as much as $2,000:** ·Police secret sergeant's report about Edward Moran, American Counsel for O'Donnell, December 7, 1883. NAI, CSORP/Police Crime, Carton 2.

306 **"at the altar ... bloody informer":** *Nation*, January 5, 1884.

306 **"When she heard us nagging ...":** *Irish Times*, October 4, 1883.

306 **"I say to you, sir ...":** *Nation*, January 5, 1884.

307 **"in a girl's hand":** *Irish Times*, September 18, 1883.

307 **"No matter, O'Donnell, you are no informer":** Evidence of Thomas Jones, Old Bailey; Tom Carey and Maggie Carey, *Cape Times*, August 1, 1883; *Irish Times*, September 18, 1883.

308 **"The result was not ...":** *Reynolds's Newspaper*, March 24 and 31, 1895.

308 **she was pregnant:** The late Niall Ó Dónaill, the Irish lexicographer and one of the most reliable chroniclers of O'Donnell's story, was led to believe by relatives that Susan's condition was the reason that the nuns who were sheltering her in South Africa had tried to prevent her from appearing in court.

Author conversation with Dónall Ó Baoill, October 18, 2016. See also "Dálach Ghaoth Dobhair" ["The Gweedore O'Donnell"], *Donegal Annual*, 1960, 209–26.

308 **"He also said if O'Donnell ...":** NAI, CSORP/Police Crime, Carton 2.

309 **challenge any members:** The identities of the jurors had been kept secret—a breach of the accused's right of access, about which Sullivan and Pryor expressed anger in the press. "For all he is allowed to know, [the jurors] may have dropped from the clouds on the summons of the Crown," Sullivan complained in the *Pall Mall Gazette*. (Undated clipping, TNA, P O'D file.) But a small ad that appeared in the December 8 edition of the *United Irishman* entitled o'donnell's murderers left no doubt about the need for anonymity: "Our friends in London will be good enough to furnish us with the names and addresses of the jurors whom the English will swear in to hang O'Donnell, also short sketches of their lives. We want to be prepared to write their obituaries."

309 **"leave it to his solicitor ...":** *Times* (London), December 1, 1883.

309 **"You are a fine fellow ... because my father ...":** November 19, 1883. Old Bailey.

309 **"a desperate man ...":** *Times* (London), December 1, 1883.

309 **"talking in a very *high* state":** Old Bailey.

310 **did not appear:** South African jurisdiction had no power to compel a witness to give evidence in England, and those who had agreed were demanding considerable financial compensation: Dr. Ensor was being paid five guineas a day to make up for loss of earnings; Nathan Marks had received an advance of £200 and £485 for the month of November. "The terms are high but we are not in a position to force him to reduce them," the colonial secretary had been told. (Alfred Carrington Wylde, resident magistrate of Port Elizabeth, August 7, 1883. WCA, 1/PEZ 1/1/1/7.)

310 **"when Carey was a staggering ...":** *Times* (London), December 1, 1883.

310 **"A man under trial ...":** Ibid.

310 **"Idle bravado":** *Times* (London), December 3, 1883.

310 **"a conclusion that needed ...":** Sullivan, *Nation*, January 5, 1884.

311 "You are James Carey . . . O'Donnell was sharper . . . virtually part of . . .": *The Life, Trial and Execution of O'Donnell.*

311 "flushed with gratitude . . .": Ensor, *Gleanings.*

311 "under provocation . . .": *Times* (London), December 3, 1883.

311 "If B has a deadly weapon . . .": TNA, P O'D file, A30424/64.

311 "in the case of a hot quarrel . . . The question I put . . .": *Times* (London), December 3, 1883.

312 "That puts the rope . . . It looks blue . . .": *New York Times*, December 17, 1883.

312 "I understand your lordship . . ." and subsequent quotations: *The Life, Trial and Execution of O'Donnell.*

312 "whatever its origin": *Times* (London), December 3, 1883.

312 "THE CLERK OF ARRAIGNS . . .": *The Life, Trial and Execution of O'Donnell.*

313 "Wait a minute, can I speak?": Ibid.

313 "Nobody ten feet away . . . Three cheers . . .": *New York Times*, December 17, 1883.

313 "stout, plump face . . . 43–47 years . . . condemned O'Donnell's morals . . .": December 12, 1883. NAI, Police Reports, 1882–1921, Box 1, 3/715/1.

313 "burying all recollections . . .": *Standard* (London), January 10, 1884.

313 "Finding her destitute": *New York Times*, June 12, 1885.

314 "a salutary and soothing . . .": Russell to Harcourt, December 10, 1883. TNA, P O'D file.

314 "a huge blunder": December 8, 1883. Davitt Correspondence 9, TCD, MS 9602/53.

314 "The conviction of O'Donnell . . .": As quoted in Tynan, 340.

314 "The conduct of O'Donnell . . .": December 7, 1883. *Devoy's Post Bag*, vol. 2, 229–30.

315 "I did think [Denman] had left room . . .": December 7, 1883. TNA, P O'D file.

315 "I have long hesitated . . .": December 10, 1883. Ibid.

316 "Is not the fearful punishment . . .": Ibid.

316 "The man committed no . . .": December 8, 1883. TCD, Davitt Correspondence 9, 9602/53.

316 "[He] put it covertly . . .": *New York Times*, December 17, 1883.

316 "If we found prisoner guilty . . .": TNA, P O'D file.

316 Denman certainly admitted: In a few handwritten lines (sent to William Harcourt), Denman said that as he was retiring from court he was told by the foreman that only one member had hesitated "for a time" about the guilty verdict. "I thanked him but said I preferred not being made a party to the secrets of the Jury box." TNA O'D File.

316 the judge left the courtroom: See *The Life, Trial and Execution of O'Donnell*, 22. "After dismissing the jury with the fatal direction . . . his lordship retired to his private room and in a few minutes returned *with the black cap in his hand.* . . . There was no longer any doubt as to poor O'Donnell's fate. The Judge knew what was coming and he was ready for it."

317 "Judge Denman's wonderfully correct . . ." and subsequent quotations: *The Life, Trial and Execution of O'Donnell.*

317 **"I am directed by the President . . .":** Copy of Lowell letter. BL, Gladstone Papers, Add MS 44198; The Irish vote had become increasingly important in American politics, numbering in New York alone around 250,000. One member of the delegation later admitted that he had gone along "merely to please the Irish"; another that he had proposed the resolution because "he represented a large Irish constituency and was forced to do something." (As quoted in O'Grady, *Irish-Americans and Anglo-American Relations, 1880–1888,* 240.) The word circulating in Washington, DC, was that the British should not take the unanimous ruling seriously.

317 **Harcourt was determined:** Patrick McIntyre claimed in his memoir that it was an open secret at Scotland Yard that, had it not been for O'Donnell's eruption in the dock, "Harcourt had intended that he should be respited." This is unlikely. Harcourt had taken exception to Charles Russell's assertion that public opinion favored commutation—"If he means *English* opinion he is entirely mistaken," he snapped to Gladstone, adding that he had received none of the usual letters and petitions for mercy, except from "one mad woman" who justified the crime. "Probably Russell refers to *American* opinion which he has done his best to work."

317 **"The Fenians would believe . . ." and subsequent quotations from Harcourt's seventeen-page "Secret" memo about the O'Donnell verdict:** December 12, 1883, BL, Gladstone Papers, Add MS 44198.

318 **". . . I do not conceive anything can alter":** The Harcourt-Gladstone correspondence ended with a fawning exchange of admiration. Gladstone: "Your letter is a proof of the conscientious care with which you discharge a duty alike delicate & important, but I should be sorry if you wrote it under the impression that I had made such a call upon you for the satisfaction of my own mind. . . . I have told Mr. Russell that upon the papers before me I should have judged & acted as you did." Harcourt: "It is on these occasions that your lieutenants have occasion to be grateful for the strong arm with which their Chief always sustains them when they are right and helps them when they are wrong." December 13, 1883. BL, Gladstone Papers, Add MS 44547.

318 **"raise his voice":** *Standard* (London), December 17, 1883.

318 **"the Queen of England . . .":** RAVIC/MAIN/D/36/122.

318 **"a strange hesitation . . . It is probable":** Ibid., 116.

318 **Victor Hugo:** *Le Rappel,* the French journal founded by Hugo's sons, had published the appeal, adding: "If ever a murderer be excusable it is the man who has struck down a traitor and made himself the instrument of justice through patriotism." *Standard* (London), December 17, 1883.

319 **"But I must add with regret . . .":** December 14, 1883. BL, Gladstone Papers, Add MS 44547.

319 **"seven for murder . . . Three of these desire . . .":** *New York Times,* December 14, 1883.

319 **"the prison physician says . . .":** *Times* (London), December 13, 1883.

319   "When all hope of saving him . . .": *Standard* (London), January 10, 1884.

320   "They're all my friends . . . Cheer up, Father . . .": Ryan, *Fenian Memories*, 111.

320   "Go on and finish it!": Corrigan (ed.), *A History of the Phoenix Park Patriots*, 111.

320   "Father, I suppose . . . A cooler man": Ryan, *Fenian Memories*, 111.

320   "I would have swung . . .": *Times* (London), August 22, 1883.

321   "very hospitable house": December 17, 1883. Matthew (ed.), *Gladstone Diaries*, vol. 11, 78.

321   "dynamite Irishmen . . . For every O'Donnell . . .": As cited in the *Irishman*, December 22, 1883.

321   "for warfare against . . . honor and judgment . . .": Undated clipping. TNA, P O'D file.

322   "The origin of these devilish schemes . . .": As quoted in Short, *The Dynamite War*, 176–77.

322   postmortem confession: *United Ireland*, January 5, 1884.

323   "Who was responsible . . . ?": General Pryor had been determined to show that the plea of self-defense was "original, natural and never for an instant abandoned, even when O'Donnell was without counsel." In mid-October, he advised that depositions from all the South African officers who had dealt with O'Donnell should be secured in order to have details of "whatever utterances O'Donnell had made" since the killing of Carey. *Times* (Philadelphia), October 14, 1883.

324   "The very important question . . . some controlling disease": Steven Penney, "Irresistible Impulse and the Mental Disorder Defence," *Criminal Law Quarterly* 60, 207–37.

324   truth of history: Also in the account is an aside of "curious interest." It claims that Tom Carey wrote a letter on his mother's behalf to her brother-in-law, giving an entirely different account of the shooting to that she subsequently gave under oath. "The production of this letter in court would have impeached mother and son, whose testimony was a fabric of falsehood. Extraordinary efforts were made to steal, beg or buy the letter, but it had been destroyed or was in possession of the Crown." *United Ireland*, January 5, 1884.

324   "terrible sprees . . . the most dissolute . . .": *New York Times*, January 8, 1884.

324   "very drunk": WCA, 1/PEZ 1/1/1/7.

324   "looked dazed, as if . . .": Old Bailey.

324   "If he drank he did not know . . .": *Times* (London), August 22, 1883.

324   "perverted . . . I am sure . . . how can it be true?": *United Ireland*, January 19, 1884.

325   Pat had repeated the circumstances: This was later published as "a statement made to his brother":

> I was sitting on the settee. Carey was leaning with his left shoulder against the boards. He said to me, "I think you know who I am." I said, "Yes, you are that damned Irish informer, Carey." . . . As I said so, Carey drew out his pistol. I sprung towards him and struck his right hand sending

the pistol over his shoulder. I would not be sure whether a shot went off or not. As he turned to pick up his pistol again, I drew my own pistol and shot him. Carey's son was the first to appear on the scene followed by Parish and Jones. Carey's son picked up his father's pistol on the floor and put it in his pocket. . . . I don't intend to make any further statement. (*The Life, Trial and Execution of O'Donnell.*)

325   **"for his soul's sake . . . His story was this . . .":** Davitt, *Fall of Feudalism*, 455.

325   **"removal . . . one of the most marvelous . . .":** *Times* (Philadelphia), August 6, 1883.

325   **"getting the follow on . . .":** Packie Manus Byrne, quoted in Hugh Shields, *Narrative Singing in Ireland: Lays, Ballads, Come-All-Yes and Other Songs* (Dublin: Irish Academic Press, 1993), 153.

326   **"broadside ballads":** Many Patrick O'Donnell songs are recorded on the website of the Irish Traditional Music Archive (ITMA), https://www.itma.ie/.

After

329   **"Umfogoclko . . . Nkalitshaana, 1885 . . . J. Carey . . . rude emblem . . .":** From an account by the English mimic and humorist Charles Duval after a tour of Southern Africa. *Dundee Courier and Argus*, July 13, 1888.

329   **"When Nero perished . . .":** Ensor, *Gleanings*.

329   **sawed off his skull . . . haunted:** "Talk" column in unnamed clipping, November 10, 1977, courtesy of Margaret Harradine, former Africana Librarian, Port Elizabeth.

329   **the informer's ghost:** When Maggie Carey died in 1897, the only person other than close relatives to attend her funeral was the family's Special Branch minder, Patrick McIntyre. He had stayed in touch and knew that the older brothers had taken their mother and sisters to an unknown location in France, where they had learned to speak the language fluently. Two of the youths remained in England, one joining the navy and the other the army. Sent to Dublin with his regiment, the soldier son was posted on sentry duty at Kilmainham, "standing guard outside the very cell where his father had been incarcerated." Both later joined the French Foreign Legion in Algiers. Maggie Carey was buried under her assumed name in the south of England, but the location of other family graves is unknown. (McIntyre.) In Dublin's Glasnevin Cemetery, a stone's throw from the graves of Skin-the-Goat and fellow Invincible Harry Rowles, is a memorial to James Carey's parents and his children who died in infancy: "This tribute has been erected to perpetuate the memory of a good father and loving mother by their affectionate son, James Carey, 19 A Denzille Street. In loving memory of the children of James and Margaret Carey."

330   **"An immense concourse . . .":** *New York Times*, January 23, 1884.

330   **the local martyr:** After three months of working as a kitchen maid for Patrick Ford's family in Brooklyn, Susan Gallagher was "taken sick" (*Irish Times*, June 30,

1885) and went to hospital—very likely a "lying-in" hospital. (The closest maternity institution was on Second Avenue at Seventeenth Street, but Boston Lying-In Hospital had a reputation for the best obstetric care in the United States and an unconventionally relaxed attitude toward unmarried mothers.) Ford had covered the hospital costs, but nevertheless, there were acrimonious money issues between him and Susan. She insisted that he was refusing to hand over the $2,000 that he had promised her if she agreed to testify at O'Donnell's trial, and his son had taken her side, saying that Miss Gallagher had "a just claim and that his father ought to pay it." (This, and subsequent quotations, *North-Eastern Daily Gazette*, July 1, 1885.) After being discharged, Susan did not return to Ford's house on Bedford Avenue but went to live out as a servant. A year later, in June 1885, giving her age as twenty-four and described by the *New York Herald*'s court reporter as "prepossessing and well-dressed," Gallagher sued Ford for the $2,000 but seemed willing to settle for half the amount, maintaining that O'Donnell had repeatedly told her that he wanted her to have £700 from his defense fund. Ford dismissed this outright. In a statement to the press he pointed out that Miss Gallagher had not been called to give evidence, as her testimony would have damaged rather than benefited the prisoner—"So the money spent in bringing her from the Cape was a dead loss." He also quashed Susan's assertion that O'Donnell had wanted a financial settlement made for her, saying that her name was not mentioned in instructions conveyed by Father Fleming. Out of charity, Ford said, he gave the young woman $500 from his own pocket. "She was not entitled to a cent." Susan did not appear to have pursued the matter in civil court as she was advised to do, and the case was dropped. According to Dónall Ó Baoill (whose great-grandmother was Patrick O'Donnell's sister Mary), she was later married in New York to a Donegal man, and "they had at least one son." Conversation with the author, October 18, 2016.

330 **"to the patriotic Rev. James MacFadden":** *Times* (London), June 24, 1885.

330 **Manchester Martyrs:** The cry of "God save Ireland" (inspiring T. D. Sullivan's unofficial national anthem), proclaimed by one of the martyr's from the dock, had been behind O'Donnell's outburst in court; just as the martyrs' mock funeral, where mourners marched behind three empty hearses, had influenced the Derrybeg ritual. *Irish Times*, November 23, 2014.

331 **"with manifest pride":** *Daily Telegraph* (Sheffield, UK), November 28, 1887.

331 **O'Donnell memorial:** Another Celtic cross was erected in Derrybeg in 1954 by a committee of Fianna Fáil, Ireland's Republican Party. Standing today beside Dan O'Donnell's pub (now Connie Coyle's), it has an Irish inscription translated as:

In memory of Patrick O'Donnell from the parish of Gweedore who was put to death in Newgate Prison in London on 17 December 1883 because of his high loyalty to Ireland.

In 1902, when Newgate Prison was demolished, its burial remains were transferred to a mass grave in the City of London Cemetery, where the National Graves

Association has subsequently commemorated O'Donnell among other "Irish patriots."

331 **"In loving memory . . .":** The inscription continues: "This monument was erected by the grateful admirers of his heroism in the United States of America, through the *Irish World* and forwarded by a ladies committee of New York. Mrs. Maggie Halvey, Mrs. F. Byrne, Ellen Ford." As cited in Ó Gallchobhair, *History of Landlordism in Donegal,* 48.

331 **"the monstrous inscription . . .":** *Times* (London), October 11, 1887.

331 **"the priest indignantly replied:** James MacFadden wanted no distraction from a private land war he was conducting on behalf of the tenants of Wybrant Olphert's Gweedore estate, as part of the nationwide Plan of Campaign launched for an abatement of rents. In January 1888, Dublin Castle prosecuted MacFadden for promoting the plan, and he served six months in a Derry prison. On his release, he continued urging support for land agitation and ignored a summons to attend what he called "a Coercion Court." In February of the following year, a large force of Royal Irish Constabulary men arrived to arrest him after Sunday Mass, and when MacFadden, dressed in his vestments, walked toward his house, District Inspector Martin took hold of him by the arm. The priest shook him off, and Martin drew his sword, prompting a cry of "He's killing the priest." The crowd closed in and within minutes had bludgeoned Martin to death. Forty-eight people were charged with murder, including MacFadden, who was released after a defense counsel bargain—a plea of guilty to obstructing the police. He was banned from political activity for five years but remained an "apostle of anarchy," the driving force behind local land battles. (Breandán Mac Suibhne, "Soggarth Aroon and Gombeen-Priest," 168) Eventually, his bishop transferred MacFadden to his own home parish—presumably where he could be kept an eye on. Ó Broin, *The Prime Informer,* 45–46.

331 **"I loathe the very mention . . .":** Ibid.

331 **"noble and fearless . . . the victory . . .":** *Irish World,* May 16, 1885.

331 **"modern Coriolanus . . . two men . . . a brave little woman . . .":** Ibid.

331 **Frank and Mary Ann Byrne:** The money was welcomed by the Byrnes, who had moved with their two children to Providence, Rhode Island, where Frank Byrne worked as a shipping clerk and supplemented his income by selling cigars. When acute rheumatism forced him quit his job, and Mary Ann was stricken with paralysis, the family was reduced to relying on the local branch of the Ancient Order of Hibernians for assistance. *Providence Journal,* February 17, 1894.

332 **"crazy for notoriety . . . somewhat of a crank . . .":** *New York World,* June 4, 1894.

332 **"One man and one only . . . the actual scene . . .":** Ibid.

332 **"Eumaeus":** The Phoenix Parks murders enthralled Joyce—"Right outside the viceregal lodge, imagine!" (*Ulysses,* 174), providing him with vivid scenes, characters, and catchwords, "Skin-the-etcetera" (744) being a particular favorite. Fitzharris is a key figure in the "Eumaeus" chapter (704–776), in which John Mallon (749),

Buckshot Forster (764), and Katharine O'Shea, "That bitch, that English whore" (755), are also referred to. "Aeolus" is set in the offices of the *Freeman's Journal*, where the editor, Myles Crawford, tells Stephen about the murders and that the *New York World* had cabled the paper for a special report. Showing Stephen a map, he says, "T is viceregal lodge. C is where murder took place. . . . F to P is the route Skin-the-goat drove the car for an alibi" (173). *Finnegans Wake* also makes much of Phoenix Park, while the murders and their aftermath inspired Joycean archetypes and coinages, such as "invincibled"(376), "burked" (ibid.), and "Number Wan" (72).

332 **"are all hallmarks . . .":** See Luke Gibbons, *Joyce's Ghosts: Ireland, Modernism and Memory* (Chicago and London: University of Chicago Press, 2015), 216–19.

332 **"Egansville":** Thomas Brown, *Irish-American Nationalism, 1870–1890* (Philadelphia: J. B. Lippincott, 1966), 158.

333 **"dynamite was necessary":** Gantt, *Irish Terrorism in the Atlantic Community*, 149.

333 **diverted $100,000:** John Devoy substantiates this in an open letter to Egan published in the *New York Times* on October 29, 1892: "In 1882 a draft from Monroe's Paris bank for £20,000 or $100,000 alleged to be from you and payable to Alexander Sullivan was deposited in a New York bank and thence transmitted to the Mechanics and Traders' Bank in Chicago." During the subsequent months some $90,000 was drawn on checks signed Alexander Sullivan Trustee "payable to Alexander Sullivan."

333 **"Sullivan's men . . .":** Ibid.

333 **"that clean-handed . . .":** Le Caron, 228.

333 **"his worthy *fidus Achates*":** Ibid., 234.

333 **"I made up my mind . . .":** *Daily State Democrat*, September 3, 1884.

333 **"the true friend of the Irish":** Paul Knaplund and Carolyn Clewes (eds.), "Private Letters from the British Embassy in Washington to the Foreign Secretary Lord Granville, 1880–1885," *Annual Report of the American Historical Association for the Year 1941* (1942), 170.

333 **"pandering to . . . The dynamite wing . . .":** June 10, 1884. Ibid., 178.

334 **"Joe Brady Club . . . All dynamiters . . .":** Ibid., 170.

334 **"an English-hating Irishman":** D. Healy, *James G. Blaine and Latin America*, 208.

334 **"others have earned . . .":** 1892 conversation with Mallon, T. M. Healy, *Letters and Leaders*, vol. I, 181.

334 **"a splendid way with . . .":** McCracken, *Inspector Mallon*, 227.

335 **"the DMP's star turn":** Tim Healy, quoted in ibid., 172.

335 **"Fitzharris could only be used . . .":** Ibid., 214.

335 **"to make herself a nuisance . . . I wish to God . . .":** Ibid., 202.

335 **"in modest but comfortable . . .":** "Sinn Féiner" George Lyons, quoted in ibid., 219.

335 **"an accursed re-echo . . . No such thunderbolt . . .":** Davitt, *Fall of Feudalism*, 53.

336 **"baneful and blood-stained monster":** May 20, 1882. Cartoon by John Tenniel, cited by Teresa O'Donnell, " 'Skin the Goat's Curse on James Carey': Narrating the Phoenix Park Murders through Contemporary Broadside Ballads," in *Crime, Violence*

and the Irish in the 19th Century, ed. Kyle Hughes and Donald MacRaild (Liverpool: Liverpool University Press, 2018), 250.

336 "I did not make an S . . .": Lyons, 387.

336 "to checkmate the most powerful . . .": Davitt, *Fall of Feudalism*, 549.

336 "Gladstone was 'Teresa'": Ibid., 619.

336 "Notes of an Amateur Detective": Davitt Papers, TCD, MS 9365/745/3.

336 "campaign of systematic calumny . . .": Davitt, *Fall of Feudalism*, 543.

336 "something of a farce . . .": Jenkins, *Gladstone*, 515.

336 "a good deal mortified . . .": Lucy Cavendish, quoted in Marlow, *Mr. and Mrs. Gladstone*, 234.

336 "If we cannot rule ourselves . . .": Bew, *Enigma*, 113.

337 "The Irish all went . . .": June 10, 1885. QVJs.

337 "these theoretical radicals . . .": December 19, 1885. Ibid.

337 "an *illiberal* Tory": Salisbury's description of himself, cited in Roberts, *Salisbury: Victorian Titan*, 334.

337 "more precious to us . . .": Speech of November 9, 1885. Ibid., 382.

337 expect nothing from the Tories: "Rightly or wrongly, I have not the slightest desire to satisfy the national aspirations of Ireland," Salisbury would tell Carnarvon, who, realizing he had been used as a tool to entice the Irish vote, tendered his resignation. Hammond, *Gladstone and the Irish nation*, 730.

338 "coquetting with Parnell": Jordan, *Kitty O'Shea*, 127.

338 "If five sixths of the Irish . . .": December 12, 1885. Roberts, *Salisbury: Victorian Titan*, 362.

338 "I determined on taking . . .": Jenkins, *Gladstone*, 541.

338 "calamitous": Hibbert, *QV: A Personal History*, 374.

338 "I told him, I feared . . .": February 1, 1886. QVJs.

339 "a really bad & worthless man": October 8, 1891. Ponsonby, *Henry Ponsonby*, 213.

339 "great, beloved country . . .": Ibid., 206.

339 "He feels so much for me . . .": February 6, 1886. QVJs.

339 Gladstone's "great comfort": Gladstone, to the queen. February 1, 1885. QVJs. Spencer was virtually alone among his contemporaries in understanding Ireland's nationalist spirit—and that patriotism was the impulse behind much of its crime—but there could also have been an element of self-interest in his loyalty to the prime minister. Many prominent observers (Charles Russell among them) were convinced that the earl, now Gladstone's most trusted ally, would be the next head of the Liberal Party. (Ponsonby, *Henry Ponsonby*, 214.)

339 "actually cut him": Edward Hamilton, quoted in Spencer, *The Red Earl*, 14.

339 "I trust you are not going . . .": Lord Powerscourt, quoted in ibid., 6.

339 "We have heard . . .": Spencer, *The Red Earl*, 13.

339 "This was one of the great . . .": Jenkins, *Gladstone*, 541.

340 "princes, ambassadors, peers . . .": Edward Hamilton, quoted in ibid., 551.

340 "undulating cadences . . .": Ibid., 582.

340 "which I sometimes have thought . . .": Ibid., 552.

340 "the disaster of 1886": Lucy Cavendish, Unpublished diary, vol. 14, postscript dated 1889, Chatsworth, DF19/1/12.

340 "What vast benefit . . .": Jenkins, *Gladstone*, 538.

340 "twenty years of resolute government . . . two deeply divided . . . Confidence depends . . . 'stupid calumny'": Roberts, *Salisbury: Victorian Titan*, 383–84.

341 "We have purposely and advisedly . . .": Le Caron, 246.

341 "the powder business . . . His lordship, beyond all . . .": John Gerard, *What Was the Gunpowder Plot?* (London: Osgood, McIlvaine and Co., 1897), 218.

341 "this plot of powder . . . great love and honour . . .": Ibid., 214.

341 "to work with Greek fire . . . Mrs. Brown's Jubilee celebrations": Short, *The Dynamite War*, 232–33.

342 "a renumeration of £2,500 . . .": "Very Secret" Memorandum. May 30, 1885. TNA, FO 5/1932.

342 satisfaction of H.M. Government: This assignment was to confirm the identity and whereabouts of the real Number One. Citing the evidence of a letter he had received, Millen names the Invincibles' prime mover as Captain John McCafferty (who in the mid-1880s was head of a team studying the feasibility of bombing England from hot-air balloons). Millen says nothing in his report about Patrick Egan—an omission that calls into question his powers of infiltration. Gantt, *Irish Terrorism in the Atlantic Community*, 149.

342 "the credit of baffling . . . so that he . . . Millen humbugged them": Bussy, 160.

342 "half dead with fatigue": June 21, 1887. Hibbert, *QV in Her Letters and Journals*, 306.

342 prime minister had endangered her life: Patrick Tynan was among the participants who traveled from the United States to France a decade later to attempt a diamond jubilee–timed attack—a plot that the British government again appears to have known about. On September 12, 1896, he was arrested in the bar of the Hotel Folkestone, Boulogne-sur-Mer, where for over a week he had been "almost constantly drunk and boasting what revenge he would wreak." (*Freeman's Journal,* September 15, 1896.) For Tynan, it was another opportunity to aggrandize himself, and it proved to be both a personal triumph and a publicity stunt. The French allowed him to return without consequences to his family in New York, and the press clamor resulting from the capture of "Number One," led to a second printing of his *Irish National Invincibles* book.

342 "What are these people waiting for? . . .": Lyons, *Parnell*, 403.

343 suspected William O'Shea: The birth in November 1884 of Parnell's daughter Katie, following a year after that of Clare, was hard for O'Shea to accept, as he knew for certain that he was not the father. He was resentful too of the couple's lack of discretion, and his letters to Katharine from 1886, when snide allusions about the affair began appearing in the press, voiced his anger at the likelihood of a scandal. What irked and humiliated O'Shea most, however, was his thwarted political ambitions. Certain that her husband was about to shatter his long silence, Katharine had sought Gladstone's help to secure him a Liberal seat, and when nothing came of this, Parnell foisted O'Shea on Galway as a parliamentary candidate, despite the

dismay of the Irish party. O'Shea resigned from a constituency that did not want him and blamed Parnell for ending his public life. "I have been treated in blackguard fashion and I mean to hit back a stunner," he had warned Katharine in November 1885. *Love Story*, vol. 2, 92.

343   "always my enemy . . .": Dungan, *The Captain and the King*, 344.

343   "the Castle people": B O'B, 441.

343   "The only man on earth . . .": Letter to Davitt, August 26, 1888. TCD, MS 9368.

343   "injured persons . . . the vaporings . . .": Davitt, *Fall of Feudalism*, 542.

343   "It is an old story now . . .": and subsequent quotations: R. B. O'Brien, *The Life of Lord Russell*, 216.

344   **appearance in court of Henri Le Caron:** Le Caron received £10,000 for his evidence but had been told to pretend to know nothing about the fee in order to be able to swear in court that he had not been paid. The Careys' minder Patrick McIntyre was brought from royal duty at Osborne to meet a "Mr. Holland" in a Paddington hotel, and for a year served as the major's full-time bodyguard. As a result of his appearance in court, Le Caron's life was under constant threat; he remained in London, and his wife and four of his six children were brought from America and given separate lodgings for their safety. *Reynolds's Newspaper*, May 19, 1895.

344   "a friend from America . . . I had heard it before . . .": Le Caron evidence. *P and Crime*, pt. 13, 9–10.

344   "Land League will have £100,000 . . .": Le Caron report to Robert Anderson, May 23, 1881. TNA, Robert Anderson Papers, HO 144 1538/5.

344   **[Parnell's] political gamesmanship:** Le Caron's evidence had prompted Gladstone to do his own sleuthing, and he had asked Lucy Cavendish to look for evidence among her late husband's papers. She wrote back on March 1, 1889, sending him documents (no longer attached to the letter).

My dear Uncle William,

I send you as you asked me to do, some data as to Parnell's having *before '81* obtained money for Land League purposes through what I called "shady" instruments. . . . I was greatly pleased to see that the defence is going to turn upon what you have always believed, i.e. Parnell's changed tune ever since he came out of prison. . . . I can well believe that Parnell & his lieutenants in their desperate want of means for carrying out legitimate agitation thought themselves justified in getting money thro' any course. They may even have pleaded plausibly tho' wrongly that it was a good thing to divert money even by such crooked ways from dynamite to constitutional purposes. All I want is that you recognize the fact that they *did* so obtain money. With all excuses & deductions & fully recognizing that there was no selfish aim or personal gain involved, the fact of Parnell, *in those past years* having so far "stood in" with such a paper as the "Irish Times" [*Irish* World] has always made me feel that a dark shadow rests upon him. If however his counsel brings up or [discloses] what I have long believed to be probable, clearly that since '82 he has entirely broken with the party of plots & violence, it will make an immense difference in my feelings. . . . I have marked with double ink strokes the passages relating to money matters. I have also marked with one stroke (with pain & grief) passages that seem undeniably to prove that Mr. Parnell *at that time*, shut his eyes to the murderous teaching of the paper that he was making use of.

BL, Gladstone Papers, Add MS 44269.

344 **"revolutionist to the backbone"**: Le Caron evidence. *P and Crime*, pt. 12, 40.

344 **"palpable yarn"**: Davitt, *Fall of Feudalism*, 610.

344 **"Have made enquiries . . . Now that I am . . ."**: May 4, 1889. Letters, Davitt Papers, TCD, MS 9368.

344 **anxious to play down his militant past**: A witness who could have testified to Egan's dealings in physical force was Superintendent Mallon. He had been called to London but refused to appear in court, cabling his Dublin commissioner after being subpoenaed: "Cannot give evidence. I prefer Waterloo Bridge [suicide]." (Bussy, 226.) Mallon gave as the reason, his duty to preserve the anonymity of his sources, but he was also protecting himself. The commission's "chief agent," William Joyce, was his nemesis at the castle and likely to have discovered damaging evidence against him. (See Ó Broin, *The Prime Informer*, 32.) At the last moment, however, the right strings were pulled, and Mallon was exempted from testifying.

344 **Irish agitator as a US minister**: Egan's term in Valparaíso, Chile, coincided with a diplomatic crisis that became known as the USS *Baltimore* affair, when the United States came close to declaring war on Chile, and the insurgents who became involved accused the new minister of gross violations of neutrality. Opinion of Egan's time there is divided. One observer dismissed him as a "biased . . . blundering diplomat" (Healy, *James G. Blaine and Latin America*, 234), while another praised his vigorous foreign policy defending American interests. But the fact that he was reporting directly to the president of the United States and his secretary of state made this period the apotheosis of Egan's career. With the change of government in 1893, he left mainstream politics and relocated to New York, where he resumed his business interests. Two years later, after the Conservatives' success in the English general election, he and Patrick Ford promised "another agitation," (*New York World* August 10, 1895) but by this point, Egan had effectively retreated back into the shadows.

345 **"Don't mention Mexico."**: Cable from Lincoln, Nebraska, February 9, 1889. Campbell, *Fenian Fire*, 354. See Campbell's book for a full account of Millen's role in the "Jubilee Plot."

345 **"marvel of smashing"**: Mary, *Diaries*, 407.

345 **"That man will not come . . ."**: B O'B, 449.

345 **Pigott fled to Madrid**: A twist to this grim ending—and one that has not been explained as anything more than a coincidence—was the presence in Madrid at exactly that time of William O'Shea.

345 **destroying Pigott**: In *Finnegans Wake*, Joyce turns repeatedly to spelling the error in Pigott's forged letters: "How do you spell hesitatatatancy" (305); "Bravure, surr Chorles! Letter perfect!" (181); "the spoil of hesitants, the spell of hesitancy" (97). He plays on his novel's central character's initials—HCE becomes "HeCitEncy!"— and still, Joyce cannot let it go: "all my hazeydency" (305); "unhesitant in his unionism and yet a pigotted nationalist" (133).

345 **"the shaking of hands"**: Kehoe, *Ireland's Misfortune*, 376.

346 **"little short of ludicrous"**: Bew, *Enigma*, 160.

346 **contempt for . . . "The Great Inquisition"**: (Davitt, *Fall of Feudalism*, 542.) Parnell, however, was said to be seriously alarmed on learning that the *Times* was negotiating with Patrick Sheridan, now living in exile on a ranch in Colorado. The panel was investigating the revelation made at the time of the Kilmainham negotiations that Parnell had known Sheridan was directing the Land War insurrection and planned to use him "to put down outrage." Sheridan had been named by James Carey as one of the Phoenix Park conspirators and, "at a minimum," writes Paul Bew (*Enigma*, 152), "was capable of saying—whether true or not—that he had sworn Parnell into the IRB on the eve of the murders." One source even alleged that Parnell had demanded that a message be sent to Egan in Nebraska asking for his help in preventing Sheridan from testifying—the implication being that Parnell wanted him "removed." As it happened, Sheridan had no intention of appearing as a witness; he had been hoaxing the *Times* and came close to obtaining a sum of £20,000.

A second charge involved a letter—a genuine letter—from Parnell to Frank Byrne. Referring to a check Parnell had obtained from the Land League in January 1883—an advance requested by Byrne "for the purposes of our organization"— Parnell was asked by the commission, "Is it true that you made this payment of £100 to Frank Byrne for the purpose of enabling him to escape from justice?"

"No."

"Had you any idea that he intended to escape from justice?"

"Certainly not."

The third charge, "that Mr. Parnell was intimate with the leading Invincibles," was true enough in the case of Patrick Egan, his former mentor and friend, who prided himself on playing the "open and secret" movements. (For the judges' report, see Davitt, *Fall of Feudalism*, 605–8.) Parnell, however, went out of his way to exonerate the league's former treasurer. Deliberately misleading the commission, he declared that his confidence in Egan had never wavered and that he had not been aware of Egan's extremist sympathies. "He never would, in any circumstances, I should think, countenance crime," said Parnell, conceding slightly: "I think with regard to physical force as a contingency in the event of the failure of the constitutional movement Egan would have gone further than I would have gone." *P and Crime*, pt. 20, 269, 71.

346 **"studied disrespect . . . lordly indifference":** Ibid., 597.

346 **the chief was triumphantly absolved:** It was Parnell's acquittal, together with his denunciation of the Phoenix Park assassins, that prompted Patrick Tynan to write *The Irish National Invincibles*. He insisted that the Invincibles had been formed "by order of the Parnellite Government of Ireland" (Corfe, 136), and his personal vendetta against its leader caused great indignation among even the most advanced revolutionists: "Doubts Cast on 'No 1'" blazed the headline of the *New York World* the day after publication of its long extract (June 4, 1894); Patrick Ford spoke out in Parnell's defense, saying that Tynan had never known Parnell and had probably been "bought over" by the Conservative government; Henry George described how he had personally witnessed Parnell's appalled reaction to news of the murders; while the political activist Marguerite Moore stated categorically, "I know—I *know* that Parnell was innocent." *New York World*, June 4, 1894.

346 **"and we find the same . . .":** Judges' report. Davitt, *Fall of Feudalism*, 605–8.

346 **"the citadel of Liberalism":** Lyons, *Parnell*, 469.

346 **"someone detonated William O'Shea":** *Great Contemporaries*, 277.

346 **"that awful scoundrel Parnell":** Lyons, 469.

346 **"a dreadful scene . . . Any further hesitation . . .":** Kehoe, *Ireland's Misfortune*, 370–71.

346 **"The stench of the divorce court":** Tim Healy, quoted in Callanan, *The Parnell Split*, 46.

347 **"A great cry of reprobation":** Lucy Cavendish, unpublished diary, vol. 14, postscript dated 1889, Chatsworth, DF19/1/12.

347 **Mrs. Harry Drew:** Mary Gladstone had married Hawarden's curate in 1886 and four years later, at the age of forty-two, gave birth to a daughter, Dorothy—curly-haired "Dossie"—Gladstone's favorite grandchild.

347 **"I feel so low, so wretched . . .":** Undated letter to Lucy Cavendish's sister, Lavinia Talbot, Mary, *Diaries*, 413; The situation brought to Mary's mind lines from Robert Browning's "Lost Leader" ("We that had loved him so, followed him, honoured him . . ."), a poem written as an expression of disenchantment with William Wordsworth for abandoning his liberal ideals.

347 **"For nearly 5 years . . .":** Lucy Cavendish. Unpublished diary, vol. 14, Chatsworth, DF19/1/12.

347 **"miserable and most cowardly . . .":** *Love Story*, vol. 2, 183.

347 **"English wolves howling . . .":** Callanan, *The Parnell Split*, 23.

348 **"reeking name . . . Mr. Parnell will not succeed . . .":** *Labour World*, December 13, 1890.

348 **"defiant, dastardly, devilish":** Mary, *Diaries*, 414.

348 **"[I] found Uncle W so astounded . . .":** Lucy Cavendish. Unpublished diary, vol. 14, Chatsworth, DF19/1/12.

348 **"It'll n'er dae":** Mary, *Diaries*, 413.

348 **"Poor fellow! Poor fellow! . . .":** B O'B, 563.

349 "I can truly say that I am now . . .": Jordan, *Kitty O'Shea*, 193.

349 "He suffered acute pains . . .": Fair, "Letters of Mourning."

350 "Let my love be given . . .": *Freeman's Journal*, October 9, 1891.

350 "affectation": *Love Story*, vol. 2, 276.

350 O'Kelly had "gone too": Ibid., 183.

350 "I have given, and will give . . .": Ibid., 160.

350 "glorious King" and subsequent quotations: Fair, "Letters of Mourning."

350 "a taste for the bottle . . . a sonsy comfortable soul . . .": Foster, "Mrs. O'Shea's Parnell," in *Paddy and Mr. Punch*, 137.

351 "ruinous infatuation": Kehoe, *Ireland's Misfortune*, 376.

351 "the happy delusion": Nora O'Shea to Henry Harrison, February 1, 1921. As quoted in Harrison, *Parnell Vindicated*, 216.

351 "a thing of long, long habit": December 20, 1885. Lucy Cavendish, postscript. Unpublished diary, vol. 14, 1889, Chatsworth, DF19/1/12.

351 "She does not advance an inch . . .": Undated letter to Lavinia Talbot, Lucy's younger sister, cited in Jane M. Renfrew, "Who Was Lucy Cavendish?," Devonshire Collections, Chatsworth, Secondary Source file for Lucy Cavendish.

351 keen interest in women's education: Her educational achievements were recognized by the University of Leeds, which in 1904 bestowed on Lucy its first honorary degree. Lucy Cavendish College in Cambridge was named after her as a tribute.

351 "odious and ridiculous": Preface to Sheila Fletcher, *Victoria Girls: Lord Lyttelton's Daughters* (London: Hambledon Press, 1997). In 1889, Lucy and her sisters signed the anti–women's suffrage petition organized by Mrs. Humphrey Ward.

351 "dragged . . . Dear Freddy . . .": Letter to Mary Gladstone, July 9, 1884. Cited in Jane M. Renfrew, "Who Was Lucy Cavendish?"

351 "I do, on occasions 'open attack' . . .": December 23, 1887. BL, Althorp Papers, Add MS 76820.

352 "on his own responsibility": Jenkins, *Gladstone*, 531.

352 "no longer a whole-hearted . . .": Foster, "Mrs O'Shea's Parnell," in *Paddy and Mr. Punch*, 128.

352 "that dangerous old fanatic . . .": Ponsonby, *Henry Ponsonby*, 216.

352 "confused and feeble": Jenkins, *Gladstone*, 583.

352 "all hope of anything . . .": Ibid., 578.

352 "much troubled & tossed about": Ibid., 600.

352 "Even among his bitterest . . .": Ibid., 603.

353 "a never-to-be-forgotten night": Marlow, *Mr. and Mrs. Gladstone*, 274.

353 "I cannot & will not add to the perils": From Gladstone memorandum, "The Plan," Quoted in H. C. G. Matthew, *Gladstone, 1809–1898* (Oxford, Clarendon Press, 1997), 603.

353 "final, disagreeable . . .": March 2, 1894. Marlow, *Mr. and Mrs. Gladstone*, 278.

353 "a good & very religious man": Ibid., 293.

353 "had a wonderful power . . .": May 19, 1898. Hibbert, *QV in Her Letters and Journals*, 337.

354   "I could not get up the smallest . . .": Marlow, *Mr. and Mrs. Gladstone,* 279.

354   "a small perturbation . . .": Matthew *Gladstone,* 610, footnote.

354   "from the sunless north": Hibbert, *QV: A Personal History,* 436.

354   "shaky and much altered": March 26, 1897. QVJs.

354   "the greatest man of the century . . . I am sorry for Mrs. Gladstone . . .": Marlow, *Mr. and Mrs. Gladstone,* 293.

354   "How can I say I am sorry . . .": Hibbert, *QV: A Personal History,* 377.

354   "falling in with the wishes . . .": Marlow, *Mr. and Mrs. Gladstone,* 293.

355   born to protect: Queen Victoria survived Gladstone by nearly three years, dying at Osborne on January 22, 1901. Among items placed in her coffin, according to her precise directions, were her wedding veil, jewelry, a number of photographs, Prince Albert's dressing gown, and, in the hand nearest her heart, a photograph of John Brown and a lock of his hair (concealed from her family with a posy of flowers).

355   "all that *concerns* . . .": August 10, 1892. Ponsonby, *Henry Ponsonby,* 217.

355   "He did at times . . .": Hibbert, *QV in Her Letters and Journals,* 337.

355   "must survive me . . .": Jenkins, *Gladstone,* 578.

355   "*Le Roy le veult* . . . And God save England too": Denis Gwynn, *The Life of John Redmond* (London: George G. Harrap & Co., 1932), 283.

355   "one of the happiest days . . .": Cited in Jane M. Renfrew, "Who Was Lucy Cavendish?"

356   go the way of all the others: As indeed it did. The failure of the Irish Convention was followed by the destruction of the Home Rule Party in the general election of 1918; the withdrawal of the then-dominant Sinn Féin party from Westminster; and the setting up of a revolutionary government in Ireland. A guerrilla war from 1919 to 1921 was halted by the controversial Anglo-Irish Treaty, but this did nothing to integrate a forever-divided island.

356   "Do not give your heart . . . That is what Ireland . . .": Fingall, *Seventy Years Young,* 69.

Acknowledgments

My book has several godparents, but one has nurtured it quite literally from conception to delivery: to R. F. Foster, the celebrated Irish historian, I owe a debt that I can never fully repay.

Creator of the first chair of Irish history in Britain (Carroll Professor at Hertford College, Oxford, from 1991–2016), Roy Foster is a specialist on modern Ireland and the author of an outstanding body of work, including the two-volume biography of W.B. Yeats. At Trinity College, Dublin he had been taught by two of Ireland's most eminent scholars, T.W. Moody and F.S.L. Lyons, and I consider myself enormously privileged to have been the recipient of sparks from this flame. Professorial emails would arrive, steering me away from clichéd interpretations of Irish "victimhood," and toward undiscovered riches:

> Do you know Samuel Ferguson's "At the Polo-Ground," a sort of Browningesque meditation about Anglo-Irish relations, traditional hatreds etc. . . . Another contemporary reflection of the times worth reading is Trollope's last and unfinished novel "The Land Leaguers" (I've written an essay about it which I'll send you). It's a pretty dyspeptic view but it's good on local conditions, violence and Irish hatreds.

Without ever being bossy or condescending, Roy provided invaluable notes at different stages of my narrative, and unhesitatingly answered my queries. In his absence at Hertford College, he allowed me to stay in his rooms, where I slept alongside "the Bridge of Sighs," and was within a minute's reach of Oxford's great Bodleian Library. His introductory emails to other luminaries in the field opened every door. The doyenne of Irish intellectuals, Catriona Crowe, then Head of Special Projects at the National Archives of Ireland, met me on my first visit; Stephen Ball advised me on nineteenth-century Irish policing; Patrick Maume, a brilliant researcher and author of numerous entries in the Dictionary of Irish Biography, helped me with an identification; Paul Bew, emeritus professor at Queen's University, Belfast, life peer and biographer of Parnell, shared his expertise over lunch in the inner sanctum of the House of Commons; Kevin Kenny, professor of history and Glucksman professor of Irish Studies at New York University, took a heart-warming interest in my project, emailing important suggestions, and even trawling through his doctorial dissertation folders in search of material that might be of use.

Both Roy and Kevin urged me to contact an Irish historian then writing a compelling micro-history of rural activism in West Donegal, his own ancestors being among the protagonists. Author of this prize-winning book, *The End of Outrage*, and recently appointed director of Acadamh na hOllscolaíochta Gaeilge [Academy of Irish Language] at the National University of Ireland, Galway, Breandán Mac Suibhne proved to be a mentor as well as a vital source. From his on-site tutorial on how to master the nineteenth-century finding system at Dublin's National Archives to the posting of alerts of interest, and an eleventh-hour close-reading and correcting of my text, Breandán has been endlessly supportive and generous with his time.

When it became clear that I needed an Irish translator, he led me to Lillis Ó Laoire, then head of Irish at NUI Galway, who in turn put me in touch with his star PhD student, Ailbhe Nic Giolla Chomhaill, now lecturer in Irish at the University of Limerick. This was providential. Not only was Gweedore the location of Ailbhe's family home, but her mother, Máirín Seoighe, had produced a 1993 drama-documentary on Patrick O'Donnell, and Ailbhe, a specialist in Irish folklore, was practiced at finding gold among the oral narratives of the past. Her initiative and enthusiasm as a researcher combined with her own personal warmth made our work together an absolute joy.

I owe an immeasurable amount to Donal P. McCracken, former Dean of Humanities at the University of KwaZulu-Natal, and an authority on the Irish diaspora in Africa. Having tracked him down after reading an exemplary article on Patrick O'Donnell by his late father, J.L. McCracken, I then discovered that Donal was the author of *Inspector Mallon: Buying Irish Patriotism for a Five-Pound Note*, a book that became one of my most important sources. A serendipitous email contact led to a meeting in Dublin and an ongoing correspondence, during which I came to rely on the encouragement and sharp insights that Donal sent my way.

My first Donegal contact was Vincent O'Donnell, who, as I sat beside him in his Inver home, translated into English a 1960 Irish article on O'Donnell that I had been desperate to find. He directed me to a local historical society and depository of books, photographs, and historic newspapers in Derrybeg, and it was there—the Comharchumann Forbartha Ghaoth Dobhair [Gweedore Development Cooperative]—that I was greatly assisted by Tony McHugh and Mícheál Ó Domhnaill, who opened up the collection to me. When the time came to choose illustrations, Mícheál, a colleague of Breandán Mac Suibhne at the Acadamh na hOllscolaíochta Gaeilge, sent me scans of superb nineteenth-century photographs by Robert Banks and James Glass, generously approving my use of a Glass image from the Comharchumann's album.

Dónall P. Ó Baoill, professor of linguistics, was described to me as someone I must not fail to contact, as being the great-grandson of Pat O'Donnell's sister Mary, he knew more than anyone else about the family's history. This I could well imagine, as I had already mined his indispensable article published in the local journal, *Scáthlán*. When we finally met over tea at the Merrion Hotel in Dublin, I came away not only with new discoveries, but with a wariness of what Dónall called "the far-fetched claims." His scholarship, empirical approach, and vivid evocations of Gweedore set a splendid example for which I thank him greatly, along with my thanks for his unstinting support.

In South Africa, I spent a day with Margaret Harradine, who was Port Elizabeth's Africana librarian for a quarter of a century, and holds the keys to archival research on her city. As the library site was under reconstruction and closed to readers, Margaret gave me access to all the relevant material in her own living room. The Africana's current librarian Carol Victor joined us with additional finds, and I am indebted to them both for their kindness.

Then there are a number of others I must thank for helping me in different ways: Anthony Appiah, Lola Bubbosh, Rose Cannings, Rebecca Carter, Anne Clarkson, Maggie Ferguson, Hyunkee Kim, Isabel Lloyd, Marge McNinch, Kerby Miller, Heathcote Ruthven, William Shawcross, and Michael Shipster. I would like to express my appreciation of the hard work of Patrick Mahoney, Fulbright scholar, currently attached to NUI Galway, who sorted out my citations, and obtained illustrations and permissions with diligence and engaging good humor.

Among the institutions whose collections have greatly enhanced this book, my first thanks must go to Her Majesty Queen Elizabeth II for permission to quote from material in the Royal Archives at Windsor Castle. I am particularly indebted to the archivist Allison Derrett, LVO, whose extracurricular assistance went way beyond the call of duty. I am privileged to have the authorization of the Board of Trinity College Dublin to quote from the papers of Michael Davitt and John Dillon, and I express my gratitude to Trinity's Felicity O'Mahony and Sharon Sutton for their help. Further thanks are due to the Devonshire Collection, Chatsworth, for allowing me to draw on their collection, and to the archivists Aidan Haley and Fran Baker, for assisting me at different stages of my research. I am most grateful to Jeremy McIlwaine, senior archivist of Archives and Modern Manuscripts at the Bodleian Library, for permission to quote from the Harcourt Papers; and to Oliver House, superintendent of the Bodleian's Special Collections.

At the National Archives of Ireland, the archivist Gregory O'Connor taught me the cryptic number trail system of its vast leather tomes, and located the two vital boxes of "B Files" that formed the basis of my research. In the Newsroom at the British Library it is entirely thanks to Stewart Gillies, News Reference Team Leader, that I was given access to bound nineteenth-century journals, several of whose evocative illustrations I use in my book.

In addition, I would like to acknowledge the use of material from the following institutions, and to single out for thanks their archivists, curators, and librarians: Neil Cobbett at the National Archives; Erika le Roux at the Western Cape Archives and Records Service; Andrew Isidoro at John J. Burns Library, Boston College; Christopher T. Baer at the Hagley Museum and Library Wilmington, Delaware; Mark Eccleston at the University of Birmingham's Cadbury Research Library; Claire Doohan at the National Folklore Collection; Conor Dodd at the Glasnevin Cemetery and Museum; Una Mathewson at the Central Library, Letterkenny; and Amy McDonald at William R. Perkins Library at Duke University. I must convey my debt to the British Library's Western Manuscript Department; to the Manuscript Division of the National Library of Ireland; and to the London Library, for the loan of key works throughout the time they were needed and for the helpfulness of its congenial staff.

Without the belief of my American agent, the indefatigable Lynn Nesbit, this book would not exist. It so happened that Ireland and the Irish had got under her skin just at the moment that I was beginning my research, and in the spring of 2017 she joined me on an exploratory trip to Dublin. When my proposal was considered "too Irish" by several commissioning editors, Lynn would not let go until she had found a publisher who saw its potential. This was Morgan Entrekin, CEO and publisher of Grove Atlantic, who talked me into tackling a far more ambitious book than the one I had originally outlined.

Morgan's personal commitment has been extraordinary, his textual judgment unfailingly right, but I owe him most thanks for choosing as my editor the brilliant young Irish-American, Katie Raissian. What I felt at first was a startlingly severe edit was in fact a masterly act of streamlining, an overview of the narrative in which I was far too deeply embedded to see clearly. Just as outstanding was Katie's skillful, sensitive approach to every aspect of the book's aftercare, and I consider myself blessed to have been in her hands.

Huge thanks, too, to Grove Atlantic's Sara Vitale, whose spot-on observations and meticulous overseeing of the picture insert helped to shape the finished book; to the managing editor, Julia Berner-Tobin, for her patience, and for assigning one of the best copy editors in town—Amy Hughes, whose insights raised the usual sniffer-dog exposure of factual errors, repetitions, and grammatical infelicities to an entirely different level of expertise. The scrupulousness of Maureen Klier's proofreading and Jay Kreider's compilation of the index is further reason for my appreciation of the Grove team's dedication to the production of my book.

In London, I am lucky to have been in the care of Clare Drysdale, the associate publisher of Atlantic Books, who has championed my book from the moment we met, and gone out of her way to nurture its author. I much appreciate the guidance of the Irish sales director, Simon Hess, and the work that the art director, Richard Evans, has put into designing the cover.

Several friends have played crucial roles. Harry Evans, the late Sir Harold, cast his genius editor's eye over early drafts; Tina Brown encouraged me—as she did with her *New Yorker* writers—to take on a subject far beyond my comfort zone; Peter Conrad, who as my Oxford don, set an almost unreachably high bar, spurred me on with his enthusiasm and inspired suggestions; the screenwriter Stephen Schiff taught me how to make a proposal enticing and was always on hand for worldly-wise advice; Grey Gowrie shared memories of his upbringing in Gweedore; Anthony Gardner provided astute editorial guidance on the opening chapters. My warm thanks to them all.

I must also express my great debt to my friend and fellow biographer, Selina Hastings. For twenty-five years we have read and commented on each other's works in progress, one chapter at a time, the pact being that we are completely honest. I have always known that I get the better deal—and never more so than with this book, which Selina launched by giving a dinner for me to discuss my idea with Roy Foster, and by introducing me to their mutual friend as a Dublin contact. A bookish, big-hearted, retired lawyer, John McBratney, gave me a base for weeks at a time—the use of his charming flat in the villagey quarter near the Canal, where I was in walking distance of the National Archives and Library. After hours John was a wonderful companion (it was he who first showed me Phoenix Park), and I know that our friendship will long outlast my publication.

I owe my discovery of Gweedore to the generosity of Brian and Anne Friel, and their two daughters, Sally and Mary, who lent me their cliff-top house overlooking the long Atlantic strand, where they spent many a summer holiday. This is the West Donegal setting of Friel's plays, the homeland of the young O'Donnell of *Philadelphia, Here I Come!* who followed my own young O'Donnell in seeking a better future in America. And while I had no idea until my arrival that the Friel's house was within a few miles of haunts I needed to explore, this happy chance was reinforced by an immersion in the mighty, ancient landscape that helped me to instill the spirit of place in my book.

Accompanying me on this Gweedore adventure was my husband Ross MacGibbon, who was just as smitten by its bleak beauty, and just as caught up by the quest. It is Ross, my rock and soulmate, who will always get my final and most heartfelt thanks.

Index